Myth and the Christian Nation

A Social Theory of Religion

Burton L. Mack

Myth and the Christian Nation

Religion in Culture: Studies in Social Contest and Construction

Series Editor: Russell T. McCutcheon, University of Alabama

This series is based on the assumption that those practices we commonly call religious are social practices that are inextricably embedded in various contingent, cultural worlds. Authors in this series therefore do not see the practices of religion occupying a socially or politically autonomous zone, as is the case for those who use "and" as the connector between "religion" and "culture." Rather, the range of human performances that the category "religion" identifies can be demystified by translating them into fundamentally social terms; they should therefore be seen as ways of waging the ongoing contest between groups vying for influence and dominance in intra- and inter-cultural arenas. Although not limited to one historical period, cultural site, or methodological approach, each volume exemplifies the tactical contribution to be made to the human sciences by writers who refuse to study religion as irreducibly religious; instead, each author conceptualizes religion—as well as the history of scholarship on religion—as among the various *arts de faire*, or practices of everyday life, upon which human communities routinely draw when defining and reproducing themselves in opposition to others.

Published titles in the series:

*Religion and the Domestication of Dissent:
Or, How to Live in a Less than Perfect Nation*
Russell T. McCutcheon

*The Symbolic Jesus: Historical Scholarship, Judaism and
the Construction of Contemporary Identity*
William E. Arnal

Representing Religion: Essays in History, Theory and Crisis
Tim Murphy

Situating Islam: The Past and Future of an Academic Discipline
Aaron W. Hughes

Forthcoming:

It's Just Another Story: The Politics of Remembering the Earliest Christians
Willi Braun

Rethinking Hindu Identity
Dwijendra Narayan Jha

Japanese Mythology: Hermeneutics on Scripture
Jun'Ichi Isomae

Myth and the Christian Nation

A Social Theory of Religion

Burton L. Mack

LONDON   OAKVILLE

First published in 2008 by
UK: Equinox Publishing Ltd, Unit 6, The Village, 101 Amies Street, London, SW11 2JW
USA: DBBC, 28 Main Street, Oakville, CT 06779

www.equinoxpub.com

© Burton L. Mack 2008

All rights reserved. No part of this publication may be reproduced or transmitted in any form or by any means, electronic or mechanical, including photocopying, recording or any information storage or retrieval system, without prior permission in writing from the publishers.

British Library Cataloguing-in-Publication Data

A catalogue record for this book is available from the British Library.

ISBN 978 1 84553 372 4 (hardback)
ISBN 978 1 84553 373 1 (paperback)

Library of Congress Cataloging-in-Publication Data
Mack, Burton L.
  Myth and the Christian nation: a social theory of religion / Burton L. Mack.
    p. cm. — (Religion in culture: studies in social contest and construction)
  Includes bibliographical references and index.
  ISBN-13: 978-1-84553-372-4 (hb) — ISBN-13: 978-1-84553-373-1 (pb)
  1. Religion and sociology. 2. Religion—Social aspects. 3. Christianity. I. Title.
  BL60.M275 2008
  306.6′3—dc22

Typeset by S.J.I. Services, New Delhi
Printed and bound in Great Britain by Maple-Vail Book Manufacturing Company, Lakeville, MA.

Contents

Preface	ix
Introduction	1

Part I
The Religions of Other Peoples

Chapter 1
Looking for Religion in the New World 16

Chapter 2
Noticing Social Interests in Myths and Rituals 48

Chapter 3
Watching Myths in the Making 82

Chapter 4
Thinking with Myths about Culture 120

Part II
The Religion of Christianity

Chapter 5
Early Christian Mythmaking 146

Chapter 6
The Social Formation of Christendom 183

Chapter 7
The State of the Christian Nation 217

Chapter 8
Religions in a Polycultural World 249

Conclusion	271
Bibliography	276
Index	284

*For Jonathan, Ron, Merrill, and BJ,
colleagues who made writing
this essay an exhilarating
intellectual adventure*

Preface

When conservative Christians entered the political arena in the United States in the last half century and then won access to power, there was very little public criticism, much less discussion of the principle of the separation of church and state. Then the event of 9/11 surfaced the languages of righteousness, power, apocalypse, and divine mandate to go to war. It was apparently not the time to quibble about the religious language used to interpret our social situation. Firming up the suspected links to al Qaeda, Islam, and the "axis of evil," the rhetoric of evil enemies was enough to justify massive military action. There were no cautionary counsels. There was little deliberation about alternative responses. Flags, patriotism, and agitation for a holy war against terrorists won the day. Politicians and the American public said in effect to "Go get them." I was stunned by the way in which our administration construed the situation in terms of good and evil, and then used the language of Christianity to justify our response. And I was dismayed by the inability of our deliberative processes to question that justification. The language of righteousness and revenge had smothered all discussion. Where is the public forum, I asked myself? Why do Christians think it is time to get into politics? Why has the language of good and evil squelched other ways of thinking about the reasons for the state of the world? Why do we in America have such a difficult time talking about religion? We needed some plain talk about religion and society, our society.

I had always known that public discourse about religion in America was shallow. I understood this to be an unfortunate result of the popular conception of religion as a matter of personal religious experience and private opinion, and also because of the taboos against its analysis and discussion. This meant that religion was thought to be of no importance for matters of social and political consequence. And the doctrine of the separation of church and state meant that religion and society had not become a subject of instruction in our public schools. Yet here were Christians writing textbooks, talking politics, reminding us that we were supposed to be a Christian nation, and using Christian language to justify a military mission. So something was unspoken. Something was wrong.

We needed to hear from our historians of religion about the ways religions worked in other societies, how and why peoples have thought their myths and rituals were so important, under what circumstances myths surfaced to rationalize public policies, and whether myths might be challenged and changed when they get out of sync with social situations. If that learning could be applied to the history of Christianity, it might then be possible to understand how it could be that a president of a democracy gets to say what the Christian's God wants us to do. It might even be possible to criticize such an authorization on academic grounds. The history of scholarship on religion is a fascinating story of a quest to define and understand it. It is a story of learning by stages, and the enormous collection of ethnographic data produced can be arranged as selected case studies and illustrations dotting the history of that learning. It is what scholars have learned about religions that could help us think more deeply and clearly about religion and society in our current social situation at the beginning of the twenty-first century.

The scholarly study of religion started with Columbus's discovery that the natives of Guanahani (christened "San Salvador") "had no religion." And it was true that they had no religion of the kind familiar to fifteenth-century Europeans. This means that the quest began with curiosity about other peoples and their religions, but with a notion of religion given by our own Western tradition. This concept, derived from familiarity with Christianity, was taken for granted and appeared to be self-evident. The quest soon ran into the myths and rituals of other peoples where the Christian notion did not fit or help to explain anything. Scholars have therefore worked hard to revise their concept of religion in order to understand the myths and rituals of tribal and other peoples. Finally it became possible to use what had been learned about the religions of other peoples to analyze the religion from which the original conception was taken, namely Christianity. To let the reader see what scholars have had to work through on their way to a social theory of religion will highlight the reasons for entertaining a social theory of religion as well as provide an explanation for the reasons we are having such a difficult time thinking critically about Christianity in our recent and current situation.

What can be learned about religion and society from the history of the study of religion may certainly exercise and entertain the reader's imagination with such concepts as "social interests," "social formation," "mythmaking," "imagined world," "myth and rituals systems," "mythic grammars," and "cultural mentalities." These concepts will need to be described, then looked at from various angles in order to settle into place as important components of a coherent scholarly theory. Finally, they will have to be applied in some way to questions about the Christian mentality in America raised by the Christian Right and its discourse about the Christian nation. It will not be possible or necessary to answer all the questions that might come to mind about religions in America and in the global world in our time, but a platform for the forum of public discussion about such questions certainly can be constructed.

I have imagined a literate public interested in the question of religion and society but without specialization in religious studies. I would like to think my topic and discursive style helpful for such readers. It is, of course, the case that I also imagined some historians of religion looking over my shoulder while I was writing. But I did not write this book for them, and many of them, supposing they also find my theory interesting, may have to wince here or there. That is because not all of us have managed to think of religions first in terms of their social significance. Many literate readers may also have trouble along the way, wondering why the scholarly mind cannot dispense with abstractions and theories. Nevertheless, I hope to have cut an interesting swath through a very impressive scholarship struggling to understand a very important human enterprise. If religion is a mode of thinking about social constructions, the thesis to be developed, then the history of religions can be described as a study of one way humans have of thinking about themselves.

My challenge has been to design the book with the non-specialist reader in mind. I have therefore taken the time to provide examples from the history of religions while developing the concepts that need to be in place before approaching our current situation. And in the case of Christianity, the religion among us that has come to speech as a political ideology that is causing consternation, I have taken the time to review its history with my social theory in mind. The result is a book that asks the reader to carefully consider the arguments for such a theory and to think critically about its application to our polycultural nation and world. In keeping with the essay format there are no footnotes, only occasional references for the documentation of specific texts or data under discussion as well as a few scholarly works that mark major junctures of theoretical importance in the history I have reviewed. Some readers might want to use these references to position the study in historical and scholarly contexts or as places to do some more exploring on this or that topic. However, I hope to have kept the reader in touch with the scholarship I have consulted without needing to do more research. I have kept scholarly references to a minimum, and those that seemed necessary or appropriate are cited in abbreviated format, often within parentheses. Full titles and details of a specific reference can easily be found in the bibliography. References of a more general nature, a mention for instance of Copernicus, the Tlingit Indians of the Pacific Northwest, or the civilizations of the Ancient Near East, are not thoroughly documented as would be expected of a scholarly monograph, nor can they be in such an essay. My assumption has been that a general familiarity with the histories in review will suffice and, if not, will be available to the reader in encyclopedias, standard research tools and engines, and the few references I make to important studies.

I would like to mention four persons with gratitude who have been important dialogue partners and who have made this study possible. They are Jonathan Z. Smith, Distinguished Professor of the Humanities at the University of Chicago, mentor and critic of long standing; Ron Cameron, Professor of Religion at Wesleyan University, Middletown, Connecticut, and Merrill Miller, Professor of Religion at The University of North Carolina at Pembroke, co-chairs of the national seminar on Ancient Myths and Modern Theories of Christian Origins, an arena of critical thinking and conversation that has sustained me for over ten years; and BJ, my spouse, cultural analyst, conversation partner, and critical reader of my drafts. What a wonderful group of intellectuals I have had as friends.

My indebtedness to Jonathan Z. Smith does need an additional comment or two. He has been my conversation partner for many years while I was working out the social logics of the religions of Late Antiquity. Now that I have used this learning to render an analysis of Christianity in the twenty-first century, Jonathan has continued to provide the critical edge to my study. His reading of my manuscript before publication, and his detailed comments, questions, and suggestions have made it possible for me to make my arguments more precise. I am deeply grateful to him.

I also want to acknowledge that I have drawn upon some earlier essays of mine already published. Portions of Chapters 1 and 7 are taken from *The Christian Myth* (pages 84–7 and Chapter Eight), reprinted here in revised form with the permission of Continuum. In Chapter 2 portions are taken from *The Christian Myth* (pages 91–5) and also from my essay on "Social Formation" in *Guide to the Study of Religion*, edited by Willi Braun and Russell T. McCutcheon (pages 283–96).

Now we shall see what other readers may make of my study of religion as a human investment in social interests.

Introduction

Thinking about religion in the United States soon runs into the problem of its definition. The popular conception, taken for granted by most people, is that religion is a private matter, a special kind of personal experience. This is sometimes said to be contact with a spiritual realm of reality, sometimes expressed as an encounter with the spirit or power of God, and sometimes experienced as a personal transformation. Studies of religion defined in this way tend toward psychologies of religion, and there are many self-help guides to spiritual wholeness that regard religion mainly as a matter of personal experience. This way of thinking about religion accords with our focus on persons as individuals. It is this concept of religion as a private and personal matter that has made it possible to think of the United States as a "Christian nation" even while concurring with the doctrine of the separation of church and state.

A second definition of religion regards it as an institution devoted to the representation of the spiritual realm in the human world. This has often been called "organized religion," referring to churches, temples, mosques, and their programs. Religious institutions are usually distinguished in terms of their belief systems, tenets, and ritual practices. Most Americans have no trouble thinking of religion both as a personal experience and as an organization, for the purpose of the organization is understood to enable and enhance the religious experiences of its members. The result has been that belonging to a particular religion has been regarded as a matter of personal preference, the ritual context within which one's personal belief system can be fostered. This definition usually includes the notion that the tenets of a religious institution should not determine the ways in which other persons, society as a whole, or the government of the United States need to think or behave.

Yet a third understanding of religion sees it as a culture, a system of symbols, beliefs, and values that a people have in common. This definition is social. It is not the customary way of thinking about religion in the United States. Scholars who study the religions and cultures of other peoples do think of religion as integral to a society and its culture. It has been difficult, however, to study religions in the United States with this concept in mind, because we are a nation of many religions and understand ourselves as a society of free and independent persons who do not share a common religion or culture.

A remarkable change in thinking about Christianity occurred during the last half of the twentieth century and the first decade of the twenty-first that challenged these traditional notions of religion and society. Christians started talking about the United States as a "Christian nation," saying that our society was in danger of losing its grounding in Christianity and that Christians should enter the political arena and work to make sure we all behaved as Christians. This violated the long-standing tradition of the separation of church and state, and it did not mesh readily with the American Christian emphasis upon religion as a matter of personal experience and piety. Christian churches (organized religion) were encouraging their members ("born-again" Christians) to take control of America (society) in the interest of Christian values (culture). This strange combination of all three concepts of religion in the notion of the Christian nation brought to the surface an unexpected manifestation of Christian mentality that is well worth exploring. It will therefore be helpful to document this recent chapter of thinking about religion in contrast to earlier statements that took the doctrine of separation for granted.

When John F. Kennedy was running for president, the question of his religious affiliation became a major issue. The Greater Houston Ministerial Association invited him to address this issue on September 12, 1960. Kennedy opened with the statement that "we have far more critical issues to face in the 1960 election...[that] are not religious issues—for war and hunger and ignorance and despair know no religious barriers." As for his being a Catholic, the question should not be "What kind of church I believe in, for that should be important only to me—but what kind of America I believe in." He then went on to deliver a speech on "an America where the separation of church and state is absolute." At the time this sounded good to Protestant Democrats, whether they all breathed a sigh of relief or not, for it conformed so clearly to the prevailing views on religion and politics. Religion was a personal and private matter that should not influence public policy-making. And the separation of church and state should not allow for a public policy to privilege a given religion. That was all that had to be said at that time. It cleared the air for the ringing of the bells and the gavel's call to order in a land where the state guarantees religious freedom, and where "no religious body seeks to impose its will directly or indirectly upon the general populace or the public acts of its officials" (Kennedy). In effect, since religion is a personal and private matter, one's religion should not matter in the realm of public service.

Since that time, however, Christians increasingly came to speech on public issues. Christian leaders talked about the "Christian Right," a "Moral Majority," and a "Christian Coalition." These terms intentionally eroded the older notions of the separation of religion from politics and purposely positioned Christians in decidedly political postures. The problem, as these Christians saw it, was that our society was in danger of losing its footing in traditional Christian values. The answer proposed was that Christians should work to make sure that public policy and laws agree with moral laws. It seems that shifts in civil rights and social practices from the period of the cold war, the effects of the civil rights movement on legislation, and the student demonstrations against the Vietnam War came to expression in ways that were

Introduction 3

frightening and offensive to traditional Christian sensibility. It was as if the unexamined notion of the Christian nation was sufficient and comfortable as long as general patterns of social practices allowed for the thought that Christianity remained the moral conscience of the people. When pockets of people emerged whose social views were critical of national policies and traditional patterns of social and political practice, and whose call for changes in the application of the traditional values of freedom, equality, justice, and the pursuit of happiness resulted in life-style practices that offended Christian sensibilities, Christians found themselves increasingly engaged in political action. This has had its effect at all levels of our society, from school boards through city and state bureaucracies to national party politics and the recent administrations.

Then there was the "terrorist attack" of September 11, 2001. Suddenly the public discourse was awash in the religious language of "evil enemies," "terrorists," "holy war," and "Islamic extremists" on the one hand, and the marshalling of patriotism and the military for a "crusade" against an "evil axis" of governments thought to threaten the USA and spawn terrorists on the other. The surge of this religious language was so sudden and automatic that its irony was hardly noticed even by Americans who were troubled by it. The irony was that the same labels were being used by both parties in their description of the other. As things developed, the term "Islamic extremists" turned into "Islamofascists," with one of their hallmarks being their rejection of secular governments in favor of Islamic states governed by their "church." The similarity of the two rhetorics, that of the Islamists and that of the US administration, did not register. There would be a Department of Homeland Security to protect the United States at home, the "city set on a hill," the "light to the nations." There would also be a "preemptive war" abroad to destroy our enemies before they destroyed us. Now there were two reasons for fear: one was sin and immorality from within our own society; the second was evil and terrorists threatening us from without. The cultivation of fear trumped deliberation, and patriotism flourished by calling for loyalty to the righteous cause of replacing "tyrannies" with "democracies." A series of books with an Armageddon theme, describing the "rapture" of the righteous and the destruction of sinners in the apocalyptic holocaust at hand, went off the charts (Frykholm, *Rapture Culture*). The fear of impending disaster, whether from God or the terrorists, apparently touched the nerve of concern for personal salvation. However, on the national front, where religion now mattered as a reason for going to war, the response was not only fear but bravado because God was on our side. As President Bush said, we were "the greatest force for good in history." A lieutenant general gave speeches on the Christian nation going to war against infidels and winning because our "God was bigger than their gods." Attorney General Ashcroft said, in effect, not to worry because Jesus is our king and "We have no king but Jesus." And our radio preachers and television evangelists said that God had allowed the terrorists to attack us because, as a nation, we had sinned and deserved the punishment. Some Americans were shocked at this religious rhetoric for generating fear and going to war, but only a few complained, and their complaint was not heard in the halls of Congress or taken up seriously in the pages of the media. Liberals, who had already been put in their place by the opprobrium of the Christian Right as weak on moral issues in public policy, were tongue-tied. And the so-called mainline Christian churches apparently did not know what to say.

So religion may matter in more ways than one. It has always been thought to matter for individuals, of course, molding character and grounding moral behavior. But now it seems that it may matter as a factor in the mentality of a people and the ways in which a society works as well. Now that we have seen violence in the names of both Christianity and Islam, we are not so sure about all the ways personal religious belief and experience work in the larger social arenas. We have little understanding of the part played by religion in a society, especially at the level of a society's shifts in rationale for political purposes. At the level of national politics religion has always been taken for granted as one of the "unalienable rights" to which the "Laws of Nature and Nature's God" entitle Americans, as the preamble to the Declaration of Independence states. That worked as long as religion was seen as one of the personal freedoms guaranteed by the Constitution and as long as Christianity could be thought of as the caretaker of personal morality. But the recent chapters of our history let us see that religion is not merely a private affair. It is no wonder that we are having trouble comprehending the social situation in which we find ourselves at the beginning of the twenty-first century.

What might we have said to ourselves about our nation under duress without the language of religion? It was used to understand what was happening, construe motivations, and devise policies in response to new situations. Christians and politicians did that by taking positions and attitudes that purportedly kept us in touch with traditional "values," standards of "rightness," and marks of personal and national "righteousness." It is not that the Christian language of good and evil was the only way we had to talk about ourselves. But that is the language that came to the surface when debating social issues, political policy, and national interests. The power of that language was such that, when used in support of political propositions, nothing more needed to or could be said. How can it be, one might ask, that a modern democracy finds itself stymied by the use of a language that resists deliberation?

And how could the Islamic "extremists" and "terrorists" have explained themselves without appealing to the religion and tenets of Islam? It is true that they also pointed to many other reasons for their anger against the United States and other Western nations, such as colonial domination, exploitation of their natural resources, and military occupation of their lands, as well as the intrusion of lifestyles offensive to their cultures. We may not recognize these reasons as grounded in a people's religion and culture. But the conflicts created by these interventions readily took the form of questions about the tenets and warrants of Islam both in the Western nations and in the Near East. Islamic scholars were quick to assure us that the religion of Islam was misinterpreted by the terrorists who spoke of jihad against satanic America in the name of Allah. So let us not turn the conflicts in the Near East into religious wars. Our president learned his lesson and made it clear that we were not going to war against Islam, just against terrorists and bad governments that threatened our national interests. And yet our global interests continued to be justified because we were a Christian nation. As David Rieff put it, "For the Bush Administration, American leadership is a self-evident moral right...[with] the conviction that America has a special mission based on the universality of its values" ("We Are the World," 34).

Many Americans would point out that neither the Islamic extremists nor the Christian Right are adequate definitions of their respective religions. So let us not target religion for critique. They might go on to say that there are many ways other than conservative Christianity to define personal and social well-being. So maybe religion does not matter even at the personal level any longer. They could also go on to remind us that the so-called culture wars on the front between conservative Christians and liberals of political and social persuasion revolved around a rather small list of issues that threatened conservative taboos, having mainly to do with sexual practices and a few symbols of the Christian nation, not with a comprehensive political agenda. So the argument is that, although the Christian Right has become a national embarrassment, it has not touched upon the really important social issues facing us, such as creating a just and sustainable society. And many Americans might go on to make the point that the conservative commitments of Christians, though expressed in matters of morals at the popular level, were taken advantage of by politicians to marshal support for causes quite different from those espoused by the majority of Christian Americans. So, with the big picture in mind, is it religion that matters, or power politics?

Not every intellectual would be satisfied with this kind of reasoning. The influence of the Christian Right in US politics might be discounted because we are essentially a secular, scientific, and rational society, or so the argument might run. But the influence of Islam in Near Eastern nation-states and others around the world has also to be explained. On October 7, 2001, Neal Gabler wrote an article with the title "An Eternal War of Mind-Sets" for the *Los Angeles Times*. Drawing upon the distinction between "mythos" and "logos" suggested by Karen Armstrong (*The Battle for God*), where "mythos" relies on "intuition, superstition, [and]...non-rational ways of knowing," while "logos relies on reason and logic, on what we call rational ways of knowing," Gabler went on to say that

> Our new war is a battle between mythos and logos. Osama bin Laden, the Taliban and their Muslim fundamentalist allies live within mythos and have subordinated themselves to it. They see themselves not as individuals with wants and needs, which is a relatively modern notion, but as operatives of Allah. For them, everything is

religion, everything faith. In fact, they don't acknowledge any other legitimate way to look at the world. They are essentially premodern and ahistorical.

In contrast, "Born of reason, America, through its economic, intellectual and military might, is the logos capital of the world, which presumably is why it is the primary target for the Islamic fundamentalists." Thus, as Gabler sees the conflict, "This may be the very first war to be fought over epistemology. As such, it may be terrifyingly intractable."

This article was apparently written in anger and consternation as a response to the terrorist attack of September 11, 2001, but it tells us nevertheless about the difficulties we have when trying to identify the significance of religion and culture in the functions and structures of a society. One might account for Gabler's views by seeing them as an intellectual's celebration of America's heritage of the Enlightenment, the Industrial Revolution, and the rise of scientific achievements in the Western world. But especially in retrospect, his positive assessment of America's rationality and designs upon the rest of the world has to be seen as uncritical. And his appeal to the terms *logos* and *mythos* is particularly unfortunate. Many will see this as an awkward attempt to borrow credibility from the Greek philosophical tradition, whence the terms originate, and historians of that tradition will know that the terms were not used by the Greeks to contrast opposing epistemologies. Logos was used to name any message, report, or speech, and mythos was used to refer to stories of all kinds as well as historical accounts. Gabler's use of the terms is a recent construction and a modernist's anachronistic view of history.

Note that, for Gabler, religion plays no role in American society, and reason plays no role in Islamic societies. It is as if the Christian notion of being the superior religion of the world has been secularized to support the American claim to being the superior power and society in the world. But none of that helps us understand the persistence of what Gabler calls the "mind-sets" that are now locked in "an eternal war." He draws upon the long tradition of debate in Western civilizations between reason and "faith," and he is right about the apparent resistance of Christian religious mentality to rational critique and the difficulty Western logic has had in making sense of religion. But the impasse keeps him from suggesting that critical thinking may actually help us explore the logic of myths and religious mentalities if only we were to focus upon the question. We don't know what Gabler would say about the role Christianity has come to play in American society and government. Would he recognize the authority of the Bible as myth for the Christian Right, as he has the authority of the Quran as myth among Islamic peoples? Would he grant the use of the term mythos for the Christian gospels, or call them histories, or deny their social logics? And we don't know how Gabler can be so sure of the "rationality" of the American "mind-set" when its self-confidence about being "scientific" hinders reflexive self-criticism. The best we can do is to read the article as a reflection of the way many Americans think about religion, culture, and society. We can thank him for that straightforward description. We are, apparently, comfortable with the idea that American culture and society are superior in every way to other cultures and societies. And yet, there it is, an American "mind-set" embroiled in approximately fifty years of culture wars within, all with persistent appeals to Christian values as arguments, and its result in a national politics and an administration that uses the rhetoric of righteousness to justify the use of absolute power abroad.

In the course of our history we have encountered many other cultures and religions, but we have still to learn how to engage them constructively. Our encounters have invariably been marred by exploitations, various forms of domination, and missions to convert them to our ways. We have seldom been interested in or able to plumb their different social logics, or to use the comparison of ourselves with them to ask about the social reasons for or intellectual investments in the construction and practice of their myths, rituals, and societies. In the case of Christianity, we have not even dared the kind of questions our scholars have asked about other religions. That should tell us something about the problems we have in coming to terms with the role of religion in a democracy. We do not think critically about religion in public forum. We do not have a tradition of education in the human sciences that includes religion from grammar school through college. Religious studies are pursued mainly in graduate schools of the academy, and the knowledge produced by these studies has not easily found its way into public discourse.

This sets the agenda for our study. We need to develop a social theory of religion in conversation with the history of the study of religions. We will do that in Part I of this book. We also need to trace the history of Christianity as a religion in order to analyze the social logics of its myth and ritual systems. We will do that in Part II of the study. At the end of these studies we will return to the question of the Christian nation and explore the reasons for thinking it an important, if troublesome, manifestation of the challenges confronting Christianity and other religions in our polycultural social democracy.

This book will share with the reader what I have learned in the study of religion. I have taken examples of religions and cultures from ethnography, Asian studies, Ancient Near Eastern studies, the Greco-Roman religions, and Northern European peoples, as well as the histories of Judaism, Islam, Christianity, and the encounters of Western civilization with other peoples since the Age of Discovery. These examples will be used to illustrate how religions work in order to develop a social theory of religion.

Before turning to a brief description of the individual chapters, it may be helpful to mention some characteristic features of religions that begin to surface when they are studied in social contexts. I would like to think that the reader will have already noticed these characteristics and that in some sense they are observations of features merely taken for granted. By mentioning them as items of importance for the study at hand, I hope to tease the reader into thinking about religion with me in ways that are not customary for its popular conceptions. The following items are not yet formulated as ingredients of a general theory of religion (leaving that for the chapters that follow), but they are observations of a kind that may prepare the reader for this study. All are generalizations taken mainly from the archives of the history of religions, frequently with the ethnographic model of a single society in view. Thus they may not appear adequate for a description of the Christian religion in its many variants, much less as applicable to the modern situation of religions in a multicultural nation-state. The strategy, however, is to move away from current concepts and definitions of religion in order to address the current situation as a conceptual problem amenable to critical analysis. I mention these features here in the hope that a fresh set of observations might generate a new set of questions that begin to call for a social theory of religion.

The first observation is that the markers of a people's religion are public knowledge. The myths, symbols, rituals, dances, feasts, festivals, and rules of conduct that we have traditionally taken together as a set of markers for a people's religion are all linked to social moments and occasions. As such, everyone within a people knows about them, and guests from without can usually find ways to observe them. Each has its part to play in what we might call the patterns of daily social activity, the seasonal cycle, the modes of tuition, the rotation of production, the life-cycle of individuals, and the history of the people. This means that the practice of religion is integral to the patterns of practices that structure living together in a society.

A second observation is that individuals may participate in the religious markers of a society in a wide variety of ways. In Christian congregations, participation has usually been thought of as predicated upon belief. However, belief is a peculiarly Christian notion deriving from the odd combination of myth and history in the New Testament gospels. The terms "belief," "faith," and "piety" are not at all adequate to describe the ways in which most people actually learn, accept, and participate in their religious markers. Some individuals may think deeply about their myths, others not at all. Some may take special delight in performing at their festivals, while others prefer looking on. No one stays away because of little faith. In a stable society, one not undergoing major change, religious markers are simply accepted as part of the pattern of social activities and become occasions for celebrating participation in the life of the people.

A third observation concerns the function of myths and rituals. What these add to the mix of systems that structure a society is a magnification of horizon and detail. Myths expand the view of the world beyond the horizon of the local natural environment. Rituals provide a lens to concentrate on the details of significant actions and watch them performed in deliberate perfection, as if set in a different world and time. The times and spaces beyond the contemporary environments and histories of a people, beyond those environments that are available for investigation by means of living memories and empirical contact, become the imagined world where agents and events can be located to reconfigure and gain some distance from social interests and issues as well as the mysteries of the natural world. Such images are often imagined as combinations of features taken from flora, fauna, and humans. We are accustomed to calling these images gods, but if thought of in terms of the Christian concept of God the term "gods" hardly suffices for the vast majority of creatures imagined to populate the unseen imaginary worlds. As a matter of fact, the superhuman beings of primarily anthropological stature, those we have recognized as gods like ours, seem to rise to the top of pantheons where societies have developed hierarchies in which powers become invested in chiefs, kings, and emperors. Of much greater incidence seem to be the ways in which most peoples have imagined their ancestors. Ancestors are often referred to as a collective, but can also be imagined as a single progenitor of the people. The stories of ancestors and heroes mark past events of precedence that are still felt to be effective or influential for the way the world is working in the present. The expanded horizon of the imaginary world is seldom filled with beings and events that form a complete and comprehensive system to account for the real world. And most of the knowledge basic to the workings of the society settles into techniques and rules of practice that are named, learned, and applied without reference to the imaginary world. Nevertheless, the imaginary world frequently becomes a kind of environment that encompasses and centers the society in its history and natural setting. It adds scope, mythic images, and mystery to a society's world. It is also frequently the case that stories set in the imaginary world tell of events in which the morals of the stories can become lessons about the right and wrong ways to act.

A fourth observation is that a combination of the mythic world, the religious markers, and the regular practices of a people create what might be called a mentality characteristic of a people. Because the combination is accepted as the way the world works, and because it is taken for granted, such a mentality is largely unconscious. Looking on from outside a given society, however, and comparing one society with another, it is obvious that a people can share a rather long list of characteristics that distinguish them from other peoples. Such characteristics can include particular attitudes, ways of thinking, values, humor, social practices, habits, and the automatic defense of a people's identity and integrity in the face of comparisons with others and challenges from without. We know about this by encounters with other cultures, and we know how easy it is to point out a few of the distinctive characteristics of another people. What we have not done is ask about the mentality that makes possible such collective characteristics. We have not asked about the social practices, religious markers, and collective investments in a people's identity that may play a role in its pervasive persistence.

A fifth observation is that, when change takes place within a society and its territory, it is frequently the case that its religious markers also change. Changes to the religious markers are often slight, occurring by increments and in subtle ways, in order to accommodate new social situations and configurations. Such change can occur in a variety of ways. The introduction of innovative technologies and the resultant change in patterns of labor and production are one way. Rivalries within the society that result in the rearrangement of hierarchies and the divisions of labor are another. Environmental change, whether caused by human or natural means, can force changes in patterns of production and social practice that bring pressure to bear upon customary myths and rituals. Finally, demographic changes, ranging from internecine conflicts to epidemics, displacements, and population growth and congestion, also become occasions for rethinking and revising myths, religious markers, and cultural symbols. In all of these cases of social change, the chances are that the religious markers will provide a sense of continuity even while both they and the social patterns are undergoing change. Myths are especially amenable to changing. That is because they and their occasions for rehearsal can be set at a slight distance from the performance of rituals or the schedule of festivals in which standards of replication tend to prevail. It is also because myths are stories requiring the imagination and embellishment of the storyteller on some occasion called for by the special circumstances of the people gathered to listen. Thus, in any given rehearsal, an assessment of the current situation of a people can make a difference to the way the storyteller paints the picture of the mythic world, depicts its characters, and relates the things that happen there.

A sixth observation is that, in situations of major social change, religious markers tend to become enhanced as identity markers. When people move or are moved into another people's territory and find themselves living within another culture, changes usually take place in both cultural traditions in order to accommodate differences and fashion skills in negotiation. Religious markers are often the only features of the culture as practiced in its original territory that can be transported. Not all of them can easily be transferred to new locations, but those that can be frequently become the mechanisms for links to the past and symbols of a persistent investment in the identity of a people in terms of its culture. If a people and its territory become the object of another people's conquest and occupation, however, accommodation may take the form of sullenness, resistance, or even hostility. That is because dominant cultures usually treat the other as subordinate, expecting acceptance, obedience, or conversion to the dominant culture's ways. It is then that resistance to the dominant culture can take the form of ideological conflict based on appeal to the authorization of traditional religious markers.

In our time a very complex mix and merger of cultures and social formations make the analysis of the roles of religions very difficult. The Western nations are heirs to their own histories of enlightenment, industrial revolution, imperial expansion and collapse, urbanization, and the development of nation-states with structures of governance in separation from the religious markers, institutions, and authorities of the cultures and societies of the past. Religions and religious institutions from the past have continued, however, now in curious and tensive relations to the nation-states within which they continue their separate existence both at home and abroad. Ideologies of democracy seek justification in humanistic values apart from anchorage in a religion even while the term "multicultural" is used to recognize the persistence of the religions and cultures of the several peoples that are now challenged to find ways to live together in peace. Despite the Western rhetoric of tolerance for other religions, and the notion that all religions are parallel ways to find the one God, the religions and cultures of the many peoples now living together in nation-states do not overlap. Older mentalities persist and the governments of modern nation-states are finding it difficult to treat all the same. Where there is a dominant religion within a nation-state, its beliefs, values, and religious symbols can be taken up by the so-called secular governors to authorize interests and policies that have little to do with the function of those symbols among the peoples who first created them, and especially within the institutions of their religions as people of a culture as well as citizens of a state. And yet, despite the complexity of the situation and the difficulty of analysis, lessons from the history of religions can provide us with comparisons that will help us spot features of the current situation we can understand. Should it be possible to answer the question of why religions matter by developing a theory about religion as a human construction in the interest of the human enterprise of social formation, we might be able to imagine taking some next steps in the construction of the social democracies we are currently trying to create.

This book makes a proposal for just such a theory. Chapter 1 will summarize the ways religion has been explained in the past one hundred and fifty years. I will work with the major theories that scholars have proposed, but also with popular notions and clichés that have settled into place in common parlance. One point will be that the need to account for religion arose in the "discovery" of other peoples in the world and their strange myths and rituals. Another will be that an implicit comparison with Christianity has provided the unexamined model of religion for the definition of terms when describing the religions of other peoples. A third is that it has apparently not been thought necessary to question and analyze the social logics of either Judaism or Christianity in the same way as we have the religions of all other peoples. A summary of the ways in which scholars have studied and thought about religions can help us see why we need a social theory of religion.

Chapter 2 will explore the relation of myths and rituals to social life and describe the concept of *social interests*. This will be a first step in developing a social theory of religion, the aim of Part I of the book. The concept of *social formation* will also be mentioned and related to social theories in general. There are many studies of religion as an important factor in the social and cultural formations of the human enterprise of living together. I will summarize some of them as a way to get the reader to think about the social logics of myths and rituals.

Chapter 3 will introduce a theory of *mythmaking*. This will build on the concept of social interests developed in Chapter 2, but then add reasons for the imaginary environment of a society within which deities can be located. The deities can be seen as imaginary agents of forces that impinge upon intersections of social interests and activities within these environments. Then it will be possible to notice the variety of deities humans have imagined, and to relate certain types to certain social configurations. The chapter will come to focus on the deities familiar to us from the ancient Near East and the Greco-Roman era of Late Antiquity, those we have learned to call gods.

The world of memory and imagination made possible by myth and ritual expands the horizons of a people beyond their current borders in both space and time. The resulting environment thus imagined becomes the place for anchoring precedent events and defining histories, genealogies, credentials, symbols, and the ways in which habitual patterns of thinking and practice fit into the rhyme and reason of the larger world as a whole. The effect is that collective identities, characteristics, and affinities of a people can be imagined apart from any given moment, experience, or event. Thus they can be recalled, thought about, and used to put familiar constructions upon new situations.

Chapter 4 will introduce the notions of *situation* and *mythmaking* in order to explore the reasons for shifts in mythic imagery during times of social change. It will be possible to illustrate both notions and show how each is related to the other. One point will be that, although myths are resistant to change at the levels of collective imagination and cultural mentality, they are a medium available for manipulation and rearrangement when (social-historical) situations call for rethinking. Another point will be to understand how religion influences debate and the marshalling of support for views to be taken and policies implemented in a time of deliberation. A third point will be that both social formations and religious myths and rituals are thoroughly human constructions. It is therefore not surprising that myths are appealed to in times of social change for arguments concerning national attitudes and policies.

Chapter 5 will describe Christian beginnings from the first to the early fourth centuries. It is important to do this as a redescription of the dominant paradigm of Christian origins. The paradigm is based on the New Testament gospels about the dramatic events of the appearance of Jesus as messiah and son of God. Critical scholars now understand the gospels to be the products of early Christian mythmaking in the interest of social experiments among schools of Jesus' followers. It was the concept of the kingdom of God that focused and energized these mythmaking projects and prepared the way for the so-called Constantinian revolution. We must take the time to review this history because the gospel is the Christian myth, and only by redescribing its production can we analyze its structure and its social logic which are still at work in the contemporary Christian imagination.

Chapter 6 will analyze the myth and ritual system of Christendom as a grammar that supports Christian mentality. The importance of the church as a religious institution will be described, and its structure as an institution of empire will be emphasized. That the concept of the church includes a universalizing mission in league with notions of empire will prepare us for a consideration of the "Christian nation" in Chapter 7.

Chapter 7 explores the social logic of the Christian myth and mentality as a legacy that is still at work among us, not only in the institutions of Christianity, but also in the concept of the righteous nation, as well as in the unexamined assumptions that determine the way in which we as a people automatically view the world and make our assessments about the way it works. The Christian myth and mythic world have functioned as the lens or frame of reference for viewing and interpreting other peoples and their cultures in ways that fail both to understand the other and to be reflexive in regard to ourselves. Many Americans now regard the worldviews of traditional Christianities as passé and of little consequence for our modern scientific and rational ways of viewing the world. And yet, features of these mythic worldviews continue to haunt our mentalities even as a so-called secular society. A summary and study of these features can help us frame the questions we might want to ask about religions in our time.

Chapter 8 presents an analysis of our social situation in the United States at the beginning of the twenty-first century. It will be a meditation on the problems we are having with Christianity and other religions in our efforts to construct a social democracy. In spite of the problems a hopeful outlook can be managed. That is because our study will have demonstrated the capacity of a people to transform their myths and religious traditions in response to changing social situations.

The Conclusion invites the reader to think with me about our future as an experiment in the construction of a polycultural social democracy that need not be a Christian nation.

Part I
The Religions of Other Peoples

1 Looking for Religion in the New World

When Columbus landed in 1492 on Guanahani, an island in the outer ring of the Bahamas which he christened San Salvador, the "Age of Discovery" began. The discoveries were of lands and their peoples that had not appeared on older maps of the world. Instead of the three familiar continents there was now a "new world" to challenge the tripartite conception. And instead of the older classification of the peoples of the three continents, derived from the three sons of Noah in Genesis 10, there was now another kind of people not mentioned in the Bible. As Columbus wrote in his log: "These people have no religious beliefs, nor are they idolaters. They are very gentle and do not know what evil is... They have no religion" (*Diario*, 143). They came to be called "Indians," in keeping with the purpose of Columbus's voyage to reach the Spice Islands of India by sailing west instead of around the continent of Africa, but it was soon clear to others that he had reached lands and peoples very different from those he had hoped to find. That did not keep Columbus or the other explorers of the sixteenth and seventeenth centuries from claiming the lands for the kings and queens of Europe, or from treating the natives as subjects of their sovereigns.

Columbus thought he had circumnavigated the world and landed in the Spice Islands, one of the sources of luxurious and exotic trade goods from the East. Another was China, the kingdom of the Kubla Khan, well known by now from the travels of Marco Polo in the thirteenth century and the lore about the Silk Road. But these goods—silk and spices—could be acquired only by laborious overland caravans or by sailing around the southern cape of Africa. Since Marco Polo had been by land to the easternmost limits of the *oikoumene* ("inhabited world"), beyond which lay ocean, once the notion that the earth was round had been accepted, it was possible to imagine sailing around the world from the western shores of Europe and its offshore islands to the eastern shores of the *oikoumene* and its offshore islands. The lands and seas had now been charted on the Catalan Map of the world, the one used by Henry the Navigator and Columbus. Where else could Columbus have landed after sailing due west except on the eastern shore of Asia?

Columbus persisted in thinking that he had reached the shores of Asia, despite the many differences in geography, flora, fauna, and people encountered, and the failure to find anything like the great Khan and his kingdom. But others soon realized that these lands were "new," previously unknown to Europeans. The story of attempts to find some place for them on the old maps, or to revise the old maps without having to acknowledge that they were faulty and incapable of containing the new information about the shape of the world, can be found in an essay by Jonathan Z. Smith, "What a Difference a Difference Makes." His study reveals an amazing stretching of the imagination of sixteenth-century Europeans in order to accommodate the reports of distinctive features of a geography and peoples that differed from those familiar to them. They unleashed an intellectual project of historic consequence for Western thinking, the beginnings of what we have come to call the academic disciplines devoted to research in the earth sciences, biological sciences, social sciences, and histories of the natural and cultural worlds. Our present study will be limited to just one discipline and set of categories generated by the discovery of the New World, those that focus upon peoples and their religions.

Peoples without Religion

Of particular interest for the subsequent quest of Europeans to understand another people and their religion is Columbus's observation that the natives of the new world had no religious beliefs and no idolatry. This is a theme repeated many times in the diary of the first voyage. In the European world of the fifteenth century, Christianity was the definition of religion, although it was known that other people also had religions, such as Judaism, Mohammedanism, and the religions of India and China. These, however, were regarded as false religions, and a fourfold classification of religions was still standard in the seventeenth century, namely "Christianity, Mohametanism, Judaism, and Idolatry." Since Christianity was taken for granted as the true religion, and all others known at the time were regarded as false religions, there was no need for Columbus to be more specific about the meaning of the term *religion*. As a category of thought and definition it had only two connotations: true and false. But to find neither religious beliefs nor idolatry among the natives of the new world confounded even this traditional classification. From reading his logs, it is clear that Columbus was having trouble comprehending how this could be. Again and again he mentioned that the Indians did not have items that belonged to the European conception of Christianity, a conception that had assimilated many of the customary marks of imperialist culture, such as clothes (they were naked), buildings (they had only palm-thatched tents that reminded him of Moorish military camps), weapons, iron, worship, prayers, agriculture, law, and a knowledge of evil. Thus the Indians had no (true) religion, but neither did they have "false religion nor are they idolaters." This astonishment was registered many times by subsequent explorers and historians (J. Z. Smith, "Religion"). And so it was that the discovery of peoples who had no religion was to become the occasion for the study of religion in the next several centuries. The first response, of course, was to think of these indigenous peoples as in desperate need of religion and civilization. Thus the request to "Your Highnesses" to send "devout religious persons...to convert the Indians...to increase the Holy Christian Religions" (*Diario*, 141). It was not long, however, before Cortez landed at Vera Cruz in 1519 and discovered an advanced civilization of the Aztecs that did not match either the Christendom of the European kingdoms or the civilizations of the Muslims and other peoples to the east of Europe. The encounter resulted in conflict, as did the incursion of Pizarro into the Inca empire of Atahuallpa in 1532 (Diamond, *Guns, Germs, and Steel*, 61–82). The Incas were considered "infidels," and the explorers became conquistadors. Scribes and priests commissioned to record such explorations found themselves curious about the "heathens" and began to keep diaries with their observations of native practices, a sort of primitive ethnography.

During the sixteenth and seventeenth centuries exploration turned to colonization and the sending of missionaries throughout the Americas and the Pacific Islands. In 1524 the Franciscans arrived in Mexico. In 1531 Zumarrage, the first archbishop of Mexico, reported the destruction of 500 heathen temples. In 1537 Pope Paul III declared that the American Indians were entitled to liberty and property, but that did not mean the missions to convert them were wrong. In 1540 he approved the foundation of the Jesuits, who then launched their many missions, from India to the Americas. Some voices were raised to question these designs upon the New World peoples. The lectures of Francisco de Vitoria at Salamanca from 1527 to 1540 criticized the conquest of the Indies on the basis of moral considerations. And in 1552 Bartholomé Las Casas, a Spanish historian and missionary to Hispaniola, published his account of the oppression of the Indians. But the conquests and missions continued, as did colonization throughout the seventeenth century. In 1620 the *Mayflower* landed at Plymouth Rock, and by the end of the century the Society for the Propagation of the Gospel in Foreign Parts was founded in London (in 1701). The logs, letters, and treatises describing the indigenous peoples from the new world and beyond began to stack up back home in Europe.

These reports, many written by Christian missionaries, entered an arena of intellectual ferment in Europe. The ferment was partly the result of the Renaissance and its new appreciation of the natural world and partly was created by the Protestant reformers and their critique of the Catholic tradition. Luther's replacement of Catholic religion with his doctrine of "justification by faith alone" became the basis for the distinction later German theologians and scholars would make between "religion" (Catholicism) and "faith" (Protestantism) as two types of Christianity. This distinction did not immediately affect the reading of the ethnographic reports with their detailed observations of Indian practices and attempts to describe their beliefs. It did, however, contribute to the questions soon to be raised about religion, both theirs and that of Christianity, by scholars on the threshold of the Enlightenment. The intellectual excitements of the seventeenth century included the advances in astronomy and science made by Copernicus, Galileo, and Newton; the "Book of Nature," as Galileo called it, that began to unfold as the field of mathematics was applied to the natural environment; and the distribution of knowledge made possible by the invention of the wooden printing press. It was becoming clear that there were many peoples in the world, from Africa to the south and the Canary Islands off its western coast through the Americas and the islands of the Pacific to the shores of Asia, who were living in communities with strange practices, incomprehensible ideas and rites, and without the benefit of "history," "religion," "civilization," a "scientific view" of the natural world, "technology," and "knowledge of God." How could that be?

The ferment speeded up during the eighteenth century. Science produced natural philosophy and the Industrial Revolution. The Enlightenment produced rational philosophy, historical research, and social critique. Romanticism produced sensibility for the arts, individual introspection, and cultural critique. Locke's treatises from the 1690s were being read: *An Essay Concerning Human Understanding* and *The Reasonableness of Christianity*. Rousseau wrote on the origin of languages, inequality among peoples, and "the noble savage." Hume wrote *A Treatise of Human Nature* and *An Enquiry Concerning Human Understanding*. It was the age of Goethe, Voltaire, Diderot, the American and French revolutions, and the first of the modern nation-states. This intellectual climate made possible questions about the ways in which humans live in the world, understand their natural environments, think about themselves, and develop different kinds of societies and cultures. Here and there treatises began to appear that tentatively proposed viewing the New World peoples as having "spiritual dispositions" common to humankind, as Fontenelle put it in his *De l'origine des fables* (1724), a comparative study of Greek and Amerindian myths. It was not until the nineteenth century, however, that major studies appeared which looked for the signs of religion among native Americans.

Signs of "Primitive" Religion

The nineteenth century saw the publication of the *Sacred Books of the East* by Max Mueller, the corpus of Greek inscriptions, the old Icelandic Eddas (mythological and heroic poetry), portions of the Babylonian creation epic *Enuma Elish*, the Egyptian *Book of the Dead*, the *Fairy Tales* of the Brothers Grimm, and various collections of European folk customs regarded as remnants from pre-Christian times. This interest in exploring the myths and rituals of the past of Europeans, Ancient Near Eastern peoples, and the peoples of India was one of the ways in which Enlightenment scholars stepped outside the orientation to Christian thought and its worldview, which had been determinative for the medieval period. Texts turned into data for the study of other religions, now to be appreciated without the disparagement of being false or inferior to Christianity. And now the ethnographic reports from the Americas could also be compared. The reports from missionaries had become quite detailed, and they were being joined by ethnographies from scholars in the field. Many native tribes were being visited for first-hand observation, questioning, and the recording of their myths, ideas, and ceremonies. The nineteenth century also saw the beginnings of archeological investigations of prehistoric Europe, such as the cave paintings at Altamira in Spain and the beehive tombs of the Peloponnesus. Mannhardt's collection and study of evidence for *Forest and Field Cults* in Europe appeared (1875–77). Frazer's *Golden Bough* burst on the scene (1890–1922). It was a twelve-volume compendium on myths and rituals from Late Antiquity, Africa, and elsewhere in which a king is killed and gods die and rise, as Frazer interpreted them. He thought the death–resurrection theme could also be seen in European folk festivals such as the Maypole, the Corn Mother planting and harvest festivals, and the fire festivals at Easter and other times of the year. These interpretations have since been criticized and set aside, but at the time the large collection of texts in these twelve volumes expanded the database for the study of pre-Christian and non-Christian religions, and they were pored over by scholars and others wondering what to think about these primitive practices (J. Z. Smith, "When the Bough Breaks").

One of the more important observations about nineteenth-century scholarship is that two complementary notions played a role in many of its fields of study. One notion was that of origins, another that of evolution. Darwin published his *On the Origin of Species* (1859) in the field of natural sciences. Using comparative philology, linguists were looking for the origins of the Indo-Aryan languages. In the study of ancient texts, since the Renaissance and Reformation the earliest was prized. Philosophers went back to the classical texts of ancient Greece for points of departure and anchorage. And Protestants had jumped over the history of Catholicism to land at the beginning and explore the New Testament gospels and the letters of Paul for the pristine origins of the Christian faith uncontaminated by Catholicism. Origins were regarded as definitional and explanatory of later "developments." The quest was to identify the first words, ideas, texts, myths, experiences, and ceremonies that had generated subsequent traditions and practices. Voilà! The Amerindians and other indigenous cultures of the new worlds could now be given their place in the history of religions at the beginnings of human time. They could now be viewed as "primitives," a designation that was better than other earlier terms such as "savages," but one that nevertheless continued to identify them negatively, solely in relation to the "higher" civilizations. The idea was that their religion, supposing they had one and that it was possible to describe it, might well reveal the origins of religion in all its subsequent developments. There was a deep irony in this move, to be sure, one which was hardly noticed. It was that the peoples who did not have religion might end up defining religion in ways that traditional Christians would be unable to recognize.

The medieval schema of human history based on the Bible was still present even if its accounts of the earliest pre-Abrahamic peoples had now to be expanded. In traditional Christian thinking the Bible documented the history of humankind as a progression that started with the creation of the world, had a bumpy start because of the sin and wickedness into which humans fell, to be given a second chance after the flood, but then narrowed in the covenant with Abraham, and finally opened out to Christendom with the advent of Christ. In Protestant thinking, Catholic Christendom was then superseded by Reformed Christianity and the Age of Reason, yielding a three- or fourfold scheme of stages from paganism through the religions of Judaism and Christianity to the Enlightenment. This notion of evolution by stages, initially tied to eighteenth-century theories of the progress of economies of subsistence (hunting to pastoralism to agriculture to commerce), was hardly adequate to account for the transitions from one to the other, but it was accepted as a general schema by rationalist thinking in many fields besides that of the history of religion. Auguste Comte published a course in positive philosophy (1830–42) in which he outlined ways of explaining the natural world in three stages: theological, by attributing creation to the gods; metaphysical, in which the philosophical concept of the absolute accounted for the world; and positivistic explanations in which natural causes were discovered by science. This pervasive origins–evolutionary scheme soon became the way in which the study of primitive peoples was taken up and focused upon the question of their religion.

Since the concept of religion in the minds of Enlightenment scholars was still defined by belief in God as a supernatural being and his worship, it was difficult to imagine that the primitives had a religion. However, the ethnographic literature on primitive societies described the ways in which primitive peoples lived in relation to their natural environments, and these features of their practices appeared to be a kind of "natural religion" or "religion of nature." In traditional Western thinking, fascination with the mysteries and beauty of the natural world was hardly the way to worship the creator, as Petrarch's fourteenth-century confession documents. His sense of guilt was caused by a momentary lapse of attention and adoration, focusing on the lovely valley spread out below him instead of on the divine world above. But after four hundred years Renaissance man had finally learned to appreciate the romance of the natural world. The old folk festivals still practiced in European villages and tied to the cycle of the seasons had traits that some said were religious. What if the New World primitives were religious in the same way? They were hardly ignorant of their worlds, having given names to the many animals, plants, and geographic features of their natural environment and knowing precisely how to treat its living creatures and natural cycles in the interest of their own patterns of life together. A kind of respect for the natural order on the one hand, and close observation of particular features of it on the other, described a mentality that, while very different from the European, was found to be intriguing. Detailed classification of the flora and fauna was matched by clearly outlined social relations related to tribal and kinship systems. The several kinship groups (clans) of a tribe could be named after different animals or birds (they are bears; we are eagles). The feathers from the eagle might be collected by the eagle clan, crafted into objects and ornaments for use on special occasions, and sometimes left as markers at an appropriate location away from the village as a reminder of their role in the patterns of tribal activity. Hunting and gathering were hardly haphazard practices and often involved group preparations that looked faintly like rituals to make sure the animals and the weather cooperated with the hunt. The clans and families knew their places in the tribal systems of kinship and the distribution of labor, how to work and live together, and how to handle conflicts. Feathers and furs, shells and wooden implements seemed to take on what might be called values for trading, dressing, and symbolizing status. They understood gifts and reciprocal exchange as a matter of course, both among themselves and when engaging the natural world in hunting and harvesting. The sly fox, the imperious eagle, the trickster coyote, and the dangerous snake all had names and stories that gave them characters and interests and designs upon the world that impinged upon those of the primitives themselves. Thus the Europeans found themselves taken with the picture of primitives responding to the natural world as alive, motivated, and encompassing. And the reports from missionaries were full of teasing suggestions about native references to the powers, forces, and spirits of their natural world. Why not describe their view of the world as a natural religion with a belief in spirits?

It was Sir Edward Burnett Tylor who put it all together as a theory of the origins of religion in the two volumes of *Primitive Culture* (1871). He knew that a redefinition of religion as "faith in spiritual beings," as he put it, required a more precise explanation of its origins than the ethnography actually provided. And, if primitive religion really was the origin of later religions, one would also have to explain how belief in spirits could turn into belief in souls and finally gods. He struggled with the several terms that had already been used to attempt a description of primitive religion, such as fetishism, awe, magic, superstition, a "disease of language" (taking their myths of natural and imaginary agents literally), nature worship, ancestor worship, and animism. Tylor settled on the term *animism*. Taken from the Latin word *animus* meaning "mind" or "spirit," it contained human psychological connotations without immediately suggesting the theological concept of the soul (which had its roots in the Greek term *psyche*), although it is not difficult to see that Tylor was much interested in deriving the concept of soul from his animistic origins theory. To do this he focused, not on the way primitives believed in all of the spirits inhabiting their world, but upon two "biological problems" that he thought the primitives would have had, namely (1) what to make of human figures in dreams, and (2) what to think about a person after its body was dead. One might consider this cheating, for it superimposed a European set of conceptual problems upon the primitives' world of thinking. It was a set of problems for which the enlightened Englishman of the late nineteenth century already had the solutions and it reverberated so nicely, bouncing back and forth between the Christian notion of soul and the English obsession with séances, ghosts, and gothic mysteries. Nevertheless, Tylor's turn to ghosts and dreams made it possible to achieve his objective, namely, to find a link between the primitive belief in spirits and later forms of religious belief recognizable to the European view. He did this by filling in a few stages in the personification of spirit from *animus* to soul and then to gods in order to end with a category of religion that the nineteenth century understood. He worked this development out by using funerary rites and sacrificial rituals as mechanisms by which the several conceptual transitions took place, even though the scenarios of such rituals had to be taken from sources that were hardly primitive. The result was that the primitive layer of the development did not look much different from the first earlier views of superstition, the idea that primitives did not think clearly. Tylor in fact worked backward from his dream and death scenarios to suggest that the two "problems" had to do with the confusion of subjective and objective reality, or the inability to tell the difference between the presence and absence of an "insubstantial" entity. Thus, for Tylor, religion rested on psychological delusion and mistaken logical inference, just as earlier scholars had thought. This fit the thinking of the Age of Reason, however, and became the major theory of primitive religion with which much of the next century had to agree or contend. The prevailing view was that religion developed from animism through polytheism to monotheism. Darwin wrote to him: "It is wonderful how you trace animism from the lower races up to the religious beliefs of the highest races... How curious, also, are the survivals or rudiments of old customs" (*Encyclopedia Britannica*, 15th edition, Vol. 18, 808).

Frazer accepted Tylor's theory of animism and the soul, but was much more interested in taboos and rituals as attempts to evade or control the forces of nature. Magic, he thought, was the origin of religion, and it must have been "pre-animistic." When primitives discovered that their own magic did not work, they turned to the gods (wherever they came from) in rituals of negotiation to ask the gods to perform for them. Andrew Lang would have none of that. In 1898 he published *The Making of Religion*, rejected Tylor's theory of animism and the evolution of religion from primitive superstitions to monotheism, and instead argued for belief in a "high god" and monotheism among primitives at the beginning, after which there was unfortunately a deterioration of religion into mythic irrationality. As the nineteenth century came to an end, some scholars such as R. R. Marett began to question the rationalistic basis of religion and the intellectualist theories of primitive religion by suggesting that the emotional responses of primitives to the forces of their environments must have preceded animism. As evidence, he referred to the description of *mana* in the reports of a missionary to Melanesia, Robert Henry Codrington, and his translation of *mana* as the "power" in persons and things that determined the ways primitives treated them. This interpretation of *mana* is no longer held by scholars (J. Z. Smith, "Manna, Mana, Everywhere and /'/'/'").

All of these attempts to describe primitive religion were scholarly projects of some magnitude, requiring the accumulation of massive amounts of data and years of research. And yet, in retrospect, they can now be seen as projects that had a great deal of trouble understanding the mentality of these primitive peoples, mainly because they were also struggling to rethink their own concepts of religion. The traditional notion of religion had run into trouble in light of the expanded scope of human histories, societies, and logics that the Enlightenment, colonial expansions, and Industrial Revolution had brought into view. It is not difficult to see that the notion of religion in the minds of these scholars was still indebted to an unexamined familiarity with Christianity as its source and definition, despite the criticisms of Catholic Christianity that had taken place during the Reformation and Enlightenment. In keeping with the early explorers' observation that the New World peoples had no religion, that is, were not like Christians, scholars of the nineteenth century thought of themselves as having put aside the traditional concept of religion while looking for its origins in the cultures of the primitives. What happened was that the cultures of the primitives became the field of play for Western scholars to work out their own problems with their understanding of religion now that the concept of Christianity was also in need of redefinition.

One can see that the selections scholars made of this or that feature of the ethnographic descriptions of native peoples were determined by attempts to find their own culture reflected in the religion of the primitives and by questions about how to proceed with its critical analysis. Most of this project was accomplished obliquely, not by direct reference to Christian beliefs and practices from which the notion of religion was taken. But the ways in which the archaic and primitive religions were thought to reflect features of traditional Christian myth and ritual are not difficult to discern. Thus, in effect, the myths of the killing of the kings in Frazer's *Golden Bough* are easily read as precursors of the Christ myth, and the frequent tracing of ritual sacrifice to magic throughout this entire period of research can easily be turned around as a commentary on and criticism of Catholic Christian ritual by Protestants. Tylor's theory of the gods as personifications of ghosts is a bit more difficult to read as an influence from and/or implicit criticism of (Catholic) Christian religion, but it does agree with the sensibilities of nineteenth-century British mentality and is not entirely removed from a Quakerly suspicion of Christian theology. Lang's theory of primitive monotheism is easily read as a defense of the biblical view of human history, where the one creator God had to exist at the beginning. The subsequent history was cast in light of a Protestant critique of Catholicism as a mythic degeneration. By working out the origins of religion in terms of belief in spirits, rituals as magic, and the irrationality of the primitive mind, eighteenth- and nineteenth-century scholars did not accomplish a reasonable description of primitive cultures, nor did they produce a theory of religion adequate for the analysis of the religions of other cultures. Nevertheless, the term religion, dislodged from its definition only in terms of Catholic Christianity, was on its way to becoming a general category in the investigation of disparate cultures.

Early Sociologies

One can trace this change taking place with even greater clarity during the late nineteenth and early twentieth centuries. The most remarkable shifts in the study of religion during this period were related to the advent of sociology and ethnology. The social sciences were stimulated by the changing configurations of social relations and political ideologies in the Western nations, and it began to dawn on intellectuals that religion was somehow related to the mentalities and cultural patterns that affected the actual workings of economic, social, and political systems. The changing social conditions brought about by the Industrial Revolution in England, where the plight of workers who had moved to the cities to work in the factories was dismal, generated a remarkable literature and public debate in quest of understanding the causes for such a radical change in English society and what should be done to humanize it. Essays and books burgeoned in descriptive critique of the social effects of the Industrial Revolution. The French experiment with democracy was always in view, but the French Revolution was seen as bloody and chaotic. This resulted in a fear of the uneducated masses of workers taking the reins of government that made cultured English intellectuals cautious. The agony of it all was felt primarily, not just in an assessment of the ugliness that the factories had produced in the cities and the lives of the poor, but in the erosion of traditional English culture and its apparent inability to address the situation. Raymond Williams has cited and discussed more than thirty English essayists from 1780 to 1950 (thus spanning the nineteenth century) in his *Culture and Society*. The writers were more than comfortable with their positions as guardians of the traditional values associated with Anglican Christianity, high-class education, moral values, literature, arts, and civil government, and their focus usually fell on the questions of how to educate the lower classes and how to persuade the newly wealthy industrial giants to treat their workers humanely. Thus, they did not produce a critical analysis of religion and society, thinking of the Anglican tradition as a necessary ingredient in English society for the inculcation of character and culture. Yet it was here in England that Karl Marx produced *Das Kapital* (1867), and the London school of social science was to emerge, striking evidence of the ferment of ideas unleashed by the social changes of the times.

In Germany, Max Weber turned an education in the history of agrarian economics into a devastating critique of the capitalist agrarian policies of the Bismarck aristocracy; he grew pessimistic about the chances of liberal thinking to change matters for the benefit of German society and its peasants, and suspected that Protestant Christianity was partly to blame. He published *The Protestant Ethic and the Spirit of Capitalism* in 1904–5, and then began a series of studies on charisma, tradition, and law as types of authority in the structuring of societies. Religions continued to fascinate him, and a collection of essays on the sociology of religions, including Zoroastrianism, Judaism, Christianity, the religions of India and China, and others was published in 1920. His comparative method treated these religions of the modern civilized world as total systems of cultural significance and ideological consequence for social structures. Weber's primary interest in comparing these religions was to determine (1) the effect of a religion on a system of economy, and (2) the effect of rational ways of thinking on what he understood to be a universal human concern with gods and their control of the world. Starting with tribal religions and Marett's theory of "pre-animism," Weber regarded natives as "enchanted" with the spirits and forces that affected the way their world worked. Rituals were essentially the magical means to influence the gods. A partial "disenchantment" took place in the later religions where priests and prophets rationalized rituals, conceptualized gods, and formulated various attitudes toward the world in keeping with the nature of the imagined god. In Weber's view, the world as human environment was problematic and incapable of supporting the human desire for "salvation." In the "stages" of "disenchantment" of the gods, various forms of salvation were distinguished, to end with a description of twentieth-century Calvinism. Protestantism fostered an ascetic ethic in the interest of demonstrating one's "election" in the face of a *deus absconditus* (hidden god) whose final judgment could not be known. Thus, rationalism had succeeded in the disenchantment of the gods, but it had not erased the human need for "salvation." In Weber's view, asceticism and mysticism were the only forms of religious experience still available to modernity. Less a social theory of religion than a sociology of the religions under review, the importance of his work was, nevertheless, to demonstrate that religions make a difference to the workings of social structures and political practices. His influence in the study of religion as an important factor in the construction of cultural mentalities and social ideologies can be traced throughout the twentieth century and is still quite strong at the beginning of the twenty-first.

Meanwhile, in Paris, Émile Durkheim, Marcel Mauss, and others were forming the French school of sociology. They were critical of the unexamined assumptions that had determined the definition of religion in the preceding century's quest for the origins of religion, namely, that religion had to do with belief in gods, the supernatural, animism, mystifications, and magic. Instead they understood religion as the way in which a people brought to expression and cultivated their social bonds. They were much interested in working with the ethnographics of primitive peoples because these societies were less complex and elaborated than those of the highly differentiated civilizations. What they looked for were the fundamental elements of a religious practice that affected the formation, functioning, and maintenance of a society. Mauss studied the logic of exchange among primitive peoples, reducing the ethnographic descriptions to the underlying principles that turned the "gift" into a system of obligations—the social obligations to give, receive, and return. By demonstrating that the principle of reciprocity was involved in the rituals, patterns of exchange, and social etiquettes of primitive peoples, he was able to merge the functions of religion, economics, and the practices of social relations into a single coherent picture. The term "religion" was retained for certain phenomena, such as ritual occasions, but the concept and definition of religion were radically socialized.

Durkheim found himself fascinated with the reports and ideas of "totemism" among Amerindians and native Australians, and in 1912 he published *Les Formes élémentaires de la vie religieuse*. *Totem* was a term taken from the Ojibwa Indians of the Algonquin tribe northwest of the Great Lakes, possibly meaning "blood kin" in reference to sisters and brothers belonging to the same clan, who were therefore not allowed to marry. But it soon came to be used for the practice of many other tribes to give their clans the names of animals and plants, mark themselves with signs of such identity, and use the emblems on ritual occasions to contract rites of passage and celebrate cross-clan negotiations. It was at first thought by earlier scholars that the relation of a clan to the animal or plant from which it took its name had to be described in terms of identity confusion, if not awe, reverence, mysticism, and union with the supernatural, thus as features of religion. In his study of totemism so defined among the tribes of Australia, however, Durkheim was able to counter these ideas in a thorough description of the "social facts" of totemism and a penetrating analysis of the "fundamental elements" of the system. The social facts included the functional relation of totemistic practices and ideas to such things as the classification of plants, animals, and geographical objects in the natural order, and to systems of kinship and clan relationships in the social order. The clan emblems called *tjuringas* played a role in male–female distinctions, dietary rules, initiation rites, ancestor memorials, and festivals of display, recognition, and tuition in which the tribe as a social unity of clans was acknowledged and celebrated. The question was whether you could call totemism a religion at all.

Durkheim saw that something curious had happened during the preceding century when the term "religion" started to be used in reference to the world religions of India and China without the denigrations usually associated with comparison to Christianity. Since it was clear that these other religions of high civilizations did not have systems of belief comparable to Christianity, such as belief in a personal god of creation, cosmos, and history, it meant that religion no longer needed to be defined by Christianity, whether explicitly or implicitly. It was still acceptable to think of all peoples having a religion, including the primitive cultures, but that no longer meant having to look for their belief in and worship of gods who populated a supernatural realm. For the entire nineteenth century scholars had been looking for the embryo of Christianity among primitive cultures. It was no longer necessary or right to continue doing that. It was still possible to look for religion among the primitives, he thought, as long as its evolution did not have to end in Christianity or other cultures. So what was the ultimate ground of religion, if it was not belief in gods and spirits of a supernatural order? It was, according to Durkheim, the encompassing reality and affect of the social facts that provided the structure for a social order. Primitives experienced this reality in terms of the bonds it established in human relations, social system supports, and principles of identity and obligation. It was a reality that "transcended" any given individual, clan, or practice and thus was "prior" to all of the elaborations of a given society and its rites. Durkheim used the term *sacré* to account for the care, respect, rules of approach, and taboos surrounding the *tjuringa*, totems, markers of clan identity, and other "emblems." Reading carefully, one can see that he used this term (*sacré*) because he wanted to acknowledge the primitives' attitudes of special attention and respect for these emblems without calling these attitudes religious. When he did occasionally use the terminology of religion, he preferred the adjective religious over the noun religion. He tended to do that whenever his description of a totemistic practice such as the imitation of the clan animal in dances and ceremonies began to look like the collapse of distinction between the human and the animal or the worship of the totem as a supernatural being. Such conclusions were invariably countered with additional analyses of the fundamental logic of the totemic system at work in the particular instance. Living together as a social unit was the prior and primary creator of its totemistic structure and systems, and it was the social unit itself that was being acknowledged and celebrated by means of the display and manipulation of the totemic emblems.

Unfortunately, the term *sacré* hardly remained uncontaminated with traditional connotations of religion, and mainly for that reason Durkheim's proposal for a radically different definition of religion was not always accepted or understood by subsequent scholars. Nevertheless, in the wake of his work, it became possible to use the term religion as a general category covering different kinds of religion, and the term *sacré* (sacred) as the description of any religion's manifestations in beliefs and practices, thus allowing for the comparative study of religions. That both terms were as yet undefined, that is, without clear conceptual or descriptive content, was hardly noticed.

Noticing Tribal Intelligence

In America the study of primitive religions took a different turn. That was because it was the land of contact and engagement with the Amerindian peoples on the one hand, and also because of the influence of Franz Boas, the founder of the discipline of cultural anthropology on the other. It was Boas who insisted on the method of studying primitive peoples that came to be called ethnography. Before accepting a faculty position in anthropology at Columbia University in New York in 1899, he had become interested in Amerindian cultures, doing research on Baffin Island and Vancouver Island. On the basis of this experience he became critical of the quest for origins and the notion of evolution current at the end of the nineteenth century. He developed instead the method of doing research in the field (fieldwork), learning the native language, living with a tribe for a period of time, and observing all aspects of its life in order to determine how each feature of its social system and culture fit together to make a whole. He taught his many students to treat a tribal culture with respect and to look for the interweaving of its many patterns of activity and thinking in its organization as a society. His students went forth to do just that, living with indigenous peoples not only in the Americas but also around the world, and producing scholarly ethnographies aimed at both detailed description and theoretical understanding. The names of tribes, their lands, and territories now dot the scholar's memory map of the twentieth-century studies along with the names of ethnologists who made advances in theory.

Reading this scholarship in retrospect, one is struck by the degree to which something called the "primitive mind" emerged as the object of study. Boas asked the question in *The Mind of Primitive Man* (1911), arguing a startling and controversial thesis to the effect that all peoples of whatever race had an equal capacity to develop societies and cultural forms. Though the Nazis burned his book in the 1930s, and although many anthropologists had to do cartwheels in coming to terms with his theses, after Boas, primitive peoples could no longer be regarded as incapable of reasoning, as had been the case in the nineteenth century. It was discovered that primitive peoples often had produced classified inventories of flora, fauna, stones, and woods that, though stored in the minds of the primitives, could easily compete with the scientific classifications of the modern world available only in detailed, scientific textbooks. And it was obvious that experimentation had taken place, for the properties and practical uses of natural materials were also matters of tribal knowledge. Then there was the amazing complexity of kinship systems known to all persons in the tribe, the rules of which governed genealogical systems and the classification of a tribe's moieties, clans, and families. Kinship systems provided rules and equations for deciding on the proper marriage partners, cross-clan changes in residence for one of the partners in a marriage, the assignment of clan membership to a child, and the ways in which a child would be initiated into the adult world and by whom before, at, and after puberty. Ethnographers were frequently stunned by the discovery that such systems, together with the various ways of working out the equations and manipulating them, were taken for granted by members of a tribe and stored in a memory system of much greater detail than could be managed by westerners, frequently including the ethnologists themselves.

As for the relations among *Magic, Science, and Religion* in primitive cultures, the title of an ethnographic study of the Trobriand Islanders by Malinowski

(1948), both "magic" and "religion" seemed to fade away as ornaments around the edges of their "scientific" achievements and practices. They had figured out the exact ratio of outrigger to canoe for peak stability and efficiency without benefit of a Western-style mathematical calculus, and they were able to transfer the knowledge of this ratio and its application to the construction of outriggers from generation to generation even though they did not refer to mathematical calculations based on numbers. As for their engagement of the natural world, they knew exactly the time of year the fish would be running. Getting ready for the fishing season was naturally a significant activity, and it presented occasions for mimetic rituals and dancing that through the eyes of the nineteenth-century scholars had looked like magic or religion. But, of course, the natives knew full well what the forces of nature were that were converging, and they also knew what and how to engage them, and what their chances were for survival and success. No primitive magic, superstition, and religion there.

It was the same with the description of the way totems worked in *The Savage Mind* by Lévi-Strauss (1966), and the way myths engaged the processes of thinking on the part of native peoples, as analyzed in his four-volume series, *Introduction to a Science of Mythology*. This list of discoveries could easily be extended. The Winnebagos' village layout, with its orientation to the north–south, east–west coordinates of the globe, revealed a remarkable skill and interest in the orientation of social structures to the natural world and its seasonal cycles. The village layout was also found to have a subtle, complex interweaving of dual clan orientation to the hierarchy of the tribe (J. Z. Smith, *To Take Place*, 42–9). The totem poles of the Haida and Tlingit were found to evoke not reverence toward nature or the gods, but honor and memorial to a tribal chief and his clan lineage. The social logic of the potlatch, in which the accumulation of wealth at the top of the tribe was divested in a ceremony that gave it all back to members of the tribe, had nothing to do with sentiments usually associated with religion. Its social logic could be worked out as making sense for their economic system of production and distribution of goods, their tribal system of organization, as well as being an occasion for all the tribe to pay extraordinary attention to a ceremony that confirmed their way of life and thinking, and that allowed for taking delight in the redistribution of goods. The shaman's knowledge of a situation and his use of a basket of feathers and stones to treat distress and disease (J. Z. Smith, "Sacred Persistence," 49–52), the reasons for a network of African villages to decide it was time for another circumcision ceremony (Turner, "Mukanda"), the social circumstances calling for a pig festival in New Guinea (Rappaport, *Pigs for the Ancestors*), and the social and strategic significance of elaborate dressings, paintings, and tattooing of the body, all these and other features of native practices were analyzed by scholars and found to have their social logics and their intellectual integrities rooted in classificatory schemes, schemes "which allow the natural and social universe to be grasped as an organized whole," as Lévi-Strauss put it in *The Savage Mind* (135).

As one might expect, there has been vigorous debate among scholars working in the field of religious studies. Not all were able to accept the trends in ethnology. Religion seemed to disappear in the descriptions of tribal cultures. And the emphasis on the primitive "mind" seemed far too intellectual to explain what looked like emotional involvement with the primitives' world of the "sacred." The problem was that religion in the minds of many scholars was still being thought of on the model of Christianity. Familiarity with the Christian religion had provided an implicit definition of the term that seemed to require a certain sensibility when meditating on the divine. It is understandable that the Christian view of the world and its extremely rich and all-encompassing history of cultural productions could not simply be set aside as being of no consequence for the study of religion. It is therefore not surprising to find studies of primitive religions and world religions throughout the twentieth century that continued to think of religion on the Christian model.

The theory of primitive belief in a "high god" or primal monotheism, as in Lang, continued to find proponents, as in the works of Wilhelm Schmidt, *The Origin and Growth of Religion*, and quite differently in Raffaele Pettazoni, *The All-Knowing God: Researches into Early Religion and Culture*, while some scholars still emphasized the pre-logical, mystical, and affective sensibility of primitive mentality. Lévy-Bruhl published a study on primitive mentality in 1922 (*How Natives Think*) in which he argued that there was a big difference between the reasoning of primitives who did not understand the relation between cause and effect and the rationalism of civilized cultures that did. Rudolf Otto took up the concept of "the holy" (*das Heilige*; "the sacred") and described the human experience of it as one of attraction (awe) and revulsion (fear), thus describing religion psychologically on the Christian model. Adolf E. Jensen argued in his *Myth and Cult among Primitive Peoples* that both myth and cult were based on the primitives' myth of a primal killing that effected a rupture between prehuman time and human time with its experiences of death, sexuality, and cultivation of plants for food. The implicit analogy to biblical and Christian themes is obvious.

Theories of "the Sacred"

Meanwhile, another attempt at descriptive explanation was emerging in the studies of G. van der Leeuw and Mircea Eliade, which was to have a profound effect on the study of religion. Both of these scholars amassed voluminous illustrations from all religious traditions of what they called the phenomena of religion, such as myths, rituals, shamans, and esoteric practices. Each was interested in pursuing a general theory of religion in order to argue for its universal presence and practice among human beings from the beginning of human history; and both of them had recourse to the then contemporary language of the sacred, a term being used to define the divine phenomenon with which all religions were understood to have been engaged. By using this term in the German (*das Heilige*), van der Leeuw extended and universalized Christian vocabulary in a massive imposition upon all religious phenomena, thinking of his work as *Missionswissenschaft* (science of the Christian mission). Eliade, on the other hand, used the language of the sacred to reconceptualize traditional Christian concepts in light of the data derived from ethnography and studies of other religions. Both infused these terms with ontological significance, referring to a real, objective entity.

Van der Leeuw's two-volume compendium, *Religion in Essence and Manifestation* (1938), presented an exhaustive list of topics and components to describe the ways in which humans have been religious. Having learned that by using the term *sacred* every human encounter with mundane objects and everyday events could become a religious experience, he found that everything thinkable did become sacred, from sacred stones, demons, and "the absolutely powerful," through medicine men, priests, and the sacred community, through souls, sacrifice, and mysticisms, to birthing, marriage, and dying, and the religions of struggle, repose, and compassion. Thus the adjective sacred was used to bring every feature of human life and thought under the rubric of religion. Time, space, love, alienation, will, obedience, and domination were all sacred when viewed as religious phenomena. This had the effect of imagining religion as a universal ontological environment within which humans lived and to which everything they did related. But if everything was religious, what was left? And was the sacred really anything at all? Stepping back for a moment from the reading of van der Leeuw, it does not take long to realize that the human experiences he interpreted as religious are much better seen as experiences we all have in the course of living together as human beings. We normally do not need to interpret social moments as manifestations of the divine. And nowhere in this discourse was it ever acknowledged that the overriding category of the sacred was vague and vaporous, or that it was a coinage taken from familiarity with the medieval Christian view of an otherworldly realm, an order of reality different from the everyday world. Unfortunately, many scholars found this new approach intriguing, for it seemed to confirm the feeling that religion was real, that it was special, and that it had to do with making contact with the divine. Exhaustive research on religion's role in social formation, thinking, and the mentality of a people was no longer so important. Thus the language of the sacred became a shorthand mystification that short-circuited other ways of asking questions about human behavior.

Mircea Eliade introduced the category of history into a phenomenology of the sacred in order to develop a theory of religion that could say why it was so important, and why it has persisted in the West despite the secularization of the Western nation-states. He wanted to merge the two scholarly traditions of religious studies, the one focused on primitive religion, the other on the world religions of the higher civilizations. The framework of his model of religion was essentially Christian, though he found neutral terms to refer to its essential characteristics in order to translate Christian concepts into terminology capable of universal applications. Thus he retained the concept of the transcendent realm. He also retained the concepts of origin and history, but without accepting the evolutionary scheme of development to account for the higher religions as more rational than the primitive. From the primitives he accepted the concept of the natural environment as fundamental for human orientation to the world and not at all inferior to the social environments created by the higher civilizations, or in need of history to produce societies in support of human well-being. As a matter of fact, insofar as history became the arena for social conflict, it described the problem that religion would have to address. He put the two scholarly traditions together in *The Myth of the Eternal Return: Cosmos and History* (1954), a theory of religion that rapidly gained adherents and became the basis for many academic departments of religious studies in the United States. The way it worked was that cosmos described the natural world enveloped by and impinged upon by the realm of the sacred. Cosmos was the way the two worlds, sacred and natural (or profane), were put together at the beginning, and linkage between the two made possible "epiphanies" (from the Greek for "appearance, manifestation") which could be understood by humans, especially primitives, who had no trouble seeing that an epiphany was evidence of the cosmic realm of the Sacred. Anything might become an epiphany: an eagle taking off to soar, the first *Schneegloeckchen* (snowbell) of spring, a broken pole. The "terror of history" threatened this original orientation to the cosmos and became the problem that religion would have to address. As Eliade collected and pored over his accumulation of primitive myths, he found stories that seemed to suggest that the primitives had thought deeply about the "rupture" that must have taken place between the two realms of the cosmos. Thus they were aware that life experience in the social and natural world was full of struggle and problems. Conclusion! Myth and ritual could relieve the sorry round of labors that otherwise had no meaning. Myths told of the realm of the Sacred and the way things were *in illo tempore* ("at that time," taken to mean "at the beginning"). Rituals were reenactments of the myths that realigned the natural and divine orders, at least for a brief period of time. Taken together, myths and rituals broke through the banal of the everyday and the terror of social history with its conflicts. It is not too difficult to see why Eliade's theory was eagerly accepted by students of religion. It came to focus on the importance of myths and rituals as the two primary manifestations of religion, thus providing categories for the interpretation of real and readily available data specific to religion. As for the concepts of the Sacred, cosmos, and history, they reverberated with the traditional worldview of Christianity and so were not immediately challenged. They made it possible for all the data under investigation from other religions, otherwise appearing strange, to have some meaning after all. Besides, the scope of Eliade's cosmos was so expansive and speculative that to challenge it as a category could only occur by offering a better theory.

Eliade's amazing erudition and prodigious labors resulted in a large collection of impressive publications, including an anthology of myths for comparative study (*From Primitives to Zen*), an *Encyclopedia of Religion*, a *History of Religious Ideas*, as well as many essays and monographs on special topics. His faculty position at the University of Chicago made "the Chicago school" famous, and his method and theory of religions came to be called the history of religions. From the 1950s through the 1970s, this school tradition was the rationale for the creation of departments of religion in many universities and affected their composition of faculties by encouraging representative scholars from different religious traditions. The overriding assumption was that all religions could be interpreted and compared in terms of Eliade's theory. Research was vigorous, books burgeoned, and it seemed that the study of religion had taken its place as an independent academic discipline. Religion was its own distinct object of study and had its own method by which to study it. However, as the new discipline produced more research and more detailed descriptions of different myths and rituals, questions about the differences among the various religions began to appear. An experience of the Sacred was not enough to understand all the motivations and persuasions that religious behavior implied. It was also the case that to study a religion without taking account of its own social context and history robbed it of its significance in the life and culture of a particular people. Thus the ethnological stream of religious studies anchored in the discipline of cultural anthropology finally challenged the history of religions. The frame of reference for studying and interpreting any religion was no longer the world of Eliade's cosmos and history. Instead, religion was to be studied in relation to the lifeworlds of real peoples in their social, cultural, and historical contexts.

The Cultural Anthropology of Religion

Again there were vigorous debates in the halls of learning. If religion belonged to a people's society and culture, what was it doing there? And what did it do there that other social systems could not do better? At first it was enough to argue that religion was indeed thoroughly integrated into the structures of a society. It was not an independent system of persuasion and behavior isolated from participation in the society as a whole and driven by the terror of history, much less an individual's need of salvation or quest for religious experience. But what, then, did religion do for a society? From the beginning of the twentieth century scholars working in the field of primitive religions had occasionally described the relation of a religion to its society by using the term *function*. Religion functioned to provide many of the occasions, ideas, and practices that made a society tick. As scholars became more convinced of this relation, and found that the language of function could be used to account for the way many systems of signs worked together in a society, including most religious phenomena, the term "function" tottered on the edge of becoming a theory.

Clifford Geertz published an important set of studies in 1973 entitled *The Interpretation of Cultures*, and a second set of essays in 1983 called *Local Knowledge*. A cultural anthropologist at the Institute for Advanced Study in Princeton, Geertz had worked as an ethnologist in Bali, Polynesia, and taught at the University of Chicago in its Department of Anthropology. Trained as a sociologist, he had grown dissatisfied with descriptive accounts of tribal societies that stayed at the level of practices and their relations to structural systems, as if that relationship was sufficient to explain social functions and discourse. He found that such things as territory, language, racial characteristics, "blood" relations, behavioral characteristics, and various kinds of codes were important features that gave a people its identity and determined its lifestyle. In Bali and Java he had noticed that both behavioral patterns and social structures worked as symbols of a shared world he called "culture." In the popular activity of the Balinese cockfight, for instance, he was able to demonstrate that the rules of play became occasions for unexpressed manipulations of status and honor related to social structures of significance to the society in general. These he called the "deep play" at stake in the betting (*Interpretation*, 412–53). As for religion, it could now be described as a "cultural system" in which its symbols worked to create the imaginary world of a people (ibid., 87–125). His definition of religion was:

> (1) a system of symbols which acts to (2) establish powerful, pervasive, and long-standing moods and motivations in men by (3) formulating conceptions of a general order of existence and (4) clothing these conceptions with such an aura of factuality that (5) the moods and motivations seem uniquely realistic. (ibid., 90)

This integration of religion and society was made possible because of the shift from social anthropology to cultural anthropology in which Geertz was most interested. However, it marked a turning point in the study of religion as well, making it possible to define the Sacred as a system of symbols that provided a society with its "conception of a general order of existence." After Geertz it was no longer possible to leave the concept of the Sacred located in Eliade's cosmos or van der Leeuw's phenomenology. Religion now was seen to function as the provider of "meanings" and "explanations" that gave a society its energies, motivations, and identity.

Those not completely convinced, or wanting more explanation, began to use the term "functionalism" in a more or less negative tenor of criticism. The arguments against functionalism were three: (1) Functionalism only worked if the society could be imagined as a single organism, living in isolation from other societies, and interested mainly in running smoothly by making sure that all interests were in harmony. But such a picture does not recognize or address the conflicts that characterize the internal workings of real societies. (2) Therefore, functionalism is not helpful if one asks about the role of religion when a society is in the process of internal change or is engaged with other societies in cross-cultural exchange, conflict, or war. And (3) in any case, a functional description is still only a description, not a theory that explains why it is religion and not something else that helps keep a society balanced, working, and harmonious.

The alternative in the minds of many was structuralism. Structuralism took note of the several systems of signs and rules that give a society its "structure." By now several systems of signs had been identified, such as language, kinship systems, clan organizations, hierarchies of authority and responsibility, calendrical and seasonal calculations, the organization of production, and practices of exchange. And since the several systems were intertwined in the workings of a society, and since the interrelationships allowed for play and shifts in balance, structuralism could handle change, conflict, and the ways in which a society continued to keep on working.

Structuralism took its theoretical point of departure from Ferdinand de Saussure's analysis of language as a system of signs (words), the use of which was governed by rules of grammar and syntax that made it possible to put words together to form a sentence that had meaning. The point was that not just any sequence of words could make sense, only those that followed the rules of grammar and syntax. And it was clear that such a set of rules was taken for granted by those who spoke the language. One learned to speak a language by processes of cultural tuition, mimicry, and trial and error in forming sentences that were understandable in communication, not by memorizing the rules of grammar or syntax. Thus the structure of a language was not a matter of obvious, collective consciousness, but had to be reconstructed by analyzing its use in spoken or written discourse. The object was to discover the underlying rules that had to be followed in order for sentences to make sense. The unconscious structure of a language with its rules of grammar and syntax was a kind of game board. It did not itself come to speech, but enabled speechmaking as if the speakers were players of the game who decided upon the moves they wished to make given their turn. It was worth the effort to analyze the structure of a language, for the importance of a language for its people was obvious. Every people had a language, and no society worked without one. Language, in fact, was a system of signs intertwined with other systems that gave coherence to a society and enabled it to work. Since working the systems on the analogy of using a language seemed to be the way societies managed to live together and make sense of their practices and culture, the analysis of a society's structure promised to uncover something fundamental about human competence and performance, something that might come close to being a definition of society as a human construction and the human as a social being.

An Intellectual Anthropology of Religion

The works of Lévi-Strauss stand out as the first major analyses of the structures of kinship, totemism, and myth. He was able to show that kinship was a primary system of signs with its own structure, intertwined with other systems of signs such as totemism, which gave many tribal peoples their social structure (*The Elementary Structures of Kinship*). He also devoted enormous scholarly effort to the analysis of the myths of the Bororo Indians of Brazil and other tribes in South and North America (*Introduction to a Science of Mythology*). His approach was to make sets of the variants of a myth as they occurred among neighboring tribes with their own slightly different environments and social practices. He understood the importance of the agents and events in the imaginary world of a myth, in keeping, it seems, with a profound knowledge of the way in which human fantasy delights in embellishing the world of the everyday in some relation to the patterns of life shared by a people. He therefore looked for the ways in which fundamental notions in the description of human behavior and thinking surfaced and were treated in a tribe's mythology. He found that the myths of the Bororo were structured by setting up oppositions such as those between "too fast" and "too slow" or between the "raw" and the "rotten", in order to recommend the better "middle way" (neither too fast nor too slow, but "deliberate"; neither raw nor rotten, but cooked). Thus one might conclude that these myths functioned as a kind of unspoken cultural tuition. Their structures were rooted in the grammar of a society's collective judgments and agreements about the best way to see and do things, their narratives providing an imaginary world of enchantment to invite yet again consideration of the rules without overt instruction. In the case of the Asdiwal stories of the Tsimshian, Haida, and Tlingit tribes of the Pacific Northwest, Lévi-Strauss found that the oppositions involved were used to focus attention on an interweaving of tribal structures having to do with kinship, marriage, hunting–fishing, and their natural environment. The most interesting thing about the stories was that they took for granted what everyone knew about these structures, then reversed their normal logics by telling a story of the disasters to follow if the rules of behavior were not maintained ("The Story of Asdiwal"). Since Lévi-Strauss it has become customary to recognize the complex interweaving of the several systems of signs that structure primitive societies and to look for what he called their logics. Lévi-Strauss's own conclusion was that the "primitive mind" was hardly primitive. It had the capacity to think very clearly indeed, even though it expressed itself in ways difficult for Western thinkers to understand (*The Savage Mind*).

What, then, about religion as a system of signs in analogy to language? Does it have its own structure or structures, and how might it relate to other systems of signs in the structuration of a society? For the student of religion who wants to understand the effective difference religion makes in a society or culture, these questions have become very important. They are, however, not easy to tackle. That is because the features of a society that have normally been thought of as religious have long been regarded as matters of mystery, not of social logic or intellectual labor. The analysis of religions as systems of signs does not have a long history of study and discourse to control the investigations. Lévi-Strauss made a beginning, but most scholars in his wake have not produced the rigorous and detailed analyses required to test his theories.

Fortunately, a historian of religion at the University of Chicago, Jonathan Z. Smith, has been working at the task of making social sense of religion for the last three or four decades, accepting structuralist theory in general, but focusing on the special ways in which myths and rituals focus a people's attention on particular practices or situations, highlighting features normally overlooked, and making it possible to think critically about them. Smith's work on religions occurs in the context of a major project on the ways humans think in general and rationalize their worlds. This project has been worked out in detail in a stunning production of essays on the kinds of knowledge we have achieved in the fields of botany, geography, history, language studies, the making of encyclopedias, academic disciplines, and the history of ideas. In every case this knowledge has been won by means of making comparisons. At a fundamental level we invariably take note of an object of interest, let us say a stalk of wheat, by finding a place for it in our systems of classification. We do this by comparing the newly noticed object with other similar objects with which we are already familiar (other grasses and grains). These will be objects that are somewhat alike, but also a bit different from the object of interest. This results in giving the stalk of wheat a place of its own in a list of familiar things, and then we try to give it a name. Giving it a name may call upon other lists of familiar things classified according to other interests, such as topographical locations (where was it found growing?), seasons of the year (when was it headed out?), whether it might be experimented with as edible, a thing of beauty, to be picked as an ornament, or left to mark a special place in the topography, and so forth. Each list of classified things is in effect a system of differences. A list consists of "similar" things distinguished from one another by means of their "differences" from one another. The listing marks each item as distinctive but also, and more importantly, creates distinction by means of the "differences" among the "similar" items. Thus it is that difference is the factor by which the classifications have been made. When two systems of differences come into play in order to "name," "acknowledge," and "understand" the reasons for one's interest in some object or list of objects, it is the gap between the two systems of differences that provides the "space" for thought. Thought can be evoked for very many reasons and left at the level of reflection and meditation. The two lists, being themselves systems of differences, do not prescribe identities or what to think about them.

Smith's turn to the history of religions seems to have been taken as a kind of challenge, both to the academic discipline of religious studies where religion was said to be radically unlike all other ways of reasoning, and also to his own intellectualist anthropology, as if he were up against a human practice that at first did not appear to make sense in the usual ways. His approach has been to tackle myths and rituals that have provided primary points of departure for major theorists and traditions of interpretation in the study of religion. His work has appeared in essays focused upon a given myth or ritual in its social-historical setting, analyzed in comparison to a second set of examples taken from a different culture or time, and discussed in terms of the history of scholarship devoted to each. Thus he has been working on two fronts, the sense historians of religion have made of a myth or ritual and the way in which these myths and rituals can be better understood to make sense in the social climates and situations in which they were generated. Invariably, the better understanding of a myth or ritual has been achieved by (1) painstaking historical reconstruction of the social context, and (2) comparison between the two examples from different cultures in order to make sure one has seen the subtle differences of function in each case. It is always the differences that throw light upon features of a given myth or ritual that make it possible to render a clear and convincing redescription. Thus context and comparison control his method. And, because of the wide-ranging sets of examples he has treated, a general theory of myth and ritual as thought-producing social activities has emerged. In the course of which he has challenged the interpretations of earlier scholars and schools that emphasized being mesmerized by the divine, and instead has shown how myths and rituals make possible thinking about social activities and interests.

In every case he has attended to the social history of the myth or ritual in question, working out the particular social situation of context and its customary practices and ways of thinking. He has then looked for the "gap" between the myth or ritual and the customary, everyday practices of the people, in order to ask about the ways in which religion may be a sense-making activity of social significance. He has shown that it is in fact a fundamental mode of reflexive thought of significance for social construction and maintenance. How might that be? Well, as it turns out, there is always some relationship between a mythic theme or a ritual practice and the social situation or practice in relation to which it has meaning. In the case of a ritual, let us say an animal "sacrifice," it is the normal practice of killing animals that belongs to herding and animal husbandry, namely, the domestication and breeding of animals for food and other purposes (J. Z. Smith, "The Domestication of Sacrifice"). In the case of a myth, let us say a story about stealing fire from the gods, the use of fire in everyday living would be the connection. What Smith suggests is a shift in the second system of differences we use to interpret the significance of myths and rituals. The second set customary for the study of religion has been a list of theological categories that play the gap between myths and rituals and their imagined worlds of the gods.

This merely describes a circle within the world of the imagination where anything and everything can happen without connection to the social world. Its dislocation from the empirical world may certainly provide a rich and complex game board for exciting adventure in the building of abstract systems such as theology and philosophy on the model of mathematics. But that way of setting up two systems of differences (both taken from the same list of "interests" in the transcendent realm) cannot produce much understanding of the social significance of these phenomena. Instead, Smith has asked us to switch our focus away from that imaginary world as the place to locate human interests, and attend instead to the practical world of everyday social life in order to redefine the gap that needs to be played (that between a myth or a ritual and the social situation it reflects).

In the case of animal "sacrifice," the gap is that between the way in which killing an animal takes place in the normal and usually messy way and the precise, finely honed, deliberate attention to detail that turns the act into a ritual. In the case of a myth about stealing fire from the gods, the gap is created by the elaborate and fantastic differences between the settings in which the acquisition and use of fire occur. According to Smith, rituals work this gap between the perfect performance of an action in a specific place marked off at a distance from the usual locations for such actions, inviting concentrated attention by those who will have the everyday practice in mind as they pay close attention to the performance. Result? A common practice is taken up into a location and atmosphere not customary for the everyday practice, but potentially provocative for thinking about its place, problems, reasons, and significance in the group's larger patterns of life.

In the case of myth, the gap is created by the difference between the "once upon a time" setting for a fantastic story and the possibly banal everyday practices that might otherwise be taken for granted. Myth works with a time distance ("then" vs. "now"), while ritual sets up a space difference ("here" in the ritual space vs. "there" where the action usually occurs). Neither prescribes anything at all, whether beliefs, dogmas, or ethics. They instead open up the thinking gaps created by their extraordinary constructions upon the everyday and leave it to the group to negotiate the differences. This does reverse the normal process of making comparisons. We usually gain advantage from the familiar in order to make the unfamiliar comprehensible. In the case of religion, it is the unknown and unfamiliar as a fantastic construction upon the known and familiar that is used to defamiliarize the customary and invite its meditation. But, as we shall see, Smith's model does work, and working it out gets quite interesting precisely because of this inversion. We can use his model, first to locate the intersections of social interests that bring myths and rituals into relation with social structures, and then to develop a theory about the kind of thinking religion makes possible. Smith's studies on myths and rituals are important for our quest, for he has developed a theory about each of them that makes it possible to relate both to a social theory of religion.

And so, since I have found the work of Jonathan Z. Smith so important for my own studies in the history of religions, it may be helpful for the reader to hear his description of religion and religious studies in his own words. I cite from a programmatic essay called "Map Is Not Territory", published in 1978 and cited with ever more frequency by scholars:

> Religion is an inextricably human phenomenon. In the West, we live in a post-Kantian world in which man is defined as a world-creating being and culture is understood as a symbolic process of world-construction. It is only… from this humane, post-Enlightenment perspective that the academic interpretation of religion becomes possible. Religious studies are [therefore] most appropriately described in relation to the Humanities and the Human Sciences, in relation to Anthropology rather than Theology. What we study when we study religion is one mode of constructing worlds of meaning, worlds within which men find themselves and in which they choose to dwell. What we study is the passion and drama of man discovering the truth of what it is to be human. History is the framework within whose perimeter those human expressions, activities and intentionalities that we call "religious" occur. Religion is the quest, within the bounds of the human, historical condition, for the power to manipulate and negotiate one's "situation" so as to have "space" in which to meaningfully dwell. It is the power to relate one's domain to the plurality of environmental and social spheres in such a way as to guarantee the conviction that one's existence "matters." Religion is a distinctive mode of human creativity, a creativity which both discovers limits and creates limits for humane existence. What we study when we study religion is the variety of attempts to map, construct and inhabit such positions of power through the use of myths, rituals and experiences of transformation. (*Map Is Not Territory*, 290–1)

This description is a succinct summary of his social theory of religion. I will use his theory to guide the present study of myths and rituals in many cultures other than Christian, in order to prepare for an analysis of the Christian myth and ritual. It will then be possible to say something about the Christian mentality of the Christian Right in America, a mentality that has awakened to aspects of the social logic of the Christian myth and ritual, a logic that, unfortunately, we will have to counter as no longer appropriate for a polycultural social democracy.

A Social Theory of Religion

Thus we come to the end of this survey of the scholars' quest to find and define religion as a common, universal human preoccupation. Nothing like the concept of religion that most scholars have had in mind has been found in non-Western cultures, and the reasons should now be obvious. As Jonathan Z. Smith has said, "religion is not a native category" (*Relating Religion*, 179), meaning that, as a concept and technical term, it was produced by Western scholars on the occasion of encounter with natives of the New World who did not seem to have any religion. That, of course, was unthinkable, and so, in due course, the quest took up many features of other peoples' cultures as if they were evidence for their religion, only to find that the scholars' concept of religion could not be superimposed. That is because the scholars' concept of religion was indebted to familiarity with Christianity, a concept that was not subjected to critical analysis similar to that devoted to other cultures. Furthermore, features of the Christian religion taken to be self-evident for a definition of religion were found not to be universal. These features included the imagination of a spiritual, divine, transcendent realm, the abode of divine agents including the high god who created the world and oversees the machinations of human history. They also included the elaborate institutions of the Church, the cultivation of an ambience of worship, and psychologies of personal piety and religious experience. One might wonder whether this history of scholarship has taught us anything at all about "religion" now that the attempt to universalize our traditional conception of religion as a category has failed. However, all is not lost.

The pursuit of knowledge about other lands and peoples has produced an exceptionally rich reservoir of learning in support of a social theory of religion not dependent upon Christianity. This learning can be summarized by making four observations. The first is that all human societies are the result of wondrously complex systems of social logic, created and maintained by amazing investments of thoughtfulness and intellectual labor. A short list of these discoveries would include:

- The social significance of "rites of passage," Arnold van Gennep, 1908
- The social implications of "totemism," Émile Durkheim, 1912
- Society as a network of social relations, A. R. Radcliffe-Brown, 1922
- The concepts of "gift" and "obligation" in archaic systems of exchange, Marcel Mauss, 1925
- The structural relation of a language to a culture, Franz Boas, 1940
- The intelligence required for calculations typical of basic technologies, Bronislaw Malinowski, 1948
- The logic of kinship systems and social structures, Claude Lévi-Strauss, 1948
- The ideology of tripartite social structures and their myths, Georges Dumézil, 1958
- The logic of dual systems of classification in social organization, thought, and mythology, Claude Lévi-Strauss, 1962
- The relation of ritual to processes of social formation, Victor Turner, 1967
- Performance and display as ingredients in urban genesis, Paul Wheatley, 1971
- The social importance of a shared imaginary world (*habitus*) and the function of the gap between it and actual social patterns of practices, Pierre Bourdieu, 1972
- The importance of a people's attitude toward land, language, and blood kinship for social behavior and the construction of cultural symbols, Clifford Geertz, 1973

- The importance of geographic and astronomical calculation for social organization and village orientation, Åke Hultkranz, 1979
- The intellectual ingredient in the formation of myths and the performance of rituals and its significance for thinking about social structuration, Jonathan Z. Smith, 1987
- The reciprocal logic of dual tribal organizations, Valerio Valeri, 1989
- Geography and climate as factors in social differentiations, Jared Diamond, 1997.

A second observation is that these studies support a description of society as structured by means of systems of signs and patterns of practices. The list includes language, kinship systems, classification systems (frequently pairing natural and human objects in two systems of differences), territorial mapping, distinguishing social identities, technologies and production, social organization and the assignment of roles, calendrical systems, and rules for behavior, rectification, etiquette, and tuition. Several things can be said about these systems. They make it possible to live together in social units. None functions without the others. Together they form the complex system of interrelated devices that structure human societies. All are human creations, though none can be attributed to a single mind or moment of creation. None are thinkable without an enormous, collective investment of intellectual labor. All function as "grammars," i.e., they provide the underlying logic and rules for competence, but without demanding a conscious mastery of the rules as rules. And none are necessary for basic biological survival. This means that the energy driving the creation and maintenance of human societies cannot be accounted for as a necessary response to "needs" of any kind, or in terms of psychological motivations. Customary references to "calorie quotients," "biological needs," "acquisitive instincts," "fear," "aggression," and "species protection" are not enough to account for the intricate systems of signs that structure human societies or the processes of socialization and tuition required to master them.

A third observation is that it is now possible to conceptualize social construction as a human enterprise, to imagine the interplay of complex systems of signs, codes, and practices that make possible the formation and maintenance of a human society. Many of these systems have been analyzed in detail, their logics worked out, and their significance for social organization and practice noted. The intellectual labor involved in the construction and maintenance of these systems is truly impressive, as are the inordinate amounts of curiosity, experimentation, and delight that have been invested in the fragile craft of living together in social units. At first it seemed that these systems of signs had purely practical purposes such as producing children, procuring food, assigning tasks, keeping track of time, foraging, and reporting. But then we noticed that such purposes are not merely practical. They already partake of interest in doing tasks together and making the performance of them interesting. There is a reflexivity built into the application of these cognitive systems by which a raft of recognizably impractical human interests becomes all but inescapable. Language, for instance, is for more than communication about practical matters. It is for talking, putting constructions on events, making and sharing observations, embellishing reports, delighting in innuendo, creating metaphor, attempting persuasion, and joking. Kinship systems do more than guarantee healthy children. They govern identity, assign social place, acknowledge generational process, and define connections to ancestry. The distribution of labors is for more than getting the job done. Because of these social role assignments, people have to circulate, be with different folks at different times, and thus have the opportunity to tell stories on one another, and learn to laugh, complain, show off, or comply. The codes of honor and shame rank individual performance. The hierarchies assign responsibilities. A calendar is not only for marking time and identifying the appropriate seasons for basic activities. It makes such collective activities as planning, anticipation, and celebration seem natural. Let us say that these applications indicate social interest. Let us imagine that the human enterprise of social formation is elaborate and interesting because humans take interest in living together in social configurations.

Finally, a fourth observation is that myths and rituals have surfaced as the two phenomena common to social constructions that we have thought of as belonging to "religion." This will give us our data for developing a social theory of "religion" that can then be used to analyze the social logic of the Christian myth and ritual system from which the notion of religion was first derived.

Personal Religion

But, first, there is the matter of the current popular definition of religion as a private experience and the means by which an encounter with a spiritual realm makes personal transformation possible. The reader may well have such in mind as this study is taken up, and the differences between the popular and the academic definitions may already have become an obstacle. What might the historian of religion say about this popular notion? It may be helpful to note that the notion of personal religious experience is used to refer to a large variety of experiences, and that the only feature they have in common is that they are understood as personal, not social, experiences. It is thus the intense and singular focus upon the individual instead of upon society as a whole that may create a problem in thinking critically about the social effectiveness of religion.

It is certainly understandable that most Americans think of religion as a matter of personal belief and experience. That is because the social histories of the modern Western nation-states have created societies in which the institutions of religion have gotten separated from the economic and political structures that actually control the material and practical workings of a society. The result has even been authorized in the constitution of the United States and interpreted as the doctrine of the separation of church and state. Along with this breakdown of the monolithic arrangements of scepter and staff that prevailed during the period of medieval Catholicism, the rise of technology and the movement of people from countryside villages and farms into cities of industry created situations in which the individual was no longer supported by small, close-knit social units and their networks. Belonging to a nation-state was not the same as belonging to a people, a culture, a religion, or a "community." At the same time, the histories of philosophy and science turned the focus of their attention upon the individual as the object for the definition of what it means to be human. Our society is thoroughly individualistic in its anthropology, psychology, and economic-marketing definitions of human existence. And so religion also has come to be thought of and experienced as a personal and private matter. One even hears of "personal systems of belief" as if systems of belief have nothing to do with public matters. In the context of the multicultural society we have become, personal preference has been the only way we have dared to account for differences in religious orientation. This is one of the reasons why a social factor in the definition of religion may not make sense to many people.

A focus upon the individual has a long history among intellectuals in the quest for what might be called "authentic human experience." A recent study by Martin Jay, *Songs of Experience*, traces this history as a "universal theme" that can be detected in the works of philosophers and other thinkers throughout the entire reach of what we have called Modernity. A review of Jay's study by Jackson Lears, "Keeping It Real," finds it possible to expand upon this theme as a Western cultural assumption that drives many of our traditions of thinking about religion, literature, epistemology, psychology, and political philosophy. The roster of indices starts in the sixteenth century with Montaigne's essay "Of Experience" (1587–88) and the Protestant Reformation's call for personal transformation through faith. It continues through the Romanticisms of the seventeenth century, the philosophers and theologians of the eighteenth and nineteenth centuries working on the question of how and whether we can know the truth about reality and ourselves, and the emergence of psychology, existentialism, and art theory in the twentieth century, to end with the questions of identity, death, and violence that have been confusing us since the two world wars. Lears paints a picture of

> a philosopher...in his study, constructing rational arguments on behalf of authentic experience—which he nearly always defines as nonrational. Somehow, he thinks, we are being robbed of primal, unmediated contact with the palpitating forces of real life. The obstacles to vitality may lie in the desiccating powers of modern science or in the encrustations of traditional religion or, if the philosopher is hostile to narratives of progress and decline, in the human condition. ("Keeping It Real," 23)

The underlying assumption seems to be that we have somehow lost contact with "reality" ("real life," "our real selves"); that we have been separated from the ground of "Being"; and that some split between body and soul, mind and matter, or consciousness and our true selves, has taken place. The answer is to experience once again our true selves, sometimes imagined as unmediated presence, sometimes to be recaptured by psychological analysis or aesthetic experience of the sublime. Schleiermacher (*The Christian Faith*) thought of religion as "a primal feeling prior to any doctrine or institution." William James concentrated on "individual men in their solitude" when writing his *Varieties of Religious Experience*. And now we have the "new age" quests of "spirituality" as the answer to the irrelevance of institutional religion.

It is therefore no wonder that the popular conception of religion focuses on personal experience. The cultural traditions of Christianity and other religions provide a very rich ambience of symbols, images, reminders, and occasions for meditation upon the world and self as viewed through their orientations to a spiritual realm. And the social histories of modernity have encouraged individualism and the personal quest to incorporate the divine spirit, the ultimate reality, in one's own experience and self. However, those who have asked about the meaning of the term "religious experience" have not been able to define it (Sharf, "Experience"), and those who have sought what has been called "authentic experience" have not been able to describe it. Both terms cover too many options, desires, and human longings that have emerged in Modernity. The pursuit of both has invariably failed to appreciate and acknowledge the fact that persons are not individuals isolated from the material world and social existence. Humans are socially constituted and find themselves always in relation to others and the natural world. Thus the popular definition of religion has not provided a point of departure for thinking in general terms about religion, society, and culture.

But now, here we are with a definition of religion that limits it to the private sphere, and the notion of a "Christian nation" that has made it difficult to accommodate or assimilate the many peoples of other cultures with whom we now are living. The peoples among us of non-European extraction have not lived through a history of the separation of church (religion) and state, and thus do not think in terms of religion as "private" and the state as having to be "tolerant" of non-Christian peoples as long as they do not try to gain access to social systems of power. These peoples have brought with them their languages, their customs and costumes, their temples and mosques, their clerics, teachings, and ways of thinking. What are we to make of this? And in the case of the culture wars that have unleashed such powerful energies, actions, and reactions, both those internal to our society and those determining our relations to other peoples and nations, how are we to account for the passions and the appeals to religious authorities instead of engaging in deliberation and discussion? The role of religion seems to be an important component in the structure of our society after all. It is therefore time to do some thinking about religion as a social construct. We need to know why religion is so important to a people if we are to live together in a polycultural society or in a global age. That is why we need a social theory of religion. The next chapters may therefore be read as a step-by-step construction of a social theory of religion, drawing upon examples from the ethnography and history of religions to illustrate and document a set of propositions that will eventually bring us back to the twenty-first century in the United States and the questions with which we began. At that point, in Chapters 7 and 8, we will again address the question of the popular view.

2 Noticing Social Interests in Myths and Rituals

Tracing the history of the study of religion has resulted in two findings of importance for our theory. One is that a religion seems to be linked to the structures and life of its society, perhaps as a system of signs and practices intertwined with other patterns of activity that affect or describe the way a people lives together. A second is that myths and rituals have come into view as the two primary human preoccupations that we have thought of as religious. This provides us with data for further investigation, and with a focus upon the significance of both myths and rituals as social constructions and practices. We now need to find some links between myths and rituals and social formations. Only then will it be possible to work out a social theory of religion and explore the questions of why and how religions matter.

Myths

The reader will know that the popular definition and use of the term *myth* suggests stories or constructions upon social practices and ideas that are not true. The reader will also know that, when anyone uses this definition to describe a story or common convention, a statement is made about those who believe the myth, namely, that they are deceived. The person making the statement is accordingly not deceived, knowing that the myth is untrue. What the reader may not realize is that the history of scholarship on myth and religion has struggled with the same issue even while recognizing that myths related to religions seem to form a separate class and need to be studied in relation to social and cultural systems, not just in relation to the question of truth. And yet, because the study of religions started with the observation of other peoples and their strange practices, and because it was driven by Western science and reason, the questions asked were always about how other peoples could possibly have believed or imagined their myths (stories that were obviously untrue).

Many theories have been proposed, including some that have found it possible to set aside the truth–fiction problem by observing other features of myths and their social functions. We have touched upon some of these theories in Chapter 1, as well as the constructive proposals of Jonathan Z. Smith that need not raise the question of belief. Nevertheless, the study of myths as religious phenomena has not found a way to say when a story is a myth and not some other kind of narrative. And so, the history of scholarship has turned to stories of all kinds as well as dreams, theories of archetypes and the unconscious (Jung, Freud), and various descriptions of overwhelming emotional experiences in order to account for the fantasies, fictions, and otherworldly symbols that myths seem to incorporate. A remarkably clear discussion of this history of scholarship can be found in G. S. Kirk's book *Myth: Its Meaning and Function in Ancient and Other Cultures*. Kirk is able to give trenchant analyses of the entire spectrum of theories and the reasons why they are inadequate. However, at the end, his alternative suggestions about the narrative embellishment of stories that somehow ring a collective bell in myths reveals his own essentially individualistic anthropology. Thus the long history of myth studies concerned with the way in which individuals entertain fantasy continues to set the question. A more recent, and much more helpful, discussion of myth and ritual studies by historians of religion is Russell McCutcheon's contribution to the *Guide to the Study of Religion*, entitled "Myth." McCutcheon builds upon the small number of studies interested in the relation of myth to social structures, such as those discussed in Chapter 1 (Durkheim, Lévi-Strauss, Jonathan Z. Smith), and understands the importance of mythmaking as a factor in the dynamic, collective processes of social formation.

Social Formation

The term *social formation* refers to a concept of society as a collective, human construct. It differs from the less specific term, *society*, by emphasizing the complex interplay of many human interests that develop systems of signs and patterns of practices, as well as institutions for their communication, maintenance, and reproduction. Social formation indicates the process by which various configurations of these systems of practices are created and relate to one another in the formation of a given society. The term is also used to refer to the resulting structure of a society formed by such a process. It is a highly abstract concept with specific connotations of importance for social theory.

The concept first emerged as a technical term in the intellectual arenas associated with the work of Louis Althusser. Earlier, in the now famous "Preface" to his *Contributions to the Critique of Political Economy* (1859), and throughout the work, Karl Marx had used the term *Gesellschaftsformation* to refer to the shape of a society that results from a particular mode of production. For Marx, the mode of most significance was economic or material production, and the now familiar theoretical model of a basic practice (*base*) resulting in a social formation (*superstructure*) was set for testing. The subsequent history of Marxist thought and political experience did not invalidate the base/superstructure model, but found that the three variable factors in the equation (practice, production, and social formation) were in need of more detailed, conceptual specification. Althusser resignified the terms of the equation by working out a complex and sophisticated concept of society as a cluster of "semiautonomous instances," whereby "instance" refers to a pattern of practice that produces socially significant systems and effects for the structure of a society and its ongoing operation (*Reading Capital*, 1970).

Althusser focused upon the major triad of economic, political, and ideological practices, and continued to posit economic practice as the mode of production that determined a social formation "in the last instance." But in order to account for the many practices that conjoin in the modern society, and the variety of social formations that can be observed in human history, he applied the equation of practice–production–social formation to any and all forms of social practice that reproduce themselves and function as substructures within a larger, encompassing, social formation. A social formation was now conceived as a "structure of structures." In Althusser's rendering, "semiautonomy" refers to the relative independence of a pattern of practice from other practices, in the sense that each practice can develop its own rationale, principles of operation, institutions, mechanisms of maintenance, and modes of production and reproduction. Since no practice can be completely independent of the others, however, bound as it is to operate within the larger "structure of structures," contradiction always attends the internal logic of a practice, and the struggle for determination of the whole defines its relations of competition and conformation to other practices. The acknowledgment of multiple practices results in a dynamic concept of society, and the notion of semiautonomy raises to the level of theoretical investigation and precision the questions of determination, power, domination, and influence among the various practices.

Classical Marxist theory worked with a concept of society imagined as ranked by classes, or as layered according to the base/superstructure model, in which material production was basic and other forms of practice (politics, arts, religion, and ideology) were related to the basic mode of production as dependent, derived, and manipulative. By introducing the notion of semiautonomy, and asking the questions of interaction, force, development, and contradiction within and among the various practices of a society, Althusser made it possible to imagine every practice as a production of social effects. The result has been a quest for a comprehensive theory of social formation pursued as a humanistic, scientific, and historical discipline (Resch, *Althusser and the Renewal of Marxist Social Theory*).

Postmodernist intellectuals have tended to veer away from the renewal of Marxist social theory as pursued by scholars in the tradition of Althusser, because the social and cultural histories of the twentieth century have (1) raised serious questions about universal theories, (2) focused upon the individual and the many ways in which individuals are determined by their social and cultural locations, and (3) drawn attention to cultural issues at the expense of political and economic critique. Nevertheless, the term *social formation* has increasingly commended itself to many critical thinkers because it connotes the dynamic processes of the human construction of social structures in ways that the older term *society* cannot. The importance of the term social formation has been recognized, for instance, by non-Marxist political theorists (such as John McGowan, *Postmodernism and Its Critics*), literary critics, and scholars at work on the relation between discourse and the construction of society (such as Lincoln, *Discourse and the Construction of Society*). As a result, the term *practice*, of fundamental importance for theories of social formation based on collective interests, activity, and pursuits, is now familiar as a technical term in postmodern cultural analysis. Unfortunately, neither the Marxist, Althusserian, nor postmodern contributions to the use and definition of social formation have shed much light on the quest for a social theory of religion. Althusser did discuss religious thought (theology) as an instance of ideological practice (Althusser, *Lenin and Philosophy*, 127–86), and he did treat the institution of the Church as a "state apparatus." This was an important advance in that religion was no longer regarded as epiphenomenal in the usual base/superstructure formulations. Religion could now be seen as a "semiautonomous instance" that belonged to the several systems of practices that determined the dynamic social formation of a society. In the wake of Althusser one might have hoped for a concentrated focus upon explaining religion as integral to the social formation of a society, a structuring device that made its own particular contributions to that formation. That has not happened. In the Marxist tradition, religion has frequently been discounted or overlooked as a vanishing practice and thus of little theoretical interest.

In the tradition of religious studies, where one might have expected interest in exploring a social theory of religion, a Marxist approach to religion has not commended itself. Instead, religion has customarily been defined as an autonomous sphere of personal experience and belief determined by extrasocial and superhuman attractions. There are, however, several streams of thought in the academic study of religion that have focused upon the question of religion and society. Two of the better-known traditions of theoretical interest are those stemming from the works of Max Weber and Émile Durkheim, as discussed briefly in Chapter 1. To these should be added the large archive of knowledge about religious phenomena in social and cultural contexts documented in the fields of ethnography and cultural anthropology. American sociologists have also produced some important studies on religious institutions and groups in modern times. Of these several streams, the Weberian tradition has been the most influential among those engaged in religious studies, but this tradition continues to define religion in terms of the human quest for "salvation," not as an integral instance of human activity in the interest of social formation.

We need therefore to build on the importance of the ethnographic studies discussed in Chapter 1. Toward the end of that chapter a list of studies was given that marked major advances in our understanding of tribal societies and their practices. We can now note that most of these advances had to do with features of social structures and practices relating to religion. These features include myths and rituals, as well as observations on the native intelligence and intellectual labor involved in the collective creation of societies with complex structures. We can use the data accumulated in these studies to advance our own quest for a theory of mythmaking and social formation. The plan will be to focus on myths and rituals, noticing the ways in which they relate to social practices, interests, and situations, in order to develop lists of social interests that can then be studied in relation to the structures of particular societies.

Social Interests in Myths and Rituals

This chapter will explore some obvious links between social structures and practices on the one hand, and themes common to myths and rituals on the other. I will call these themes matters of *social interest*, a concept to be discussed more fully after a review of myths and rituals from many societies in which such interests can be noted as themes. A short list of such mythic themes and ritual practices will be followed in order to arrange the review. A given myth or ritual cannot be limited to a single theme. Myths and rituals are complex configurations that bring together images relating to clusters of interests in the life of a people. By arranging them thematically, however, in order to exemplify certain social interests, it will then be possible to consider their importance in relation to the construction and maintenance of societies with many social interests. We will not be able to answer in this chapter questions about how myths and rituals may be created in the first place, or how they work in the maintenance of a society. Such questions will be addressed in subsequent chapters. In this present chapter my concern is limited to illustrating the thematic links between myths and rituals and what I call social interests, a concept which is not common and needs to be developed slowly. The short list of social interests includes territory (or the land), the people, the organization of the social unit, rites of passage, food production (such as agriculture and husbandry), ancestors, and memorial festivals. The list will need to be expanded in subsequent chapters, where societies of greater size and complexity develop specialized interests in keeping with their new technologies and expanded social systems. In this chapter we will stay fairly close to the tribal societies of importance for the early study of religion (Chapter 1), taking a few steps into more diversified societies in order to expand the sets of examples we need to develop the concept of social interests.

Territory

It is important to realize that interests taken in a people's environment, though readily seen as involving intellectual and practical interests that one might want to trace only to individualistic and practical pursuits, are also social interests. This is true, for instance, in the case of territory. A people's land is the place where its members live and have lived. It is marked, mapped, and storied. Its contours are in memory; its workplaces familiar haunts; and its places of burial memorials. It is home to the people as a social identity, and if it is attacked or invaded by another people it may well be defended by those living there. A people's interest in its land as territory and habitat should be fairly obvious in what have been called creation myths or cosmogonies. However, these traditional designations are somewhat problematic. That is because both terms carry connotations derived from the biblical and theological traditions of Christianity. They can still be used, as long as we avoid thinking of them as pre-scientific attempts to explain the origin of the natural world. They are better understood as one of the ways in which the human imagination extends the horizons of time and space to see a people's land as a remarkable place in which to live, a place where they have lived "from the beginning."

A fine example of land turned into territory is found in the myth cycles of the Aranda and other native Australian tribes. I begin with this example because the native Australian tribes are so familiar to most of us, having served the scholarly and popular imagination as the most primitive of all tribal peoples known to ethnography, and therefore thought to be the closest to the origins of human cultural evolution. Primitive has meant no buildings, no cities, no social hierarchy, no constructive technologies, no sense of history, and only the most meager sensibility to anything like the realm of the Sacred. Jonathan Z. Smith has done much to change this picture, particularly in one set of observations having to do with their myth cycles (*To Take Place*, 1–13). According to these stories, their ancestors emerged from the earth during the *Dreaming*, a time during which the ancestors traversed the land and marked its topographical features by leaving traces of their having been there on some occasion, and eventually by transformations of themselves into the more noticeable features of the topography, such as mountains, caves, outcroppings, rocks, valleys, waterways, and other configurations, as well as into certain plants and animals. The stories of these wanderings and the names of these places turn the landscape into a memorial land upon which the Aranda live with their ancestors always in mind. In this mythology there is no need of a single event at the beginning of the world, or of fussing with the question of the before and after of a dramatic creation. Thus, the usual designation of these stories as "creation myths" is not helpful. The territory is simply already lived in when any new generation comes along. The *Dreaming* is the overarching concept that links the living with those who have gone before. It does this in two ways. One is that the stories of the ancestors such as their wanderings, their camps, their staffs (poles or sticks marked with clan identifications, some carried along, some stashed in hiding places here or there), their meeting with others, and their interests and behaviors are remarkably similar to the Aranda's way of life in the bush. The second is that the Aranda who are now alive have also come "from" the *Dreaming* and will return to it at death. In the meantime, life is full, rich, and challenging, despite what Westerners have imagined life to be like in a terrain as inhospitable as arid central Australia. That is because the Aranda are relaxed but alert, and their terrain is not at all inhospitable. It is precisely the opposite. Living in the bush is living in very close contact with the clan and its ancestors. The combination of territory, clan, and ancestors describes their home, and it supports a way of life and a social structure as complex and viable as any of the known tribal peoples. The notion that they were the most primitive people, or as the Germans called them, *Aboriginal* ("at or from the very beginning"), was a result of scholars looking for the Western concept of religion in the wrong place. Interested only in that question, scholars overlooked the Aranda's profound achievements in constructing an intricate social system on the basis of a limited set of markers that turned their territory into their native land.

The stories of interest in one's territory are somewhat different in the case of the indigenous peoples of the southwestern United States. Their land was mythologized as a fertile mother earth which produced both people and their corn. Interest in hunting and gathering did not stop, nor did the telling of stories about the eagles and bears, but watching the corn grow (!) and noting the difference corn made in the patterns of living together caught their mythmaking attention. The earth mother and the corn maidens were the central figures in many of their stories. A particularly telling creation myth succeeded in bringing the three major themes of territory, people, and the production of corn together (Eliade, *From Primitives to Zen*, 130–7; Carr, *Mimbres Mythology*, 7–11). In the beginning every living thing was wriggling in the darkness deep inside the earth. The earth was like the body of a woman, and the emergence of the people to the light of day was a slow and painful journey up through the "four earth caves," for mother earth was in travail. Along the way various "helpers" were needed to make it possible for the people to negotiate the darkness, slip away from the snakes and monsters, and climb up and out. Then there were helpers that pointed the way to the middle of the earth where the people were to settle down, and helpers that taught them the songs to sing when they got there, planted the corn, and celebrated the harvest. Now the stories of the corn maidens could be told (Carr, *Mimbres*, 35–40). There were seven of them, for there were seven types of corn from which to choose—yellow, red, blue, white, black, speckled, and sweet. The maidens were so lovely and tempting they had to be approached and handled with great care. Those who could not resist the temptation came to bad ends. We learned about these stories from the Zuni and Hopi, descendants of the Anasazi, but it now seems that they were quite widespread and popular among the many tribes of southwestern North America (*ibid.*). Each tribe imagined its territory differently, and in some stories their chthonic ("from the earth") origins tended to merge with half-remembered lore of the journeys they had made from other regions to the "middle" of the earth, where the helpers, more recently called the Great

Spirit, had led them. Many were cliff-dwellers who raised corn, beans, and squash along the edges of a nearby stream. In the case of the Hopi, the middle of the earth was their Second Mesa in northeastern Arizona where they were protected from other tribes.

Some scholars have found the stories of the seven corn maidens a curious addition to stories about the origins of the people. Recalling what we have learned about the way totems functioned among many tribal peoples, however, it is quite possible that the seven ears of corn of different colors, storied as the corn maidens, referred to seven clans of a tribe or moiety. If so, these myths can be used as examples of interests in territory, tribal structure, and food production all at the same time.

Yet another interesting mythology of a tribal society's territory is that of the Tlingit, Haida, and Tsimshian tribes of the Pacific Northwest. They occupied the narrow strips of habitable land between the glacier-covered Rocky Mountains to the east and the Pacific Ocean to the west, moving up the Skeena and Nass rivers in the summer for hunting and gathering, then down to the sea for the candlefish run and seal-hunting in the fall and winter. This terrain, their territory, is the setting for their stories of adventure while pressing the limits of social taboos and natural cycles. Protagonists include imaginary animals who drop from the heavens, turn into people, take the wrong wives, and wreak havoc with the social order, as well as heroes who can swim with the seals and live under water. But the moral is always that the protagonists do the wrong things, that the territory calls for other ways of behaving, and, though bounded by inaccessible regions, that it is a good place to live. It is their home. The people know what it takes to live there as a tribe, and living there by keeping the rules of social and natural proprieties is good (Lévi-Strauss, "Asdiwal").

The land as territory is also a major theme in the cosmogonies of the so-called high cultures, such as those of Egypt, Japan, and the ancient Near East. While it is the local landscape that is still in view, here the social formation is that of a kingship, and the land is the place where the construction of cities, temples, and memorials to royal power takes our attention. A larger natural world also comes into view, expanding horizons to include the heavens above the earth and the waters beneath it. At the beginning, gods are imagined to have separated the earth from the heavens, formed the people, constructed the temples, installed the kings, then taken their places to control the heavens, the underworld, and the kingdoms on earth. The land as territory is still clearly of interest, but surrounded now by a cosmic topography.

In one of the several Egyptian cosmogonies, the earth appears as an island rising above the waters, brought to life and light by the rising of the sun and the cry of a water fowl in flight over the waters. In another, the emerging sun god is at first a primal male cosmic glob floating in the waters "before heaven ever existed, nor earth came into being." This sounds a bit like the amorphous mother earth of the Amerindians, except that, in this case, the process of generation will be a bit more complicated. He goes through a series of weird dismemberments and relocations, all the time complaining about his circumstances, condition, and his first creations which he has managed to eject and spit out. Finally, however, his children and viziers help him settle into his sun barque so he can take charge of the daily and yearly cycles of light and life (Bonnet, "Weltbegin," in *Reallexicon*, 864–7; Mack, *Logos und Sophia*, 34–42). As the Hymn to the Sun from El Amarnah describes the result of this cosmogony,

> Beautiful is your appearing in the horizon of heaven, you living sun, the first who lived. You rise in the eastern horizon, and fill every land with your beauty. You are beautiful and great, and glisten, and are high above every land. Your rays, they encompass the lands, so far as all that you have created. You are Ra, and you reach unto their [the lands'] end and subdue them for your dear son [the king]. You are afar, yet your rays are upon earth. (Erman, *Ancient Egyptians*, 289)

One can see that a number of observations about the natural world belong to the set of interests involved in the composition of this mythology. The sun is the cosmic corollary to royal authority over the lands. Interest in the lands and the kingship is taken up into a cosmic cultivation with a tight link to the social function of the pharaoh from whom, back down on earth, social light and life radiate. To imagine the sun as the "first who lived" is a myth of fantastic reach in the interest of adoration of the Nile valley, bewonderment at the daily cycle of the sun, and aggrandizement of the pharaoh's kingdom in the lands of Egypt. The concept of the "lands of Egypt" is a synecdoche for Egypt as a society located just in those lands, thus a social notion. The social interests expressed in this mythology are seen through the eyes of the scribal and administrative elite of the kingdom, but they have in mind the wellbeing of the people and the performance of the kingdom as a whole sustained by the terrain and its natural climate.

In a Japanese cosmogony, two gods in heaven above bend down over the waters below and, with sticks, stir up a foam that congeals to form the islands of Japan (Eliade, *Primitives*, 94–5). In this myth the islands were created for the Japanese by the gods. It is not a theory of creation; it is a myth of fascination with their islands as the territory upon which the Japanese find themselves living as if it were meant to be.

In the ancient Near East, the cosmogonies include accounts of the first children of the gods getting out of hand, needing to be corrected or subdued, confusing the divine parents over what to do, and finally chopping up the cosmic mother to construct the world, the city, and the temple of the victorious king-god from and upon her body (Pritchard, *Ancient Near Eastern Texts*, 72–99). These cosmogonies can also be told in the form of a slaying of the deep sea dragon, the coming down of "kingship" from heaven to establish its earthly center in a certain Near Eastern city, and the account of the separation of the "heavens and earth" by a god who says "Let there be light." The fantastic features of these stories of origin are the result of delight in exaggerating the ways the world is known to work. There is the rising of the sun, the washing of the surf, the work required to produce the foods, the struggles for power, and the building of cities. Thus the fertile lands of Egypt appear as the waters of the Nile recede, the islands of Japan rise out of the ocean in all their glory, the ramparts at Uruk are made of burnt bricks just as the gods had made theirs at the beginning, and the destiny of Adam's progeny will be the promised land. The land as territory is always in mind.

As a matter of fact, the familiar biblical story of the creation of the cosmos and humankind is actually the proem to a story of struggle and wandering in search of a land by a people who formed a tribal identity long after other peoples were already there. The stories of other gods in charge of the cosmos and their peoples were already known, and other peoples already claimed the promised land. The story of an unnamed deity of supreme command creating the world by pronouncement, and a struggling people making mistakes on their journey to the land in the face of other powerful nations—that would be a very skillful casting of an epic for a new tribal arrangement and identity.

So these stories are not really creation myths, attempts to explain how the world began, as if these were the best the Aranda, the Amerindians, the Japanese, and the peoples of the ancient Near East could do to explain how the universe came into being. They are stories that create an imaginary beginning of a world in which the people, their activities, their predecessors, and their land can all come together in a set of relations appropriate for their place on the earth. Insofar as stories such as these remind the people who they are in terms of a given territory, the reminder is accomplished by means of distortion and thoughtful translation. The events recounted are imagined far enough in the distant past so as not to get in the way of the work at hand, but enveloping enough to count on being understood when used as metaphors or reminders when talking about their projects among themselves and telling others who they are. Note that the theme of the land is not isolated as something that has its own inherent value and interest. It is, rather, the place where people pursue their many activities and interests. It is important as that place, that location in the larger world, that terrain upon which a people's history is set, the terrain that still supports the productions necessary for living together as a people. As such, the stories told about the territory merge with all the others told about the people themselves.

The People

Many myths tell of the first people or the first man and woman. From tribal societies to the civilizations of the ancient Near East, the appearance of humans is often combined with the emergence of plants and animals, most frequently in myths of origin from the earth. As Euripides put it in the context of a classical cosmogony imagined as the sexual union of earth (female) and heaven (male): "Heaven and Earth were once one form, and when they had been separated from one another, they gave birth and brought up into the light all things: trees, birds, beasts, and spawn of the sea, and race of mortals" (*Melanippe*, frg. 484; from Martin, *Hellenistic Religions*, 7). These myths of origin "from the earth" and "into the light" combine analogies from agriculture, human sexuality, and birthing, as well as observations about living things as wondrous combinations of "life," "light," and in the case of humans, "breath." They can also reveal attitudes toward the earth as the land upon which the people live and work "under the heavens" in the light of day. It is therefore possible for such a myth to include metaphors of technology and construction, such as "pinching off" a bit of clay and "shaping" it to form the first humans. In the cosmogonies of the ancient Near East humans were imagined as a mixture of clay from the earth with the life substance of a god. The story of Adam and Eve in the Genesis story of the Hebrew Bible is an example of such a mixture, in this case of "dust of the ground" and the "breath of life" (Genesis 2:7). The theme of mixture is one of the ways in which people have imagined themselves to have "come from" and thus "belong" to the earth (their land). As the reader probably knows, the cosmologies of the ancient Near East imagined the earth floating on the waters under the earth, thus in the middle between the heavens above and the waters beneath, the realm of chaotic and inhospitable seas and dragons as well as the abode of the dead. Thus these myths are the result of profound meditations about the many environments, forces, and interests that must come together in order to think critically about human beings on earth. They are a way of locating one's own people in the past, from the beginning, as always already belonging to the nature of things in the world. One can see how the givenness of a tribal people and their place on earth would be accepted and taken for granted by any subsequent generation.

Social Structures

Then there are the interests people take in the very structure of their society as composed of families, kin, and other subgroups. In tribal societies, the kinship system is cultivated constantly by means of social placements, clan assignments, and the transfer of individuals from clan to clan through marriages. There is also the assignment of special responsibilities for caring for children that include others beyond the immediate family and the consideration of clan identities. It is important to know that studies of tribal kinship systems have not demonstrated the structural importance of what we have called a "nuclear family" (defined as father, mother, and children). Instead, the nurture of children usually involves responsibilities assumed by the brothers and sisters of the parents. Uncles and aunts, especially, belong to the basic structure of many tribal families. The resulting relations, though difficult for Western scholars to comprehend as systems and to keep in mind while tracing an individual's relatives, are nevertheless known to all in the tribe as the ways in which individual members have their particular place and identity in the society (Lévi-Strauss, *Structural Anthropology*, vol. I, 48).

Kinship systems and clan classifications need not appeal to origin myths. However, mention has already been made of totemic classifications of clans within a tribe, and these can be depicted in a wide variety of insignia, emblems, costumes, bodily paintings, and markings, all rich in connotation because of stories and analogies drawn from other systems of signs, especially from the fauna of their territory as habitat. In the history of the study of totems, touched upon briefly in Chapter 1, it seemed to scholars that these emblems and stories, and their displays on ritual occasions, must have had something to do with religion. It must be that the emblems, taken as they were from the natural order of their environment, were symbols of an early human sense of the sacred, vague and mistaken though such a sensibility must have been. There were many speculations about the awe that the natives must have felt before the mystique of the animal totems, and the aura engendered by the totems as the natives enacted their identities. Critical scholarship has called all of that into question. There is no need to think of these costumes and accoutrements as the result of mystifications of the natural world or of the natives' confusion about identities. Underlying systems of classification reveal their intellectual integrity, and the related kinship systems demonstrate the logic of their repeated applications to social structures and social life. The works of Durkheim and Lévi-Strauss have already been mentioned in regard to kinship systems and theories of totemic classifications as having social and structural significance. It can now be emphasized that the underlying logic of a totemic system can be conceptualized as the comparison of "two systems of differences" (Smith, *To Take Place*, 85). Until the work of Lévi-Strauss on totems and of Jonathan Z. Smith on the importance of difference in the making of comparisons, scholars assumed that the relation of a clan to its totem ("we are the bears") was one of identification on the basis of some similarity. It now turns out that the comparisons in a totemic classification of clans have less to do with a particular clan's similarity to its mascot than with differences among clans. Tribes made comparisons between their clan structure and the natural orders of fauna. These were made in terms of the *differences* among clans as being "like" the *differences* between "bears" and "eagles," for instance. Thus the social logic of the totem system was directly related to the structures of the tribe divided into clans, set forth in analogy to the differences among the several animal kingdoms, and thus available for the recognition and discussion of their own differences on an objective plane. These structures and their symbolisms play a role in rites of passage and rituals of celebration. The social interest emphasis is upon ritual instead of myth. It is as if the replication of the structure of a society is regarded as the ritual responsibility of each generation, not the result of an origin myth. This would mean that kinship and totemic structures are thought of as generated and maintained within the society itself in the course of its projects and productions. It would be the implicit acknowledgment of the human construction of the society in the interest of social existence.

There is, however, a large and complex class of myths of origin for clans, clan names, and stories of separations within tribes to form new, particular clans. Also among such myths are those that account for the present set of clans as a coming together of clans that once belonged to other tribes. The ancestral myths of the Aranda account for the multiplicity of clans as well as the topography of the land as the place where they all live. This means that myths telling of the origins of a people often reflect a social interest in their social structure.

A good example of the integration of myths, rituals, social practices, social construction, orientation to their territory, and awareness of social interests is given with the Winnebago. We have already mentioned their dual system of clan classification, the topographical orientation of their villages, and the symbolic significance of their village layouts with respect to their two moieties and clans (see pp. 30, 51). We can now mention the fact that the ethnographer Paul Radin was given two different descriptions of a village layout depending upon the moiety to which an informant belonged (*The Winnebago Tribe*). Jonathan Z. Smith has been able to clarify the reasons for this. There was a hierarchy in the relation of the two moieties that complicated the picture of balanced reciprocal relations. The division of responsibilities and powers, such as which moiety always provided the chief in charge of external threats and relations and which moiety provided the chief responsible for internal order and operations, determined a ranking. The chief's moiety, called the Thunderbird people (designated "A" by Smith) was understood to be "above" the Bear moiety ("B"). When a representative of the Thunderbird moiety was asked about the village layout, it was always described as clusters of teepees divided by a line that ran through the village with two ruling teepees, one from each moiety, toward the middle and providing a sense of balance between the two halves. When a representative of the Bear people was asked, the description was that of concentric circles, at the center of which was the ruling teepee of the Thunderbird moiety. "Thus," Smith writes, "it is from a perspective of power that A sees the village as symmetrical and reciprocal; it is from a position of subordination that B pictures the village as hierarchical. A's position [Thunderbirds] is one of relative clarity; hence the mirror-image character of its picture of the tribal organization. B's position [Bears] is ambivalent; hence, its more highly valenced 'concentric' diagram" (*To Take Place*, 44).

Rites of Passage

Closely related to structural systems are a rather large number of generational interests, such as births, puberty initiations, marriages, clan and tribal leadership installations, and deaths. Births attract social interest because another life requires space and place in the larger systems of social identities, relations, and responsibilities. The entrance of a new human being into the families of a tribe is usually marked by rituals of recognition and naming. Initiations not only register, but actually transact the changes in status that must occur as the many roles required to keep a society working have to be reassigned. The assignment of traditional roles and responsibilities, as well as the ways in which hierarchy is authorized, also counts as social interests, for without a social function playing such roles would be meaningless. This includes marriages, various changes in status and leadership, as well as the installation to high offices such as that of chief or king. Death creates an absence of a person who not only will be mourned and missed, but whose responsibilities will have to be taken by others in some rearrangement of relationships. The funeral is not merely an occasion for remembering the life and virtues of the departed, or for coming to terms with his or her absence. It is also, and primarily, an occasion for family and group to gather and start the process of rearranging the relationships and responsibilities important for their life together. A remarkable example is given in the Hebrew Bible stories of a patriarch's blessing upon his children just before his death.

One of the ways in which the dynamic process of maintaining a social structure takes the form of ritual performance and mythmaking is in the initiation of boys to their new roles as young men. I will use the example of a circumcision ritual among the Ndembu described and documented by Victor Turner in his *Forest of Symbols* ("Mukanda," 151–279). Among the Ndembu the rite of circumcision was called Mukanda. It consisted of several events in preparation for the rite that could take a period of several weeks, coming to climax in a three-day ritual for the performance of the circumcision itself, to be followed by periods of seclusion for the boys, their healing and instruction, with a final celebration of introduction and reentry into the society calling for a great festival. Although the procedures for the ritual were well known, there was no definite calendar or script for its proper performance. Instead, when it became clear to the elders that the boys were "too old to be hanging around the women's quarters," the headmen of the villages in the district began to talk among themselves and with the fathers of the boys old enough to be circumcised about where and when they might have another Mukanda, and who would be responsible for which tasks that had to be performed. As Turner describes the process, it becomes clear that subtle changes had taken place in the relative status of villages and tribal leaders since the last Mukanda ten years before. These changes had resulted in latent tensions regarding honor and the authority to take the lead in assigning tasks among the adults and determining rank among the boys. Which village, who would construct the arbor in the forest, how much beer to make, whether the "chief circumciser" from the last Mukanda would be selected for this one or whether he had grown too old and shaky, and whose son would be the first to be circumcised (thus projecting a future role of leadership for him) were some of the issues. The honor of many persons and villages was at stake in all of these issues. In most cases the issue was resolved when one of the contenders for a position of honor simply took charge, announced what would happen or actually performed an action, leaving the tribe with a fait accompli. Thus the boys did get circumcised in the right place, on the right log, under the newly constructed arbor made of the right materials, and were secluded in the right enclosures, given the secret instructions pertaining to male lore and responsibilities by the right teachers, and led triumphantly back to the society gathered for the festival of reentry. Since, however, the processes of "deciding" upon the "right" places and authorities for the ritual were issues of competition and contention, gossip, slander, and grumbling accompanied the entire process of assumed authorizations until the very last day of celebration. Then it was decided by all that the village hosting the event had done a fine job, and that it had been a "good Mukanda." Thus the boys stepped into their new responsibilities as adult males, and the rankings of honor and leadership in the society were established for another period of time.

The rites of passage have been regarded by scholars as "religious" because they are indeed rituals taking place out of the ordinary pattern of activities and are accompanied by symbolic accoutrement, secret instructions, cutting of the body, metaphors of "killing," and sometimes the killing of an animal or fowl to obtain materials for the rite and the festival to follow. The symbols involved are often traceable to myths that tell of the gods and imagine the horizons of a tribe's place in the larger world of the imagination. But caution needs to be taken lest the focus fall on what to us has appeared to be the manipulation of mysteries in transactions with the gods, namely, religion as we have traditionally understood it. Instead, the focus is clearly upon the rite of passage for the individuals involved and for the changes that take place in the social roles assigned. That a rite of initiation can be performed as a rite of circumcision is also worth considering. It is an example of a social logic that, though complex and seldom fully articulated, could be rationalized in a number of different ways. The point must be, however, that whatever the rationalizations, whether they have to do with health, sex, procreation, or the bloodletting trials that must be suffered when joining a male association or club, the distinctive effect of a circumcision from the society's point of view is that a body has been marked "irrevocably" as one of its own.

Among the Aranda of Australia the *tjuringa* is used to mark the difference between the before and after of an initiation. The *tjuringa* is a flat piece of wood carved with geometric markings and capable of being swung in a circle to make a "roaring" noise, hence it is sometimes called a "bullroarer." *Tjuringas* are kept hidden from children and women, stashed in hiding places, taken along by the men on hunting parties away from home bases where men from other clans might be encountered with their own *tjuringas* and distinctive markings, and used apparently on some ritual occasions. It is clear at least that the bullroarers made their noises from beyond the confines of the camp during the earlier parts of an initiation. Then, at the time for the sharing of adult male secrets, the boys would be shown the *tjuringa*, perhaps presented with one (?), told that it was the bullroarer, and that the geometric patterns were the distinctive marks of their clan. Before this was known to ethnographers, there were discussions about the *tjuringa* and its geometric markings, for it seemed to be the only object of the Aranda that could be regarded as artwork. The questions were about its markings, how geometric markings related to natural representations, and whether the *tjuringa* served as a symbol of the Sacred. Now we know that the *tjuringa* was a clan identification card, created to document and display clan classifications, and that it had a distinctly social function (Smith, *To Take Place*, 106).

Food Production: Agrarian

Shifting the focus from mythologies and rituals having to do with interests in the territory and the people as a social entity, I now turn to rituals associated with the food production of agrarian and herding societies. There are two major types of ritual that have played important roles in the life of these societies and in the modern study of religion: the festivals at the times of planting and harvesting of grain crops; and the feasts associated with animal husbandry. In the modern study of religion and society these rituals have called for attention because they seemed to document precursors to the Christian concepts of "offerings" and "sacrifice." I choose to discuss these rituals because of this general familiarity with them, and also because the scholarly attention devoted to them will allow me to make the point about the social interests they reveal. However, these rituals belong to another, and parallel, scholarly typology of societies that limits the large and instructive picture of food production to just these two practices. This parallel typology has given each of them an exceptional privilege linked to what have been termed "revolutions" in the staged "developments" of human societies. The "agrarian revolution" has been seen as an advance on "hunting and gathering" societies, and so forth. None of these standard descriptions of staged development of society types related to food production works any longer. We now know that tribal societies, traditionally assigned to the pre-agrarian and pre-husbandry level in an evolutionary schema, consciously engaged in many forms of food production that required technologies to enhance the natural environment's production of plants and animals. Examples include the "fire-stick farming" and eel farming among Australian natives (Diamond, *Guns*, 309–10), tuber crop technology in Ceram and throughout Polynesia (J. Z. Smith, "A Pearl of Great Price"), combinations of animal domestication, terracing, and rock-garden farming on Easter Island and elsewhere (Diamond, *Collapse*, 90–3). The recent study of civilizations in the Americas before the Western conquests by Charles C. Mann (*1491*) is a startling critique of the traditional notion of American Indians as sparsely settled or nomadic hunters and gatherers. Instead, there were high civilizations of complex societies engaged in multiple technologies of food production such as the conscious alternation of soils in the Amazon jungle to plant fruit trees (*1491*, 337–49). This means that myths, rituals, practices, and technologies of food production cannot be limited to harvest festivals and animal sacrifices. I have selected these rituals from among the much larger picture of human modes of food production because they are better documented in our scholarly tradition and can serve as examples of the social interests reflected in their myths and rituals.

The domestication and cultivation of corn in the Americas resulted in fairly large settlements with evidence of concentrated labor projects and supervision from chieftains. The highly structured and diversified civilizations of the Maya, Toltecs, and Aztecs were developments of earlier agrarian cultures in the Yucatan and the inland valley of central Mexico where fertile lands were made arable by clearing forests and building irrigation systems. There is evidence of similar corn-producing projects in North America from the southwestern regions to the Ohio valley. Unfortunately, we do not have evidence of the planting and harvest rituals of these cultures, only evidence of the mythologies associated with these agrarian economies. One example has been cited above in the "creation myths" of the Zuni and Hopi.

We are much better informed about the myths and rituals of grain production in the ancient Near East, Greece, and European countries. In British English, the term *corn* is used as the generic name for cereal crops in these lands, even though the grains of importance are wheat, barley, and rye. A large selection of myths and rituals about the Corn Mother and the Corn Maiden was collected in Frazer's *Golden Bough* (525–87). Many of Frazer's examples have to do with folk festivals at the times of planting and harvesting. In Europe, for instance, the farmers in a local district would race to complete the cutting of the grain lest they be the last one to finish, and so be "honored" with a wreath of wheat stalks to hang on their door and be called "the old Corn Mother" for the coming year. Greater festivity and more congenial social consequences were possible when Maypole dances were staged and the village youth selected for pageantry. In the Near East, agrarian rituals and festivals were resignified in the course of social histories that centered in temple-states. Offerings of food products at the temple were taken up into systems of assent to authority, the rectification of wrongs, and the keeping of accounts of personal failures and achievements. As the Hebrew Bible shows, older agrarian practices could become the markers of a yearly cycle of ritual occasions to remember and celebrate important moments of a people's epic history in relation to their temple-state.

One example of myths and rituals that retained their close relation to agrarian production through a long history of civilization is that of Demeter and Persephone at Eleusis, located 15 miles west of Athens. The importance of Eleusis as a center for celebrating the planting and harvesting of wheat is related to the fertile plains of nearby Thriasia, the major source of wheat for Athens and its lands. Eleusis was the village where the wheat from the Thriasian plain was collected and stored, giving rise to a tradition of families who controlled the collection and distribution, and to the festivals at the times of fall planting (*thesmophoria*) and spring harvest (*thalysia*). At some point Athens must have taken control of the economy and the organization of the festivals, for they marked major dates in the Athenian calendar and drew large numbers of people to Athens twice every year. However, the festivals remained centered at Eleusis, where an impressive institution of priesthood and ritual developed. Scholars have called this institution a mystery religion or cult, in keeping with its attraction as a place of pilgrimage where a combination of myth and ritual was focused on Demeter's "secret" until well into the Hellenistic period.

The myth of Demeter (probably meaning "earth mother") and her daughter Persephone (or Kore, "maiden") is well-known (Eliade, *Primitives*, 63–6; Martin, *Hellenistic Religions*, 65–72; Burkert, *Ancient Mystery Cults*, index, see 'Demeter'). Persephone, alone in a meadow picking flowers, is abducted by Hades, Lord of the underworld. Demeter goes looking for her, is told what has happened by the moon goddess, and, grief-stricken, wanders aimlessly alone, disguised as a mortal, until she finds herself at Eleusis. Her grief and wandering away from the company of the gods create blight on the land and the cessation of offerings to the gods. So Zeus intervenes and negotiates with Hades to let Persephone come back for two-thirds of the year to be with her mother. Thus the so-called "lesser mysteries", dedicated to Persephone, were celebrated in Athens at the time of the spring harvest festival (*thalysia*) and the "greater mysteries," dedicated to Demeter, were celebrated in Eleusis at the time of the fall planting (*thesmophoria*). The *thalysia* at Athens involved a public sacrifice of pigs and feasting. The *thesmophoria* in September was a ten-day festival involving preparations in Athens for a jubilant procession to Eleusis, where those properly prepared were allowed to enter the Telesterion, a large enclosure, for the showing of Demeter's "secret." This was the high point of the ten-day festival for initiands, and not to be revealed to those who had not experienced the night-time drama. Nevertheless, the object of the secret itself was said by some to be merely the showing of a stalk of wheat. If so, it must have been held over from the spring harvest, unthreshed and ready now for the grains of wheat to be sown. Thus the object revealed was hardly a mysterious symbol: it was the real thing. It was given ritual significance by means of its relocation from the fields and threshing floor to the Telesterion for contemplation and by means of the festive time away from the fields set aside for a major urban festival. The secret could now symbolize the entire round of cereal production, mark its importance for life in the Greek polis, note the mysteries of the natural processes of growth, and link the whole to the larger horizon of the cosmos and its gods. The ritual display of the wheat stalk was no doubt a solemn occasion, but it was also food for pensive thought as well as a reason for jubilant festivities. Talk about religion and social formation!

It is important to recognize that this famous example of agrarian myth and ritual was cultivated over a long period of time in the context of social formations in which interests and issues focused on aristocratic estates, kingships, the Greek city-state, the temple-states and aristocratic empires of the Near East, and the Roman empire. It should not be seen as a "remnant" from an earlier stage of agrarian civilization. Grain agriculture was important as a technology of food production in parallel to the construction of kingdoms and the city-states. We have not yet discussed myths and rituals focused upon these social constructions, but it can now be noted that the simultaneity of civic and agrarian rituals in Greece was one of the ways in which a contrast of social practices and interest provided the means for reflection and reflexive thought about the social formations themselves.

Food Production: Pastoral

We can now turn to a concept that has overwhelmed the study of religion and implicitly defined the meanings of a large number of rituals, namely, those that appear to be a sacrifice. The reasons for the prominence of this concept are understandable. They have to do with the facts that the notion of the "sacrifice" of Christ is so central to Christian myth and ritual, and that Christian myth and ritual have in effect defined religion for scholars in the tradition of the history of religions. But, of course, neither the long history of theology nor the concentrated history of the study of religion has ever found it possible to explain the logic of this concept applied to the death of Jesus. It rides along as an undecoded cipher of what is held to be a profound transaction between the human and the divine, not to be explained in purely human terms. How this strange configuration of myth and ritual came about will be examined in Chapters 5 and 6. For now, those ritual killings thought to be precursors need to be discussed.

Scholars have wanted to see the ritual killing of animals in hunting cultures as the precursor of the practice and concept of animal sacrifice in Greece, the ancient Near East, and in early Christianity. Walter Burkert has looked for the ritual killing of animals in hunting cultures in order to locate the origins of religion at the early stages of human development, thinking of religion as rooted in the notion of sacrifice (*Homo Necans*). Unfortunately for this quest, the facts reveal no evidence of it. An important set of studies by Jonathan Z. Smith has made it clear that the ritual killing of animals cannot be traced to hunting and gathering cultures ("Bare Facts of Ritual"; "Domestication of Sacrifice"). Instead, the ritual killing of animals begins with the domestication of animals among herders and in agrarian societies. When certain animals are bred for food, both the procedures for breeding and the production of food require killing some animals. It is important to keep in mind that meat was not a part of the regular diet in societies practicing large animal husbandry. It could not be preserved and so had to be consumed on the occasion of the killing, thus becoming the occasion for a feast. It is also important to realize that the killing of breeding animals only took place seasonally. It is therefore not difficult to imagine how, on those special occasions when an animal was to be killed, roasted, and consumed by everyone in the family or village, both the killing of the animal and the feasting to follow would take on the features of a display and celebration. It is this reconstruction of the history of sacrifice that reveals the practical and social interests involved in the eventual setting aside of a time and place for the collective performance of the perfect killing and the celebration of the feast to follow. Naturally, as a social unit changes, the economies become more complex, the experts at killing the animal display their finesse, the fathers and kings assign servants to prepare for the feast and then remind the people gathered of their lineage from heroes and how fortunate they are to belong to the district of this estate. Thus the occasions become calendrical and memorial, and the performances become grand, formalized, and institutionalized.

A study of the social significance of animal sacrifice in ancient Greece has recently been published by Stanley Stowers ("Greeks Who Sacrifice"). In Greece this ritual occasion was called a *thusia*. A *thusia* was performed at the tomb of the local *hero*, the term used for an early or founding ancestor of a district's leading family. As we know from the huge reservoir of stories, songs, and written descriptions of heroes in Greek antiquity, their social and cultural roles were so taken for granted that the imaginative embellishment of their escapades produced genres of literature for celebration, entertainment, pedagogy, and even allegorical and philosophical treatises. The ritual consisted of a meal for which an animal was killed and roasted, and to which the people who lived in the district were invited. Since meat was not eaten regularly as part of the daily diet, the roasting of an animal marked the meal as a feast. Oblations were made at the tomb of the hero or ancestor of the leading family of the district. The tomb was frequently covered by a round flat stone with a crevice to receive the wine. This physical gesture of refreshment was the way in which the Greeks acknowledged their sense of indebtedness and connectedness to the ancestral tradition of which the hero was the prime representative. As the animal was prepared for roasting, certain parts were thrown into the fire as a gesture to the gods who also belonged to the larger "family" and district of those present. But the rest of the meat, meal, and wine was then consumed by the people as a banquet. Judging from the general descriptions of Greek *thusiai* and banquets, it was a grand occasion for stories, song, socializing, and drinking.

The people took part and were served according to rank reflecting the hierarchies throughout the district. The father of the leading family provided for the feast from the resources of the estate. As the Greeks described it, he was the one who sacrificed or gave the feast, although the dirty work of building the fire, killing and roasting the animal, and preparing the meal surely must have been done by the servants. It was customary for the father to ask one of his sons to sacrifice with him. It is this aspect of the *thusia* that Stowers thought curious and worth further investigation. What he found is a very important clue to the social functions attached to the ritual. The father's invitation to his son "to sacrifice with him" was the way in which the head of the estate announced his choice of an heir apparent. It was his will and testament, so to speak, and functioned as a legal contract. In cases where siblings may have contested the right of that son to inherit the estate and manage the family's financial affairs, the son needed only to have a witness that he had in fact sacrificed with his father. Thus the ritual was the occasion for linking the past with the future by insuring the generational continuity of the district's aristocracy. It also confirmed or reconstituted the social structure of the district as a whole, centered as it was on the memorial of the district's hero and with an invitation to all the people, as well as the gods, to be present.

Ancestors

In the history of the study of religions, it has often been thought that primitive peoples had no history. One of the reasons for such thinking is that the Western concept of history is so closely related to written texts and driven by an interest in the documentation of facts. It has therefore been difficult to recognize that a tribal myth of origins, or stories about some hero, much less folktales set in the past, provided a tribe with its precedents and history. This may be one of the reasons why the widespread concept of ancestors has been slighted as a significant mythic theme. It is true, of course, that there have been many ways in which ancestry has been imagined, including several concepts of the ancestors themselves. We have already noticed what might be called pre-human ancestors, as in the case of the Aranda's concept of the *Dreaming*. Ancestors as progenitors would be another type, as would the honored dead. In each of these and other ways of conceptualizing ancestry, different modes of imagination, myth, and ritual can be noted.

Another reason for the failure to recognize ancestry as an important mythic theme (the point I want to make in this discussion of social interests), is that the scholarly definition of myth is a story about superhuman beings and superhuman agents. As the *HarperCollins Dictionary of Religion* states, "No story about superhuman beings, no myth" (749). This definition is understandable as an attempt to distinguish myth from other stories in the scholarly tradition concerned with the category of "divinity" (or the gods), but "superhuman beings" who "can do things humans cannot do" is only one of several characteristics that define the stories I am calling myths. Stories or images of ancestors, together with memorial rituals, whether the ancestors are imagined as superhuman agents or not, count as myths that reveal social interests. In the archaic cultures of Western antiquity, where the concept of the gods is distinguished from the concepts of humankind, ancestors, and heroes, the distinctions were not always clear. This range of anthropomorphic agents was taken by philosophers as an invitation to set up a cosmic grid or game board to explore the various combinations possible between humans and the gods, or better between the stories of the gods inhabiting the imaginary worlds above and below, and the life of humans on earth. There is no reason to limit the definition of myth to the stories of deities located in the cosmic dualisms of antiquity or in the subsequent Christian imagination of an ontologically transcendent realm of the spirit. After all, the main difference between an anthropomorphic deity storied in a people's myths and a human being living in that society has little to do with the late Western notions of divinity, transcendence, and a superhuman order of reality. Rather, it has to do with the difference between an imaginary world that encompasses the past, the present, and the future on the one hand, and the world of everyday experience on the other. This distinction will be discussed in Chapter 3, where the definition of myth will focus on the concept of social interests rather than on a particular characterization of superhuman beings as gods.

I want, therefore, to emphasize the importance of ancestors for the construction of the mythic worlds of most, if not all, human cultures. Ancestors need not be storied in elaborate myths, although some are. They need not be memorialized in festivals marking their birthdays, although many are. And they need not be given a credible genealogy in order to be memorialized by later generations, although genealogies abound and many are for just such a purpose. Ancestors, heroes, and "fathers" of various traditions and cultures have to be in the picture as we explore the function of myths, for they are an important index for the ways in which the mythic imagination expands the horizon of a society's imagined world beyond its present and everyday borders to include its past, where precedents were set, as well as its orientation to the cosmic and chthonic realms and the future. It is frequently the mythic memory of the precedents set by its ancestors that not only accounts for the way in which a society is constituted in the present and accepted as normative and good, but also continues to influence the ways in which one thinks about present circumstances and the decisions required to negotiate them.

Ancestors have been imagined and memorialized in a large variety of ways. We have already noted the close connection between the ancestors and the topography of the Aranda. The Chinese practice of maintaining a household shrine with the pictures or emblems of the four most recent past generations of the fathers is another mode of memorial. Remarkable in its appropriateness for an agrarian peasantry, the daily ritual of placing a candle on the table-shrine is described as routine for the wife and mother of the present generation. But one can hardly be blamed for imagining the moment as touching and significant when the image or symbol of a recently departed father is added to the panel and the most remote in time and living memory is removed.

Among the Tlingit, Haida, and Tsimshian of northwestern North America, where tribal organization of chiefs and clans supports a seasonal rhythm of hunting, fishing, and gathering in separate locations, the importance of a line of leading chiefs can be displayed in the construction of an elaborately carved and painted totem pole. As for clan relations and the significance of kinship roles, the memories and memorials cannot be focused on a single chief or family. Instead, a mythical hero named Asdiwal and a mythical heroine named Evening Star find themselves making the rounds of the yearly encampments and occupations, relating to one another, and experiencing the natural forces of the change in seasons, in a story of fantastic exaggeration and marvelous transformations. In Chapter 1 this story was mentioned as an illustration of the sophisticated logic of tuition by negative example in a folktale, and earlier in this chapter the stories of these tribes were mentioned as evidence of their knowledge of and attitude toward their territory. Here it can be noted that a "once upon a time" can function as a mythic past in which a pair of memorable characters portray what might be called the founding events of tribal society in obvious distortion for the purposes of entertainment and pedagogy.

In the ancient Near East, tribal and clan structures had been overlaid by petty kingships and aristocratic families, which governed large landholdings worked by servants, peasants, and slaves. Tribal and family ancestry was therefore much more difficult to maintain. Imperial relations encompassed simpler ways to keep in mind the human past of a family or people, through variety of fictional and mythic mechanisms. Kings, cities, and mighty warriors were the locations of social security and structure, and the cosmic horizon of the heavens was in view to comprehend the unimaginable arrangement of powers in a kingdom and its expanse. Thus the links to a primeval past were now traced through the histories of kingships, and this enriched the sense of a people's ancestry to include both patriarchs and kings. This was made possible in part because the role of the king and his court was viewed on the model of a family. Since the families of the district aristocracies and the peasant/workers within a kingdom also continued to be important for the people, two social systems co-existed simultaneously, thus giving rise to comparison and, because of their differences, creating occasions for thought. Important studies of family religion in the context of the kingdoms and empires of the ancient Near East have been published by Karel van der Toorn (*Family Religion*) and Mark Smith (*The Origins of Biblical Monotheism*, Chapter 3).

Among the Hebrews, descent from tribal patriarchs was still the main way of imagining a people's ancestry. Stories of the patriarchs were created in order to imagine how a collection of tribes had formed with claims upon the land of Israel. Genealogies of leading families were devised in the interest of claims upon proper descent for social roles, clan membership, and land ownership. The genealogies created for Jesus in the gospels of Matthew and Luke are familiar examples of such fictions.

In Greece, the combination of aristocratic landholders, the emergence of city-states, and continuing differences among old tribal traditions, local histories of rural districts, and the displacement of peoples in the post-Alexandrian and Roman eras created a most confusing situation for tracing ethnic ancestries. And yet, the importance of belonging to a particular people and its culture is everywhere in evidence. The poems of Pindar celebrate the victors of the games by memorializing their illustrious (*mythical*) family histories. The yearly feasts and festivals in honor and memory of the ancestor (or hero) of an aristocratic family were still held at his tomb in the district where the family had its roots. In the cities, writers were tracing the histories of peoples, cultures, cities, kings, and emperors all the way back to the beginnings of civilization. It is no wonder that, along the way, some heroes were separated from their tombs, some gods and goddesses imagined as the inventors of this or that technology were given shrines in many locations, and stories were told of the ways in which the ancestors were born from the gods.

A particularly interesting example of the way in which ancestry continued to be imagined and cultivated among leading families of the Semitic Near East is available in descriptions of a funerary ritual called the *marzeah*. There are texts that mention the "men of the *marzeah*," their banquets, and their leader. Other texts describe a *marzeah* as the ritual banquet for a funeral. In the so-called *rephaim* texts from Ugarit, the gods are depicted banqueting at a *marzeah* (Patrick Miller, "The MRZH Text"). Still other texts suggest features of the funeral ritual that involved calling upon the ancestors to be present for the banquet. Loren Fisher has brought these texts together in his description of this ritual in his book, *Genesis, A Royal Epic*. These features tell us that the transition from the world of the living to the world of the dead created a shift in representation that resulted in imagery we usually associate with the gods. On the occasion of the death of the patriarch of a district, tribe, or petty kingdom, the sons and other leading men would gather for a *marzeah*. The spirits of the ancestors would be called to be present, and the name of the patriarch, now deceased, would also be called in order to give his blessing to those still alive. The blessing was for the general well-being of the people, but especially for the sons of the patriarch, that they would in turn have sons and so assure yet another generation. The patriarchs were called by using their personal names, as for instance in Jacob's call upon the God of Abraham and Isaac, his ancestors, to bless Joseph and his sons in Genesis 48:15–16. *Elohim* is the term used most frequently in the Hebrew scriptures to refer to what we have understood and translated as "God." It is this term that occurs in the blessings of Jacob and Joseph. Although it is a plural form, it usually occurs in grammatical constructions that assume a single entity and it was the generic term for the spirits of the ancestors as a collective. We know that the patriarchs of particular tribes and families were remembered by name even though they were also included among the unnamed *rephaim* and *elohim* as collectives for ancestral spirits. As for the concept of named patriarchs, we know that the singular figure was storied as an individual but understood as a collective, a condensed symbol of a people as a whole. Sometimes this mental shift from an individual to a corporate characterization was acknowledged, as in the case of stories about Jacob who was given the name of Israel, a generic designation, in a blessing by the *elohim* (Genesis 35:10). It could also happen that a generic designation of a people came to be treated as a name and storied as a single person. Such was the case with Adam, for instance, a term which simply means "the human," or "humankind." This mode of abstraction, representing a social entity in a single figure, was a typical and very important intellectual pattern of thought in the ancient Near East. If this is so, it does appear that the concept of God in what we have come to call the Judeo-Christian tradition may well have roots in ancient Near Eastern myths and rituals in which patriarchs and kings joined the company of the unnamed dead. If so, the *marzeah* would best explain the process and best be explained by a theory of religion as social interest. What we have translated "God" would be the mythic form of attributing agency to a people's collective ancestry (Mack, *The Christian Myth*, 97–9).

Social Interests as a Concept

The human enterprise of social formation is a marvelous and complex collective achievement. One of the ways in which we have sometimes taken note of this achievement is to make a listing of types of societies by focusing on their primary means of production. The list usually starts with hunters and gatherers, then herders, and then small-scale agrarian societies. Production in these cases refers to modes of acquiring and distributing foods, even though the notion of "tribal" structure is usually not far away at the beginning of this evolutionary schema. Then, with the success of an agrarian enterprise, features other than the production of food come into view and foul up the classification based only on foods. For now the list goes on to mention year-round settlements, chieftainships, kingdoms, and finally empires, nation-states, and, more recently, global networks of corporate power. In these cases the social formations are defined by the social institutions required to organize labor for large-scale undertakings such as irrigation projects, cities, monuments, temples, and armies. Thus the term "production" wears thin if thought of only in relation to foodstuffs and markets. Societies can be organized to produce much more than food, and all societies can be seen to have done so, including the primitive tribes upon which we have focused in this chapter. Societies can also be organized to support technologies, inventions, and new configurations of human resources for social purposes. Familiar examples include the so-called "agrarian revolution," in which the cultivation of grain crops produced much more than a steady and abundant supply of food. It also produced permanent camps, grain storage, increase in population, labor assignments, calendrical markings, supervision, kingship, and support for persons involved in occupations other than the production and distribution of goods. Other obvious changes occurred in the emergence of the ancient Near Eastern civilizations and others from Asia, Mesoamerica, South America, and elsewhere, such as the territorial expansion of centralized power, the construction of administrative centers (cities), hierarchies of executive power, and professional classes of warriors, scribes, priests, and artisans. One could also easily add to the factors of social change such inventions as tools, technologies, books, calendars, sciences, arts, architectural design, cuisines, and defense, all with their attendant changes in social formation. In each case, supposing it were possible to set up a project of comparative social structures and their cultures, it would surely result in noticing that changes in mythologies and rituals have accompanied changes in social configurations. But, as important as some of these observations may be for the work of explaining the relationship between social formation and mythmaking, it is obvious that the most marvelous feature of human ingenuity has been overlooked in all of these classifications. What is that? It is the fact of social construction itself.

From tribes to empires to global corporations dealing in oil, arms, and money, all societies are human constructions. Since the construction of a society cannot be traced to a single individual of genius or to a great moment of discovery, crisis, or fear, we have not been able to imagine how social formation can be the result of a collective human enterprise. There is at least no technical terminology or discourse available for describing such a process. Part of the reason is that all of our vocabulary of invention and construction has had the individual in mind and not a collective. It is also the case that the construction of anything by an individual frequently includes the aspect of motivation. Thus the notion of producing something is implicitly beholden to our individualistic psychologies of desire, intention, planning, testing, and accomplishment. The whole process is understood to be conscious, even in the case of allowing for "discoveries" in the place of "inventions." So it is that, even though social formations are obviously collective human constructions, not accountable to natural law or divine creation, we find it difficult to imagine how humans have managed their creation. And yet, the histories of societies available to us for observation require us to find some way to acknowledge collective complicity in their construction and maintenance. What if we dispense for the time being with the notions of creative purpose and conscious motivation, stemming as they do from our individualistic psychologies, and start instead with some observations about the ways in which societies are put together as collective formations? After all, we do know quite a bit about some of the structural components of a society. Let us see where this kind of knowledge might lead us.

Societies are composed and maintained by the interweaving of structural devices such as a language, a kinship system, systems of tuition (education) for passing on the knowledge of production technologies, some system for the distribution of individuals to the various tasks required to sustain the society, calendrical systems, mathematical systems, systems of exchange, the distribution of goods, rules of etiquette, and some way of ranking roles and authorizing hierarchies. We have stumbled upon many of these features inadvertently in the course of this chapter. Now it can be said that, upon closer analysis, each of these ways of giving structure to a society is not only a structuring device, but also a semi-independent structural system in its own right. This is most clear in the case of a people's language, for we now know that a language is a system of signs structured by its own rules of grammar and syntax, as well as the device by which people create and maintain other systems and talk to each other meaningfully about the relationships that govern life together in a society. As a matter of fact, language is the structuring device of most importance for the construction of many other systems of signs, each of which also has its own structure and mechanisms for application. This is true, for instance, with the way in which humans classify, name, and accumulate information about the use of the flora and fauna of their habitat or territory. It is also true for the way in which language is used when distinguishing the places in which persons, families, clans, moieties, and tribes fit into a kinship system and help it work out its own logic in the passing of generations. Rules of etiquette are found to be grounded in the shared wisdom of myriad experiences over a long period of time, reduced to workable codification of the type: "We don't do that; this is what we do." A system of exchange will have its own language and rules as well as some logic to the ways in which it affects the quality of life in its society as a whole. Systems of production, distribution, governance, warfare, and construction will all have their own language and logic as well as complex interrelations with other systems of signs and practices in the composition of a people's life together. All are taken for granted as the working parts of a society as a whole, but all can also be watched carefully as distinct structures or systems to see how their operations affect other systems at work in the maintenance of the whole. All are invested with collective interests, energized by projects, and made possible by intellectual labor. Language is fundamental for every system and for the ways in which the several systems interact and fit together. Language is the way in which thinking takes place by making comparisons, giving things names, and deciding what to say and do about them. Thus these structuring devices are intertwined in giving a society its overall structure. All of them are there all the time and, as we shall see, there are a few other structuring devices still to be mentioned such as those belonging to the imaginary worlds where time, space, myths, and rituals may be located. Not all the possible combinations need to stay in place for all time. There is a churning and twisting of combinations as social histories experience shifts in circumstances, interests, and authorization (Schatzki, *The Site of the Social*). And yet, even when they are experiencing unacceptable social circumstances, strategies and tactics for survival within the given social structures seem to be the way humans respond. There is apparently no other option for living as a human being. Even those who withdraw from society and live as hermits, or those who become "anti-social" persons do not negate this fundamental condition. What then might be the glue that keeps a society's structuring devices attached to each other through thick and thin? How can we understand the interests humans apparently take in constituting themselves collectively as social creatures? What is it about a society that makes it possible to count on the fact that others will understand one's moves, and make their own moves in response according to the constraints and incentives customary for living together within the society?

Well, we need a term to acknowledge the collective investments humans make in the construction of their societies. We do not have such a term because humans generally think of the structures of their society as already given, not as a result of human construction. It is not exactly that humans deny their collective complicity in social constructions. After all, the history of human societies and the history of our own Western civilizations can hardly be understood any other way. It is the large-scale, complex, drawn-out process of changing and maintaining social structures, so difficult to comprehend much less analyze, that brackets the notion of humans doing the work of constructing their societies. The thought of such collective endeavor is merely consigned to the realm of the unexamined as inconceivable. Yet, if we want to explain a social theory of religion and ask about its function in ways similar to other social structures, we need a shorthand term to acknowledge the unconscious interest humans take and have taken in the collective construction of their societies. By itself, the term *interest* will not do. That is because "interest" comes with a large set of connotations, most of which imply conscious motivation of the kind that involves personal planning and investment with a view to reward. The collective interest that needs to be named, and that is so taken for granted by a people as to be something of which they are hardly conscious, may be better expressed by a pair of terms such as *social interests*. Since the collective investments in the construction of societies and the way in which the results are taken for granted do not cancel each other out, they are not uncritical oppositions. They define a mentality required for social existence. By using the pair of terms, "interest" would not have to be understood as a term of conscious motivation on the model of individualistic psychologies, but instead as the predicate of the collective social, and "social" would be understood as the location for the collective agreements taken for granted that give a society its structure. Thus the term social interests can help advance our quest, for it parries the slippery question of motivation that usually attends the term interest even while it takes up the otherwise overlooked factor of the collective human investment in the construction of society. Since this factor has to come to the fore in order to imagine myths and rituals as human constructions related to social interests, I dare to suggest the formulation. It is the observation of the structuring devices in the overall structuration of society that makes it possible. Only in this way can the enormous investment in energies, social experimentations, intellectual labors, and the negotiation of agreements be acknowledged. Only so can the logics of the several structuring devices and their applications allow us to see how the dynamic process of social formation proceeds as a viable enterprise. And only with some concept like this in mind can the possible links between social formation and mythmaking be acknowledged. It is a necessary concept if we want to explore the social function of religion as important for life in the everyday world.

Finally, it needs to be emphasized that all of the above social interests are also matters of intellectual interests. We have already toyed with the idea that all of the structuring devices in view are not only products of intellectual investments, but also provide grammars that require intellectual activity in their applications. Now it is important to see that intellectual interests merge with social interests in the construction and maintenance of a society. To find an object, a person, a situation, a task, a problem, a mode of thinking, a set of rules, a calculus, a classification of flora and fauna "interesting" is an intellectual activity. And so, we are very close to saying that social formation is the result of the interests humans take in thinking about living together and thinking about the world in which they live. As we shall see in the case of myths and rituals, the intellectual component in the range of interests involved in the social construction of societies invites elaboration and even makes it possible for a given social grammar to become a game board for play with or without practical consequence.

This chapter has presented a selection of myths and rituals from many cultures to illustrate their social functions and develop the concept of social interests. A social theory of religion is not yet fully in view. There is enough, however, to suggest that myths and rituals are embedded in social practices and thinking. They mark moments of social significance and reconstitution and appear to belong to a system of signs that may have its own structure and may be one of the systems that structure human societies. As a system of signs, myths and rituals enlarge the empirical world of a society to include a world of the imagination that encompasses the past and future of the people, the forces of nature that impinge upon the practices of the people, and certain junctures among all of these orders that help focus the interests of a people as a social identity. What we need now is a closer look at the imaginary world created by myths and rituals, for it is in that world that the social interest humans take for granted in the everyday world can be acknowledged and manipulated. It is also in that world that the imaginary beings we have called gods appear.

Myths, Rituals, and Social Interests

When compared with the other systems of signs and patterns of practices that structure human societies, systems of myth and ritual manifest three distinctive characteristics: (1) they focus attention upon figures and actions in orders of time and space at a distance from the everyday world of activity; (2) they exaggerate the descriptions of the figures and activities that inhabit those imaginary worlds in ways that mark them as different from their counterparts in the world of actual experience; and (3) they may include the attributes of intention and performance of the frequently powerful agents located in those imaginary worlds. In sum: imaginary world; fantastic features; powerful agents. We can turn these characteristics to theoretical advantage by noting that they stretch the imagination beyond the parameters of everyday experience, empirical observation, and access to confirmation. It is the relationship of this imaginary world to the everyday world of social experience that provides the answers we seek about the relations among myths, rituals, and social practices.

As for the way in which myths and rituals expand the horizons of the normal senses of time and space, several observations can be made. Myths are frequently set in the past, sometimes in a "once upon a time," sometimes at or before the very beginning of the world, sometimes in the chthonic realms beneath the earth, and sometimes in the future. Rituals are actions that take place in the present time, but in places that are marked off from the everyday. Thus the horizon that controls the outward limits of credibility may be as vast as all of imaginable time and space. The logic of these manipulations of the ordinary, everyday experience of time and space has been worked out by Jonathan Z. Smith. According to Smith, ritual takes an ordinary activity away from its ordinary place in the everyday and performs it in microadjustment in a marked-off space. Attention is drawn to the difference between a "perfect performance" of the activity and the customary, an invitation to critical reflection upon the everyday. Myth sets up a contrast between the "now" and the "then." Ordinary figures take on extraordinary features when transposed into the mythic world. Attention is drawn to the differences in such a way as to underscore the inaccessibility of precedent-setting agents and events, as well as to invoke thoughtful reflection on the structures of the ordinary. By design, then, myth and ritual manipulate ordinary orientation to space and time in the interest of bringing critical thought to bear upon the ordinary. They do this by marking differences in perspective that invite comparison and create a space for critical reflection. In myths, the concentration of an unlikely combination of features in a single figure can bring thought to focus intensely on a particular, perhaps heretofore unexplored, configuration of social forces. In the case of ritual, an action common to the everyday will be slowed down and unraveled into moments so minute that time stands still and the space becomes otherworldly. It thus appears that myths and rituals are designed to exercise the imagination by placing ordinary objects in extraordinary settings, and extraordinary figures in ordinary settings. They fill both the long reaches of the past, the vastness of space, and often the future world with figures and moments that, though distant and detached, are very much present to the imagination and bear some relation to everyday life. Let us say that the contrast between the everyday world and the imaginary world not only prompts reflection upon aspects of actual social situations which otherwise may not have been noticed, but also creates a certain fascination with the strange and interesting figures inhabiting that imaginary world. Pierre Bourdieu has helped us see the importance of this expanded world and has given it the name of *habitus*, that is, the imaginary world in which a people's collective agreements about living together reside.

Why would a people want to do that? Well, what if the process of social formation creates and draws upon social interests and forces that cannot be explained by reference to any contemporary source or cause? What if a people recognizes that, for any given generation, the structures governing their lives together were already in place? What if belonging to human society is not merely a matter of voluntary association, but a coming into a world set by circumstances prior to anyone's doing? Why then, any attempt to give an account of oneself living within a social formation would require pressing beyond the borders of the observable and known. Such would be the case, for instance, when reflecting upon one's sense of belonging to a people; sharing a particular attitude toward the land; accepting, marking, and honoring genealogical loyalties; cultivating the memory of forebears whose influence cannot be accounted for simply in terms of biological descent; wondering at the "cosmic" and natural arrangements of the world that determine the pace and direction of activities; experiencing the constraints of another's views in the way in which judgments, construals, and "memories" redound; looking for reasons for ranking and the assignment of tasks; noticing the shared world of the imagination in which reports, plans, questions, curiosities, jokes, and intellectual achievements are located and managed; and wondering about the effects of gift-giving and obligations. Myths and rituals are the ways humans have of acknowledging the complexity of the social by locating social determinations outside the world of the everyday, even while configuring them in such a way as to cast their reflection back upon the everyday.

The Fabrication of Myth

Now, an odd thing happens when the interests derived from the other systems that structure human societies are transposed into the imaginary worlds of myth and ritual. We have noted that the themes typical for mythologies correspond to these social interests. Kinship, classification, calendrical orders, territory, production, and so forth, are all there. The remarkable thing about these themes in mythic mode, however, is that their transposition into the once upon a time of myth triggers a transformation of the theme. Interest in kinship as a system may shift to interest in ancestral legends, genealogy, and descent. Mapping one's territory is often transfigured as an account of creation. Technologies of production are imagined as discoveries, inventions, or first-time stories. Tuition takes the form of example stories set in a fantastic world or past. The alreadiness of social arrangements is often accounted for in terms of origin stories in which precedence is established by patriarchs, powers, and authorities not accessible for questioning. Thus the imaginary world does not reflect the faces one actually sees in the everyday social world, nor is the imaginary world as lovely, sensual, detailed, and inviting as the natural environment of a group and its polished artifacts. The mythic world is much too large for normal comprehension on the one hand, and much too grotesque to serve as a mirror on the other. Can these fantastic features be explained?

The fantastic configurations of the world of myth are the result of compressing many social forces and features into imaginary figures and moments of agency. The mythic world allows for recognizable features of the social world to be exaggerated, concentrated in odd configurations, parceled out and distributed among several agents, set in situations of conflict, and observed in moments of narrative transformation. I have already noted that the complex systems of signs and patterns of practices that structure human societies cannot be the creation of individual agents. But attribution of agency is a primary mode of accounting for things that appear and happen, and agency is one of the main ways we have to attribute purpose to an event. If a people wants to think of its social structures as having purpose and design, mythic moments and agents will have to be imagined, and the forces or agents will often have to be imagined as "persons," even while establishing social circumstances of which no real person is or could have been capable. It should not be surprising, then, that the agents who populate this expansive world of the imagination look strange. That is because they are imagined as agents of and representative figures for social roles and forces that structure a society as a whole. What kind of an agent might be imagined as the culture-bringer, law-giver, arrangement-setter, terrain-creator, or "person" responsible for all the little cracks in the natural–social system where mistakes, failures, jokes, tricks, and serendipities happen? Just to ask the question lets the familiar mythic figures appear.

Thus the mythic world cannot be a perfect reflection of the social world. Neither is the mythic world the picture of an ideal society with which the social order is to be constantly compared. The imaginary world of a people is a motley conglomerate of disparate images that vary in intensity and clarity of profile. The mythic world does not inhibit the energies required to manage social relations and practices in a dynamic social formation, though it may set limits for acceptable conceptual and behavioral experimentation. In a situation of social and cultural stability, the gap between the social world and the mythic panoply may be thought of as creating a space for play, experimentation, thoughtful meditation, as well as a bit of cheating, winking, and/or calling one another to task. But creating a space and backdrop for the theatre of human activity is not the only way a mythic canopy functions. It may also be treated like a collage in which the arrangement of its figures is susceptible to reconfiguration. In a situation of social and cultural change, the mythic world can become a battlefield for ideological advantage. Because the symbols within the mythic world can be manipulated, they can either be highlighted in order to argue for traditional ways and values, or reconceived and rearranged in the interest of calling for social change.

The Technology of Ritual

Thus far we have described the ways in which rituals relate to social practices and interests. We have also noted that a ritual's construction of time and place creates a difference between the ritual performance of a practice and the everyday performance of that practice. This difference, we have emphasized, creates a space for thinking about the practice, both in its everyday settings and in its performance as a ritual. We have also noted that the performance of a ritual provides an opportunity for "unraveling" the practice into its many smaller actions and moments in order to reveal their relations to one another, take care in its execution, refine its techniques, and display the skills required for its perfect performance. We can now develop the concept that Jonathan Z. Smith has named "the technology of ritual" (private correspondence). What he means by this is not only that rituals are occasions for the display of a performer's technics and technical skills, but that the performance of rituals can be seen as a technology in the construction of social occasions that affect the patterns of social interests and thinking involved in social constructions themselves. Examples can be given to sharpen this concept.

In the cases of the *marzeah* and the *thusia*, funerary rituals do more than celebrate a rite of passage. They actually recreate the structures of an aristocratic society by confirming the contemporary genealogical relations and hierarchies of the group in relation to the traditions that were at work in the last generation. The celebration is a way of replicating this structure and guaranteeing its acceptance and logic for the future. It does this without overt instruction or the application of force or threat. People take their places as a matter of course by participating in the celebration as if it were a festive or pensive occasion. In fact, the ritual occasion creates a virtual reality that invites participation without having to explain the placements or philosophize about them. It is a "technology of caring" (Smith) with implications for the future everyday world.

In the case of the rituals associated with Demeter and Persephone, their design created yearly occasions of festival and drama that displayed the power of the *polis* and mysteries of agriculture for a large number of people dependent upon both. Participation in the festivals was also an acknowledgment of Athens' influence far beyond its borders, as well as an individual's implicit acceptance of a kind of citizenship or sense of belonging to its civic authorities. It would therefore be possible that slight changes of procedure or assignment of roles in any of the many activities might be noted, and translated into codes of honor, status, and future authority. The planning and performance of the rituals would constitute a technology of social engineering by means of participation in festivities that result in all-but-guaranteed acceptance of one's place in the society. Similar technologies of urban rituals might be found in Paul Wheatley's studies of urban genesis, cited in Chapter 1. He came to the conclusion that rituals and religious performances were the attraction that established the centers around which cities developed. Clifford Geertz found that the palace of the king in Negara was built as a stage for ritual performances that celebrated and confirmed the social cohesion of the society (*Negara*).

A particularly interesting example of ritual as technology is found in Roy Rappaport's description and analysis of a pig festival in New Guinea (*Pigs*). It was decided to have a festival when the pigs were too many, out of hand, and rooting in the gardens, but plans for the feast also included invitations to neighboring tribes to attend an event at which there would be games and mock battles. The invitations were a gesture of friendship, but the games and battles were understood by all to be rather serious matters of competition, by which the winners and losers would be ranked in that order until the next festival in the district. One neighboring tribe did not attend, effectively announcing tensions among the tribes, if not some hostility. The festival proceeded with jubilant participation, and the mock battles were taken as occasion for the display of skills in hunting and tribal warfare. But as soon as one of the contestants was hurt, even slightly, the game was called off and the feasting could begin. Latent tensions about territory, hunting rights, and intertribal rivalries were resolved in the ranking, and the pig problem was solved.

This means that myths and rituals should not be thought of as practices that cultivate "religious" interests in contrast to social interests and practical interests. They are the ways in which the expanded *habitus* of human societies is acknowledged, memorialized, manipulated, and contested. Religion thus explained is not only part and parcel of the systems that structure human societies; its distinctive functions appear to be essential extensions of the other systems of signs and patterns of practices. Myths and rituals are not only generated by social interests, they are the ways in which social interests continue to be shaped, criticized, thought about, and argued over in the ongoing maintenance of a society.

3 Watching Myths in the Making

In the popular understanding religion is defined by a belief in gods. In our study of the scholars' search for religion among tribal peoples we have not encountered many gods. Instead, we have noticed social interests and the many ways in which these interests have been recognized in myths and treated in rituals. We are now ready to take another step or two in our quest for a social theory of religion. We need to notice that, instead of gods, tribal peoples sometimes told stories about animals or other features of the natural world as if they behaved like humans and/or might be taking interest in the human world. We need to describe what can be called the mythic imagination. We need to account for the emergence of what we think of as gods in the imaginary worlds of myth, and the sense of exchange with influential forces in the performance of rituals.

We will begin with a description of the mythic imagination as the world in which the gods can be located. This will draw upon the illustrations of myths and social interests given in the last chapter, working mainly with examples from ethnography. Then, however, it will be possible to shift our focus to the aristocratic empires of antiquity in order to show how a world of the gods was created in the mythic imagination and given cosmic dimensions. It is important to make this transition from tribal societies to kingships and aristocratic empires, for it is there in our remembered history that gods familiar to us were imagined. It will be possible to make this transition by means of some observations about the ways in which changes in social formations create shifts in social interests and thus in the configurations of myths and their gods. Toward the end of the chapter some consideration will be given to the Hellenistic age, where yet another set of social formations and conceptions of the gods can set the stage for our consideration of Christianity's beginning in Part II of the book. For the moment, however, it is the way in which myths are made and deities imagined that we need to consider. We will see that they are understandable products of intellectual labor, thoughtful engagements of significant moments where human interests and activities encounter natural and social forces that are difficult to fathom. Then, in Chapter 4 we will explore the ways in which existing myths and rituals can be used and manipulated in the analysis of situations of social change that need to be rationalized.

Environments

Mythic imagination begins with an awareness of two environments, the natural world and the social order. Both environments are taken for granted. And yet, there is a great deal of difference between the requirements of living with and within each of them. Neither environment is fully available for manipulation and questioning. Both need to be engaged and handled in the pursuit of the human enterprise of social formation. But each needs to be handled in a particular way.

The natural environment is much too large and complex for comprehension. It is also in motion, so that only certain features, such as topography, appear stable. Some features such as the yearly cycle of seasons are changes that seem to be regular, but other changes, such as storms, fires, comets, and earthquakes, happen as surprises. It is, however, possible for certain environmental features of particular interest for a people to be studied in detail and turned to practical advantage. The knowledge required to maintain the practice of agrarian production, for instance, is a system of relations discovered among several orders of natural reality such as astronomical regularities, seasonal cycles of weather and growth, types of grasses, grains, and soils. In the course of these discoveries, experimentation would have occurred with the manipulations required to turn this knowledge to advantage for the production of food, for example, the best ways to till and plant, harvesting technologies, silo construction, distribution methods, and cuisines. The point is that both the practical and scientific knowledge involved in grain production, while in some ways detailed and explanatory, is layered in relation to knowledge about (and the mysteries of) the rhythms and life-producing forces of the natural world. The larger world of nature had to be imagined as mysterious and wonderful even while the focus on grains produced a rather precise knowledge about ways to manipulate the natural process.

Managing life together in the social realm also involves detailed knowledge of its social structures, such as relations among clans, families, social roles, tasks, taboos, and etiquette. Much of this knowledge becomes available to children in the course of their introduction to the social world. And yet, because the structures are already in place for any given generation, the reasons that can be given for them and for specific patterns of activity are limited since they are buried in the history of the collective contributions to social formation. It needs to be emphasized that the reasons for the accepted and traditional ways of life in a society are also not available for explanation. The reasons usually given are mostly observations about "proper" behavior and reminders of traditions. That seems to be enough to satisfy most questions and get on with the work of living together. This larger encompassing world of tradition, especially in relation to memories of ancestors, stories of heroes, and precedent events of the past, actually works to define the characteristics of a people, its way of life, and its identity. But traditions are available only to the memory and imagination of a people, sometimes cared for by assignment to specialists who can be asked about them when it seems important to be reminded of them. The combination of memories, stories, and the resulting constraints upon behavior in a structured society determines a sphere of influence larger than the arrangements of the everyday. The everyday can be filled with tasks, talk, observations, and banter unaffected consciously by the constraints and influence of the larger imaginary world. But without that receptacle of the knowledge gained by a long history of experiments and agreements reduced to selective memories and the storied rationales for structural arrangements and social habits the everyday patterns would not cohere.

Both of these environments, the natural and the social, surround the empirically available orders of reality with systems of knowledge and awareness that can reach to the limits of what is possible to know or imagine. People do not usually distinguish between empirical and imaginary ways of knowing about their environments. But it is quite important for our purposes to realize that the world of nature and the history of one's own people cannot be grasped as environments on the basis only of testable, present-tense knowledge. Imagination enters the picture as soon as a natural environment of large scope or a social situation with some history is to be considered. Since both environments encompass the everyday available orders by means of extensive horizons that have to be imagined, the two environments coalesce in what we can call an imagined world. It is within this imagined world that the gods appear; and it is at the intersection of the two environments where myths and rituals mark moments of social interests, social practices, and the cultivation of customary habits of thought.

The fact that the scope of the imagined world extends beyond the everyday world as experienced and observed, and that it includes past events and stories of the gods, does not hinder the full exercise of intellectual, practical, and social interests in the present, nor does it mean that interests focused on the manipulation of the intersections of the two environments are uncritical about the dynamics of the influence of each. As Malinowski demonstrated in the case of the Trobriand Islanders, precise practical knowledge required for fishing did not erase interest in ritual celebrations invoking mythic deities associated with the sea, fish, and weather. Nor, in the case of the elaborate myths and rituals of Demeter and Persephone, did it mean that the farmers did not know exactly what was required to raise a crop of wheat. Thus myths and rituals point both ways. They mark social interests of practical value and influence and they do that by setting them in the context of the larger, encompassing worlds where the mythic imagination can focus attention upon them. Even though this larger, encompassing world is complex, consisting of both social and natural environments, each layered in terms of accessibility, orders of knowledge, and human skills, it is comprehended and accepted as a single environment within which people know themselves to be at home.

Fictional figures appear in the imagined world personifying forces, influences, constraints, and powers that impinge upon the world of the everyday but are beyond the reach of its control. Such figures may also represent the unknown reasons for such impingements or influences, which are of many kinds. They include such things as the mysteries of weather cycles and changes, the rise and fall of the waters, the growth of flora and the behavior of animals, and the effects of the sun and moon by day and night. They also may include past events that have become social precedents, the memories of ancestors whose influence continues to affect ways of thinking about a people, the constraints of the social structures in place and some account of how they came to be, the authority invested in those who are given the right to say what should be done, and the unspoken rules governing honor and shame. The everyday world is touchable, manageable, and partially testable to the degree that those living within it have the curiosity, intellectual capacity, and skills to comprehend and control it. But the facts that the forces of nature are not of human making and are beyond human control and that the social world is rooted in traditions created by humans from the past and is open to contention and internal conflicts mean that the intellectual labor of a people will focus on those features of its social existence and its engagements with the natural environment where the environmental impingements most readily affect social interests. Living in such an environment need not obstruct the patterned way of life or the exercise of practical thinking. But at those junctures where the larger imaginary worlds overlap the social interests and practices of the life and thought of a people, the imagination of the influential forces can result in the personification of agents we have come to call heroes, ancestors, and gods.

The Gods

In the previous chapter I listed three features of the world imagined in mythic mode, one of which was the appearance of agents we customarily call gods. I used the term "agency" as if we might take it for granted, for it is a common and self-evident concept. It seems that this concept occurs automatically whenever we ask ourselves how something came to be. It is involved in accounting for events, actions, inventions, constructions of various kinds, and in application to all the ways humans have changed the natural environment to produce foods, buildings, cities, and states. It is also one of the ways in which we question things that happen, especially things that happen to us serendipitously, or perhaps as a threatening circumstance ("Who or what did that?"). The current interest in biology and cognition has found that agency is a primary intuition, which can be documented from the very early stages of child development. Applications of this concept and finding to the analysis of religious mentality can be found in Lawson and McCauley, *Rethinking*

Religion. A more recent discussion that explains the mythic notions of gods as both intuitive and counterintuitive responses to a world perceived as intentional is Luther Martin's article on "Cognition and Religion." Cognitive theorists interested in the origins of religion have suggested that this counterintuitive response can help us understand how the concept of superhuman beings occurs in children and functions in religions. Thus, the appearance of "superhuman" agents in myths and other stories may well be accounted for in part as the way connections are made between biological and cultural mechanisms. It is, however, the function of these agents in the stories we call myths that I want to pursue. The challenge will be to emphasize the factor of social interests in order to narrow the selection of stories with superhuman agents to those we normally think of as myths. This will allow us to treat the superhuman agents that appear in these stories as a result of a distinctive social logic, one in which the common use of the term "agency" and the customary use of the term "gods" come together.

But, first, a word about the term "god" is needed. There is no single, universal concept of god by which to define such a one or recognize one when you see it. As a matter of fact, the term God in Western and current discourse is a curious combination of name and concept. Used as a proper noun or name, God denotes the Christian God. It has also been used, of course, as a designation for the Gods of Judaism and Islam. Used as a concept, the term becomes an abstract generalization capable of connoting universal features of "divinity" as well as indefinite references to a god or other gods in the plural. This confusion of terminology and use, and the fact that the Christian name-concept is not applicable to other cultures, means that its use to refer to other gods cannot escape subtle comparison with the Christian God, a comparison that usually assigns other gods to inferior positions. Since other cultures do not imagine their gods in ways that match the Christian concept, some scholars have bequeathed the terms God/gods to theologians and substituted "superhuman beings," as the *HarperCollins Dictionary of Religion* suggests. I will, however, continue to use the terms *god/gods* in keeping with popular usage in order to treat together all the stories with agents we have traditionally called gods. The task is to sort through this accumulation in order to form a subclass related to collective social interests of significance for social formations. This will in effect add an important feature to our definition of myth, as well as call attention to the many kinds of mythic beings that cultures have cultivated.

Thus, there is a great variety of personifications depending upon and relating to different types of social formation, their environments, and their worldviews. Even our brief survey has touched upon many mythic beings: ancestors of several kinds, earth mothers and fathers, folktale figures, animals, tricksters, creator gods, solar deities, corn mothers, divine-human kings, and so forth. The list could easily be extended with other figures more familiar to us: gods associated with the vine and wine (Dionysos), protection at sea (Isis), victory in war (Athena, Yahweh), questers (Gilgamesh, Odysseus,

Theseus), dynasty transfer (Osiris, Horus), royal hierarchy and family conflict (Babylonian pantheon, Greek pantheon), fire (Prometheus), hearth protection (Vestal Virgins), highway protection (Hermes), authoritative teachings (Moses, Yahweh, the Seven Sages in Greek lore), healing (Asclepius), and so forth. Most of these more familiar figures are depicted as anthropomorphic agents at those intersections of the two environments where forces are imagined to have influenced, and perhaps continue to influence, human thinking and activity. This means that the ways in which the mythic world is thought to affect human activity and well-being are projections of the ways in which humans see and understand themselves. Many deities are portrayed as "persons" who see, judge, desire, plan, purpose, decide, act with intent, and have power to accomplish their purposes. Since these deities have been placed at junctures of social interest and human well-being, the effect of the stories told is that the gods also have taken interest in a human project and have intended their influence to be used in the interest of that project. Thus the imagination of the gods is related to thinking about social interests by means of narrative embellishment.

Myths

These observations about the gods as personifications of impingements upon human interests and endeavors can now be used to shed some light on the way myths are made and work. Myths take the form of narratives in which deities are protagonists of actions that take place at a juncture where the human world and the natural environment are imagined to meet in dynamic relations. The creation of an imaginary character, scene, and action has little to do with a "belief" in the gods as supernatural beings. The creation of an imaginary character is a human intellectual activity that we normally take for granted and use constantly to share our stories about the way people behave and the way the world seems to be working. It is no doubt related to the marvelous functions of human consciousness with its capacities for memory, conceptualization, language, communication, and planning. The scope of human consciousness extends the present into the past as a memory and into the future as an anticipation. It also comprehends a present situation as a place and time in relation to the larger worlds of social belonging and orientation to the natural realms. As we know, however, in order for a story to invite our attention, selections must be made from the vast worlds of awareness and experience in order to focus upon aspects of a certain situation, a particular interest, a task, or project. The small talk of everyday life is easily teased into observations about situations and other persons that can give rise to imaginative descriptions, analogies, humor, and truisms. It is this exercise of the imagination that produces interesting images and fictive stories to enhance observations and thinking. A particular situation or impingement can also provoke curiosity and lead to stories told apart from immediate experience. Stories can be thoughtful elaborations of precedent events, encapsulations of memories, common occurrences, fictional reconstructions of human situations, or theoretical curiosities to be worked out in scenes that seem to be set completely beyond the bounds of human experience.

Looked at from this perspective, the stories we have called myths belong to a much larger class of fictions, all of which can be understood to enhance awareness of environmental features of interest and social dynamics worth exploring. Thus we have fairy tales in which the personifications can range from imaginary creatures (such as leprechauns), and animals (Mother Goose characters; coyote tricksters), to innocent children (Grimm's fairy tales). From ethnography we have stories of personified tubers (Hainuwele), grains (corn maidens), seals (Asdiwal), and coyotes (Amerindians). Then there are dragons, giants, and heroes with exceptional powers or helpers galore in Western epic romances. Added to these examples we have the cosmic gods imagined in the myths of highly articulated civilizations. There is at first no reason to draw a line between myths and fairy tales as if only the myths are stories of "supernatural" or "superhuman" beings. Many imaginary beings are "supernatural" in the sense that they are not "natural" and can do wondrous things. And there is no reason to distinguish between myths and fairy tales as if fairy tales are only entertaining while myths are serious business. All fictional narratives, including myths, have to be entertaining in order to capture and hold attention and be memorable. Studies of fairy tales have demonstrated how very serious they can be in terms of tuition, for example, Bettelheim's study of Little Red Riding Hood (*The Uses of Enchantment*, 166–83). The story is cast in terms of a little girl and a wolf, but analyzed from an adult perspective; the dangers are suggestive of real-life encounters yet to be experienced by a little girl. Thus, the imaginary engagement with the story as a child, an engagement Bettelheim describes as "enchantment," works as a tuition in advance, one that can be understood both at the imaginary level of the child and at the level of memory when real-life experiences occur. The concept of enchantment can even be used to understand the effect of memorable fictions in the long tradition of Western novels. They range from hero epics of the ancient Near East (Gilgamesh), the Greeks (Odysseus), the Germans (Siegfried), and the English (Lancelot, King Arthur), through the Hellenistic tragedies and romances, to the later Gothic novels, "high mimetic" fictions (a description coined by Northrop Frye in his *Anatomy of Criticism*), and the more recent genres of fiction that explore human situations in many diverse cultural and social contexts. We sometimes refer to a book or movie as "captivating" or "powerful," and we mean by this that it explores human situations and social relations, creates new insights, and engages reflection in such a way as to be memorable and invite discussion with others who also have experienced the story. Thus we need to think more deeply about the stories we call myths, and ask about the features that may set them apart as stories of the gods that belong to religion.

Jerome Bruner has studied the way in which the structure of poems and stories "triggers" the reader's response of reimagining and thinking about a story in relation to one's own experiences and customary views of the everyday world (*Actual Minds, Possible Words*). He talks about the gap between a story and everyday experiences and develops a profound thesis about the way in which narrative works as a mode of thinking. He is able to show us that narrative is a primary mode of thinking fundamental to the ways in which humans make sense of the world, and that it is quite different from our orientation to customary logics with their interest in facts, propositions, and truth. The term he uses for the intellectual link between personal experience and narrative portrayals is "verisimilitude," the invitation to reimagine a fictional situation or plot as an exploration of human situations and dynamics already in mind and cast in a narrative mode. Myths use the narrative mode of thinking in that they story human situations in fictional portrayal. There is, however, an important difference between the myths we are tracing and other forms of fiction. It is that the situations addressed are social moments, and the stories (myths) are those shared by a group in the interest of practices and relational issues of importance for the functions of their society.

We have already considered Jonathan Z. Smith's description of the way in which myths set up a comparison between a "then" and a "now" in order to focus attention upon a particular situation, action, or practice. We will see that the "then" of myths is only slightly different from the "once upon a time" of fiction. Both provide the "distance" or "gap" which is the comparative mechanism required for thinking about a situation. The difference between them has to do with the relation of the mythic scene to the social interests and structures of a people as a collective, as well as the way it becomes a customary mechanism for acknowledging and thinking about those interests together. Myths are narratives set at the borders and overlaps of the two imagined environments where social interests and human projects meet the constraints located in the imagined environment. The normal process of the narrative imagination is sufficient to create a myth as long as it treats this intersection of environments in ways appropriate for focusing on the social interests and projects involved, and does so in ways that make it possible, if not necessary, to give such a project concentrated thought and critical attention. Myths can do this by creating a space between the narrative account, set in an imaginary time, and the current situation as the occasion for telling the story. Rituals do it by comparing a customary action of a project with a perfect performance of it as if within the imagined world. Either way, the result is that the practical and everyday features of a socially significant human situation or activity can be compared with a scene from the imagined world. In the interest of setting up this kind of comparison for the purpose of pondering the human project, the impingements and constraints from the encompassing environments can readily become fictionalized agents. The constraints and impingements are real, and thus their personifications can be imagined as agents about whom appropriate stories can be imagined and with whom appropriate exchanges can be made, such as wondering about intentions, asking for help, saying "Oh, I see," or expressing gratitude. It is the location of a project at the borders of the environments and the cultivation of the project as a collective social interest that make it possible for deities to be imagined and engaged.

We can now account for the bewildering variety of fictionalized agents in the history of social formations, all of which have sometimes been classed together as gods or deities. From the mud turtle of the Amerindians to the myths of Marduk, Yahweh, and Zeus, the differences in characterization relate to differences in social formation, social interests, environmental horizons, the location of intersections along the borders, and the focus on particular constraints and impingements from beyond the borders. We began our studies with tribal societies in which the social interests were cultivated by imagining the intersections of social and natural environments. We also noted that the intersections of natural, social, and ancestral worlds provided the setting for an exceptionally rich production of stories among the Aranda. As we now approach the mythologies of the highly articulated societies of the ancient Near East and Late Antiquity, yet other foci of social interests and other intersections with imagined environments will come into view. In the case of the social fractures and multicultural mixtures of the Hellenistic age, the cross-cultural intersections of competing social environments will become the location for novel configurations of social interests that can generate new cross-cultural mythologies.

Thus we can begin our quest to theorize the mythic functions of the gods as we have imagined them by describing the systems of myths and rituals in the civilizations of antiquity. That is where examples can be found of myths in the making that let us see the social interests involved and their collective acknowledgments. It is a good place to begin for another reason as well: these myths and their gods are familiar to us as the precursors of our own Western civilization, and their gods had their place in a worldview of cosmic dimension that provided the context for the mythmaking of early Christianity. With these civilizations of antiquity we can imagine the moves that must have been made from pre-aristocratic societies with agrarian and herding myths and rituals to highly developed hierarchies of power in control of extensive social administrations. It is here that we can see how gods were given their places within a cosmic realm, yet made available for social contact by priests, rituals, shrines, and temples. If we follow these developments briefly from the ancient Near Eastern kingdoms, through the Hellenistic period of social and cultural shifting, and into the periods of the Roman Empire and Christendom, we will be able to see how the Christian God, the one that we still have in mind as we think about religion, came to be imagined as the "one true supreme being, god of creation and history," as the traditional and popular definitions have imagined him.

Social Scope and Class Distinctions

Before we take this step, however, a cautionary word is in order, lest we use our pictures of these civilizations as sufficient descriptions of life and human activity at all levels of social organization. As we will see, the pictures painted of the gods and histories sketched of the kingdoms in the ancient Near East were creations of an intellectual elite we call scribes. They were certainly interested in mythmaking that encompassed the large scope of a kingdom's place in the cosmos, as well as social interests that had the people of the kingdom in view as a collective. However, this large-scale view was a perspective given with their social position "at the top." The scribes were palace and temple functionaries, and, as such, their mythologies rationalized the kingdom in terms of the importance of the kings and priests for the collective well-being. In analogy to the difference between the way the Thunderbirds and the Bears viewed their village plan among the Winnebago, we can suspect that our scribal texts from the ancient Near East do not tell the whole story. As a matter of fact, careful explorations of other artifacts have brought into view an altogether different, pulsating, and dynamic picture of domestic religion (Toorn, *Family Religion*). The household was the location for family religion that produced its own mythologies, practices, and modes of critical attention to social interests and relations on the local scale. This difference between "official" religion and other more local or "domestic" religions will be mentioned here and there throughout the book. However, the emphasis will be upon the "official" religions, not only because they are those that have left the legacies for us to ponder, but also because we want to end our study with a critical analysis of the "Christian nation." As we will see in Chapter 7, the conflict between "official" and "local" mythologies is a major factor in the culture wars unleashed by Christians in the United States. In the traditions of Western civilizations, the view from the top and its mythologies assume and justify sovereignty and power as the source of social order. It is the history of that mythology we need to track.

Myths of the Temple-State

The kingdoms of the ancient Near East were highly structured societies centered in cities with a temple and a palace. The temple was the earlier and more important construction, for it served as the center for the administration of the kingdom. This included the organization of food production; the keeping of accounts for business transactions; the distribution of goods, lands, and labor; the archive of historical records; and the calendar of festivals and ritual occasions. Priests, scribes, and specialists in laws, rituals, divination, and cosmology served as counselors to the king, creators and interpreters of myths, and officiants at rituals and public celebrations. Palaces for the king began to appear in the second millennium B.C., for he was the locus of authority and power that made the entire system work. He was charged with the defense of the city, construction projects such as city walls, irrigation systems, and the repair and maintenance of the temple buildings. He was in control of an army charged with the defense of the kingdom and its lands, as well as the conquest of other kingdoms when conflict or reasons for expansion occurred. Scholars have called this type of society a temple-state and remarked on its cohesive unity as a highly diversified and structured society, its grand monumental buildings, its impressive art, and its rich production of literature, laws, and mythologies. Even though the history of three millennia tells us of the rise and fall of many kingdoms in these lands of the two rivers, the persistence of the structure of the kingdoms as temple-states gives us a fairly clear picture of the social context within which a remarkable system of myths and rituals provided rationale for the maintenance of working relationships at all levels of the society.

We are not sure of the myths that may have belonged to the local prehistories of these temple-states, myths that may have been elaborated and transformed by the priestly scribes in the interests of the new social hierarchies. But, judging from the incidence and types of creation myth in many agrarian societies, and noting the importance of grain agriculture and animal husbandry for the ancient Near East (Diamond, *Guns*, 180–6), we can conclude that this type of myth probably preceded the elaborate cosmogonies written by the temple-priests. These cosmogonies are available to us in written texts dating from the middle of the third millennium B.C., or about the time that temples began to appear in the ancient Near East. As for the rituals, they appear to be transformations of rituals typical of agrarian and husbandry societies, for they took the form of sacrifices and offerings even though they were sometimes dislodged from their agrarian contexts and reinterpreted to mark political, social, and historical moments of importance for the new social arrangements. And, of course, agriculture and animal husbandry did not go away just because kingdoms formed. They remained as the primary means of food production throughout the entire period of aristocratic kingdoms in the ancient Near East. Since the structures of a kingdom required supervision at the top and chains of authorization all the way down and out to the borders of the kingdom and beyond, and since such power invested in a king required extensive and repeated rationalizations, the scribal imagination had much work to do. However, the myths these scribes composed let us see that they did find ways to rationalize the powers of kingship in relation to the forces that were imagined to control the world of nature, now conceptualized as a cosmos (an ordered system). A link between the two loci of power was imagined to have been forged at the very beginning, when the creation of the world, the building of the temple, and the establishment of the kingdom all occurred. So the temple-scribes visualized a cosmogony in which a family of gods created the world, humankind, and the plans for the temple-state.

We have the texts of the Babylonian creation epic on tablets from the first millennium B.C., but many scholars have reasons to think that it stems from early in the second millennium B.C. It is referred to as *Enuma Elish* ("When on high") from its opening line, and in English translation continues through fourteen double-column pages in the third edition of Pritchard's *Ancient Near Eastern Texts* (60–72; 501–3). The setting is given in the first lines of the poem: "When on high the heaven had not been named, Firm ground below had not been called by name." A primordial pair commingling as a single body gave birth to the gods. As the family of gods increased, contentions developed, rankings took place, leaders appeared, and a separation of loyalties took over, some to Apsu, the primordial father, and some to Tiamat, the primordial mother. Rowdiness and noise disturbed both parents, who differed on what to do about it. Apsu wanted to destroy the gods and return to the calm they had enjoyed before they brought them forth, but Tiamat said, "No." Since the clamor continued, Ea, the god of wisdom (in the second or third generation from the pair), devised a plan that included getting rid of the primordial pair and installing a strong monarch to bring the gods to order. Ea then slew Apsu and engendered Marduk, the "Sun of the heavens," the "loftiest of the gods." "When he moved his lips, fire blazed forth." According to Ea's plan, Marduk was to refashion the world and fashion humankind to "serve" the gods. But Tiamat and the gods that rallied to her were still to be vanquished. On hearing that Apsu had been slain, and stirred by anger and rage at the continuing commotion among the gods, Tiamat held counsel in an assembly of the gods loyal to her and made plans for a battle against the gods loyal to Ea. Tiamat's company marshaled weapons, dragons, vipers, and so forth, and none of the gods was able to do battle with her except Marduk, who killed her, cut her in half, and made from her body the heavens and the earth. He then took charge of all the gods, giving them "stations" in the heavens. From one of Tiamat's company, charged with guilt for leading the rebellion, he took the blood and fashioned humankind, "the black-headed ones." He also had the gods build Babylon, the temple and its walls of "burnt brick," so that the gods would have their "cult hut" and the black-headed ones would serve them. The poem ends with a glorification of Marduk's "fifty names," all gods with stations and powers that keep the cosmos running. Marduk will "shepherd the black-headed ones" and teach them how to tend their sanctuaries. Their sanctuaries will be "a likeness on earth of what he has wrought in heaven." Then the poem turns to address the black-headed ones:

> Let the wise and the knowing discuss together [Marduk's fifty names of the cosmic gods he incorporates].
> Let the father recite [them] and impart them to his son.
> Let the ears of the shepherd and herdsman be opened.
> Let him rejoice in Marduk, the Enlil of the gods,
> That his land may be fertile and that he may prosper.

The strategy is clear. The priests were in charge. Memorizing and discussing the names of fifty gods to keep the fields fertile was surely enough to keep everyone in line, especially the kings.

So the personification of forces impinging upon the social world from the larger worlds of the imagination, images we have been calling deities or gods, did not fade from the scene just because humans had learned how to construct a temple-state. Reading the creation myth in reverse, taking the picture it presents of the gods at war with one another as a projection of the human history that can be imagined as the temple-state came into being, and as kingdoms fell and new kings came to power, one might have thought that the human struggles, contentions, and investments on the way to the accomplishment of a civilization would have been so obvious, so hard-fought over such a long period of time, that gods would no longer be needed in order to take pride in the accomplishment. But no. Not only did the gods not go away, they multiplied, acted just like humans—contending for honors, hearing rumors, being piqued and angry, calling assemblies, laying plans, demanding loyalties, going to war, and killing one another in order to build the world, a world that still needed non-gods to "serve" them. If we turn it around once more, what was it, we may ask, that the black-headed ones still needed from the gods?

Well, for one thing, they needed to imagine how it could be that the king had such power and authority. Royal authority always needs to be rationalized, and the way it was done in the ancient Near East was to imagine that the king was chosen and authorized by the gods. But with the king having such authority, you did need to watch him, making sure that he understood his obligations to the temple, the kingdom, its laws and productions, and the well-being of the people. Many are the texts that give glory to a king for performing just these functions, all of which surely were not among his personal primary interests. But since, on his soft side, the king desired honor, the scribes certainly knew how to handle him. A clear example of giving the king credit for the codification of laws that only the temple-scribes could have written is the so-called *Code of Hammurabi*. The prologue tells how Hammurabi was chosen by the gods "to make equity appear in the land." It is written in the first person and begins with Hammurabi recounting the decision of the gods to install Marduk as their king in a scene set at the creation of the world, as it is in the *Enuma Elish*. Hammurabi reports this as if he were there, for in the next strophe it says:

Watching Myths in the Making

> At that time Anum and Enil named me
> To promote the welfare of the people,
> Me, Hammurabi, the devout, god-fearing prince,
> To cause justice to prevail in the land,
> To destroy the wicked and the evil,
> That the strong might not oppress the weak,
> To rise like the sun over the black-headed ones,
> And to light up the land.

The law code was engraved on a stone stele at Babylon, on which the image of a god, probably the sun-god Shamash, is seen giving Hammurabi symbols of his authority as king. Framed in this way by the gods, the scribes were able to let the king glory in his position as the author and executor of the laws of the land, even while they made sure that the formulation of the laws and the administration of the social order remained under their control (Pritchard, *Ancient Near Eastern Texts*, 163–80).

Hammurabi was king of Babylon from 1728 to 1686 B.C., and was the sixth of eleven Old Babylonian kings. To collapse the "then" time of the creation myth with the "now" time of Hammurabi's reign has to be seen as a most remarkable and daring example of scribal imagination. But to depict Hammurabi in the presence of the gods before the gods had actually fashioned the world and the black-headed ones is astounding. His commission was imagined to have taken place in the period when plans were being laid, but before their execution. The tight link between the present Hammurabi and the pre-existent commissioning has to be seen as scribal aggrandizement in the interest of authorizing the laws they had written for Hammurabi and the systems of justice they were proposing for his rule. The prologue continues with references to additional reasons for Hammurabi's authority, including royal descent, a catalogue of achievements in construction and war befitting an ancient Near Eastern monarch, and relations with various gods who took delight in him and granted him wisdom.

Suppose we read the *Enuma Elish* and the *Code of Hammurabi* together. Talk about a perfect example of our theory on social formation and mythmaking! First, let us notice the social interests that appear when we consider the impingements of the world of the gods upon the world of the temple-state. The first is power, power to create and build, but also to command and order, as well as win at war. Then there is ranking, leaders and loyalty, hierarchies of authority, and the execution of tasks. Glory and honor follow nicely, with the approval of one's "father," "the fathers," and the "assembly" playing the biggest roles in ascribing honors. Were it not too great a digression, numerous examples could be cited at this point of charming depictions of the gods dressed out in human ostentations. It is clear from afar that the scribes were having a great time, laughing while they came up with a scene in their scriptorium, then reading it reverentially to the king in his chambers. Not to undercut the seriousness of mythmaking, you understand, for the power of the *Enuma Elish* as a whole is clearly in the interest of rationalizing the temple-state by glorifying, not only the powers of the king, but also the temple "service" to the gods, the very niche in the whole system of primary interest to the scribal-priests. What a myth! With a cosmic order so imagined, the gods at their "stations" among the stars and constellations, and the "plan" for a kingdom linked to those gods at the very beginning of the created orders, what more do you need?

Well, you might want to fill in the gap between the royal gods of the cosmogony and the human kings and their histories to acknowledge the differences between them. The scribes did not want to tarnish the picture of the divine kingdom constructed at the beginning of the world, and they did not want to erode the authority this gave their own king, but they needed to see the king as a human being, one who sometimes failed in his endeavors. They were able to do this by writing a story about an early king at Uruk who, because he was descended from the gods, went on a quest to join the heavenly company and so find eternal life. This story of Gilgamesh became a popular epic of some length, reworked many times from the second millennium B.C. through the first. Even though he had gone to the ends of the earth, the bottom of the sea, and had slain the dragon of the dark forest in the mountains, Gilgamesh did not find a path up the mountains leading to the heavens above. So he finally had to return to Uruk, a hero who failed. There at Uruk "All his toil he engraved on a stone stela." The reader is then invited to visit the walled city and the temple of Anu and Ishtar where, apparently, the stela was to be found. "Behold its outer wall... Peer at the inner wall... Go up and walk on the walls of Uruk, Inspect the base terrace, examine the brickwork: Is not its brickwork of burnt brick? Did not the Seven [Sages] lay its foundation?" (Pritchard, 73). So there it is. Even Gilgamesh, two-thirds god, learned that the glories of Uruk, with its city walls of burnt brick and the cornice of the temple like copper, will be enough for mortals. And look, "Did not the Seven Sages lay its foundation?" Whether by sages or the lesser gods under Marduk's command, the Near Eastern city was built at the beginning, when the world was created and the plans were laid for civilization on earth to mirror the world of the gods who controlled the cosmos (Pritchard, 72–99).

Putting the three texts together, the *Enuma Elish*, the Prologue and *Code of Hammurabi*, and the *Gilgamesh Epic*, we might take note of the fact that both the kings and the gods also have been put in their places. To get the stories going, the gods are imagined in their own world. It is a world completely outside the bounds of the social and natural orders. As the story of the creation ends, however, the gods are stationed as "guards" of the natural forces, heavenly bodies, and constellations, agents of control. They are cosmic gods, placed far away from immediate contact by humans. They do have kings and priests who act as intermediaries in the social order. And the priests pay them homage in the daily rituals and the ceremonies and festivals that mark the calendar of the kingdom's year. Voilà! The human enterprise of social formation created a highly structured working society whose social interests as seen from the top focused on the attribution of authority to make it work, not on the junctures between tribal, agrarian, and natural orders we have been considering. The gods are far away, with only the temple-priests to keep them in mind and make sure that the society continues to work smoothly. The making of myths, the performance of rituals, and the influences of the gods have been institutionalized. The political authorities and what we now might call the religious professions have reached an agreement on a division of labor that actually structures the society as a whole. With this development, we will have to keep our eyes on the priests and scribes, for some of the gods may be at their disposal.

This chapter of human history cannot be summarized adequately in a few short pages. It covers a time span of at least three thousand years and a history of many kingdoms and several empires dotting the lands of Sumeria, the Tigris–Euphrates valleys, the Levant, and Egypt. Nevertheless, the picture just drawn of the temple-state as an empire, with its myths and rituals, is a responsible generalization of social and cultural accomplishments that were still in place at the beginning of the Hellenistic period. The picture I have drawn does differ from that customary for the last generation of historians of religion. The older "pan-Babylonian" school interpreted the ancient Near Eastern cultures as an exceptionally clear example of human religion and religiosity prior to the advent of Christianity. Of special interest to these historians were such things as the single sovereign "high" god, the creation account, the notion of the temple at the center of the world, a yearly re-enactment (as they understood it) of the *Enuma Elish* as the reestablishment of the king's divine authority by reinstallation, and the temple as an institution of religion with oversight of "theological" and "ethical" instruction and of "worship." It might be mentioned that an important, if oblique, corrective of this interpretation of Babylonian religion was given by Henri Frankfort and others in their book *The Intellectual Adventure of Ancient Man*. It was a study that accounted for the various cultures of the ancient Near East in terms of their differing natural environments, the intellectual adventures of social construction, and how they handled the gap between societies and their natural environments. Happily, the pan-Babylonian school of the history of religions no longer dominates the picture of the religions of the ancient Near East, and it is now possible for us to consider their imagination of cosmic gods as mythmaking in the interest of rationalizing social hierarchies.

Myths of the Polis

The ancient Near Eastern temple-states came to an end during the Hellenistic and Roman periods. It was a time when many cultural traditions met and merged under the overarching influence of the Alexandrian and Roman empires. It is hardly possible to trace the histories of all these cultural traditions through this period in order to mark the changes that took place in regard to concepts of the gods and ritual practices, but a brief reminder of the Greeks and their gods can prepare us for a discussion of the Hellenistic period, where a number of observations can be made relevant to our quest for a social theory of religion and its application to Christianity.

The Greeks did have a pantheon, but their gods were more earthbound and atmospheric than cosmic. Even Zeus, the ruler of the world and father of the gods, was imagined to be in the clouds above Mount Olympus. Poseidon was right there in the ocean, Athena was ducking in and out of Athens and Sparta, following the troops on their marches, Hermes was either flying about on some mission as herald or marking the roads with signposts of protection, and Apollo was busy keeping lyres in tune and making sure the priestess at Delphi got the grammar and syntax straight for the cryptic oracles. Then there were scores of other deities identified with local districts, cities, and shrines, associated with powers to watch over particular human activities and make sure every eventuality worked out right.

The reason for this pantheon of deities, associated with particular locales and functions rather than cosmic stations, was related to the social histories of the Hellenes. The centers of settlement in Greece and the islands were separated from one another by a broken and mountainous terrain. Each district was controlled by an aristocratic landowner, and small cities emerged where the leading landholders of the surrounding districts formed an assembly (*synedrion; ekklesia*) to administer their collective interests in governance, commerce, and defense. Some of these cities, such as Athens, Sparta, and Thebes, became what we call a city-state (*polis*) and played leading roles in larger areas covering several smaller districts. These cities and the representatives of their districts codified laws, built fortifications, organized armies, built temples to patron deities, and developed loyalties under the insignia of traditional tribal constituencies, the emblems of the patron deities, and the symbols of the city itself. Thus the city-state was not only a social identity but engendered a civic loyalty that came to expression when one said, "I am an Athenian, a Spartan, or a Theban."

It is important to realize that this contrast was a result of differences in the two natural environments. Mesopotamia was able to construct temple-states because of the economic surplus created by the river systems, irrigation, and ample land available for agriculture and herding. Hence the temple-states were centers of bureaucracies that managed extensive landholdings, developed writing to keep accounts, assigned priests to look after temple rituals that not only marked the kingdom's calendar but also encouraged the social cohesion of the people, had scribes to adjudicate conflicts and violations of the law in human relations, and courtiers ("friends" of the sovereign) to preside over the many classes of workers and artisans. Thus the distinctions between the "imperial" governance of the ancient Near Eastern monarchies and the "democratic" political organizations of Greece can be understood as resulting from differences in their natural environments and their means of food production.

There were, however, many temples and shrines across the land in Greece, some far from a city. A temple or shrine would be built by the leading family of a district and dedicated to a deity appropriate to the place and of importance to the family tradition. It was not uncommon to dedicate a local shrine to one of the more familiar gods or goddesses and to add an adjectival cognomen descriptive of some feature or function appropriate for the locale, such as Artemis Potnia Theron ("Lady of Wild Things"). Those we have called priests and priestesses were often members of the family who looked after the district shrine, and who could explain the proper procedures to a traveler. When entering the precinct of a shrine representing the patron deity of a district and its families, it was customary for a visitor to make an offering to show respect for the local traditions. Before some new venture was undertaken, the appropriate deity might be acknowledged by an offering at its shrine or temple. For those who had a special need, such as illness, worry about a family member abroad, or uncertainty about a decision, the shrine of an appropriate deity could be visited to leave a votive offering and request help. Temples were also places where festivals were held with dancing, mimes, and feasting. Many of the Athenian public festivals marked seasonal and agricultural activities, such as the planting and harvesting of grain (Demeter) and the pruning of the vines and harvesting of the grapes (Dionysos). Some city festivals were a yearly acknowledgment of its patron deities (Athena, Apollo), and many included a sacrifice to an appropriate deity that became the occasion for feasting. We have already mentioned the sacrifice (*thusia*) at the tomb of a district hero or ancestor of the leading family in a country district occupied with herding and agriculture, and we have already noted that the killing of an animal or some special handling of produce was a practice that became ritualized in agrarian and herding societies to mark and celebrate transitional moments in their collective activities. In Greece during the first millennium B.C. these rituals apparently became the customary way to acknowledge deities personifying special interests other than the strictly agrarian, so that a devotion (ritual offering) to a deity on a certain occasion became a mark of what the Greeks called piety (*eusebeia*), having respect for the local traditions symbolized by their patron deity.

Since the Enlightenment, the scholarly view of Greek religion has focused upon the very large number of deities, festivals, shrines, and temples, and the way in which the gods seem to have been taken for granted by the people, their historians, poets, and philosophers. This has given us a general impression of the Hellenes living in a world teeming with gods who might be encountered or appear at any moment. This perception of Greek religiosity needs to be toned down. Three observations are in order. One is that most of the moments in which gods are mentioned are exactly what we have theorized as intersections of the imaginary and everyday worlds, where social and human interests encounter influences or circumstances beyond human control. That there seem to be so many moments is partly a result of the Greeks leaving written and archeological records, partly a product of exhaustive Enlightenment research into the "classical tradition," and partly a selective interest concentrated on Greek religions. Naturally, the compilation of a thousand years of the Greek practices of piety seen as examples of Greek religion creates the impression that the Hellenes were interested mainly in religion.

A second observation is that, looked at more closely, the Greeks considered an offering to the gods as a pro forma matter. An acknowledgment of the gods was what you did in order to let others know that you knew where you were and what you were supposed to do according to the systems of loyalties and constraints that held together the network of Greek political and ethnic relations. The performance of an offering to the local deity was regarded as an obligation determined by the circumstances. One does not find any evidence of the later Christian sensibility of devotion as worship.

The third observation is that, during the period of Christian formation, to be discussed in Chapter 5, Greek philosophies and mythologies became important ingredients in the mythmaking and theological writings of the so-called "apostles" and "fathers" of the church. This gave privilege to Greek texts and documents in distinction from the large literary and intellectual productions from the ancient Near East. Scholars are well aware that early Christians were deeply indebted to these intellectual traditions, especially those from a large and vibrant production among Jews during the Persian and Alexandrian periods. But because of early Christian polemics against the Jews and the Jerusalem temple-state in order to argue for their own right to the heritage of Israel, and because of the more modern notion of Christianity's uniqueness, scholars have wanted to interpret Christian origins as uncontaminated by Jewishness and thus have preferred influence from the Greeks as a kind of "buffer" against Judaism (J. Z. Smith, *Drudgery Divine*). The one exception was the continuing influence of the Hebrew scriptures. As we will see, however, the early Christian reinterpretation of these scriptures to create the Christian Bible and epic was accomplished by means of Greek philosophy and allegory, driving yet another wedge between the relative importance of the Jewish and Greek influences in the minds of Christians. So it was that Greek texts and documents of Greek philosophy and religion were given privilege when "rediscovered" in the Renaissance, Reformation, and Enlightenment periods. The reader would not be wrong to add other examples of this protectionist mechanism against influence from other traditions throughout the course of our two-thousand-year history. The inability to acknowledge and learn from the amazingly rich scientific and cultural learning of Islam during its classical period in the tenth to fourteenth centuries would be one example. Another would be the treatment of Egyptian history and culture as a kind of exotic interest. In any case, it is primarily the Greek tradition from which we are accustomed to trace our intellectual history of Western civilization.

Because we need to discuss these Greek traditions as a preparation for the Hellenistic period in the next section of this chapter, and for the beginnings of Christianity in Chapter 5, it is important to temper and correct the popular view of Greek religion and philosophy, lest our customary regard for its piety and rationalism treat it as exceptional. A remarkable study by Jean-Pierre Vernant, *The Origins of Greek Thought*, can help us here. He works with three important events in the history of the Greeks: (1) the arrival of the Dorians from the north and the end of the Mycenaean palace monarchy (c. 1100 B.C.); (2) the rise of the city-state; and (3) the beginnings of natural philosophy in Ionia (sixth century B.C.).

Before the arrival of the Dorians, Mycenae and other centers of power in mainland Greece, Crete, and Anatolia were monarchies on the model of the Mesopotamian, Levantine, and Egyptian civilizations, and were thus part of a large area of Near Eastern kingdoms connected by trade routes over which other forms of communication also traveled. This network provided the foundations for Greek thought. The rich intellectual traditions of the natural sciences, astronomy, law, writing, communications, and history were all shared by the pre-Dorian monarchies. The structures of these monarchies were also similar in that the king was sovereign over his lands, army, courtiers, people, and all aspects of his kingdom. The Dorians brought this system to an end so that the Achaeans (with the exception of Sparta) had no monarch, no center of governance and power. They were scattered throughout the lands in estates and villages, eventually forming cities without kings. The concept of sovereignty vanished and in its place rulers were chosen from among the many aristocratic landowners who formed the counsels of the city-state.

The virtues and skills required by the city-state were speech (*logos*), persuasion (*peitho*), judgment (*themis*), wisdom (*sophia*), equality (*isotes*), and equality of rights (*isonomia*). These determined the *ethos* (culture, ethic) and *paideia* (education) of the new cluster of social interests. *Arete* (virtue, excellence) took the place of obedience to a monarch that had been characteristic of the older system of monarchy, and in this process of forming the city-state the world of the gods was reconceived. Instead of the older imagination of creating order out of chaos by means of royal battle and the assumption of power by a single sovereign at the top of a hierarchy (*monos-arche*), the Greek gods became a pantheon in which family feuds had to be negotiated just as conflicts had to be worked out in the polis. Vernant's intriguing thesis is that this experiment in democracy resulted in the concept of a dynamic and orderly arrangement (*cosmos*) of the city-state, the elements of which worked together in reciprocal relationships to form a *koinonia* (community, harmony). This experiment in social formation was the second origin of Greek thought. The Ionian philosophers were indebted to both intellectual traditions.

The Ionian philosophers had the concept of the *polis* in mind when asking about the arrangement of elements in the natural world. They did not create a "natural science," as was previously thought, for they did not use experiments in the quest for natural laws. Instead, they translated the ancient Near Eastern monarchical cosmogony into a cosmology. As we have seen, the cosmogony told of an original divine pair generating the gods as their own children, who then battled for supremacy and created the world by sovereign power. The Ionians used the term *arche* (first cause, first principle) to translate the myth of sovereignty into a political and architectural concept. In the *cosmos* of the *polis*, *archons* functioned as legislators and designers of polity (Cleisthenes); in the *cosmos* of the natural world, the *arche* was conceived as a first principle from which pairs of elements proceeded to form the world in dynamic and reciprocal relations. Thus their *cosmos* was the result of a double translation, from the *polis* and from the ancient Near Eastern cosmogony.

Vernant's analysis provides us with another outstanding example of our theory about the relationship between social formation and mythmaking. In this case, however, the mythmaking produced a conceptual world of abstractions as the agents related to the interests of a social ideal based on deliberation and persuasion. When we refer to the classical tradition of the Greeks, it is largely the rise of this intellectual tradition that we have in mind. The Greeks exercised a capacity for rational analysis in the investigation of the political system of the polis, the logic of deliberation and argumentation, the rules of rhetoric, theories of education, the histories of their indigenous peoples, and the cultures of other peoples. Also, in concert with the intellectual traditions of the ancient Near East, they constructed cosmologies, developed mathematical systems such as geometry and trigonometry to measure the distance of the earth from the sun and moon, and tracked the rotations and risings of the planets and stars (Teresi, *Lost Discoveries*). When questions about the gods arose, several approaches were taken. The mythographers and historians collected myths from other cultures to compare them with the more familiar Greek myths, in effect asking about their relations to cultural differences.

The tragedians allowed the gods their roles in the family histories of descent from the famous heroes where, of course, they had their origins and primary functions, even while exploring those same family histories for circumstances in which the gods were not much help, or even in unexpected consequences of decisions and untoward eventualities in which the gods represented human desires and interests in conflict. Their treatment of the gods as stock characters in their studies of royal family intrigues shows us the degree to which the gods could be used as objective representations of common psychological complexities (Aphrodite, "sexual interests"; Artemis, "chastity"; Zeus, "father's authority"). There is no critique of the existence of the gods per se, but the way in which the tragedians cast them as actors and agents in the human drama is most revealing. They were treated as if they were agents involved in the creation, maintenance, and resolution of the human situation under review. However, the mechanisms by which these gods affected the situation are completely unexplored and left to the imagination, as they should be. Still, the gods are allowed to speak, explaining their position within the family of the gods and their interest in the human situation at hand. The result is the creation of an imaginary world of the gods in reciprocal relation to the human world, often with several different gods in conflict in their world, just as the human situation is in conflict in the real world. The relation between the two worlds is not a matter of reflection in either direction, as if one could be understood as a mirror image of the other. On the contrary, the back-and-forth of making observations on both scenes in dynamic reciprocal relations is at work all the time. It is as if the world of the gods is projected as an "objective" frame for exploring the psychological dynamics from one point of view, then used to look back upon and interpret the dramatic events in the play. That is mythmaking and manipulation in the interest of analyzing a complex human situation that is difficult to understand, uncover, and talk about objectively. It works by letting all the actors, including the choruses that represent collective perspectives, respond to the tragedian's suggestions of the gods as agents. But as the actors respond to the situation, observing it from the two perspectives of the god's impingements and the human decisions, an otherwise hidden set of human interests is revealed and explored. The agency of the gods is never portrayed or explained. The strategy of combining myths, the tragedians' own mythmaking, and human thought about a human situation is obvious and very cleverly executed.

During the Hellenistic period, the Stoics developed allegories of the gods, creating etymologies of their names and interpreting their attributes to argue that they were, in reality, metaphors of natural, physical phenomena and/or of human psychologies. Thus Zeus was translated as fire or ether, the topmost element of the atmosphere of the world. Hera was air, the atmosphere closer to the earth. Apollo was the sun, Artemis was the moon, and Athena was wisdom. The Greek philosophers did not, however, succeed in supplanting the gods, temples, and practices of piety with their philosophical schools. Not that they ever intended to. They took for granted that the practice of piety belonged to political and social life, and they knew themselves to be a kind of intellectual elite separate from the life and thinking of the people at lower levels of privilege. They had, nevertheless, intruded upon the customary scope of the mythic imagination with their propositional logics in ways that were different from the narrative mythmaking approaches of the ancient Near East, and so they eroded much of the arena customarily thought of as the home for the gods. This was to have an effect in the post-Alexandrian and Roman eras—a mixture of narrative thinking and propositional abstraction with which the gods from Egypt and the East, including the Christians' god and his son, were imagined taking their places in the new *oikoumene* (inhabited world).

In order to appreciate this changing worldview, it will help to remind ourselves that the ancient cosmology of a three-decker universe, consisting of the heavens above, the earth beneath, and the waters below, was being reimagined as a geocentric universe, with the rotations of the moon, the sun, and planets around the earth in concentric spheres at ever-greater distances from the earth, with the "fixed" stars yet further beyond. It was during the first half of the second century A.D. that Claudius Ptolemaeus, a mathematician, astronomer, and geographer, gathered up slightly earlier astronomical works by Apollonius and Hipparchus to set forth a mathematical demonstration of the new geocentric theory. In its articulation as a scientific theory, this cosmology can hardly be said to have changed the thinking of the Greco-Roman era overnight. But the abstraction discourse of the philosophers in general, and the changing social worlds just unleashed by the Alexandrian age, did create an awareness of the large-scale cosmic world of profound significance during the Hellenistic age and of great importance for our question about the locations of the gods and how they came to be imagined.

Myths of the Hellenistic World

The Hellenistic period can be dated from the death of Alexander the Great, king of Macedonia, in 323 B.C. His conquests of Persia, Asia, the Levant, and Egypt had created a temporary empire that brought all indigenous ancient Near Eastern kingdoms to an end. His program was to unite all peoples under the culture of the Hellenes by establishing Greek cities throughout the lands. His successor generals continued this program, and Greek cities were founded throughout the eastern Mediterranean with their schools, theaters, games, and councils. But the generals also divided the empire among themselves by establishing kingdoms, the Ptolemies in Egypt with their capital at Alexandria, the Seleucids in Syria with their capital at Antioch, and the Antigonids in Greece. Thus the Hellenic empire of Alexander also came to an end, and the polis was no longer a Greek city-state, but an instrument of colonization and the control of foreign peoples. Nevertheless, despite the wars among the successors over territory and the incursions of the Romans, who began to nibble away at the Peloponnesus in the mid-second century B.C., destroying Corinth in 146 B.C., and eventually took control of all the Greek lands, the post-Alexander period did see a lively merger of cultures and new social formations. Commerce burgeoned, Greek became the common language, theaters filled with audiences, sports were important, schools flourished at all levels, and libraries collected the works of scholars and the literati. It was a time when all peoples found themselves living in a much larger world than they had known in their traditional lands and localized societies, and many caught sight of the larger universe that now expanded their horizons. Some talked about being cosmopolitans, citizens of the world.

However, the big house (*oikoumene*) was not inhabited by a single people, nor had the project of Hellenization erased traditional cultures. Everyone was inhabiting a world with several cultures merging and several levels of administration jockeying for control of district lands, their peoples, commerce, and taxes. In addition, there was the movement of peoples across more or less open borders. Armies marched and set up camps and fortifications in occupied lands. Merchants and tradesmen travelled the highways and created networks of business contacts in other cities and lands. The Seleucids transported Macedonians to populate the newly created *poleis* (plural of *polis*) in Syria and the Levant as their only franchised citizens. Many people moved to important, large cities in other lands to pursue their businesses and lives in the urban environments created by the overarching administrations of the Greeks and Romans. Many found themselves living in two or three cultural worlds at the same time. Although citizenship became an issue in many cities where a displaced group of people sought a voice and more control over their own patterns of association and circumstances, no one was in control of the continuing cultivation of traditional cults and cultures that soon created a multicultural world.

Many ways were found to stay in contact with the old country and traditions (*ta patria*). Networks of communication with friends and acquaintances in one's native land were common. The formation of associations among relocated peoples could take craft, ethnic, and cultural interests as a focus. Customs, clothing, and personal emblems of a person's cultural heritage could be carried along when moving to another country. And local deities (idols) could be transported to take their place in new shrines and temples abroad when finances and other arrangements made it possible. Established temples and those in or close to urban settings might now be dedicated to several deities, and gods from several cultural traditions who were found to have similar functions or attributes could be given hyphenated names and understood to be the same. Thus the merging of cultures affected the gods as well as the peoples who learned to accept the multicultural mix as a fact of life. Piety now included respect for other peoples and their gods as well as one's own, and the festivals at most temples were public displays of theater, dancing, mimes, and feasting for all who wished to attend. The buildings and parklands around a sanctuary were also available for groups to gather and talk, for banquets and symposia, and to accommodate pilgrims who might travel some distance to participate in a festival. Cities found it good to have multiple temples and to allow or finance major festivals. Thus it was that temples became centers for enculturation in the new multicultural world of the Roman Empire, since there were many temples representing cultures far from their homeland, staffed by priests from that homeland, thus marking the contrasts among cultures throughout the empire. There is evidence that people did flock to the temples as a place for social gatherings and activities. And the patron deities who retained a bit of their older functions as symbols of particular peoples and cultures located in their traditional countries were well advertised with idols and inscriptions, both dedications and instructions to the visitor of the proper approach and offering to be made. The impression one has when reading the inscriptions, Hellenistic authors, and modern historians of the period is that this mix of peoples living together in the Greco-Roman world was taken for granted by most and taken advantage of by many. Yet, in the midst of this very lively atmosphere of the celebration of multiethnic traditions and the pursuit of a cosmopolitan way of life, an underlying sense of cultural uncertainty seems to have been pervasive. That cannot be surprising, given the dislocation and fragmentation of the traditional social and cultural systems.

One indication of this sense of uncertainty is the frequency with which the term *Tyche* ("chance," "luck," "fortune," "fate") occurs in reference to cities and persons. Tyche was a concept in Greece before the Hellenistic period, usually qualified as either "good" or "bad" luck, and only infrequently personified as a deity. But during the Hellenistic period Tyche was recognized as a force or influence prevalent in the ways the world was working. Naturally, one hoped for good luck, and when used in naming or describing a city (*Tyche Tegeas*, *Tyche Romes*) or a person (*Eutyches*) that was the connotation suggested. But even good luck happened by chance and it was chance that Tyche came to symbolize, not only for the way in which the political, social, and personal worlds worked, but also for the way in which the cosmos itself operated. The Ptolemaic universe was having its effect, and the heavens were no longer the abode of cosmic gods who gave the Romans the authority to rule the empire under the supervision of powers interested in social well-being. The atmospheric deities of the Greeks had been unsettled when their city-states were rationalized in other ways, and then conquered by the Romans. Instead, the rotations of the concentric spheres ruled blindly, mechanistically. Tyche took the place of the cosmic gods insofar as those traditionally associated with the planets, stars, and kingdoms were now so far away and inscrutable that the "inhabited world" (*oikoumene*) below seemed to be pretty much on its own. The Romans did keep order, but mostly in their own interests of empire-building and by means of their armies and tax collectors. In his treatise on "The Fortune of the Romans," Plutarch, a Greek writer, describes how Tyche,

> when she had deserted the Persians and Assyrians, had flitted lightly over Macedonia, and had quickly shaken off Alexander, made her way through Egypt and Syria, conveying kingships here and there; and turning about, she would often exalt the Carthaginians. But when she was approaching the Palatine and crossing the Tiber, it appears that she took off her wings, stepped out of her sandals, and abandoned her untrustworthy and unstable globe. Thus did she enter Rome, as with intent to abide, and in such guise is she present today, as though ready to meet her trial. (*De fortuna Romanorum*, 317F–318A)

The "trial," according to Plutarch, was the current contest between Arete ("virtue," "achievement," "excellence") and Tyche ("chance," "fate").

Another indication is given with funerary inscriptions. To be buried in one's homeland was for many no longer possible. And although most associations had as one of their purposes the proper burial of their members, it was difficult to imagine joining those who had gone before when one was buried far away. As for other conceptions of an afterlife, Hades was predominant, but no one would want to go there, and there was no conception of or desire for what later Christians would call immortality or eternal life. Therefore, the grave inscriptions generally honored the person for his or her piety and/or left an epithet such as: "I was, I am not, I do not care." The impression one has when reading these inscriptions is that, having been removed from one's ancestral lands (*ta patria*), an individual felt disconnected and alone in life as well as in death.

A third indication can be seen in the popularity of the teachings of the Stoics. Stoicism was a philosophy in the tradition of Zeno of Citium (335–263 B.C.), a Phoenician who traveled to Athens and studied with the Cynic Crates, the dialectician Stilpon of Megara, and at the academy. His teaching in the Stoa Poikile ("painted porch") gave rise to the tradition of Stoic philosophy. This attracted large numbers of followers, some well trained, others with enough education to serve as teachers in the local public schools that every Hellenistic city and town found ways to support. In the open air, and in public view, these teachers lectured the young, taught reading and writing, and had their students practice dances and choruses for the upcoming temple festivals and performances in city theaters. The philosophy focused on what we would call an ethical anthropology. The goal was to live a good life, virtuous and satisfying, completely independent of the vicissitudes of fortune (*Tyche, Fortuna*). At the level of theory, it was held that humans were capable of reason or wisdom, and that the exercise of reason would lead the individual to see that he or she could live in harmony with nature and be happy, untouched by untoward circumstances, desires, extravagant pleasures, the actions of others, the impingements of fate (*Tyche*), or even death. At the popular level these philosophical ideas were available in scores of small works packed with one-liners ("Only the wise are virtuous") and brief explications of the good life, its rationale, and strategies for attaining such. From the public schools to the emperor's court, Stoicism was the philosophy that addressed the problem of Tyche and counseled how to be virtuous and happy despite the way the world seemed to be working. At the level of cosmology, it was also possible for the Stoics to imagine that reason (*logos*) and wisdom (*sophia*) were somehow operating in the cosmos and natural world. It was because of this link between the human *logos* and the *logos* of the cosmos, no matter how difficult to comprehend, that one could be sure of finding harmony and happiness by leading a virtuous life according to reason. Thus the program of the Stoics can be seen as a profound achievement in ethical theory. It can certainly be seen as a remarkable response to the uncertainties of social life in the Greco-Roman world, but an ironic twist can also be noted in the way it addressed those uncertainties. It did so by saying that they did not matter—they were matters of indifference (*adiaphora*) to the person of reason and virtue. This meant that the social world was no longer in philosophic view. In the traditions of Greek philosophy, the paradigmatic configuration of *cosmos–polis–anthropos* had given rise to critical thinking. With the Stoics the *polis* had been removed from the schema and the individual was presented with the challenge of living according to nature (in harmony with the cosmos), untouched by social constraints or interests. The result was that the Stoic as an individual could stand tall, but in the arena of the social world Tyche had won.

Not everyone wanted to be a Stoic, and there were other approaches to coping with the new *oikoumene*, some of them quite constructive. One was the rise of a social grouping called an association (*thiasos, ekklesia, collegium*). Associations formed in urban environments, usually among persons whose native land was elsewhere. A shared interest might be a common craft, an ethnic extraction, a cultural pursuit, or perhaps the need for a place to socialize and talk about issues and strategies for living in a multicultural urban environment. Associations usually numbered about 20 to 40 members and met once a month for business and banqueting. They had officers, collected membership dues, wrote rules for behavior at the banquets, had bouncers, discussed their interests, kept in contact with the larger world, and when the occasion arose made arrangements for the burial of their members who had died. There are two observations of importance that can be made for our study. One is that, judging from the popularity and similarity of the many associations that emerged during this period, associations made it possible to keep practical and cultural interests alive that otherwise were in danger of being lost. Cultural identity and belonging to a social group, now frequently referred to as one's "brothers" (or fictive family), had to be cultivated away from one's erstwhile land and people. An association was the cultivation of a group's particular and traditional social interests in the midst of the many other interests and uncertainties of the larger, surrounding Greco-Roman world. The association could be both a real and a symbolic substitute for a remembered homeland. It was a little society, a buffer that worked to ameliorate the chanciness of the larger social environment (Kloppenborg, "Collegia and Thiasoi").

A second observation is that most of these associations called themselves by the name of some deity, such as "The Company of Heracles." It is this feature that has confused many scholars into thinking that these associations must have been some kind of cult on the model of the Hellenistic mystery religions. We will discuss the mystery cults in the next section. Here it is enough to note that the purported similarity has usually been found in the fact that associations had banquets and that it seems to have been a rather common practice to recognize the patron deity with a glass of wine or oblation as the banquet got started. Such a gesture is hardly a cultic ritual, for banquets of all kinds, including the symposium at a private home or estate, had their toasts and oblations. But that leaves us with the question of the patron deity. One might well suspect a bit of playfulness or social savvy in the process of selecting one of these deities as a namesake. Most of those selected were well-known, traditional gods, now of universal presence throughout the *oikoumene*. All of them had become markers of the dispersion of patronage from primary cultic centers to shrines and temples throughout the empire. Piety had taken the form of respect for all of them as symbols of the cultural forces that had to be recognized and lived with. There seems to be little cultivation of the myths and rituals that once belonged to deities of the Greek pantheon in associations that took one of them for a namesake. Attributes, perhaps, played a role, suggesting the appropriateness of this or that appellation. But it was the common interests of a group, not its attraction to this or that deity, that were the main reasons for forming an association, and it was this feature of the associations that made the rulers uneasy. The Romans especially were very suspicious of *collegia*, regarding them as potentially subversive. Associations had members, met privately, and promoted their own interests, which might well be imagined to be at odds with the political and economic interests of the administration. Craft guilds, especially, might find ways to put pressure on a local economy and cause unrest, while the special interests of an ethnic group in what we might call a big-city ghetto could create troubles for an administration. Looked at from this perspective, for an association to take the name of a well-known deity as patron was in effect to tell the Romans and the world that it was acceptable, that its members were responsible citizens of the *oikoumene* and loyal to the Roman authorities. If so, the emergence of associations can be seen not only as an example of social interests driving social formations; they were also examples of the human capacity for living in two or three cultural worlds at the same time, belonging equally to both and negotiating the differences creatively. Further, they can be seen as a sign that the traditional gods and heroes had lost much of their importance as personified agents presiding over particular junctures of external impingements and influences where mythic imagination and rituals had been the customary responses.

Myths of the Mysteries

But now we come to the so-called mystery cults. They also can be seen as a response to the Greco-Roman age with its overarching canopies of Tyche and imperial power. The customary list includes the mysteries of Demeter (and Persephone), Dionysos, Isis (and Osiris), Aphrodite (and Adonis), Cybele (and Attis), and Mithras. Two of these were ancient Greek cults related to agriculture and fertility (Demeter, Dionysos), but the others had their roots in cultures to the east: Phrygia–Anatolia (Cybele), Syria (Atargatis; Aphrodite), Egypt (Isis), and Persia (Mithras). None of the deities from the east retained their native functions, so that their entrance into the Hellenistic world as new cultic formations is of some significance to our study. It is also important to note that the Greek cults of Demeter and Dionysos thrived during the period despite the general pattern of attenuation experienced by many of the other Greek gods as their cults realigned in keeping with the Roman culture of patronage for civic and political power.

However, the importance of these mystery cults for our study is quite different from older interpretations that put them together in a class called *mystery religions*. Since the term "mystery religions" is now common in popular parlance, I need to explain why current scholarship no longer thinks of them as such. Two notions largely determined the older view. One was that mystery referred to a profound ritual experience of personal salvation or transformation offered by initiation into the cult, usually thought of by earlier scholars on the analogy of the Christian promise of a blessed life after death. The other notion was that all of these cults had rituals in imitation of the myths of "dying and rising gods," a phrase that Sir James G. Frazer coined in *The Golden Bough*. Neither of these notions has been supported by a closer scholarly reading of the myths. The term *mystery* is now understood to refer to the explanations and instructions given to an initiate during the performance of a ritual. Since vows were taken in some of these cults not to disclose the experience of the ritual to those who had not been initiated, these instructions and explanations were held secret, thus the "mystery." As for the notion of "dying and rising gods," it is true that a death of some kind can be found in each of the mythologies of these cults, but none of them describes the deity's destiny as one of dying and rising. Persephone is abducted, then lives alternately in the upper and lower worlds, as does vegetation. Dionysos does not die in most of his myths, though his vine gets pruned, his celebrations were ecstatic and orgiastic, and one of his animals might be killed and eaten by Maenads (female votaries of Dionysos). Only the Orphics imagined that the Titans killed, roasted, and ate Dionysos before Zeus incinerated the Titans, and from their ashes arose the human race, part evil from the Titans, part divine from Dionysos, thus calling for an ascetic way of life. Adonis is killed by a wild boar and mourned by Aphrodite in some versions of his myths; in others he spends part of the year with Persephone in the underworld. Attis pledged his fidelity to Cybele, the Great Mother of the wild mountains, but fell under the spell of a nymph, and so, in a frenzy, he castrated himself and thus became immune to human desires. Osiris was the mythic king of Egypt, killed by his brother Seth and "awakened" by Isis to father Horus the next king, but he remained in the underworld as its sovereign and judge. Mithras does not die, though he slays Taurus the bull as a sign of his cosmic and military powers. So it has become clear that Frazer and other scholars misread these myths and rituals. They had the crucifixion and resurrection of Jesus in mind when reading them, and thought of the mystery religions as precursors and parallels to Christianity, offering eternal life on the basis of a myth–ritual dramatization of a violent death and return to life. In no case did one of these mythic figures return to life as a resurrected deity, and in no case has a mystery ritual been reconstructed or a description found that regards the death and destiny of these gods as a script for ritual reenactment or that promises that the initiated will experience the same destiny (J. Z. Smith, *Drudgery*).

However, it is possible to use these familiar cults to make a point or two about their attraction during the Greco-Roman period. The collection does not make a set of mystery religions, as once thought, nor does it exhibit a set of myths and rituals that have a common theme. What they do have in common is an independence from erstwhile, traditional cultures on the one hand and from the control of the Roman imperium on the other. The cultures from which they came had been sustained by political systems in control of more or less organic societies that understood and accepted their place in a rationalized worldview. The Roman Empire had disrupted the political foundations of all these cultures and had not succeeded in creating a new cultural identity sustained by loyalty to Rome. The spread of its military and political governance was universal and accepted by the many peoples it had conquered in deference to its powers. But power alone could not replace the cultural practices, social structures, ethnic identities, and remnants of social institutions of importance for the many displaced peoples. They were left in place and provided the resources to rethink social interests in the new world of imperial power. One of the major centers for the organization and cultivation of traditional cultures in the Near East was the temple, where a people's priests, intellectuals, myths, rituals, rules, archives, business transactions, supervision of the economy, rules of protocol and conduct, and thinking about the society as a whole were lodged. In Greece, many of these social and cultural functions were distributed among shrines and other social institutions not directly under the control of the temples at the cities, but with traditional practices that linked them all together in a single culture. The Romans made many moves to recognize the continuing importance of local temples and shrines as centers of economic and political power with which to negotiate, and they also built several temples in Rome for peoples and deities from other lands as gestures of reception and assimilation.

But the new worldview was full of holes and fractures that created intellectual dis-ease and invited contemplation and experimentation. There was no longer any link between political power and cosmic powers. There was trouble finding a place for the atmospheric gods in the new Ptolemaic cosmology. The worlds of nature and the cosmos of the stars had come apart, and the world of nature, now spread out to the very borders of the inhabited world, at distances most had never imagined, much less traveled, seemed to have more wild things than domestic products. And what, really, should the working relationships be between different peoples? Is it okay to laugh at theriomorphic deities? Can the cult of the ancestors work away from the district tomb? Does working with the Romans tarnish ethnic identity? What can a woman in the diaspora do to keep family and cultic traditions alive? Where does one go to mourn, to pray, to offer a votive, to make things right, or to find a teacher who knows the old traditions? What about offensive cults and festivals of other peoples? What about the interminable wars? What about sexual relations and marriage, now that the old rules do not quite apply? And how should one think about the Romans? What gods gave them such power and put them in charge? Are we destined to second-class citizenship forever? What kind of a world is this?

We need only recognize the partial dismantling of traditional social and cultural systems in order to see that the Roman world could be both heady and disconcerting. The mystery cults can then be seen as experimental explorations of myths at the seams of social interests by focusing on ancient rituals, and this was not the only way people were playing the gaps that had occurred in their older worldviews. Entrepreneurs took up many of the religious functions that had originally been part of the temple-state or city-state systems. There were specialists in dream interpretation, divination, magic, and healing. Wandering philosophers offered wisdom, sage advice, and might even be watched for an unexpected miracle or two. Gnostics emerged, worried about the ultimate powers of the cosmic universe, now that it was known to have controlling planets traversing spheres at ever-receding distances from the earth. Surely the supreme power or powers were yet beyond the ogdoad, the eighth sphere of the stars, but must have left some sparks of their essence here on earth at the beginning when they created everything and gave birth to humans. Others, troubled by a similar view of the cosmos, began to imagine it possible, nay inevitable, that some kind of message or messenger must come from beyond, sent by the supreme beneficent god, to let humans know about their creation and destiny. But if there is no god, or messenger from god, what does that say about the creation and the world we live in?

As for questions about the Romans and how it was that they came into power and built such an empire, Plutarch could not appeal to any of the older gods, cosmic signs or powers, or humanistic justifications. His answer was Tyche, as we have seen, an impersonal force deciding rather capriciously to end up in Rome after having swept through the kingdoms of the ancient Near East and the Mediterranean. Plutarch knew that the Romans would not be pleased with that construction, so he also introduced the notion of Arete (virtue, in the sense of "accomplishment") and praised all of the leading men of Roman history by name for being virtuous. But the mark of virtue to which Plutarch returned again and again, from Romulus and Remus on, was their ability to rise to the apex of the hierarchy of political power and build an empire. At some points Arete and Tyche join together in imagining some historic battle or event, but most of the time they are said to be in a contest, with Tyche the winner. It is very important to note that the Greek penchant for personification of abstract concepts is at work in this treatise, and that the personifications of both Arete and Tyche are imagined and storied on the model of the Greek gods who presided over Athens. Yet neither is a deity on the older model, with cult and celebrations, and the winner of the contest is an abstraction of a concept that is neither divine nor human. This is a fine example of Greek rationalism, of course, which Plutarch represents, but it is also an example of the way the Roman imperium was seen by Greeks and other non-Romans. Their empire was a political structure of power difficult to rationalize in terms of erstwhile mythic imaginations of the natural and cosmic worlds, and the myths that were created for the Roman imperium hardly produced answers to the social and cultural issues of its governed peoples.

Thus, the myths and rituals of the deities of the peoples' native lands were cultivated. Some deities, dislodged from their older national, cultic, and ethnic systems and locations, were reinvented, and their rites were opened to receive other people. They were those that focused on the seams in the social fabrics and mythic imaginations left exposed by the Roman imperium. Many were marked by experimentation at the margins of traditional constraints and proprieties, pressing the limits of human capacities for dealing with uncertainties. Others addressed the desire for certainty and security by testing the evidence for some conception of the natural and cosmic worlds that might indicate interest in and support for human well-being. All of these experiments were focused on inviting individuals to explore the contingencies where the impingements of forces beyond human control might be encountered, explored, and pondered. In the process, degrees of exaggeration seem to have been common.

Among the many older festivals in celebration of Dionysos, for example, it was the Bacchanalia of the rustic Dionysos that spread and made its way to Rome. An original revelry of women alone in the forest at night cultivating the excitements of the intoxicating deity was opened to males as well as females and became a kind of Mardi Gras, suspected of gross sexual licentiousness and outlawed by the Roman senate in 186 B.C. The cult of Cybele, on the other hand, which had exaggerated the sexual attraction to the mother among her sons and her jealousy when, as youths, they fell in love with another, seems to have become quite sedate in Rome as a festival of the Magna Mater, goddess of fertility and protectress of her people. It is probable that Cybele, whose cult was originally from Phrygia, but spread to Greece, Egypt, and Rome, was reimagined along the way by identifications with Demeter and Isis.

It was Demeter and Isis who represented another concept of the feminine, one that infused the mythic imagination of the times with an attractive alternative to the control of male and martial power. We have already discussed the mysteries of Demeter as an agrarian cult. Now it needs to be mentioned that some Hellenistic authors said that initiation into her cult promised happiness in the afterlife. The analogy of the cycle of vegetation to the cycle of human life and death is not unusual, and the myth of Persephone does include the imagination of her time in Hades alternating with her life on earth with her mother. It must be this analogy that gave rise to the thought that the rites made possible the idea of happiness after death, even though popular conceptions of life in Hades, as well as those satirically portrayed by the Greek tragedians, were not happy scenes. But since the analogy can hardly be sustained, it seems better to think of the continuing attraction of the mysteries of Demeter during the Hellenistic period as a retreat from the everyday and commercial worlds, and a resort to an old and honored festival of the goddess caring for the interstices between the classical polis and its agrarian foundations. There one would find crowds of festive people from all over the *oikoumene*, spending some days in Athens around the Acropolis, reminder of the golden years of the city-state under the protection of Athena with its assembly, philosophers, schools, tragedians, and theaters. A feast of roast pork and a procession to Eleusis with camping out and preparations for the drama in the Telesterion (place of initiation) would complete a wonderful vacation.

As for the mysteries of Mithras, the link to Persia is uncertain, although the name Mithras certainly has a Persian ancestry. There, and earlier in India, Mithras was the cosmic god of life and order, the protector of kings and their armies, and the ordainer of social righteousness. There is some evidence of interest in the Persian cult on the part of Alexander the Great and his successors in Pontus, six of whom had the name Mithradates. Thus there must have been some connection to the Persian god and his cult. However, the later cult seems to have been an invention of the Roman period, for it flourished in the Roman west during the first three centuries A.D., and its archeological remains are found only there and throughout the expansion of the Roman empire into north Africa, Gaul as far as the Limes (a line of fortifications across southern Germany from the Danube south of Regensburg to the Rhine south of Coblenz), and Britain as far as Hadrian's Wall. The cult was open only to male initiates, some holding rather high civic and political positions in southern Italy, and even one emperor (Diocletian), but its members were mostly military personnel and others who accompanied the Roman troops while away from Italy. They formed cells and met in rather small enclosures, either hewn out of a rocky cliff or constructed to simulate a cave, with a vaulted ceiling and a standard layout. There were benches along either side with a table in the middle, presumably for meals. At the far end was the famous carved relief, or sometimes fresco, of Mithras with knife in hand, about to kill the bull he has overpowered. On either side there are torchbearers and other symbols such as a raven, snake, dog, and scorpion. The sun and moon are often in the upper corners, and frequently around the edges are the signs of the zodiac forming a map of the heavens centered above by the constellation Taurus. Scholars have not been able to reconstruct the rites of initiation, but the grades to which a series of initiations led are known. There were seven grades, from Raven and Nymph at the beginning, probably symbolizing initial instructions, through Soldier, Lion, Perses, Runner of the Sun, to Father. It must have been very popular as a male military fraternity, for there are scores of archeological remains of Mithraeums and, given its distinctive character among other Hellenistic cults, it must have served Roman and military interests in a search for cosmic authorization. It is important to note that generally Hellenistic cults were in the process of exploring social questions by means of feminine deities as mothers. Here, in the case of Mithraism with its astronomical orientation in the interest of rationalizing military power, the ranking, which may well symbolize an ascent through the universe to the highest cosmic power, ends in the highest grade of Father. Luther Martin concludes his study of Mithraism, in his book on *Hellenistic Religions,* with the following: "Mithraism apparently complemented the hierarchic and disciplined structures and values of its male members...with a new integrated view of the cosmos now completely structured in terms of masculine attributes and in support of Roman imperial rule" (118). A thorough and penetrating analysis of the intellectual labor involved in the construction of Mithraism and its logic is available in Roger Beck's study *The Religion of the Mithras Cult.* However, it all came to an end with the edict of the Christian emperor Theodosius against all pagan cults in 391 A.D.

The cult of Isis marks another attempt at reconceiving the whole world, including the cosmos, this time in the interest of human well-being at all levels of the *oikoumene.* Her temples and priests were found throughout the Greco-Roman world, her myths were well known to historians and essayists, and aretalogies inscribed on *stelai* (stone posts or upright slabs) in major cities and seaports recited her virtues and accomplishments for all to read. She appears to have been the most popular goddess, and perhaps deity, during the Hellenistic period. Her sovereignty filled the void left by the retreat of the cosmic and atmospheric gods; her demeanor was thoroughly positive and constructive with regard to urban social life; and her feminine attributes were clearly those of a goddess interested in the well-being of family life. Isis was originally a goddess of fertility associated with the Nile. She was then the mythic Queen of Egypt, protecting the lands and people from the threatening encroachments of the desert, which were personified by Seth, and searching for Osiris, the king who had been tricked and killed by Seth, to make sure that their son Horus continued the dynasty and governed Egypt well. During the early Hellenistic period in Egypt this pageantry was dramatized in special rooms and buildings adjacent to urban temples called Birth Houses. It is no doubt from this dramatization that the myth of Isis and Osiris became known to the Hellenistic world, but as her cult spread, with Egyptian priests performing daily rituals in her temples, votives displayed from sailors praising her protection at sea, aretalogies listing all the effects one could wish for in a cosmic power who ruled in the interest of social health and happiness, and public processions and festivals of great color and festivity, some wanted to make sure she would not overlook them, and so rites of initiation were offered.

The mid-second century A.D. author, Lucius Apuleius, put together a collection of Milesian tales (short stories often called Hellenistic romances) under the title *Metamorphoses* or *The Golden Ass.* It is the story of Lucius, his namesake, who is turned into a donkey by drinking a magic potion gone wrong in the house of a friend far from home. He is taken here and there as a beast of burden, suffers untold humiliations by robbers, and on the way overhears the many tales he now repeats, one of which is the famous story of "Psyche and Eros". At last he learns of Isis, shows up at one of her processions as instructed, is offered the crown of roses he is told will end his trials, is changed back to himself by eating the roses, and then is initiated into the cult of Isis. There is a fairly clear description of an initiation into the cult of Isis, and putting it together with Plutarch's full treatment and interpretation of the myth in his treatise "On Isis and Osiris," as well as with the aretalogies and other records and reports, scholars have been able to reconstruct the cult and its attractiveness for the Hellenistic populace. It is also a fine example of mythmaking in response to the Greco-Roman world as we have been considering it. It will therefore be helpful to cite a few lines from the recension of a Memphis aretalogy found at Cyme (Asia Minor) in the second century A.D. The aretalogy consists of over fifty lines, all describing the virtues of Isis, and almost all in the first person. It begins:

> I am Isis, the mistress of every land...
> I gave and ordained laws for men, which no one is able to change.
> I am the eldest daughter of Kronos.
> I am the wife and sister of King Osiris...
> I am the mother of King Horus...
> I divided the earth from the heavens.
> I showed the paths of the stars.
> I ordered the course of the sun and the moon...
> I made strong the right.
> I brought together woman and man.
> I appointed to women to bring their infants to birth in the tenth month.
> I ordained that parents should be loved by children.
> I made with my brother Osiris an end to the eating of men.
> I revealed mysteries unto men...
> I broke down the governments of tyrants.
> I made an end to murders.
> I compelled women to be loved by men.
> I made the right to be stronger than gold and silver.
> I ordained that the true should be thought good...
> I established penalties for those who practice injustice.
> I decreed mercy to suppliants...
> With me the right prevails.
> I am the Queen of rivers and winds and sea...
> I stir up the sea and I calm it.
> I am in the rays of the sun.
> I inspect the courses of the sun...
> With me everything is reasonable...
> I am called the Lawgiver...
> I overcome Fate.
> Fate harkens to me.
> Hail, O Egypt, that nourished me! (Grant, *Hellenistic Religions*, 131–3)

It is obvious that intellectuals well acquainted with Greek, Hellenistic, and Egyptian cultures had their hand in this mythmaking project, a project that may have begun soon after Ptolemy I became monarch in the late fourth century B.C. It draws upon both Greek and Egyptian mythology, underpins Egyptian and Near Eastern family values with Greek-sounding concepts, translates the Egyptian desire for social stability (*maat*, "rightness") into Greek-like legislation, and understands the need to come to terms with the new Ptolemaic cosmology. Of special interest are the last lines in which Isis says "I overcome Fate [*Tyche*]. Fate harkens to me." But neither the cult of Isis, nor that of Sarapis, the product of a similar mythmaking project under the first two Ptolemies, a project designed to provide a Macedonian monarch in Egypt with a Greco-Egyptian god and its authorization, could make a place for itself in the cultural and political mix of the Greco-Roman age which was similar to the temple cults of the older temple-states or the official temples of the Hellenic *poleis*. They remained what we would call subcultural formations, taking their place among other ways people had of exploring the mythic and cultic imaginations responding to the times.

This concludes our discussion of the so-called mystery cults and gods. It can now be noted that not all of them in the traditional list had secrets to guard, and the practice of initiation in some of them can now be understood as a signal to their new initiates and to the world that they offered a particular view of the world among the many others available. To belong to the god or goddess of the cult was a special favor, setting one apart, if only for a short period of time, from a disenfranchised existence in the Greco-Roman world. If so, it means that the list could be expanded. It would not be difficult to include the Jewish synagogue, Philo's Therapeutae, the Gnostics, and early Christian associations. And yet, these do make another class, for they all left a legacy that the mystery cults did not. We will touch upon some of these at the beginning of Chapter 5. For now, it is time to summarize our study of where the gods reside.

Where the Gods Reside

The gods reside in the mythic imagination where human activity and social systems engage their environments. These environments include the natural world, the cosmic order, the sense of the social system of one's own people, the traditions and memories of the past history of a people that impinge upon the present, and the presence of other peoples with social systems and cultures different from one's own. We have emphasized the human construction of societies, and noted the complex system of structures involved in the workings of a society. And we have used the notion of social interests to mark the collective investments in features of the environments that together form the social world. We have also taken examples of social interests and mythic imaginations from very different kinds of society. We have looked at tribal societies, several forms of agrarian societies and petty kingdoms, the highly structured kingdoms of the ancient Near East, the city-states of Greece in both the classical and Hellenistic period, and the emergence of the Roman Empire. Moving from one to another we have noted that different social systems imagined their environments differently, and that each configuration of environments imagined its social interests differently. Thus the personification of forces, influences, and imagined agents in the encompassing mythic world produced deities of different kinds. In the ancient Near East, for instance, cosmic deities demanding the "services" of humans provided the "then" that allowed for contemplation of the "now" in which a temple-state needed the services of its citizens. And as for rituals, we have noted that they focus attention on certain actions and behavior thought to be important for the workings of a society by marking a particular time and place as the "here" and "now" for a careful performance. They need not reenact the myth of the deity that may be imagined in the "then" time of a myth associated with the ritual. But a deity may hover around a performance in the imagination and provide an additional distance from the performance for the purpose of heightened awareness and thoughtful contemplation. We have also seen that a more or less stable social system can produce institutions that provide supervision for myths and rituals as well as for other programs and structures of the society. On occasion we have used the term culture to indicate the total complex of the mythic imagination in support of the habits, symbols, taboos, and values taken for granted by a people which give them their sense of identity.

Alexander's attempt to transplant the culture of the Hellenes into conquered lands can now be seen as a remarkable experiment in cross-cultural encounter that opened the way for the multicultural Hellenistic age. The response of the many conquered peoples illustrates the human capacity for negotiating differences and rethinking one's own traditions. Scholars have called the negotiations at the level of mythologies syncretism, and we have mentioned several examples. We have noted the fact that the new social world could not entirely supplant older traditional cultures, and that exercises in assimilation found their limits at junctures where the interests and values of traditional cultures were no longer supported by the new *oikoumene*. And so, some social interests, once rationalized by traditional mythologies and normalized by ritual codifications, became matters for reexamination. Some of these have surfaced as explorations in mythmaking, social formation, and ritual practices. They include questions about gender, sexual relations, family values, ethnic identity, citizenship, the individual, the other, associations, other deities, other rituals, festivals and theater, the natural world, the wild, power, authorization, armies, and what to think about the cosmos.

It is completely understandable that a variety of explorations, debates, and experimentations characterize the intellectual and social climate of the

Greco-Roman world. It is also understandable that, of the two environments composing the mythic imagination, the one encompassing the social world seems to have been more pressing than the natural and cosmic environments. It was at the level of the people that explorations took the form of participation in festivals, attendance at shrines, and consultation with specialists in healing, divination, and magic, all of which appealed to the gods for authorization. At the level of the intellectuals and the official institutions of governance, the questions of kings and tyrants, *anthropos* and *physis* (nature), political theory and ethical theory, as well as the marks of human excellence (*arete*) could be explored without taking much notice of the multicultural world and its challenge to traditional mythic imaginations. When they did take notice, it was possible to allegorize the mythologies by translating the names of the gods and their attributes into concepts belonging to the philosopher's own rational systems for accounting for the world. Thus there were not only several levels of social placement in these remnants of aristocratic kingdoms, but also several levels of thinking and rationalization of the social and cosmic worlds. One might have thought that the rational approach would render a devastating critique of the mythic, but the relationship between Hellenistic intellectuals and the gods was similar to the noncompetitive concurrence of knowledge and mythologies about the processes of food production. The intellectuals did not criticize "belief" in the gods per se, though some did dare to wonder whether the gods really existed. They recognized the importance of the mythic imagination of their culture for social life even while borrowing the authority of the gods via various modes of allegorization as a kind of argument for their more rationalistic worldviews. This is a most interesting finding. It joins the other evidence we have been looking at regarding the persistence of cultural traditions even after their political structures have been dismantled and their peoples find themselves living in a multicultural world. We have used the notion of "rethinking" cultural traditions. Now we can focus on the phenomenon of persistence, the persistent cultivation of a cultural tradition in situations that are different from those originally rationalized by the culture. In the case of the gods we have been thinking about, questions may be asked about circumstances in which some fade away, some are not allowed to fade away, some are reduced in function, some are reassigned, and others are reinvented by various strategies to resume powerful positions in a mythic imagination. We will address ourselves to some of these questions in the next chapter, which will focus on the social situations and circumstances in which thinking *with* myths takes place, cultural traditions can be transformed and reproduced at the same time, and a people's persistence in the cultivation of its myths and rituals can be described as a mentality. The plan will be to develop the social logic of the mythic imagination as a canopy or encompassing worldview that provides a people with a grammar for thinking critically about its social situations.

4 Thinking with Myths about Culture

In the last two chapters we have been exploring the reasons for myths and rituals in relation to the human enterprise of social construction. The emphasis has been upon the interests humans have in living together and upon the intellectual labor involved in the construction of the many systems that structure the activities of a society and keep it working. A theme has been followed in the descriptions of the construction of myths and rituals, namely, that they too are a result of intellectual labor and are to be seen as no different in this respect from other systems of signs and patterns of practices fundamental for social existence. The suspicion has been that myths and rituals are important, if not necessary, ingredients within the sets of signs that structure a society, but that suspicion has not been explored until now. Since this emphasis upon social interests and the intellectual labor involved in the imagination and construction of myths and rituals differs from popular conceptions of religion, it has been necessary to move slowly in the development of alternative concepts and terminology. We are now ready, however, to consider the function of myths and rituals within a society and to explore the specific contributions they may make to its construction and maintenance. This can be done by developing the concepts of (1) the imagined world, (2) thinking with myths, (3) transforming myths, and (4) a mythic mentality.

The Imagined World

A mythic imagination of the two environments, social world and natural world, can now be called an imagined world: the world as perceived and imagined within which a people finds itself at home. We have sometimes called this a worldview, meaning thereby a picture of the world as a people sees it. The world viewed in this way has often been thought of as composed of a collection of snapshots, an objective reality based on observations. Once the imaginary features required by both environments are noted, however—that they merge with one another at junctures of social interest, and that their reach extends to the horizons of imaginable time and space—the picture metaphor is hardly helpful. It is stretched by the complexity of the fabric it is supposed to depict, and it is made unworkable by the resulting layers of intellectual systems required to comprehend it. This is especially so because the deities we have discussed in the last chapter also have their places within a people's worldview. Thus the scope of an imagined world intends a comprehension of a universal order of natural phenomena, social structures, histories, as well as a home for the gods.

Not all of these social realities, natural phenomena, and imagined beings can be present to one's consciousness at the same time. Selections must be made on occasions when particular configurations of interests and curiosities recall them for review. Because such an imagined world is the result, not only of present-tense observations, but also of memories, stories, precedent events, maps, myths, and rituals, as well as plans for the future, the metaphor of an environment is better than that of a picture. It is when all of these features are taken together that the world in which a people resides can be seen as an important factor in the process of thinking. The imagined world is the location and vehicle for precedents that continue to influence thinking, authorizations that sometimes require recognition and affirmation, symbols that mark social values for observation and reflection, and in general the images that provide reasons for the fact that the social structures at hand are already there for every new generation. Within this world the deities represent the personification of the forces or agents imagined to be involved, as well as the rationalization of influences that impinge upon human interests.

We can now suggest that the imagined world of a people provides the framework for its sense of identity and self-understanding. If a people are those who live in this world, have imagined this world, have invested in this world by constructing it of practical observations, memorable moments, and personifications of forces that impinge upon social interests, it is more than their home. It is their record of living within a world encompassed by the two environments. It is their writing of themselves into the tapestry of their imagined world, a world imagined to be large enough and composite enough to hold all the observations and stories there may be, yet highlighting a selection available for re-reading. This mechanism for the cultivation of the socially fashioned self-identity of a people is a marvelous and mysterious human phenomenon. Like a text under discussion in a classroom, observations about the imagined world become the way in which persons reveal to themselves and to others how they understand each other. This happens when they say what they think about the world. Features of the imagined world become the "third partner" in any thoughtful meditation or dialogue about living together in such a world.

In the last chapter we distinguished myths from other imaginative fictions by using the concept of social interests and by making the point that both myths so defined and social interests so conceived had a people in mind as a collective. The examples we have pursued of myths in the making and of myths at work in societies emphasized the collective as a structured whole. As we turn now to the topic of thinking with myths, I want to remain at this level of collective interest and mythic function, for only so will I be able to relate the function of myths so defined to the concept of a people's mentality. There are, to be sure, a number of caveats. One is that myths, once in place in a society, also affect interests and thoughts at a personal level. Another is that the myths of a people as a whole also affect the ways in which specific moments and situations of individuals are interpreted and handled. Another caveat is that thinking with stories is not at all limited to myths, as we have noticed in the previous chapter. These issues will engage us more directly toward the end of our study, as we take up the question of individualism in relation to the popular conception of Christian experience in the United States, but for now we need to investigate the ways in which thinking with myths takes place at the collective level.

I have used the terms *environment* and *tapestry* to add some necessary dimensions to the customary conception of a worldview. Environment adds the sense of encompassing, and also a kind of thickness or density, to the world within which a people know themselves to be living. Tapestry can suggest a surface into which observations and images may be interwoven or upon which images can be projected for analysis. It is also helpful in suggesting a certain distance from social situations under review, a distance that turns the tapestry or canopy into a kind of mythic collage or "text" that allows focusing upon just certain features of the world at a given time and on certain occasions, leaving the rest to a kind of peripheral vision. Thus the gods, or a precedent event, or a rule of behavior embedded in the collective knowledge of the way the world works (and thus available for rehearsal in a folktale) are not always in mind during the everyday. We might think of this as if the gods recede into the background of a layered panorama of the worldview while attention is focused on more immediate and practical features of the social world. But when occasions arise, the gods can come to mind as reminders of the more expansive environments, as invitations to think about a particular practice or specific situation, or even as items for the reconsideration of the myths and rituals woven into the tapestry of the imagined world. A certain sensibility of the encompassing world of the imagination enables awareness of one's place within it, and the imagined world can provide images with which one's particular circumstance can be compared, understood, and thought about.

Thinking with Myths

As for the images associated with myths and rituals, there are two fundamental mechanisms for producing critical thought. One is the way in which myths and rituals work within a stable society; the other is the way they work when social change occurs, especially when a people encounter another culture. Toward the end of Chapter 1 the studies of Jonathan Z. Smith on myths and rituals were mentioned. We need to recall the basic principles and conclusions of his work with myths and rituals and emphasize two features of the way they work. One is that they work in relation to a social practice or "situation"; the other is that they work by creating a gap or space between the situation and the imagery of the myth or performance of the ritual. This gap is created not only by the distance of the myth or ritual from the situation, but also because of differences and distortions between the two, differences that are notable and evoke consideration. We now want to develop the concept of "thinking with myths."

We are accustomed to the importance of concepts, terms, logics, and ideas for "thinking." We sometimes say that we think "with" ideas, images, abstractions, and so on, meaning that concepts, like words and technical terms, are the intellectual tools and ingredients for thinking "about" situations. "Thinking with myths" works somewhat differently. Recalling our discussion of narrative as a mode of thinking, and of Jerome Bruner's distinction between the narrative logic of verisimilitude and the propositional logic of facts, the logic of myth can be placed right in the middle between these two logics. Since myth is a narrative mode of description, it relies on the function of verisimilitude to create the link intended between the everyday world and the imagined world. But the factor of distortion in the mythic mode of description creates a different kind of gap. Mythic gap creates questions about, new perspectives on, and/or invitations to bewonder or ponder a situation or practice. It does not propose the "right" way to construe such practices, and thus does not translate its descriptions into the propositional logic of facts, but it can invite analytic thinking about the reasons for the practices and constraints so described in relation to the structures of the society and its imagined world. This analytic thinking can use propositional logic. If we are careful to notice that both the "verisimilitude" of mythic description and the "propositional logic" it can invite are consequences of mythic distortion at a second level of function, we can say that myth shares features of both the other two primary kinds of thinking but cannot be reduced to either of them. We can do this by identifying myths as (1) constructions that result "from" thinking about situations, (2) constructions that invite thinking "about" situations, and (3) constructions that can be used "in" thinking about situations. Myths are a language created by and for intellectual activity that focuses upon social situations from the perspective of the imagined world. The perspective of the imagined world is that of the encompassing environments within which situations need to be addressed.

In a stable society, myths and rituals can provide their own occasions. Rituals take place at certain times and places according to a schedule of social events. Myths also are usually reserved for reminder and retelling on special occasions of public celebration. Both types of event can be understood as imaginative elaborations of common practices and typical situations of significance for the workings of a society. Thus, a myth or ritual occasion not only provides an elaborate commentary upon a real-life situation in the society, it also replicates previous myth and ritual occasions as special events in the calendrical rounds of the life of a society. The common practice and typical situation made special by the myth and ritual are still common and typical in the everyday world, but the myths and rituals can distance themselves from the common or the practical by means of their elaborations of it and their settings in the imagined world. Thus the real-life situation upon which attention has focused, and its elaborations in mythic mode and ritual performance, create a gap for comparison, a space for switching perspective back and forth, an opportunity to ponder or rethink the social logic of the common practice in the everyday world.

Myth works by calling attention to what happened "then" in a story about the gods. This story bears some relation to the way things happen "now" in the everyday life of the people. However, the stories do not match exactly, and they dare not. That is because the myth is an exaggerated description of a process involving imagined forces. The exaggeration creates a distortion and sets up a comparison in which the difference has to be noted. The distance between the "then" and the "now" also contributes to the gap between the story and the social situation. The gap provides the space in which thinking about the differences results in reflection upon the social process. When the myth of Dionysos was recalled on some occasion in which wine-making or the drinking of wine occurred, attention was drawn not only to the myth but also to the human processes and activities at hand. The result might well be a thoughtful awareness of and a bit of reflection upon this human activity, as well as upon the work of vintage, the social etiquettes of wine usage, and the conviviality it was known to stimulate. Thinking of this sort may not result in the search for reasons and theories about how it is that humans know about winemaking, or why it is that drinking wine plays such an important role in social life, but a heightened awareness of and reflection upon participation in the process are surely possible. As a matter of fact, it was the gap created by this myth that allowed for the playful banter without which the Greek symposium or banquet would not have been festive and convivial. The Dionysia mentioned in the last chapter went further. They were explorations of and experimentations with social relations under the canopy of the Greek worldview in the context of the new *oikoumene* in the Hellenistic age. Thus the social logic and effectiveness of a myth or ritual can change when cultivated in the context of new social situations.

As for rituals, we have already used the example of animal sacrifice to note the relation of a ritual to a common practice. The ritual occasion differs from the common practice in at least two ways. One is that it takes place in a controlled space, which Smith calls "here" in distinction from the "there" where the common practice takes place. The other difference is that the ritual slows down the action by calling attention to each feature of the normal dispatch, and controls both the pace and the gestures in ways prescribed by the proper performance. The proper performance includes the persons who know how to do each of the actions and the precise, finely honed, deliberate attention to detail that turns the act into a ritual, such as the preparation of the animal and place, ornamentations, approach, positioning the animal, taking the knife, and so forth. Smith refers to this as a "parceling out" of what otherwise would be a swift and messy activity. Proper performance may also include consideration of the place, such as the tomb of a patriarch or an altar in a temple precinct. It is this specific place, marked off at a distance from the usual locations for such actions, that invites concentrated attention upon the perfect performance by those who will have the everyday practice in mind. It is also the case that the occasion can be made special by marking moments of significance in the yearly or social calendars of a people. Looked at in this way, rituals can focus attention on the perfect performance of an action in relation to its common occurrence, or on a significant action in relation to an important occasion. Either way, the concentration of attention can be understood to enhance awareness and thoughtfulness about the social significance of common activities (Smith, *To Take Place*, 96–117).

Transforming Myths

We shall turn now to examples of social situations created by cultural encounters in which another kind of mythic thinking can be seen. Instead of the ways in which myths and rituals work in stable situations by enhancing awareness and thoughtful reflection about a society's customary practices and structures, changing patterns of social activity, and especially incursions from other cultures, will challenge the social logic of the customary practices and focus attention upon the myths and rituals themselves. This can result in the reimagination of traditional myths and the recasting of traditional rituals in application to the changing social situation. This kind of thoughtful engagement of the social world is not really different from the mythmaking and social analyses we have already considered, but it may seem different for two reasons. One is that the concept of mythmaking will be stretched in that the focus of attention will no longer be solely on the social situation of interest, but will include thinking about the traditional myths and rituals themselves. Old myths may be revised in the new mythmaking process. Another reason is that the clearest examples come from the encounters of Polynesian cultures with Western colonial expansions, thus providing stark contrasts between the two cultures that required rapid and exaggerated responses. These will all be situations in which the dominant Western cultures encountered native cultures that were treated as subordinate. The inequality between the two partners in transactions of cultural differences will be obvious in the ways in which myths were used to think about and negotiate untoward situations. And yet, it is just because of the inequality that we can illustrate our thesis about thinking with myths.

Captain Cook in Hawaii

The stories we have of Captain Cook's arrival in the Hawaiian islands are well known, memorable, and unsettling. They are memorable as accounts of the first encounter of Europeans with the Hawaiians, the natives of a group of islands that eventually became possessions of the United States, and that have marked significant moments in its history. The stories are unsettling because we have yet to fathom the reasons for what happened. On the arrival of Captain Cook early in 1778, and again upon his return from a visit to the Pacific Northwest about one year later, the Hawaiians received him and his seamen with open arms, lavishing upon them gifts, foods, hospitality, and the sexual services of their young women. This was the behavior from December 1778 through January 1779, climaxing in extravagant ritual meals in several temples before Cook's planned departure on February 4. But then a change of circumstance and mood took over. The *Resolution*, one of Cook's ships, had trouble with its foremast, and both ships had to return for repairs. They found the cove empty where they had just been treated as royalty and gods. When they did encounter the people, the Hawaiians were sullen and the chiefs hostile. Thievery, skirmishes, and violence occurred. When a tender was stolen, Cook blockaded the cove and went ashore to find the chief and demand its return. The final event was an inexplicable convergence of angry natives upon Cook. He was killed, dismembered, and cooked. The remaining crewmen sought his body and a dispute developed over the possession of his remains, only to be "resolved" when his bones were returned to the crewmen ten days later before the ships left. As incredible as these stories have seemed, the subsequent history of friendly relations with Vancouver, whalers, traders, the missionaries who arrived in 1820, and other colonists is even more mysterious. And so we have always wondered what these Hawaiians must have been thinking.

Fortunately, a study has been published by Marshall Sahlins, Distinguished Professor of Anthropology at the University of Chicago, which accounts for the encounter, including the details of the many exchanges and events, by reconstructing the social system of the Hawaiians and their mythology. The study has the title *Historical Metaphors and Mythical Realities* (1981), and describes an extremely complex social system tightly intertwined with an elaborate mythic worldview and an intricate calendar of rituals. I want to summarize the major features of Sahlins's explanation of the Cook events, in the interest of our exploration of thinking with myth. I will add a background detail or two from *The Island Civilizations of Polynesia* by Robert C. Suggs.

The mythology of the Hawaiians is similar to the general pattern found among Polynesians in imagining the events of the arrival of the first chiefs and peoples to their island. That they come by sea from beyond the horizon is no surprise. That there are already people on the islands with their chiefs in charge when the "first chiefs" and their companies arrive is a slight mythic exaggeration. It is required, however, in order to account for the internecine battles that are also located at the beginning of the island's history. This compounding of themes in a single mythic scene is not at all unusual in folktales and myths. In the case of origin myths it is absolutely necessary to cheat a little by setting a scene for the origin events that includes features that could only result from the events. In any case, the description of the civilizations already there is fully in keeping with features and histories of these tribal peoples. They were originally from the Indochina coastlands, colonizing by degrees the so-called Polynesian triangle through the Fijis, Samoa, Tonga, the Cooks, Societies, Tahiti, Tuamotus, and Marquesas Islands as far as New Zealand in the southwest corner (the Moa and Maori), through Easter Island in the southeast, to Hawaii in the far northeast corner. In the case of Hawaii, there is archeological evidence for Polynesian occupation from around 120 A.D. on the island of Hawaii itself, with later settlements through the island chain to Kauai around 1200 A.D. Whether there were several migrations from Tahiti or the Marquesas to account for the difference in these archeological datings, or movements of original peoples from island to island over the course of time, are matters of scholarly dispute. Either way, the isolation of Hawaii, and its freedom from intrusion by other peoples for at least one or two thousand years, can help us understand how the extremely complex social structure and its very tight incorporation of a mythic worldview could have developed.

There was a class of chiefs at the top of the social order with proprietary rights to various topographical areas of an island. Under the supervision of a major chief were the male members of his tribe unrelated to the two "families" of the chief, and regarded as commoners. One family of the chief consisted of his brothers and uncles; a second family consisted of his progeny. Males from both families were considered legitimate contenders for the major chiefdom. Thus there were many potential chiefs, all of whom could be recognized as "chiefs" in distinction from commoners, and who might have designs upon the top position. One of the ways in which the potential for competition was partially controlled was a distinction between males who belonged to the chief's own family and his progeny who belonged to his wives' families. These family groups were treated differently by the chief, who apportioned official duties and land supervisions to them depending on his assessment of their loyalties to him. This, however, set up a distinction between two ways of inheriting his office: one was to usurp the position by killing the chief; the other was by appealing to natural descent. Thus there were many "chiefs" ranked in terms of closeness to the main chief. It is also important to realize that in all the other islands there were other main chiefs, often in competition and conflict with one another. The women formed a third class, surrounded by taboos that kept males and females apart even while taking meals. However, it seems that any woman could enhance her status by having a son sired by a chief, thus moving into the group of the chief's wives and possibly thinking that her son might one day become a chief. It is not at all clear how all of these registers actually worked in practice. What is clear is that the behavior of the young women when prevailing upon Cook's seamen for intercourse was motivated by the thought that Cook and his men were gods, the gods storied as the first chiefs of the Hawaiian people.

This brings us to the mythology. There are two basic myths, each with several variants. One is about Paao, forced to leave his original homeland because of a quarrel with his older brother Lonopele that resulted in Paao's killing of Lonopele's son and a long arduous journey by sea until he reached Hawaii. There he deposed or killed Kapawa, the indigenous chief who was benevolent to his people, cared for an agrarian way of life, and who did not condone human "sacrifice." Paao also slaughtered all the existing priests, built temples for human sacrifice, and installed a new ruler from Kahiki, the land beyond the western horizon (or the sky). The ruling chiefs of Hawaii trace their descent from this chief installed by Paao, and regard one of Paao's company, the feather god Kukailimoku, as their personal conqueror god. The other major myth is about Lono and Ku, two gods who alternate presence and power during two different seasons of the year. Lono represents the time of the original indigenous chief Kapawa and the season of fertility renewal and agricultural production. It is celebrated during four lunar months, roughly our December through January, called Makahiki. Ku represents the social system established by Paao and marked by the taboos that pertain during the rest of the year under the rule of the chief. During Makahiki the taboos are lifted, human sacrifice is banned, and the chief goes into seclusion while the people celebrate a kind of saturnalia. Emblems of Lono are taken in procession around the islands for about three weeks, stopping at temples for festivals as a sign that the god of the indigenous culture has returned to reclaim the lands for the people. At the end of the Makahiki, a symbolic death is enacted, the temples are returned to Ku, the chief comes out of seclusion, and Lono leaves for Kahiki to return again the next year.

This brief summary of Hawaiian imperial society and its mythologies at the time of Cook is certainly not sufficient as a description of the rich cultural ambience of daily life, but it may be enough to explain their encounter with him. By coincidence Cook sailed in from beyond the horizon on his "floating islands" just about the time Lono always returned from Kahiki. That was apparently enough to start thinking in terms of the mythic categories. The correlations were not exact, but close enough for them to think of Cook as Lono. Cook was surely a new appearance, acting like a god–chief. He immediately asked for the chief of the people and the chiefs received him with presents as befitted exchanges among chiefs. Cook ate their food and gave gifts to the people, among which the new iron spikes were found to be wonderful and especially useful. His lesser chiefs (petty officers) did finally receive the women who sought to have children by the gods. And Cook circled the islands, just like Lono, as if to take possession of the lands for the Makahiki, letting the priests invite him to the Lono temples wherever he landed for the traditional songs and feasts. Then he planned to sail away just as the Makahiki was ending. Had his visit ended there the translation would have seemed correct. However, before he left, Cook was asked when he would return.

He could have had no idea of what the Hawaiians were thinking. He therefore used his own categories to understand these people. They were at first seen as uncivilized barbarians. As Captain Vancouver was to say after his own visit in the 1790s, it would be good to make them Christians, but first they would have to be civilized. That meant teaching them to read, write, dress, behave, and think like the British. This process had already begun during Cook's visit. They were quick to learn enough English to ask about the far-away island from which he came. When told it was England, and that it was ruled by King George, a ranking was inevitable: as the ruling chief of Hawaii was to the Hawaiians, so King George must be to the ruling chief. Both Kalaniopuu, the ruling chief while Cook was there, and his son Kamehameha, who ruled after him, as well as later chiefs during the period of whalers, traders, missionaries, and American colonists, thought of themselves as "brothers" to King George and rulers of the islands under his dominion. Kalaniopuu had already aspired to take on British ways and, when it was known that Cook was preparing to leave, asked for table settings and clothing so he could dine just like King George. Cook must have thought that the Hawaiians were becoming civilized.

Then, after sailing away on schedule, he came back the next week and found a change in mood that he was not able to comprehend. The seasons had changed, the Ku temples had been reopened, and the ruling chief was back in power. Lono should not have reappeared. When thievery took place and his men on shore sought to stop such "insolence," some resistance and roughing up occurred. When the tender was taken, Cook marched ashore himself to take Kalaniopuu hostage until the boat was returned. It was while Cook was leading Kalaniopuu to the shore boat that the women descended upon them screaming, others rushed around, Cook fired a shot, a call came that a chief had been killed trying to breach the blockade, and one of the men killed Cook with an iron spike. As Sahlins notes, the killing of Cook was neither premeditated, nor an accident: "It was the Makahiki in an historical form" (*Historical Metaphors*, 24). It was set up by Cook's behavior, which could only be understood by the people as a battle with Kalaniopuu as rival chiefs. As soon as it happened, the mythic categories of Ku and Lono took over. Kalaniopuu was given the credit for the killing, seen as the victor on the model of usurper chiefs in descent from Paao. This was the reason for the treatment of Cook's remains, why his bones were later said to be in a casket carried around the island in Lono's procession at the beginning of the Makahiki.

Thus the Hawaiians assimilated the event into their mythology. They would continue to ask later traders if they knew when Lono (Cook) would return. As for the chiefs, the recent dispatch of the god–chief from England only enhanced their image as conqueror–kings without affecting their continuing interest in British ways or the practice of trading they had learned. Sahlins's remarkable study of the subsequent history of trading with the British and

Americans is most unpleasant to read. For the chiefs, trading became a way of accumulating emblems of prestige in relation to their own people, evidence of their desire for equality of status in relation to Europeans, not the practice of an economy in the interest of the well-being of their people. Their native categories were not sufficient to comprehend the effect of trading as they understood it upon their people and lands. At the end of this period the lands had become the private property of foreigners, and the social structure of the Hawaiians had gone through several transformations. Subsequent chiefs appropriated the powers of enhanced contact with Kahiki in different ways, used the guns obtained from the British to conquer the chiefs of Maui, Molokai, and Oahu, appealed to the superior culture of the British to abolish taboos, administered trade with foreign merchants and naval vessels in competition with their own people, and assumed the mythic credentials associated with descent from first one and then another of the original god–chiefs. The result was a radical transformation of the Hawaiian social system and its traditional taboos, structural constraints that marked relational distinctions and appropriate practices.

Nevertheless, we can learn several things about mythic thinking in cross-cultural encounters from this history. One is that the mythic structure of a worldview provides the categories and logic for interpreting a situation in a self-evident manner. It does this automatically, it seems, without calling attention to itself as if it required analysis in respect to appropriateness for the situation or explanations that those of the other culture might find helpful. In the case of Cook's approach, the Christian myth had already been translated into self-evident categories of British culture and its civility. As Sahlins describes the encounter from Cook's point of view, there was evident curiosity about the behavior and thinking of the Hawaiians, but in every case their practices were first interpreted on his own terms of social protocol. It is clear that he and the Hawaiians entered into practical exchanges for different reasons, and that neither fully grasped the other's cultural system or logic. As Sahlins puts it: "People act upon circumstances according to their own cultural presuppositions, the socially given categories of persons and things" (67).

A second observation is that, in the actual engagement of practical exchange, one's categories are stretched in order to accommodate the differences noted in the other's behavior and interests. Again, as Sahlins describes this, "the worldly circumstances of human action are under no inevitable obligation to conform to the categories by which certain people perceive them. In the event they do not, the received categories are potentially revalued in practice, functionally redefined" (67). Thus the categories by which the Hawaiians were accustomed to think about taboos, sacrifices, prestations, chiefs, and social relations changed to accommodate new experiences and the interests they evoked even as the categories were used to negotiate the new circumstances. These categories stayed in place, for they were grounded in their cultural system and its social structures, but they suffered a re-valuation when used in relation to actions of exchange with the other culture.

A third observation is that the mythic logic of the Hawaiian cultural system also suffered significant re-valuation. I have been using a distinction between the structure of a worldview given with the grammar of its myths and a people's accumulation of knowledge about itself and the world based on observation and reasoning. Sahlins uses a distinction between categories by which persons and things are designated in practical terms and those indicating the constitution of the culture itself. In both sets of terminology, the point here is that changes at the level of categories and practical knowledge may effect changes in the worldview of a people or its cultural constitution. As Sahlins describes this: "According to the place of the received category in the cultural system as constituted, and the interests that have been affected, the system itself is more or less altered. At the extreme, what began as reproduction ends as transformation" (67). The Hawaiian mythology was altered in keeping with its application to Cook as Lono, the British kingdom as Kahiki, the rationalization required to assimilate the killing of Cook into the typology of chiefs and their mythic descent, and the mythic precedent for human sacrifice. And yet, the basic structure of the system remained the same.

This brings us to a fourth observation. It has to do with the persistence of a mythic system even when it is required to change. Sahlins used the terms reproduction and transformation. Elsewhere he calls the process of reproduction and transformation of a cultural system the "structures of the conjuncture." By "conjuncture" he means the encounter of a cultural system with a social circumstance that requires negotiation in thought and practice because of some interest. By "structures of the conjuncture" he means that negotiation at the level of practical exchange proceeds by engaging structures of thought and practice, and that the conjuncture of these follows the logic of structural systems. In the extreme case mentioned above, "reproduction" refers to the way in which a people revises a cultural system to reproduce itself structurally even while undergoing a transformation. By "transformation" Sahlins means the reevaluation of component parts and their application of categories of thought and practice. His point is that the historical process is a constant engagement of changing circumstances in which a reproduction of a culture is at the same time its transformation. In our terms, the persistence of a cultural or mythic system even in the process of change is the human phenomenon to notice. And since we have developed the theory of the importance of such a system for social practice and identity, we might now say that, in the case of the Hawaiians, their identity as Hawaiians was at stake as well as familiar social structures able to keep the society working. The traditional structures of myth and society were therefore not dispensed with, even though the several transformations of their culture eventually supported radically different ways of thinking about themselves and their engagement with the world.

Cargo

A story from Ceram, an island in Indonesia, about Hainuwele (coconut girl) was first published in Dutch in 1927, then in German translation by Adolf Jensen in 1938 (*Hainuwele*) after an ethnographic expedition to Ceram to collect native stories. Jensen's interest in the Hainuwele story produced a major study in 1951, with an English translation in 1963 entitled *Myth and Cult among Primitive Peoples*. The story as recorded by Jensen and his interpretation of it as a document for the origins of ritual sacrifice among paleocultivators caught the attention of scholars and produced numerous theories of religion based on the notion of ritual killing as fundamental. In 1976, Jonathan Z. Smith published an essay called "A Pearl of Great Price and a Cargo of Yams," in which he registered a criticism of Jensen's interpretation on the basis of a detailed reconstruction of the social situation in Ceram during the early twentieth century. I want to use his study of the story, because it exemplifies so clearly the fact that mythmaking is a mode of thinking about social circumstances. My own interest must focus on the story as reflecting the period of Dutch colonization in relation to the story's themes as they would have sounded before that time. Unfortunately, Jensen's account, which I must use to argue for the earlier form of the story, is much too long to reproduce, and besides it is obviously pasted together from many versions and additions in the interest of Jensen's own theory of the narrative connections as interlocking episodes in a single tale. An abridged version of the story is given by Mircea Eliade in his anthology of myths titled *From Primitives to Zen* (18–20), but as an abridgement it merely reduces Jensen's composite narrative to those items that support Jensen's interpretation, and leaves out a number of items that should be included. I shall therefore recite the story as Smith summarizes it and then make my own observations about its earlier content and logic. In Smith's summary he includes a few verbatim sentences from Jensen's account and indicates these with quotation marks. He also uses italics to emphasize the item of importance for his own interpretation. It reads as follows:

> An ancestor (one of the *Dema*, the Marind-amin term for ancestor...) named Ameta found a coconut speared on a boar's tusk, and, in a dream, was instructed to plant it. In six days a palm had sprung from the nut and flowered. Ameta cut his finger and his blood dripped on the blossom. Nine days later a girl grew from the blossom and, in three more days, she became an adolescent. Ameta cut her from the tree and named her Hainuwele, "coconut girl": "But she was not like an ordinary person, for when she would answer the call of nature, her excrement consisted of all sorts of valuable articles, such as Chinese dishes and gongs, so that Ameta became very rich." During a major religious festival, Hainuwele stood in the middle of the dance grounds and, instead of *exchanging* the *traditional* areca nuts and betel leaves, she excreted a whole series of valuable articles, Chinese porcelain dishes, metal knives, copper boxes, golden earrings, and great brass gongs. After nine days of this: "The people thought this thing mysterious...they were jealous that Hainuwele could distribute such wealth and decided to kill her." The people dug a hole in the middle of the

dance ground, threw Hainuwele in, and danced the ground firm on top of her. Ameta dug up her corpse, dismembered it, and buried the pieces. From the pieces of her corpse, previously unknown plant species (especially tuberous plants) grew which have been, ever since, the principal form of food on Ceram. (Smith, "Pearl," 96–7)

In Jensen's longer account, followed by Eliade, the story is a myth of the origins of human time, sexuality, paleocultivation, killing, death as a sentence, and two modes of life after death. Jensen makes two moves in order to arrive at this interpretation. One is that he appends another story about another *Dema* named Satene as a sequel to the killing of Hainuwele. Satene takes her place in the middle of the dancing ground, makes a door of the arms of Hainuwele, and announces: "Since you have killed, I will no longer live here. I shall leave this very day. Now you will have to come to me through this door." The story goes on to say that "after her going men would meet her only after their death." The other move Jensen makes is to understand the term *Dema*, not as referring to an ancestor, but as a generic title for beings living in a prehuman time. Thus, all the episodes in the story become events that took place in *Dema* time to inaugurate the human time. In a parenthesis, Eliade notes that this *Dema* time "cannot be considered paradisal" (20), revealing that both he and Jensen had the Genesis story of the Christian myth in mind while reading the Hainuwele story. Jensen notes in his introduction that some of the native informants were actually Christians, and that in the course of hearing, translating, and recording these stories his practice was to ask questions, enter additions, and in general work toward a story that made sense to the ethnographer. In his large collection of stories, the Hainuwele stories are placed just after stories of "creation" and "sun, moon, and flood," but before stories of "ascent to heaven," the "realm of the dead," and the "secret society." It doesn't take much imagination to see that Jensen was thinking of the Christian myth and its focus on "ritual killing," finding it extraordinary that a root-crop people (so near the beginnings of human history!) had already developed a myth–ritual combination centered on "ritual killing." And what a discovery in the midst of the confusion about theories of religion that had plagued the nineteenth and early twentieth centuries!

Smith rightly puts this "sequel" story about Satene aside. Even in Jensen's rendering the Satene story is obviously tacked on in order to answer the question of why the people killed Hainuwele, and to give an account of the consequences of the killing. However, in Jensen's set of twelve different Hainuwele-coconut stories (from among 443 stories in all, classified according to twelve mostly "theological" topics), one finds the names of the families who "killed" Hainuwele plus the name of the village in which they live, and the Satene story seems to be based on the division of humankind into two classes, now used to describe a twofold destiny after death. In both cases, it is probable that a story about the Maro festival, when all the people would have been there, was used for making a point or two, some not so friendly, about different moieties. This is not unusual in folktales.

Among the motifs in the Hainuwele story recited above, there is the discovery of the coconut, the command to plant it, the palm shoot as a girl-child, the Maro festival at the dancing place, and the distribution of gifts during the dancing. All are stories about how you acquire things; all are separate scenes of different kinds; all could be elaborated to make complete stories of their own; all delight in the fantasies imagined, most allowing for a twinkle in the eye while listening; and all are very typical of the folktale mode of imagining times, places, and events in order to think about features of social life that cannot be explored any other way. In this case all these mini stories have been brought together, probably by Jensen himself or the ethnographers in his party, to construct a single coconut story. From reading the whole set in Jensen's recording, it is clear that coconut stories were of some interest to the Ceramese. Cultivating coconuts and tubers was their livelihood, and a coconut story could take up any number of interesting practices for entertainment. As a matter of fact, the sequel to the killing of Hainuwele, in the story as summarized by Smith, has Ameta digging up the buried Hainuwele to cut her up and do some more planting. First the coconut, then the tuber. One can certainly imagine the narrative images stacking up in an informant's mind, teased out for telling by a curious and naïve ethnographer, and then understood by the ethnographer as a single storyline. But even if a storyteller chose to put these stories together for a native occasion, the transformations from coconut to palm tree, to palm blossom, to Hainuwele, to tuber, to different kinds of tuberous crops, would not have caused any discomfort to the listeners. Transformations of this kind are the bread and butter of the teller of folktales.

So Hainuwele is the personification of all the important features of paleocultivation. Such a personification is not a mysterious figment of the imagination. It is in fact the way fairy tales, folk tales, and myths come to be, as we have seen. As an important stock character in many of the coconut stories, Hainuwele may well have had a number of associations that could pop up to add some interest and flavor to a given scene. In our case the central scene is the dancing place at the Maro festival. Much could happen there, but the main thing was the distribution of "gifts." Eliade leaves out the part about the Chinese dishes and gongs, and Smith reminds us of the "exchange" of betel leaves and areca nuts as that which would have been customary and expected. He is right. From Jensen's version, it is clear that it was the custom during the dancing for the women to sit inside the circle as well as around the outside, exchanging and chewing betel leaves and areca nuts, and passing them out to the men as they danced around. It is of some interest, if not importance, to note that both betel and areca are the products of different kinds of palm tree. And so, again from Jensen's version of the Hainuwele stories, the people did expect Hainuwele to distribute such items. Thus the story draws upon traditional practices and expectations regarding the Maro festival, and could well be a striking rewriting of a traditional story in which Hainuwele stood in the middle of the dancing ground to pass out betel leaves and areca nuts. That she did not do so in our version of the tale is the contrast that first catches our attention. Then, however, the fact that she excretes Chinese porcelain to distribute has to be found hilarious. But what is it about this that finally makes the people angry? In Jensen's version, the distribution of very valuable objects to everyone present continues for nine nights. So the reason given for their anger cannot be right. They are the ones, not Ameta, who have received the wealth. They are therefore not envious of Ameta for having a coconut girl who produces so much wealth for *him*. That has to be a swerve to keep the prying eyes and ears of the Dutch from seeing the point. The natives' point is rather, as Smith lays it out, that Hainuwele is providing trade articles, not exchange goods. The story introduces a sharp contrast between the native system of exchange economy and the economic system introduced by European traders and colonists. Capital, cash, and the accumulation of wealth are all part of a system that is diametrically opposed to the principles of reciprocity basic to the native system of exchange. Smith notes that during the period 1902–10 the Dutch put tremendous pressure on the natives of Ceram, forbidding many practices and rituals, and levying a tax that had to be paid in cash. So what is the point of the Hainuwele story? It is, as Smith puts it, a story about "dirty money" ("filthy lucre"), a way of making commentary on European trade ("cargo") as a thing worthy of disgust and anger. One was expected to take the story (and perhaps the Maro festival, supposing it was still allowed) as an occasion to think about the situation they were in, recognize that other Ceramese were also fully aware of the conflict of culture, and render appropriate critique.

I need only point out that this is an excellent example of thinking with myth. As Smith notes,

> The Ceramese myth of Hainuwele does not solve the problem, overcome the incongruity, or resolve the tension. Rather, it results in thought. It is a testing of the adequacy and applicability of traditional patterns and categories to new situations and data in the hopes of achieving rectification. It is an act of native exegetical ingenuity, a process of native work. ("Pearl," 100–1)

Cargo Cults

When Europeans began trading with the inhabitants of the Pacific islands, the various peoples responded in many different ways. Some, such as the Hawaiians, quickly accommodated the new situation. Others grew restive because the balance of trade did not make sense and was soon out of control, as in Ceram. Still others wondered how it could be that peoples far away had goods to trade that they themselves had not learned to produce. It was such a question, posed to Jared Diamond by Yali, a native of Papua New Guinea and a local politician whom Diamond met by chance while walking together along a beach in New Guinea in 1972, that sent him searching for an answer that could account for the disparity on some basis other than superior intelligence. His search finally produced the remarkable book called *Guns, Germs, and Steel* with its subtitle *Fates of Human Societies*. He was able to show that the differences in natural environments made a difference in the ways in which humans have been able to develop different technologies, products, and societies. In a subsequent study called *Collapse: How Societies Choose to Fail or Succeed*, Diamond gives us several examples of societies coming to an end because their interests and leaders developed practices that overreached, abused, or destroyed their natural environments without understanding the consequences of their violations. Diamond's studies can help us understand the social and intellectual issues generated by the arrival of the Europeans among the Pacific peoples. For the Europeans trading meant one thing; for the Pacific Island peoples it meant something altogether different. At the level of practical transactions, one-sided as they were, the obvious object upon which to focus from the natives' point of view was the goods these foreigners brought to them as items of value for trading. They called them *cargo*, a generic term for goods that came to them in ships to be exchanged for native resources such as sandalwood, shark fins, hardwoods, and produce, all of which meant extra labor on the part of the natives in order to have something to trade. It is not surprising that some peoples learned to want more cargo than they were receiving and sought to do something about it. One of the responses was the cultivation of a mythic mode of pondering the situation and the introduction of hopes for some solution in what Western scholars have called a *cargo cult*.

At first scholars thought of Pacific Island cargo cults as new religions arising from the desire for more Western goods, influenced by Christian preaching about the return of Christ, and based on the hope, expectation, or some promise of another cargo ship arriving with the goods they wanted. The fact that missionaries always arrived soon after trading and colonization began made it natural to think that Christian mythology had been at work, especially because, in Protestant terms, preaching the word comes first and is thought to be the effective agent in converting people and inaugurating "communities." And so the studies focused on the comparison of cargo cults to early Christianity, where apocalyptic thinking was thought fundamental, and upon apocalyptic sects in the history of Christianity. These were misguided studies. They did not explore the ways in which indigenous peoples used their own myths and social structures to think through the new situations, and they did not adequately appreciate the ambivalence natives always had in accommodating Western practices. In any case, most cargo cults faded away, and most scholars lost interest. Sahlins, Smith, and others have been asking another set of questions about these island peoples, and their descriptions tell another story altogether. According to Sahlins, the Hawaiians responded to the encounter by translating the practice of trading with the British into their own traditional system of myth, sacrifice, and exchange, a mental and practical process that transformed their own system even while reproducing it. Smith called the circumstances of the Ceramese during the time the Hainuwele story was set a "cargo situation without a cargo cult." This described the situation as provoking a native response on its own terms, using its traditional myths and rituals to ponder the situation and make a statement about the disparity of the exchange, thus letting us see the dynamic of cultural encounter and change in a new light. Smith notes that, among the Ceramese, there were other ways of responding to the Dutch traders and missionaries, including some attempts at outright rebellion. This means that we may take another look at the cargo cult phenomenon.

A very interesting example of a contemporary cargo cult has been described by Paul Raffaele in a recent issue of the *Smithsonian* ("In John They Trust"). The people of Tanna, a small island in the Vanuatu group, having experienced the presence of the US military during World War II, now practice a cargo cult in honor of John Frum, who, they imagine, will come again from America with industrial and military goods. Chief Isaac Wan is the leader who presides over a little hut full of emblems, such as the American flag and a globe of the world, as well as native art objects and a blackboard with instructions regarding the "office" for the cult. On John Frum Day, February 15, the American flag is raised on a mound overlooking a bamboo-hut village, men march with bamboo rifles in review, and the people clap and cheer. The people of Tanna were obviously overwhelmed by the arrival of American ships, planes, and equipment to build barracks and other buildings. The material wealth just descended upon them, and when the military decided to leave, they simply bulldozed vehicles and equipment off a point of the island and into the sea. One of the men explained that "John promised he'll bring planeloads and shiploads of cargo to us from America." Another, while saluting the flag on John Frum Day, said that the cargo would be: "Radios, TVs, trucks, boats, watches, iceboxes, medicine, Coca-Cola and many other wonderful things." So who is John Frum?

Raffaele was not able to determine exactly when and how the cult started, but he did learn that John Frum had appeared to a group of the elders one night in the late 1930s while they were drinking kava. Chief Kahuwya, leader of the Yakel village, said: "He was a white man who spoke our language, but he didn't tell us then that he was an American." What John told them was that he had come to rescue them from the missionaries and colonial officials:

> All Tanna's people should stop following the white man's ways, should throw away their money and clothes, take our children from their schools, stop going to church, and go back to living as kastom [custom] people. We should drink kava, worship the magic stones, and perform our ritual dances.

The people got the message, threw their money into the sea, and cooked pigs for grand feasts and dancing to celebrate John Frum and their freedom. This, of course, got them into trouble with the joint British and French colonial rulers, who put the movement's leaders into prison at Port Vila on the island of Espiritu Santo. When the Americans came in 1942 with their PX (military general store), candies, and pay for a day's work, John Frum appeared to the leaders in prison at Port Vila and told them he was an American. Upon return from prison, after the war was over, the leaders told the people what they had learned from and about John Frum, and the present configuration of the cargo cult developed.

Although the practices and mythology of the cult before the war are vague, it is clear that this first chapter of the movement was an invention of "kastom," a revival of "traditional" ways in opposition to colonial rule and its missionaries. "Kastom" was the pidgin term they took from the colonialists and used to describe what they imagined life was like before the colonialists arrived. It might be helpful at this point to underscore the intellectual labor necessary to reinvent a people's past that has been disrupted by colonial conquest. The Anthropological Museum in Mexico City is an excellent example of the attempt to reconstruct the pre-Spanish history of remnant native peoples after a disruption of four hundred years. The genre used for all native peoples is that of an Indian tribe, depicted in natural settings and romantic style as living a sane, simple, and beautiful way of life. The attempt to locate distinctive features of each tribe appears to have started with slight differences in settings and practices among some of the remnant populations. But the genre itself is clearly a result of superimposing modern stereotypical (and false) descriptions of Indian tribal culture on an erased and forgotten past that, as we now know, had produced high civilizations of wondrous accomplishments, huge populations, many technologies, and scenes of bustling activity (Mann, 1491). The visitor easily recognizes the sense of loss intended by the recreation of these cultures. As a visitor, one can hardly avoid another sense of sadness, not only a kind of shared mourning over the loss, but also a kind of despondency over the naïveté supporting such romantic reconstructions.

The period of disruption in Tanna was not as long as that in Mexico, but the erasure of their traditional culture by the colonialists appears to have been as drastic. In any case, it was "kastom" that the colonialists had suppressed. It was the colonialists' view of the people that let them see themselves as "kastom" people reflected through the colonialists' eyes. And it was "kastom" that John Frum said was taken away by the colonialists and should be revived. One can imagine the excited, exhilarating, cautious, daring, experimental mental and practical proposals that must have erupted before settling down into some agreements about what the "kastom" had been, was, and what was to be done about it. This first chapter does not appear to have taken the form of a cargo cult as it did after the war, thus raising the question of how it managed the transition. It seems that naming John Frum's country of origin played an important role. That change at least gives us the chance of seeing how mythic thinking may have been involved. It is probable that the first appearance of John Frum was possible because of a widespread mythology among the Pacific island peoples. This mythology is a form of ancestor memory. The Lono myth of the Hawaiians is both an elaboration of this myth as well as its detailed integration into their ritual and seasonal calendar. Others are not as precise or integrated, yet the fundamental structure is recognizable. The island people "remember" the way they came to their islands, many generations ago by sea. The first arrivals become their ancestors, but they too once lived far away before their journey to the new land. And, as the reader may know, the arrival of the Europeans by sea, and their appearance as white people, elicited recognitions in many instances of ancestors and the thought that they had returned. We need to know that the ancestors were already imagined as white people, not only because of memories somehow kept alive of extraction from the peoples of southeast Asia, but also because of an association of the sun on the western horizon as the way to and from the ancestral lands. There were apparently stories of ancestors staying in touch by means of visits from the west. That John Frum was seen as a white man who spoke the native language, and that he instructed them to return to their old ways, fits this mythology. If so, the first revival movement can be understood as a result of mythic thinking.

What then of the postwar cargo cult? While the leaders of the movement were in prison, the people were being treated very well by the American military. The war with Japan was taking place far away. Tanna was a base for operations with a great deal of military and naval traffic. Many of the good things from the PX were available to the people, some generously distributed as gifts. And, instead of colonial taxation, when the Americans needed some help in constructing a building, they paid their laborers. It is also the case that John appeared once again, this time dressed in white as a navy seaman, and said he was from America. So the cult took a new turn. Now the land of their guardian spirit was America and the American cargo was good. To stay in touch, Chief Isaac said he talked to John on occasion, sometimes after drinking kava at night with the other elders. He also visited the active volcano where John was sometimes present in the gases that spewed forth. Thus a promise to return, this time with American cargo, was kept alive. When asked what he would like to have should John come with the cargo, Chief Isaac said he wanted a fishing boat with a 25-horsepower outboard motor. When pressed with the remark that it had been a long time since John had made his promises, and then asked how he could continue keeping "faith with him," Raffaele writes: "Chief Isaac shoots me an amused look. 'You Christians have been waiting 2,000 years for Jesus to return to earth,' he says, 'and you haven't given up hope.'"

Mythic Mentality

We have looked at three situations of encounter between Westerners and the peoples of the Pacific islands, exploring the strains put upon the native cultures, and looking for the ways in which their traditional mythic systems provided the framework for engaging another culture both at the level of practical exchange and at the level of understanding. In due course the traditional mythic systems suffered transformations, even as they were reproduced in application to the new circumstances. There was no need for the peoples to explain to themselves why and how the old system had to change, even as there was no explanation given of its reproduction as foundational. That was because there was a social logic to the mythologies that the people wanted to leave in place. They were embedded in systems of practice, ritual rounds, class distinctions, and normal productive activities that defined an entire way of life. What we have been calling social interests are obvious, and the resulting sense of belonging, identity, and rootedness in a people and its place and history is clear. We have called this sense of belonging and its resulting way of thinking a mentality. It is the way a mentality works, even in the course of radical challenge and the transformation of a people's mythic system, that we now want to question and bewonder.

In an earlier section of this chapter, it was suggested that the imagined world of a people provides a framework for its sense of identity and self-understanding. We can now consider the fact that an imagined world is usually taken for granted, seldom noticed as a system inviting examination. Instead, it is the objective markers of cultural identity that are used for display, elaboration, and comment about one's social (often ethnic) identity. Habits, dress, cuisine, gardens, building design, ornamentation, artistic styles, and artefacts register the ways a particular people shapes its physical and social environments. Many of these practices and images are transportable when people move to another country. There is an Italian restaurant in San Pedro, California, where Italian dishes are served in a setting of mosaics and art objects reminiscent of the old country. The placemats, however, are photographs of the old days in San Pedro when an Italian immigrant population contributed to the shaping of a new port city. Thus the immigration did not erase the desire to retain the distinctiveness of a cultural identity, even though the only marks available for display were some pictures, music, and special dishes. It is the same with many other immigrant populations in the United States. When one moves from one public place to another, both mythic and cultural emblems will be found: the replica of a Darvish mystic, a Virgin Mary, or a Buddha, as well as the fleur-de-lis, a picture of Zapata, or a Japanese tea garden. In every case, everyone knows that, beyond the display of such objective markers, there is a whole worldview in memory and imagination of the way of life in their former country. The fact that the imagined world is there, although taken for granted, explains the ease with which a person can say that he or she is British, African-American, Persian, Japanese, etc. If one is careful in probing a little, it is often the case that remarkable differences among cultural systems can be noticed in such things as a people's values, virtues, ways of thinking, making judgments, the sense of the right way to do things, humor, and in general the approaches taken in the accommodations and negotiations required to manage living in a different cultural environment. All of these are practices, attitudes, and sensibilities often not noticed as distinctive to their culture by those living within its system. Noticing that cultural identity is taken for granted in this way opens a feature of social existence well worth exploring.

I want now to propose a theory of cultural mentality in which myths and rituals play a predominant role. We have seen that myths are made to mark and manage social interests where a people engage the natural orders or seek to rationalize the constraints, structures, and significant practices of their social order. They mark the dynamics of social practices and interest where the two environments overlap and the influence of unexplained agencies is encountered. Rituals mark the events of significance in the seasonal and social calendars as worthy of notice, reflection, and celebration. A myth does more than attend to a particular situation in the real world; it adds images and a scenario to the world of the imagination. As such, a mythic image takes its place along with other myths in the imaginary world of the environmental canopy that gives a worldview its own set of myths, scenes, and agents. These myths may not appear to form a comprehensive system, for different interests, deities, and versions of myths can reside there seemingly unconnected. And yet, if they continue to be cultivated by a people, even if on separate occasions, they do contribute to the tapestry of the imagined world, thus making it possible to treat them as if linked together. The relationship between the tapestry of the imagined world and the structures and life of a society is not that of a reflection or mirror image. The mythic images in the tapestry are related to social interest situations that may be occasional within the life of a people. And not all of the structures of a society may be acknowledged with myths. Thus, although the tapestry of the mythic world and the society in the real world do not match perfectly, the relationship is reflexive, and the comprehension of the whole is that of a single environment.

The notion of a culture as an environment with consequences for practices and thought is not uncommon among social theorists. We have mentioned Clifford Geertz's concept of religion as culture, with its implications for several interlocking systems of symbols that determine both practices and their meanings among a people. We have also mentioned Bourdieu's concept of *habitus*, the congeries of agreements about proper and accepted behavior that serve as a set of rules and rationales for a people's way of life. Anthony Giddens uses the term *locale* to designate the extent of a social arena within which a specific center of power, organization, authorization, or information has its effective influence (*The Nation-State and Violence*, 12–17, and throughout). Theodore Schatzki has used the term *site of the social* for the place where the organizations of a social structure are in motion through the actual practices of the people involved and the dynamic relations that result between and among various organizations (*The Site of the Social*, ix, and throughout). Jonathan Z. Smith uses the term *situation* in order to describe a social setting as a circumstance with "historical" configurations and dynamic encounters of peoples, interests, practices, and thinking in need of "negotiation." And, of course, the use of the term *mentality* is common in popular parlance. I am using the term *mythic mentality* to add myth to the mix of social structures and practices, in such a way as to focus attention on the function of a mythic system as a grammar for thinking about social situations.

It remains now to suggest that, though frequently unexamined, a worldview so imagined supports patterns of thinking among the people who live under its canopy. These ways of thinking include taking certain habits as a matter of course, using customary language to express opinions, approaches to new situations, modes of humor, popular clichés, standard topics of discourse, typical arguments when addressing social issues, and ways of rationalizing attitudes taken with regard to other cultures. It is seldom the case that a people's worldview is acknowledged as the frame of reference for patterns of thinking. That is because the mythic world need not be called upon consciously in the normal exercise of making observations, judgments, and transactions. And yet, if the mythic world is a construction of intellectual labor in the interest of the workings of a society, a worldview is actually a conceptual system with its own structure and logic. As the environment for a people it provides the large-scale framework for understanding social realities, for understanding practices and events, and for making judgments about plans and proposals. Even the cluster of rationales for values, the bases for honor and shame, modes of tuition, and the ethos and ethics of a social system are anchored in the contours and images of a mythic system. And so, we might think of the pattern of the tapestry of a mythic system as a kind of grammar for thinking about and conceptualizing the social world. In analogy to the way language works, the mythic system is learned in the process of growing up in a family, social tuition, and enculturation. Although it is not noticed as a grammar, just as the grammar of a language is not consciously employed in common discourse, it can become the object of investigation and, as with the grammar of a language, described by careful analysis. Thus, in the case of a mythic system, the fact that the gods recede and that myths are not always in mind does not mean that patterns of thinking among a people are not beholden to the mythic structure of their worldview as a kind of grammar. Like the grammar of a language that is used to construct and understand sentences, the structure of a mythic system is used to think about, make judgments upon, and in general understand social situations. That, I suggest, is the function of a mythic system, a grammar that makes possible the social logic of the thinking and mentality of a people.

It is obvious that the examples discussed in this chapter are not enough to establish such a thesis. That is because the studies of these moments of "thinking with myth," though clear and persuasive, have focused only upon certain social-historical situations, not upon the social logics of entire mythic systems. If we want to do that, we need to analyze the relations among a myth–ritual system, its imagined world, and the social history of its culture in some comprehensive way. That can only be done in detail by historians with special expertise in a religion and its culture. Since we have been aiming at just such an analysis of Christianity, our task becomes a bit more complicated. In the first place, Christianity has never been the object of the kind of analyses that historians of religion have devoted to other religions. Recall that, in the examples of the transformations and reproductions of myths and cultures described in this present chapter, the focus was upon the native tribal cultures, not upon the Western ways of thinking or the ways in which Western thinking engaged these social-historical encounters. In the second place, historians of Christianity tend to be specialists in a particular period of history or theology, not in Christianity as a complex whole. In the third place, we discovered in Chapter 1 that Christianity could not provide descriptors or categories capable of describing or understanding the religions of other peoples, and that we would have to develop our own concepts for the study of their myths and rituals. So now, and this is a fourth factor that complicates our task, an irony lies in the application of what we have learned from other religions in order to explain Christianity. But still, what would happen, or so my question has been, if we turned around and made Christianity the object of our quest to understand religion, and asked about *its* myths and rituals, its imagined world, its set of social interests, the social logic of its mythic system, and the mythic grammar that might be suspected to underlie Christian mentality?

Now that we know where the scholarly concept of religion came from, and now that we have learned from other peoples how myths and rituals work, whether we call them religious or not, the implicit comparison between Christianity and other religions that has driven our curiosities for four hundred years will also have to be turned around. We will have to use our scholarly familiarity with other religions, partial and perspectival as it may be, to make comparisons with Christianity as if it were the unexplained and unfamiliar object of our investigation. Yet, it is just because we are so familiar with Christianity that we will be able to analyze its myth–ritual system in greater depth and comprehension than has been possible with other religions and cultures. So, instead of the partial investigations of the myths and rituals of other cultures in Part I of the book, we now turn to investigate a religion where some native familiarity and academic expertise can attend our analysis of a large and dynamic religious system.

Part II
The Religion of Christianity

5 Early Christian Mythmaking

We now want to consider Christianity as a religion. The reader will have noticed that occasional references have been made to Christianity as the unacknowledged source for the concept of religion in the Euro-American study of religions. A familiarity with Christianity has been taken for granted as the definition of religion in the scholarly study of religions, giving rise to an unexamined concept that has repeatedly run into problems when applied to the religions of other peoples. I have therefore developed a set of categories to explain the social interests and intellectual investments at work in the myths and rituals of other peoples. I have emphasized the relation between mythmaking and social interests, whereby the two environments of the social and natural worlds expand the horizons of the imagination to provide a canopy for mythic imagination to position the gods. The gods are personifications of forces beyond the empirical world within which limited control of social formation and production occurs. The point has been made that the social interests are basic, the inexplicable forces are real, the imagined personifications are appropriate acknowledgments of these forces, and the intellectual labors are constructive. The time has come to apply these categories to a redescription of Christianity.

Before we begin, a word needs to be said about the term *Christianity* used in the singular. There are, in fact, many Christianities. Not only are there many types of Protestant Christianities, but within the Catholic traditions there are also several Christianities, including the Roman Catholic, the Orthodox Churches, and the Armenian, Syrian, and Coptic Churches, each with many sub-formations. Major differences in social formation, mythic grammar, and ritual practice surface when they are analyzed for their distinctive cultural mentalities. I am using the term Christianity in a rather narrow focus upon the myth and ritual system that settled into place after Constantine, was elaborated in Roman Catholicism during the medieval period, and continued as definitional for Protestant Christianities from the Reformation to the present. I do this because I want to engage the popular concept of Christianity in the United States and describe its mentality in relation to the medieval and Reformation systems of myth and ritual, where the evidence for their structures and social logics is more readily available.

The challenge will be to keep track of the various cultivations of Christian myths and rituals through the long history of a complex institutionalization in relation to different social situations and interests. This will require making a selection of just those moments and features of its history that allow us to assess the social logics of its mythologies and the intellectual labors invested in reactions and responses to other interests, endeavors, and institutions that also mark the history of Western culture. This approach to a redescription is called for if we want to include Christianity in our quest for a social theory of religion. It is also called for by our quest to identify and understand *Christian mentality*, a concept that is hardly customary, but one toward which we have been working throughout the book. Because we will want, at the end of this study, to return to the questions raised at the beginning, and because those questions have to do with the Christian ingredient in the mentality of Americans who think of the United States as a Christian nation, it will take some careful work to describe this phenomenon and let it surface for analysis and discussion. Our goal in Part II of the book is to develop this concept in such a way that it can be recognized as a factor of significance in the social, political, and cultural discourses of the twenty-first century. In order to do that, however, the legacy of Western Christianity will have to be made clear. Since the history of Western Christianity has taken some decisive turns that affect what we will want to call Christian mentality, I will have to span that history in segments to make the case for its modern formation. Thus the history of Christian thinking will have to focus on its imagined worlds and their mythologies at different times of their transformations and reproductions.

The present chapter will trace the beginnings of Christianity from the earliest evidence to the time of Constantine. The point will be made that Christianity as we know it now did not start as a new religion during the Greco-Roman age, and that one cannot speak of a Christian mentality until well after the establishment of Catholic Christianity under Constantine. I will therefore need to explore the intellectual and social experimentations that took place during those first three hundred years, revise the standard descriptions of Christian beginnings, recast the pre-Constantine period of the so-called "church fathers," and put a different construction upon the Constantinian revolution than has been customary, in order to arrive at the establishment of Catholic Christianity as an institution with a particular social logic. Readers unacquainted with New Testament studies, a major source for this chapter, may final it helpful to consult my book, *Who Wrote the New Testament?*

Chapter 6 will focus on the edifice of the Christian church, its myth and ritual systems, its social and political liaisons, and the pressures upon its imagined world, universalized during the medieval period, then stretched, if not broken, by subsequent turns of history such as the Renaissance, the Protestant Reformation, the Enlightenment, the Industrial Revolution, and the emergence of the nation-state. By tracing this history with our categories in mind, it will be possible to define modern Christian mentality as a legacy of that history. The reader will see that, from its beginnings, Christianity has been a human construction in the hands of specialists and intellectuals for reasons of social interests that are quite different from those we have noted from ethnographic studies. The encompassing environments have been more political and cosmic than the combination of tribal and natural worlds we have been considering earlier, and the relation of the social formations of Christian units to the worlds of politics and empires describes a kind of double mythic grammar to the Christian mentality that eventually settled into place. One use of the mythic grammar will be the ways in which Christians imagined relating to the cosmic orders; the other, the ways in which they related to their political and social worlds. Nevertheless, our categories will be able to handle the twists and turns of Western history with the search for a Christian mentality.

Chapter 7 will discuss the notion of the Christian nation in relation to our description of Christian mentality; Chapter 8 will discuss the challenges to this mindset resulting from our multicultural world at the end of the age of empires.

The Kingdom Schools

The standard picture of Christian origins includes the appearance of Jesus as the Messiah, his message about the kingdom of God, his gathering of a group of disciples, his journey to Jerusalem at the time of Passover, his crucifixion at the hands of the Romans (with some instigation by the Jewish establishment), his resurrection from the dead and appearances to Peter and the disciples, their formation of the "first church" in Jerusalem, and the outpouring of the Holy Spirit to commission them as apostles. Critical scholars have not been able to document any of these eight points as historical events. That is because the picture is a composite of early mythologies, primarily those of Paul, Mark, and Luke. Together they form what Christians have always called "the gospel." The social logics of these mythologies describe subsequent situations experienced by associations that cultivated the teachings of Jesus and thus do not reflect the social circumstances of Jesus' time. The gospel accounts cannot be read as history. However, because the gospel serves the Christian church and imagination as the authoritative account of Christianity as a religion, it is not surprising to find that most New Testament scholars have had difficulty understanding it to be Christian mythmaking when asking about Christian origins. The task is complicated by the fact that the gospel does place its mythic events in historical time. It is this feature of the gospel that has made it so difficult to set aside, because to do so threatens the Christian claim to special status by means of both its divine origin and historical documentation. Recently, however, many New Testament scholars have been able to account for Christian origins in ways that recognize the gospel as myth, ways that give the early mythmakers their due as serious intellectuals seeking authorization for the various schools of Jesus' teachings. It is this emerging map of the first century that we need to have in mind at the beginning of our quest for Christian mentality.

I have already said that Christianity did not start as a new religion during the Greco-Roman period. It started with the teachings of a Galilean Jew, teachings that caught the attention of other like-minded intellectuals who found them timely as a way to think and talk about living in the social situation created by the mix of cultures and political powers that impinged upon them. The teachings attributed to Jesus can be found in the Sayings Gospel Q, the Gospel of Thomas, and several pre-gospel reconstructions of sets of parables and pronouncement stories (Mack, *The Lost Gospel*; *Who Wrote?* 43–73). Scholars have studied these teachings to determine their tenor and content. It has become clear that Jesus was fully aware of the social situation in Galilee and its cultural mix. He knew about Roman control, understood Hellenistic culture, spoke Greek, and construed Jewish sensibilities with his references to the kingdom ("rule," "sovereignty," "domain") of God. But he did not engage the question of Roman occupation directly, offer a critique of the political problems of the Judean temple-state, or promote any social program as an alternative to the political situation. Instead, his teachings were marked by a pithy aphoristic style that others took as a prod to wake up to their social situations, pay attention to the logic (or lack of logic) of common current practices, notice the ways in which the many current codes of behavior had become artificial, and use their own sense of humor and integrity to respond as individuals in control of their own lives. A combination of Cynic insight into the artificiality of social decorum with a Stoic view of convention as of no importance if one wanted to live as an individual of ethical integrity gave a remarkable tone to these teachings. "Let the dead bury the dead," he said. "Don't judge and you won't be judged"; "Bless those who curse you"; "As you want people to treat you, do the same to them." Most of the one-liners in aphoristic style sound like utterances made in public, at a village market or the agora. There must have been comrades who quickly caught on to the point or style of this discourse and started talking that way with each other.

While we have learned much about the multilayered social situation in Galilee under the Seleucids, Maccabees, and Romans, the precise social circles to which Jesus belonged have not been determined. That is because the texts we have were not written for that purpose. There may well have been some disaffection among certain classes of people that could account for the attention given his teachings at the beginning. However, the rather rapid spread of small groups interested in this mode of discourse tells us that it must have struck a chord appropriate for the general social climate. Those who have asked about the attractiveness of these teachings have noted their remarkable cross-cultural sensibility. Without making a point of doing so, the teachings of Jesus drew upon values fundamental to both Jewish and Greek traditions of thought and ethic. From the Jewish side, the notion of the kingdom of God with its roots in the collective or corporate concept of the people of God, and its deep commitment to social ethics, would have been noteworthy. From the Greek side, the address to the individual to take responsibility for his or her actions in response to the real world, together with the mode of argumentation and its implicit grounding in a constructive anthropology, would have been readily understandable. So even though Jesus' teachings did not contain a program, ideology, or social critique aimed at changing the world, it must have resonated with people who were alert and concerned about the social-political situation of the *oikoumene* as it affected life in Galilee. The description in Chapter 3 of the Greco-Roman world and the dislocations of peoples and cultures should be kept in mind as the general setting for the emergence of the Jesus schools. There may well have been a niche in the cultural mix into which the kind of discourse we have in the Jesus schools would have been attractive.

It will help to recall the social setting during the Greco-Roman world, a time of cultural mixing, overlays of governance, many gods and temples, and experimentation with associations, cults, schools, and philosophies focused on the challenge of living in a multicultural world. Many of these experiments took place in the diasporas away from traditional homelands and peoples. The early schools and associations cultivating the teachings of Jesus had this larger world in mind, and even though they did not address the problems and possibilities of this world directly, their energies were focused on finding ways to live within it creatively and sanely. We noted the general sense of dis-ease among many peoples, apparently because of the fragmentation of older traditional kingdoms and cultures after Alexander's campaigns and the Roman annexation of many lands accustomed to their own administrations. We noted as well that the times were nevertheless vibrant with activities which took advantage of the mobility, mix, and commercial opportunities created by the Hellenistic–Roman world. The early Jesus people sensed the reasons for the dis-ease and must have enjoyed their experiments with the art of living in the Roman world. They did this by casting the teachings of Jesus as instructions for their experiments in small group formations. There is no doubt about their discussion groups becoming attractive to others, or about the liveliness of the associations and their networks that soon formed, for the spread of the phenomenon is well documented. What we do not know in detail sufficient to satisfy our curiosity is what they talked about in addition to discussions of the teachings of Jesus, when and why they decided to form associations on the Greek model, and what their purpose was in relation to the larger social worlds around them. What we can say is that neither their experiments in social formation nor their mythmaking projects in drawing together the God of Israel, stories of Jesus, and their concepts of the kingdom of God could possibly have prepared them for their later transformation into an institution of empire.

What happened first among those listening to Jesus requires a bit of inferential reconstruction. There may have been others around Jesus who constituted a kind of Galilean Chelsea (meeting to share pointed observations about daily life in Galilee and discuss ideas about coping with its complexities), but the picture that developed later of Jesus having disciples ("students") cannot be documented and, in any case, is improbable given the lack of a program to his teachings. Nevertheless, when we do have a chance to catch sight of those who collected, embellished, and arranged his teachings in the several traditions available to us, we find that their interests and behavior fit the pattern of a Hellenistic school of popular ethical philosophy on the one hand, and that they were fascinated with the idea of the kingdom of God on the other. The two concepts, ethical philosophy and kingdom of God, actually went together quite well, not only in the teachings of Jesus but also in other Hellenistic traditions of thought as well. As was the common practice with the schools of the Stoics, or the Epicureans, or the Cynics, those who were more familiar with the teachings of Jesus became interpreters and instructors, passing the teachings on to others and elaborating upon them by coming up with similar sayings (Mack, *Lost Gospel*, 191–205). It seems that small groups formed that found Jesus' teachings a crisp discourse about a lifestyle appropriate for the times and in touch with a vague but suggestive concept of divine order that was not controlled by the ruling powers.

The fact that the collections of the teachings of Jesus are quite diverse, and that there were many ways in which his name came to be used as the founder figure for different groups, has intrigued scholars. It now appears that some followers of Jesus thought that a movement of sorts was the right thing to pursue, asking others to join their group as "kingdom people," and thinking perhaps that if there were enough kingdom people it might make a difference in the social ambience of the times (the "Sayings Gospel" called Q). Others engaged in debates with the Pharisees about the rules of purity and questioned whether they were binding now that the rule of the temple-state was in serious trouble (the so-called "pronouncement stories"). Still others formed small groups of meditation on the sayings of Jesus as a way to gain insight into a noetic kingdom of God and cultivate knowledge of themselves as its citizens apart from the turmoil of the times (Gospel of Thomas). Others apparently became discussion groups within diaspora synagogues, proposing that Jesus be thought of as a new Moses, and daring a comparison with the Maccabean martyrs (Mack, *A Myth of Innocence*, 78–97). The conservative Pharisee Paul had a revelation that, if the Jesus movement he had encountered included gentiles, there was no reason not to go out and tell the gentiles that God wanted them to belong to his people. In his mind, a mission to the gentiles would be the flowering of the promises of God to Abraham and Israel (Cameron and Miller, *Redescribing Paul and the Corinthians*).

When the Romans sacked Jerusalem and the temple in 70 A.D., Mark concluded that God had allowed it as a judgment against those who had killed Jesus, and he wrote a brief biography of Jesus to imagine how that could have happened. Others found his story irresistible. Even Matthew, still grounded in a Jewish milieu that had found a way to combine the teachings of Jesus with the teachings of Moses, and who should not have needed to link the death of Jesus with the destruction of the temple, found Mark's biography most interesting, and integrated his own group's collection of the teachings of Jesus into the story. Then Luke, a fairly well-educated Greek living somewhere outside Palestine in the early second century, perhaps in a city on the Aegean Sea, took Mark's story as the "fulfillment" of Israel's epic history and embellished it with teachings for what by then could be called gentile Christians concerned about their place in the Roman world. He also added a sequel or second volume known as the "Acts of the Apostles" to follow the story through the journeys of Paul as far as Rome.

The Myths of Christ and the Kingdom

A reading of this literature from the first century of Christian beginnings reveals an amazing investment in the teachings of Jesus and in myths about Jesus as the founder of the Jesus schools. The usual approach among New Testament scholars has been to notice the many ways in which the founder figure Jesus was imagined, characterized, and mythologized. Even though the many characterizations, from a prophet like Moses to cosmic Lord, cannot be compressed into a single, composite profile, the conclusion has been to think that, taken together, they say something about the singular figure of the historical Jesus, namely, that Jesus must have been some awesome charismatic. The inability to sort through these early Jesus mythologies and account for them in relation to the social formations and interests of different Jesus schools is a direct result of the concentrated fixation on the figure of Jesus as imagined in later Christian myths and thinking and the continuing investment of New Testament scholars in Christian thinking about the singular importance of the "historical Jesus" for Christian origins. There was, however, another focus to early mythmaking, one that has been taken as self-evident in much New Testament scholarship and therefore left unexplored. This was the concept of the kingdom of God. The mythologies of Jesus as wisdom's child, divine man, son of God, *christos*, martyr, resurrected one, and cosmic Lord, all have their place in relation to various attempts to conceptualize the kingdom of God. The Jesus schools were working on the problem of what to think about the heady concept of the kingdom of God, and where to locate it in relation to themselves, the God of the kingdom, and the Roman world. That was a big order, given the fact that the notion of the kingdom, though startling and intriguing as an atmosphere within which to experiment with the alternative behavior and thinking that each Jesus group had encouraged, was actually vague, indistinct, and indefinite.

We have two kinds of evidence for these experiments in mythmaking that we can trace for the first one hundred years. One is the variety of social groups these followers of Jesus' teachings formed, which can be arranged in rough sequence as a kind of development. The other is the tenor, content, and application of the concept *kingdom of God*. This term appears to have been the only abstract generalization used by these people to conceptualize and refer to what it was they represented. By noting the several junctures where this term and a social formation come together, we can answer some of our questions about the social interests of these people to prepare us for the later myth and ritual system of the medieval church.

The earliest layers of the traditions of the teachings of Jesus do have references to the kingdom of God. In these traditions the meaning is vague and without definite, concrete reference, whether empirical or mythological. The term itself was not a new coinage of Jesus or the Jesus people, for it occasionally occurs in both Jewish and Greek texts of the time to suggest that various orders of reality, from political structures to ethical and noetic ideals, could be thought of as perfect if only God were in control. The concept of the kingdom of God seems to have been taken up in the teachings of Jesus with layered connotations to suggest better ways of living together than the current kings and tyrants made possible. At first it seems to have meant nothing more than, "Look, you don't have to worry about the power and authority of the rulers of this world. What do they know about human well-being and integrity? You don't have to obey them or their rules of conduct. God is the sovereign who counts. Do what you know to be right were He in charge." It must have sounded sage, good, and possible, despite the fact that the god in question was hardly defined, and what his domain might look like, wherever it might be located, was left unaddressed. It was not long before both of these questions began to be answered.

The concept of God as cosmic sovereign was not a problem, and that seems to have been the way the Jesus people thought of him all along. After all, every kingdom, empire, and culture throughout the ancient Near East since the Sumerians and Babylonians, and every city-state around the Mediterranean basin since the Greeks and Romans, had imagined a sovereign high god to be in charge both of the cosmos and of the kings ruling the kingdoms of the world. And yet, all of these high gods had names, attributes, extensive mythologies, and quite precise mechanisms for contact with the kingdoms they controlled. In the case of the Jesus people, all of that was missing. We have to assume that the God of their kingdom was a Hellenistic hybrid combining features of both Jewish and Greek traditions. On the Jewish side there would have been interest in the people of God as a collective and their ideal kingdom as a temple-state; on the Greek side would be an interest in the cosmos and how it could be a home for humankind. Many Jewish authors of the Hellenistic period had not found it difficult to merge the one God of Israel and the temple-state in Jerusalem with the Greek philosophic concept of the divine power throughout the cosmos. So that part of the equation was no problem. But what if the Jesus people found themselves as a social formation more and more involved in representing their notion of the kingdom of God in the real world? That would force changes in thinking about the God of the kingdom, as well as about the manifestations of the kingdom. That, of course, is exactly what happened.

Various conceptions of the kingdom of God were entertained by the early Jesus peoples depending upon their particular constructions of the teachings, in what circumstances they found themselves forming schools of thought, and how they began to think of themselves as associations in a tradition of discourse stemming from Jesus and his teachings. For some, a rather open-ended definition of the kingdom as descriptive of ethical practices seems to have been enough. For others, a cultivation of the teachings as a way to internalize a profound understanding of oneself as belonging to a spiritual realm defined the kingdom. Others, however, came to think of their association as a formation of the people of God in the tradition of Israel. It was in groups such as these that their differences from other contemporary ways of representing the traditions of Israel turned into issues of identity and quests for rationale. Many Jews were working to salvage or translate essential features of the Jerusalem temple-state, which was threatened with disruption. Others in diaspora synagogues had already found ways to represent the heritage of Israel independently of the temple establishment. Paul seems to have drawn upon Jesus associations that had been in contact with diaspora synagogues, on their continuity with the heritage of Israel, and their representations of the traditions of the fathers. Mark drew upon Jesus schools that had been in debate with Pharisees about the authority of the teachings of Jesus in light of temple-state purity rules. In both cases it seems clear that social formations had been created within which issues of group identity produced claims upon the heritage of the Israel traditions, some internal structures of organization and leadership, and some notions of having markers that defined those inside as different from those outside the group. It would have been in situations such as these that what we have been calling social interests came to focus on issues of self-identification in relation to other contenders for representing the heritage and history of Israel. This would have meant a rather serious discussion of the kingdom of God as they understood it.

If these groups represented the teachings of Jesus about the kingdom of God in distinction from the kingdoms of the world, and if they were now thinking of their associations as legitimate heirs of the people of God, how should they now think of themselves as a social formation in relation to the kingdoms of the world and other groups representing Israel? The evidence we have from the several early Jesus schools indicates that all of these groups had been working on social ethics and practices thought to be appropriate for the teachings about the kingdom of God. We have to assume that they understood themselves as kingdom people experimenting with what we might call the ethics and ethos of kingdom teachings in practice. If so, conscious claims to being the people of God in the tradition of Israel, taking their place in the real world as a quasi-formal social unit, must have marked a major juncture in this early history. In order to think of their associations as the social location where the kingdom of God was to be manifest, or actualized, or represented within the real world, they had to do some mythmaking.

Not wanting to give up on their claims to having become just what the God of Israel and the God of the kingdom of God intended for them and their times, both Paul and Mark took up these mythmaking tasks as intellectuals and leaders within different circles of Jesus associations. These two mythmakers cannot have been the only intellectuals at work on the identity issues we have outlined during the first century, but both were influential in subsequent Christian thinking, and their myths rationalized a social logic that would eventually make it possible for the Jesus associations to become Christian churches, the churches to become the establishment church of the Roman empire, and the establishment church to formulate creedal statements of what Christians were to believe.

We need not rehearse the details of these mythmaking projects, for they have been analyzed rather thoroughly elsewhere (Mack, *Who Wrote?*; Cameron and Miller, *Paul and the Corinthians*). However, it is important to emphasize that one of the strategies was to work with the five entities of importance, namely, (1) Jesus, (2) the kingdom of God, (3) the God of the kingdom, (4) the God of Israel, and (5) the associations imagined as the people of God. The trick would be to link them together in such a way as to legitimize these congregations as social configurations intended to take their place in the real world of the *oikoumene*. Both Paul and Mark started with the God of the history of Israel and found ways to imagine that Jesus, his teachings about God's kingdom, and the Jesus associations as kingdom people and the people of God were all part of a plan that Israel's God had from the beginning. Paul did it by applying God's promise to Abraham, that "All the gentiles [nations] shall be blessed in you" (Gal 3:8), to his Christian congregations. Mark did it by starting with God's words to Isaiah the prophet about sending a messenger (John the Baptist) to "prepare the way of the lord" (Jesus), who then stepped forth to announce that the "kingdom of God has come near" (Mark 1:1–15). That was enough to imagine that the God of Israel had long thought about the coming of Jesus and regarded the Jesus associations as belonging to his people, Israel.

But both Mark and Paul thought it necessary to make sure God's hand was there on the launching of the new kingdom of God people. Both did this, in slightly different ways, by imagining that Jesus died as a martyr for the cause of the kingdom, and that God had raised him from the dead and taken him up to be with his Father in heaven. If God could be imagined to have done that, the social logic of a martyrdom could be applied to Jesus and his followers. For these intellectuals to imagine that required them to make some odd combinations of mythic ideas and extravagant leaps of narrative logic. The problem with thinking of Jesus as a martyr was that you had to imagine the Romans killing him because they thought his teachings were seditious. That was quite a stretch. There is no indication in any of the collections of Jesus' teachings that his followers knew he had been killed by the Romans or that his teachings had to be kept under wraps because they were politically dangerous. And the problem with thinking that God raised him from the dead was even more audacious. In the first place, the very thought of a dead person coming back to life in any form whatsoever was disgusting and fearful to all peoples of the Greco-Roman world. In the second place, the imagination of the "resurrection of the dead" (in the plural) belonged only to scenarios of the final judgments at the end of time in apocalyptic writings. It was hardly imaginable as an event in the recent past experienced by a single person. Nevertheless, extravagant claims were called for because the stakes were high. The concept of the martyr was common in Greek traditions to honor warriors and teachers (e.g., Socrates) who "died for" their countries and teachings. The historians of the Maccabees, a Jewish priestly family who rebelled against the Seleucid king Antiochus IV in the second century B.C., portrayed them as martyrs for the "traditions of the fathers" and imagined some kind of postmortem vindication for them. If Jesus could be imagined to have died for his teachings about the kingdom of God, and if God could be imagined to have vindicated him by means of some dramatic intervention of which only God was capable, that would do. Jesus' teachings about the kingdom of God would count as the cause "for which" he died, Jesus himself could be recognized as the hero who died for the kingdom, and the Christians' notion of the kingdom of God would be justified (Mack, *Myth of Innocence*, 102–13, 315–24; *Christian Myth*, 109–14; "Rereading the Christ Myth"). By another stretch of the mythic narrative, Jesus could be imagined as king of the kingdom, Lord of the world, ruling the world from his throne in heaven above. So that took care of the God of Israel, the God of the kingdom, the teacher of the kingdom, and the Christians as the people of God and kingdom people at the same time. But what, then, of the older concept of the kingdom as a universal domain such as would be appropriate for a sovereign god? This created some problems. You couldn't claim that the formation of the Christian congregations was all there was to it. Not if God was God, the concept of the kingdom was universal, and the kingdom itself was announced as an alternative to the kingdoms of the world. If it was supposed to be actualized within the real world, not only as a popular philosophy and ethic for individuals, but as a kingdom society among the kingdoms of the world, surely the Christian congregations were not enough. What to think and do?

Two major mythmaking moves were obviously intended to answer these queries. One was to postpone the "appearance" of the kingdom of God to the end of history, a sequel to an apocalyptic judgment planned for all peoples. The other was that, in the meantime, Jesus was imagined as a royal figure, ruling the kingdom from heaven above. Thus the kingdom people in the congregations below could now think of their king reigning above, and imagine a time in the future when "every knee would bow" to his sovereignty (Philippians 2:10). This did amount to a kind of partition of the kingdom of God, located now in different places with different functions until the time in the future when everything would finally be united in a kingdom over which God himself would rule.

I can now suggest that this mythmaking project, though understandable in some ways as a solution for the intellectual problems confronting the early associations of Jesus people who wanted a legitimate place in the *oikoumene*, had consequences of unimaginable magnitude for their subsequent histories. It was an extremely narrow lens through which the entire world, including the natural, cosmic, social, and historical orders, would be viewed. Nowhere is the natural order acknowledged as a significant environment for human existence. Nowhere is the normal, everyday order of social enterprise and production in the picture. And in the heaven above, though it is suggestive of the cosmic world of ancient Near Eastern and Hellenistic conceptions from which the Christian notion of the heavenly Lord was taken, one sees a single sovereign seated in the center to whom the astronomical and cosmic rulers of the world (*archons*), so taken for granted by the Greco-Roman world, have been subjected (1 Corinthians 15:25–27). This conception of a cosmic sovereign is very strange. By the third and fourth centuries Christians were making the claim that "We are exalted above Fate, and in the place of the planetary daimons we know but one ruler of the cosmos" (Tatian, *Oratio* IX, cited in J. Z. Smith, *Map*, 165), and by the time of the medieval view of the heavens, to be sketched in Chapter 6, a single sovereign reigns above with no suggestion of the "planetary daimons" at all.

And so, recalling our theory of social interests becoming noticeable and generating myths and rituals at the intersections of environments, we have to say, in this case, that the intersection was a two-pronged impingement upon the early Jesus associations, neither prong of which revealed constructive interest in the natural environment or the social world of the *oikoumene*. One prong was the mythic concept of the kingdom of God that substituted for the natural, cosmic, and large-scale social environments; the other was the intersection of the Jesus associations rubbing against other social configurations thought to be in competition for recognition in the social orders. That created identity issues. In neither case was the impingement one of the normal circumstances of interest to the human endeavor of social construction. Thus the social interests generating this mythology were focused solely on imagining the Christian congregations as the only people in the whole world with claim upon the only kingdom of ultimate destiny under the rule of the only sovereign in the universe.

Were these congregations to become Christian churches, and were the Christian churches to become the only legitimate religion of the Roman Empire, one might want to ask about the fate of all other peoples, their religions, their gods, and their cultures, as well as about the natural world, the natural sciences, the Ptolemaic cosmology, the classical traditions, philosophic enquiry, political theory, and matters of money and trade. It would depend upon whether the Christian myth system and worldview could ease up, broaden out, and make room in the picture for orders of reality other than the Church. We know, of course, that that did not happen except in the case of the later arrangement with the Roman Empire. So, from this early juncture of social formation and mythmaking in the late first century to the microcosmic environment of the medieval cathedral, we need to ask how the myth worked in the real world.

Social Formations

In our study of peoples and their mentalities we have been looking at worldviews, mythic systems, social structures, and ritual practices that describe an accepted environment for a people. These features of a culture were no longer in place as a comprehensive system for any people during the Greco-Roman age. As discussed in Chapter 3, bits and pieces of cultural traditions were cultivated under the Romans in various homelands, and some were transferred to other places in the *oikoumene* as attempts to display and keep in touch with one's former cultural identity. All of the obvious manifestations of Hellenistic cultivations of myths, rituals, festivals, and temple practices had older, pre-Hellenistic roots in distinct cultures. The followers of Jesus did not. They had no single country of extraction from which to transport emblems of cultural identity. Because of the importance of the emerging "biographies" of Jesus, such as the Gospel of Mark, Galilee could be thought of as the place where Jesus had lived and from which "disciples" went forth as "apostles," and Jerusalem, now in ruins, could be remembered as the city where he had died. But the only emblems with potential cultural sensibilities that the Jesus schools took from Galilee as they spread throughout the *oikoumene* were Jesus' teachings and some conceptual attempts to link Jesus and his teaching with the history of Israel. They apparently elaborated Jesus' teaching about the kingdom of God as a legacy from the history of Israel, and they did seem to continue a high regard for ethical values similar to those that were characteristic for the Jews. But these features of an emerging mentality were more sensibilities than the result of their own mythic system and social structuration. This meant that the challenge of identity in relation to other peoples, cults, associations, and the Romans could not be answered in ways that peoples of other traditional cultures were able to employ. Christians had no homeland; their people were not of a single ethnic extraction or cultural tradition; and their myth of heritage from the history of Israel was soon in trouble because of their differences from the synagogues.

What they did have were loose networks of groups of Jesus people meeting together in various countries. Some, it appears, had become associations, a kind of club with membership rules and officers typical of the Greco-Roman world. Many of these were under the supervision of "bishops" (the "shepherds") and "teaching elders." In the welfare vacuum created by the Romans, who installed only troops and tax collectors ("procurators") in their provinces of occupation, the shepherds had begun to take on the role of looking after the "widows and orphans" according to ancient Jewish ethics.

This meant that some associations were providing a quasi-social and legal service, thus a social formation worth thinking about in relation to the Roman world. They also had traveling teachers who brought news of other groups, their ideas, and practices. It does not appear that Christians had buildings during the first and second centuries; but they did meet together, mostly in the homes of patrons. Some shared a Jewish disparagement of idols and other gods which they called demons. Thus, many apparently eschewed the public festivals, feasts, and sacrifices of others around them, and that of course was part of the reason that the rest of the world saw them as a problem. They met in "secret" and were thought not to be participants in other social and religious activities, even though such activities were open to all and participation was a sign of piety and social trustworthiness. It appears that some of the Jesus associations did take meals together as any association would, but their meetings must have followed the pattern of symposia, reading one's poems, discussing their ideas about the kingdom, as well as talking about social issues of the times. One can imagine the discussions that must have followed. They were still a kind of school, making their livings in the normal ways within the province of Roman governance. Some did form enclaves in attempts to retire from the world and cultivate citizenship in the world of wisdom, but most continued to live in the everyday Roman world while, at the same time, imagining themselves as kingdom of God people. This meant that living in the world and belonging to a Christian congregation challenged more normal ways of defining oneself in terms of social and cultural identities. It was not simply a matter of living in two or several worlds at the same time. That is something many subordinate peoples have been able to manage. The problem was that neither the Roman *oikoumene* nor the Christians' kingdom was by itself a complete, comprehensive social-mythic environment, and together they were hardly compatible for the long run. The Christians were apparently fascinated with the notion of a single God and his universal kingdom, but they were still a subcultural social formation in a very large, lively, and pluralistic world. It was not at all clear how their kingdom was to be represented in the real world and how it might relate to the Roman world. Thus there was work to do in self-identification, marking their distinguishing characteristics in contrast to other cults and cultures, and building a working relationship with the Romans. Work to do, that is, as long as their curious interest in their fictive Christian family, soon constituted of many ethnic and cultural extractions, included the thought of themselves as kingdom people with God as their sovereign.

By the early second century there were associations of Jesus people who had attracted the attention of others. Some had called them "Christians," which may have been intended as a slightly derisive label, but since they had not come up with any other name for themselves as "Jesus school people," they apparently accepted the designation with pride. The Romans first thought of them as *collegia* associated with or similar to Jewish synagogues. The Jews had worked out arrangements with the Romans to practice their ancestral traditions away from home, and so the Romans were not worried about Jewish synagogues. They were, however, worried about other associations and collegiae that might foment unrest or even harbor movements that could be considered dangerous or seditious. Since the Christians were now separating themselves from Jewish views and synagogues, and since they were meeting together as "Christians," a name referring to their founder-teacher as a curious kind of "king," the Romans were understandably confused. Were these Christians loyal or seditious? What may have been a few unfortunate incidents of failing to satisfy Roman officials of their loyalty, such as refusing to perform the customary ritual gesture of an offering in honor of the emperor, resulted in some executions. Christians regarded those so killed as martyrs ("confessors"), and a genre of literature began to appear that scholars have called "martyrologies." So, needing to give an account of themselves to others, and having produced some martyrs, Christians found themselves seriously challenged about their place and purpose in the larger world of the empire. It was a challenge that took the next two centuries to resolve.

The Gospel and the Cosmos

Responding to this challenge took the form of vociferous polemical battles among leading bishops and intellectuals. The bishops were busy turning their Christian associations into assemblies (*ekklesiai*, "churches"), with regular patterns of practices, treasuries to care for the poor, and "elders" to oversee the churches in a district. The leading bishops were located in major urban centers such as Alexandria, Jerusalem, Antioch, and Rome. Intellectuals were drawn to these centers of learning and administration in order to write, lecture, and do battle with one another. As might be expected, these and other centers developed their theologies and practices in distinctly different ways. The question for some was how to adjudicate differences. There was no overarching mechanism for the discussion of Christian self-definition, much less for solving issues of authority. When reading the "fathers" of this period, one sees a marshalling of energies and seriousness that is astounding. The polemical tirades against one another were often ranting, sometimes vicious, but always ad hoc, that is, without argumentation from agreed-upon premises. Yet, they were all engaged in what appears to have been a delicious confrontation with one another, and the vociferous debates and argumentations seem to have been a kind of serious game. There was no supervision, creedal authority, tradition, or clearly marked goal to keep them in line. Nor were there any directions for playing the game. The game board was vast and open, the sky was the limit, and the project was entirely experimental.

Before having a look at three important players in this intellectual gaming at the middle of the second century, it will be helpful to note some features of the game board that called for the plays. One was the scope of the board, which by now included all of the imaginable cosmos and history. This was a result of many attempts on the part of different thinkers to find anchorage somewhere in the past, in the cosmos, or in the philosophical traditions of the time in order to claim their place in the larger world and say who they were. Another was that, on the immediate plane of history, problems with the Romans and those now being called "pagans" made the playing field quite rough. A third was that the board had not been marked for play. There was no contour to the scope of cosmos and history to mark the dangers and victories for any move. Since the object had something to do with locating and arriving at the kingdom of God, the lack of a model for the object was most embarrassing. Neither the polis nor the temple-state could provide a template for marking the board, now that the Romans had swallowed them both up in its empire. There was something about the expanse of the empire under a single monarch, and the fact that since Caesar Augustus an age of peace, prosperity, and civil order had come into being that was appealing. But, of course, the Romans were the problem, weren't they? For the Christian associations to try to deal with the Romans when they were a loose collection of networks under the supervision of bishops who were competing with one another for intellectual and political leadership was hardly thinkable as the first move. You had first to know who you were before you could play ball with the Romans.

There were, to be sure, some features of the cosmic-historical landscape from which to start sketching a framework for the people of the kingdom to imagine the world as the place in which they lived, if not their permanent home. Such a framework could not possibly be a clear sketch of the kingdom itself, for the notion of the kingdom had not yet been adequately conceptualized, much less described and located in relation to the social and natural environments of the Roman world. There were only some markers around which to start a sketch. The most important was the gospel story of Jesus, now taken literally as an account of God sending his son to inaugurate the Christian time. The second was the notion of his disciples, whom Luke had cast as "apostles" in his imaginative fiction of the birth of the first Christian congregation soon after Jesus' departure. To think of Jesus' disciples as apostles was an understandable mechanism by which the significance of the appearance of Jesus could have become known to others. A third feature of the Christian landscape was the God whose sovereignty they thought to represent. It was, however, not at all clear what this God was like, given the links that now had to be considered: to the history of Israel, the synagogues, Jesus, the new notion of the kingdom, the gentiles, the Romans, and the final judgment. Besides, where in heaven might God be, now that the old three-decker universe was being reimagined by some on the Ptolemaic model? The main thing, of course, was that he was the only real God, meaning that all of the others were *daimons* (soon to become demons), mere figments of pagan superstition. That did simplify matters.

It is worth a pause at this point to notice how very different and audacious this mythology was. No other people had dared such a thought or claim. All others had come to terms with the multicultural mix and its many gods. The usual solution, supposing one wanted to emphasize the superiority of one's own god above the others, was to rank one's god above the others, as in the Isis aretalogies, or as in the case of the Jews, to leave the other gods and peoples to their own devices while insisting on a monotheistic arrangement for one's own people and culture. The early Christian view was no doubt the result of a combination of Jewish monotheistic thinking and a Greek conception of a universal cosmology in the interest of the expanding scope of the Christians' worldview. This does not, however, account for the strict division between the one true god and all the others, or for the harsh consignment of all the others to the realm of the demonic. The reasons for these moves have to be found in the necessity to claim legitimacy as a people without traditional arguments to sustain such claims.

The first move made by the bishops did not advance the project of working toward a kingdom plan, but it did put them on the board. This was the scramble for authorization of their own teachings by claiming their possession of a tradition of the teachings of Jesus from a given apostle. The notions of "disciples" and "apostles" were images from the last half of the first century that developed quite naturally as attempts to forge links from the time of Jesus to teachers who found themselves in need of authorization. What happened in the second century, however, was that different schools of thought began to claim descent from different disciples in attempts to outmaneuver other schools and their teachers. In retrospect one wonders how conflicts over teachings, many of which were understood as the basis for particular ways of being Christian, could possibly be adjudicated by such an invention. Yet, reading the ways in which various disciples came to be cast, one sees that the invention unleashed an amazing amount of energy on the analysis of the gospels' pictures of the first disciples. The questions had to do with how closely a particular disciple was related to Jesus, what it was that made the teaching of a disciple special, and how it was possible for a bishop to have authorization by means of the teachings of an apostle, instead of from the life and teachings of Jesus. These were not easy questions to answer. But imagining the disciples of the gospel story taking the role of apostles after the birthday of the church as storied in the Acts of the Apostles turned out to be a control of sorts for keeping the bishops talking to one another, and it set up an investigation of the gospel as a charter for Christian congregations. Thus a bit of innocent, if polemically motivated, appeal to the disciples as apostles for authorization actually launched these Christian bishops and teachers on a very large-scale project of finding a place for Christian congregations in the history of the Roman world (Mack, *Who Wrote?*, 225–50).

The gospel story had been written in desperation by Mark and his fellow intellectuals in the interest of a Jesus school or association during and after the Roman-Jewish war. Jerusalem and the temple were exactly where the entire history of Israel was supposed to end in glorious fulfillment of God's grand project to set a city on a hill as a light to the nations. The Jesus school to which Mark belonged had been debating with the Pharisees about purity rules. That means that Mark and his school must have thought of themselves as legitimate citizens of a kingdom of God in relation to the history of Israel and the model of the Jerusalem temple-state, treating the teachings of Jesus as an application of the kingdom's social ethic. When the Romans sacked Jerusalem, Mark's group, as well as many others, was confronted with a major problem of identity. Mark's gospel was his attempt to save the day for the Jesus people and their concept of the kingdom of God. He did this by agreeing to the standard rationalization, namely, that God was implicated in the destruction of the Jerusalem temple. Many thought it a punishment for having illegitimate high priests acting as kings (the Hasmoneans). But then Mark added a second reason, namely, that the temple authorities had instigated the crucifixion of Jesus. "Look," he said. "God vindicated Jesus when they killed him. And that means that the kingdom Jesus talked about is exactly what God had and still has in mind, even though its glorious appearance will now have to wait for another intervention of God in the future." So the gospel of Mark has to be seen as mythmaking in the interest of Mark's Jesus school. As a myth, moreover, its social logic determined a strange relationship to the world for the Jesus school now existing in a time circumscribed by two extraordinary events of divine intervention in human time, and the logic of its plot, including the reasons for Jesus' appearance, death, and resurrection, is fraught with contradictions. It was, however, read by others as a coherent account, perhaps enchanting as a narrative, and remarkable for the way in which it offered the imagination a very large range of incidents to consider while thinking about the importance of Jesus in history. It was this myth, embellished somewhat by other gospel writers, that every Christian thinker of the second and third centuries had in mind when working on the problem of the logic of Christianity as an intellectually credible philosophy or theology. No wonder they were having trouble. The gospel story had replaced the earlier orientation to collections of the teachings of Jesus and became the standard account of the origins of many of the Christian movements. It was taken as history, and the task was to account for everything in the world by means of its analysis.

One can read the entire production of literature during this pre-Constantine period as contentions about the gospel story—attempts to use it as an event from which to imagine the structure of the cosmos, the purpose of history, a universal anthropology, and how Christians should see themselves in the midst of the Roman world. It was their myth, though they preferred to call it their *logos* and thought of it as actually having happened. As with any enchanting story, found to be provocative and inviting discussion, the gospel actually functioned as the text that kept the church fathers talking to one another. They argued with one another about the gospel, how Jesus could be God's son, what to make of the resurrection, and especially about the way the story inaugurated the time of the church. Thus, the Christian movement provided a marvelous, if messy, arena in the very middle of the Roman *oikoumene* for uprooted intellectuals with philosophic interests to take on the world and find a hearing.

Comprehensive Mythmaking

Around 150 A.D. three major players in the mythmaking enterprise of pre-Constantine Christianity converged on Rome as the logical place for their philosophical theologies to be heard: Marcion of Sinope in Pontus (in northern Asia Minor), Valentinus of Alexandria, and Justin of Samaria. Slightly later, several more joined the fray with voluminous literary output to argue for other conceptions of the new religion: Irenaeus, born in Asia Minor and writing from Lyons, but with thoroughly Roman loyalties; Clement of Alexandria, originally from Athens, who laid the foundation for Christian philosophy as head of a catechetical school in Egypt; and Tertullian of Carthage in North Africa, who defended the gospel against everything Greek, Jewish, pagan, Gnostic, and immoral. The apostolic myth would survive, but only as part of a much larger, more complex, attempt at understanding history and the world than the earlier bishops could have imagined. It is clear that the Christ associations were now fully aware of the need to give a rational account of Christianity in terms of Greek philosophy, but in distinction from Greek religions, other cultural traditions, and especially the Jewish synagogues. The entire Roman world was in view as the battles among these intellectuals were waged.

Marcion's view was that Christianity was a completely new religion, whose God had not been known until Jesus appeared. The only apostle that got it right was Paul, and the only gospel that told the story correctly was Luke's. As for the others, they made the mistake of thinking that the God revealed by Jesus was the god of the Jews. "Look," Marcion said, in effect, "the god of the history of Israel was not the god of all people. He was the god of an exclusive people, a jealous god, vindictive, and interested only in judgment. The Jewish god, creator of this hostile world, was not worthy of worship. The God revealed in Jesus Christ, on the other hand, is the universal God of the entire human race, loving, and interested in the spiritual well-being and salvation of all people. The proof of his presence in the world is the outpouring of his Spirit as recorded by Luke and emphasized by Paul, the divine Spirit now available to any and all who want to live a clean, moral, upright, and righteous life." That was enough to make other Christian thinkers nervous, and they soon began writing treatises against his views. But the startling features of Marcion's preachments did not stop there. He actually constructed the first New Testament canon (a selection of "standard" or "authoritative" texts) by including only ten excised letters of Paul and an abbreviated version of Luke's gospel. What he left out in both cases were portions of text thought to have been inserted by other apostles partial to the Jews. Marcion had a significant following, building congregations throughout Asia Minor which became, in effect, a social formation of early Christianity that was to last several hundred years.

Consternation reigned among other intellectuals, for there were no ready answers to the questions Marcion had raised. To make matters worse, Valentinus appeared in Rome about this time from Alexandria, the center of books and learning, where a Gnostic form of Christianity had emerged. Gnostics were attracted to the Platonic distinction between the physical world perceived by the senses and the noetic or ideal world of transcendence known by the mind. Plato's myth of the creation of the world in *Timaeus* was also found to be intriguing. In this myth the plan for the world in the mind of god was used by a second god, or demiurge (craftsman), as an archetypal pattern to create the physical world as its copy. Christian Gnostics used this myth to interpret the Genesis story of creation. Since, however, they had come to the conclusion that the physical world was a hostile environment in which to live, the demiurge had obviously not done a good job, and the creator in the Genesis story could hardly be the highest God. With a little help from the Greek philosophical cliché of "the body is the tomb," drawing upon traditional distinctions between "flesh" and "spirit," it seemed to them that the creation of the physical world entombed them, causing them to forget their true origins in the world of spirit and light. The emerging cosmology of Hipparchus and Ptolemy may also have been at work. As mentioned earlier, this cosmology of concentric spheres through which the planets moved in their rotations around the earth challenged the earlier pictures of the hierarchy of divine sovereignty typical of the three-decker universe in ancient Near Eastern mythologies. In the ancient Near East, as well as in Greece, the pre-Ptolemaic cosmology allowed for occasional traffic on the part of the gods from their heavenly stations to earth. The three-decker universe also allowed special humans, namely, kings, sons of a god, and heroes, to be given a postmortem destiny among the stars; for the rest of mortal kind the destiny was still chthonic, or as the Greeks said, in Hades below. The Gnostics, however, were able to imagine the supreme God very far above the created universe, outside of it in fact. This did make contact much more difficult to imagine, especially since the seven spheres encircling the earth (Moon, Mercury, Venus, Sun, Mars, Jupiter, and Saturn) were part of the physical creation and under the control of quasi-divine forces with no interest in letting humans discover their natural birthright from above. But now there was Jesus, the son of God who came down to earth from the realm of light to awaken humans to their true origin, and to reveal the destiny of those who become enlightened as a making of one's way through the heavenly spheres to the world of true being above.

Valentinus said that Christ had made it possible, not only to know *about* God, but to know him by "acquaintance," as Bentley Layton translates *gnosis* (*The Gnostic Scriptures*). And this acquaintance was intimate. Christians were to understand that they were disoriented in this world, chafing under the cosmic "rulers of this world," because they were the lost children of God far from home. They had, moreover, always been God's children, though they had forgotten it because the forces of fate had blinded them to the "spark" of divine life within them. They belonged to a strain of the human race whose genealogy stretched back to the foundation of the world when humans were first created. They had come from the true God and their destiny was to return home to God, their divine parent, the original source of life and light, the place of eternal belonging. Valentinus agreed with the Gnostics that the world had been created by Error, a personified quasi-divine being at the lower levels of a series of divine emanations called *aeons*, powerful concentrations of time and space that finally spiraled down and away from contact with the divine source. This meant that the appearance of Jesus as the son of God and revealer of the divine realm was the only source of wisdom and *gnosis* in the world, a divine manifestation in the midst of a world born of tragedy and error.

Justin Martyr was born near Shechem, called himself a Samaritan, but was apparently from a well-to-do family of Roman citizens. He was schooled in the Greek tradition, spending some time with each of the major schools of philosophy before converting to Christianity. He traveled to Ephesus and then to Rome as a Christian itinerant philosopher, and he never gave up the philosopher's cloak. In Rome he ran into Marcion and the teachings of Valentinus and found himself engaged in writing *Apologies*, rational accounts of what he understood to be the system of Christian thought to which he had been converted. This system assumed that the Christian God was the creator of the world and the father of Israel, whose sending of his son Jesus Christ had always been intended as the way to expand the boundaries of the people of Israel to include the entire human world. Thus the Christian way of life was exactly what God had had in mind for all humankind all along. Marcion's rejection of the God and history of Israel and Valentinus' theory of a world created in error and tragedy were startling challenges to Justin's assumptions. The problem was that Marcion had exposed the naiveté of thinking that the transition from the God of Israel to the God of the Christians could simply be assumed. The gospel accounts could not explain this "change of mind" on God's part. Valentinus had forced the questions of (1) how the new race of Christians could be understood in terms of Greek anthropologies that did not include the notions of predetermined destiny and divine origin, and (2) how the God of the gospels could be located and made to fit into a scientific and philosophic view of the cosmos. Neither thinker had found much help in the Hebrew scriptures and the Genesis story of creation.

Justin went to work and found himself preoccupied with the gospel texts and the Hebrew writings. He found all the places in the Hebrew scriptures where it appeared that Jesus had been predicted by the prophets or mysteriously anticipated in hidden allegories where God was found talking to the Israelites. In order to comprehend how the prophets could have known why God's spirit used allegory, and why the Israelites did not get the message, Justin turned to the Hellenistic concept of the *logos*, a term that meant thought, reason, logic, and speech. The *logos* had been used in philosophical circles as an abstraction to conceptualize the rational order of the cosmos, and it had sometimes been personalized as a quasi-divine agent in the creation of the world and to signify important events of history. The *logos* was a common concept in both Stoic and Hellenistic–Jewish literature of the time, and Justin had no trouble identifying its presence in the Hebrew scriptures, especially when read in Greek translation (the Septuagint). He traced its agency from the creation of the world, throughout the history of Israel, and into its incarnation in the person of Jesus Christ. Hence, in order to answer Marcion, Justin said that the Christian God was not "new," and that the God of Israel did not change his mind. His plan, mind, and message had been the same throughout history. It is true that the Israelites did not get the message: that was because they were dense and intransigent. But that fact explained why the God of the Israelites appeared different from the God revealed in Jesus Christ. God did not want to give them the law and threaten them with judgments and destruction, but had to because they were so "stiff-necked" and disobedient. His *logos* was always talking to them and they turned it down. God was not the problem: the Israelites were. As for Valentinus' silly view of individual Christians needing to be saved from the rulers of the world by escaping to a realm of light far away and removed from the cosmos, what about the history of God's efforts to bring his people to a life of purity and holiness on earth? The fact that the Romans did not yet understand the Christians, while the world seemed godless with pagan temples and orgies all around, did not mean that God did not want his people to be good citizens of the world. The Christian way of life was what God had in mind all along.

Satisfied that the whole world should now recognize God's *logos*, Justin explained to the Greeks that they looked foolish for having gods who were proud, envious, licentious, and deceitful. Instead of participating in orgies and drunken festivals, they should lead virtuous lives as their philosophers taught. As for the wisdom of their philosophers, didn't they know that their philosophers got their wisdom from Moses? And now that Jesus Christ had revealed God's *logos*, they should become Christians and learn to lead the kind of virtuous life that the one supreme God demanded.

Justin also wrote an *Apology* to the Emperor Antoninus Pius and his son Marcus Aurelius, whether they ever saw it or not, to the effect that the Christians were good for the empire because they were moral, law-abiding citizens, and that the Roman government should not think of them as other pagan cults and religions. His point was that the Christians' kingdom was not of this world, and so the emperor need not worry about their disloyalty to the kingdom of this world. As a matter of fact, since Jesus Christ had been predicted from the creation of the world, and since even the destruction of Jerusalem had been prophesied, the Romans were already in the Christians' picture. Why not see how surprisingly good the Christians would be for the Roman empire?

The big picture had come into view. For those schooled in the traditions of Greek philosophy, the attempt to make sense of the gospel in relation to the cosmos, *theos* (the Greek abstraction for god or divinity-likeness), the *logos*, and *anthropos* stretched the mind and the story of Jesus to the limits, while the whole *oikoumene* was now seen as the world in which Christians must find their place. Pagans, Greeks, and Jews all became targets for polemical writings that never tired of lambasting their "orgies," "licentious gods," and "stubborn sinfulness." As for the Greek philosophers and the Romans, every treatise was written as if both were listening, eager to understand just how rational, ethical, civil, and good for the empire these Christians were. Yet, reading this literature now, it is impossible to see how it could have been found instructive outside the bounds of inner Christian discourse. The arguments were actually contrived in a desperate attempt to convince each other that the gospel made sense. After Justin came Tatian in Syria, Athenagoras of Athens, Theophilus of Antioch, Melito of Sardis, Dionysius of Corinth, Irenaeus at Lyons, Hippolytus of Rome, Tertullian of North Africa, Clement of Alexandria, Origen at Caesarea, and others who filled the pages of the next one hundred years. The apologetic and polemical genres stayed the same, as did the arguments.

There are two observations to make about this chapter of pre-Constantine intellectual activity. One is that later church historians and theologians have always been impressed by the writings of these "fathers" of the church. The reason is that they translated the gospel story and creed into comprehensive systems of thought on the model of Greek philosophies. Greek concepts were used to create theological categories to explicate the universal plan of salvation held to be implicit in the gospel. The topics included the creation of the world, the nature of God as revealed in the gospel, an anthropology of humans in need of salvation, the revelation of Christ as divine savior from sin, the concepts of the Holy Spirit and trinity, the church and the sacraments where grace and forgiveness were found, and the significance of human transformation to insure obedience, humility, and purity of heart in preparation for the final judgment. These conceptual categories became doctrine (the truths that were fundamental for "the faith") and the system was comprehensive in that all known orders of reality were subsumed and rationalized. Church historians have therefore credited these early theologians with the definition of Christianity, as a system of rational thought to be explored and subjected to exegesis by subsequent theologians from that time until the present.

A second observation is required, however, in order to characterize this activity in relation to the larger world of the Greco-Roman age and the way in which it prepared for the Constantinian revolution. This has to do with the astonishing combination of a universal system of reality with a narrowness of interest in salvation. These intellectuals were adamant about the truth of the gospel. The universal system was their way of arguing for its truth, and the employment of abstract Greek conceptuality left no room for dissent, thus creating "heresies," a term that came to be used for those who got it wrong. The narrow focus of interest on the salvation of individuals meant that all other interests as well as other ways of thinking were consigned to error and godlessness. In Chapter 3 we considered some of the many experiments in thought and practice that were bubbling up in the Roman world. All of them can be considered options for coming to terms with the multicultural world. From diaspora synagogues, associations of many kinds, and schools of philosophy; through various scientific vocations, scholarly and literary activities, and civic and business enterprises; to cults and the cultural production of theatre, festivals, and civic celebrations—the Roman age was bursting with energies and interests focused on learning to live together in a polycultural society. At the popular level the Christian option certainly had some benefits because of the social formation of congregations and their welfare practices, but at the intellectual level of theological formations, one has to notice the extreme contrast between its turn toward dogma and all other available ways of thinking. Greek philosophical traditions were deliberative; the teachings of Jesus, long since left behind by the fathers, were tactical; the school traditions of the Cynics, Sophists, and others dealing in popular philosophies taught skills in the rhetorics of contingencies; and emerging rabbinical thought was working creatively with the balancing of alternative interpretations of a given principle. The church fathers adopted the logic of the singular and buttressed it with a universal system of authorization from a single God. Mythic imagery was turned into conceptual categories. Their theological embellishment of the creed was not an allegory of the gospel. There was no gap left for constructive pondering, disagreement, or laughter. On the contrary, the tenor of this discourse became adamant, serious, and demanding of assent. A tone of imperiousness runs throughout that might be understood as an innocence created by the tension between an incredible claim and the logic of philosophical argumentation. Perhaps it was a kind of unrestrained exuberance at having found a way to negotiate a serious cross-cultural impasse. Yet, one wonders what might happen if theologians of this sort were ever given positions of power and authority in the society at large.

I have used the phrase "logic of the singular" to describe this literature and its mode of argumentation. It resulted from a tight combination of the concepts of the one God, the truth (as opposite of the false), and the absolute (as in the Greek concept of the *arche*, or first principle, from which all else is derived). In this case, the concept of the truth was understood as that revealed in the gospel. Thus, there was only one truth and one correct elaboration of the absolute principle when working out a systematic view of the world, including cosmos, *theos*, *logos*, gospel, *anthropos*, and *krisis* (judgment). It was this logic of the singular (Greek *monos*, "one," "single," "alone") that addresses the reader of this literature in declarative tenor as a demand for assent.

It may be helpful to contrast this logic with the many other logics or ways of thinking with which we are familiar, and which we often take for granted. Many other logics work with the concept of the dual, such as the pro and con as two sides of an issue; "on the one hand" and "on the other" as alternative ways of viewing an issue; or as dialectic in the finding of a synthesis between thesis and antithesis. In the fields of scientific research there are several logics of experimentation, induction, and deduction, all of which invite further investigation. In the course of our investigations of the kinds of thinking that myth and rituals normally enable, the categories of observation, attention, difference, gap, classification, the comparison of two systems of difference, translation, transformation, reproduction, application, and allegory have allowed us to see the intellectual labors involved. In the case of the dual in application to socially constructed "opposites," studies have shown that an overriding concept of similarity turns the dual into a category of reciprocal relations determined by sophisticated notions of the singular containing the dual and generating dynamic and reversible relations between "opposites" (J. Z. Smith, *To Take Place*, 39–46; Valeri, "Reciprocal Centers"). Keeping these in mind, the encounter with the early Christian logic of the singular is startling. There appears to be no room for engaging the complexity of the multicultural social world in deliberation, negotiation, compromise, or an appreciation of other ways of being in the world and thinking about it.

The Meals Ritualized

There is one other item to report from the time before Eusebius and Constantine conspired in the establishment of Christianity as a state religion, a development that created the Christian worldview and mythic system that have continued until our time. This is the question of the emergence of a Christian ritual of the meal. Scholars have raised some serious questions about the traditional assumption that all early Christians performed a meal ritual in memorial of Jesus' death. Studies of the "Lord's meal" text in 1 Corinthians 11:23–25 have found no evidence that it was intended or used as a script for ritual reenactment. It was instead an etiology for the common practice of eating meals together as a Jesus association that had come to think of his death as a martyrdom (Mack, "Rereading"). The story of the "last supper" of Jesus with his disciples in Mark 14:17–25 has traditionally been taken as the historical event to which the Pauline text referred, but Mark's last supper story belongs to a separate tradition of mythmaking. It is clearly cast as an episode constructed to present the plot against Jesus by the temple authorities, thus reflecting a post-70 A.D. fiction. A second interest for the inclusion of this story in the gospel account is to give instructions to Mark's Christian association to remember Jesus' martyrdom while waiting for the coming appearance of the kingdom of God. It cannot be used as evidence for an early practice of the Eucharist as a ritual of participation in the death of Jesus as a "saving event." The first text that documents a thanksgiving prayer at a ritual meal for a Jesus association is Didache 9. It gives thanks for the knowledge that they are a living embodiment of the "holy vine of David," or members of Israel, the people of God. There is no mention of the death and resurrection of Jesus.

During the course of the second and third centuries, however, the practice of meeting together for meals, and the apparent cultivation of the customary breaking of bread and pouring of wine as reminders of Jesus' death, now understood as a martyrdom on their behalf, encouraged bishops and Christians to think of their meals as more than memorials. They actually entertained the notion of "sacrifice" as a way of putting a vicarious construction upon the martyrdom. The common understanding of a martyrdom, influenced by the traditions of Greek warriors who died for their country and of Socrates, who died for the truth of his philosophy, was that a martyr "died for" some cause. Early Christian interpretations of Jesus' death as a martyrdom had imagined the cause to be his teachings about the kingdom of God. There is no evidence that a ritualization of the meal as a memorial of Jesus' martyrdom must have intended a reenactment of the last supper story, or even of the crucifixion itself as a sacrifice. The earliest elaborated evidence for a bishop, now called a priest, taking Jesus' place and presiding over the thanksgiving meal as a "sacrifice" is found in Cyprian, a bishop of Carthage, of the mid-third century. Nevertheless, on the way to such an institution, meditations on the symbols and the eating of them must have been working, and many must have been somewhat tortuous. The impression one has when piecing together the snippets of reference to meals and prayers of thanksgiving from the second and third centuries is that the development of Christian meal rituals took place in local congregations under the supervision of their bishops, somewhat apart from the intellectual arenas of the cosmic philosophers. It seems as if, at the popular level, it was the traditional meal taken when meeting together as an association that became the focus for concentrated thinking about Christian identity and practice. That this practice eventually became elaborated as a ritual of collective identity is understandable. It may have been the only practice available to the majority of early Christians in which they were invited to think of themselves as belonging to followers of Jesus according to the gospel story.

Before citing an example of this thinking from Irenaeus, it should be noted that scholarly efforts to determine the natural metaphoric link between bread and body have never been able to discover any such association in any of the language systems of the Greco-Roman era, and the only association between wine and blood has to be their color, an association that does not extend to drinking either of them. Thus the struggle to interpret each in relation to the other as the meal ritual came to focus on the death of Jesus, an early and innocent extravagance that, unfortunately, seems to have settled into place as traditional, sent bishops and theologians into pious spirals of metaphoric abstractions. Popular Christianity at ritual meals was a context and forum quite different from the schools of the philosopher–intellectuals we have been considering. This was a context in which what the people thought about what they were doing appears to have been debated in ways that the philosophic theologians tried to sidestep.

We should take a moment here to consider the importance of these two levels of intellectual activity. The arenas of the cosmic philosophers and theologians we have been following describe an elite level of thinkers concerned with relating the gospel to the *oikoumene* and its large-scale social administrations. The bishops involved at this level of thinking were primarily those with congregations in large urban centers, providing leadership and supervision for the several other congregations of their districts. Bishops at this level of supervision were concerned with the relation of their administration to the Romans and their administrations of the provinces. Underlying the concerns and intellectual activities of these bishops were questions of place and power within the Roman world. The vehicle used was mythmaking in relation to the *logos* and kingdom revealed in the gospel as a justification of administrative control.

The thinking related to the meal ritual was quite different. The social focus was the congregation with local bishops caring for the people. Overseeing the ritual meal as a memorial "sacrifice" apparently came to be thought of as taking the role of a "father" (of the congregation as a family) or "priest" (as the presider at a "sacrifice"). This combination of a bishop as priest and the ritual meal as memorial "sacrifice" meant that an altogether different kind of authority had to be rationalized than that required for the bishop as the administrator of a district or province. The images and emblems available for meditation and mythmaking were those of the bread and wine storied in the gospel, and these became symbols charged with significance as the "elements" that made contact possible with the gospel as an event of salvation. This level of intellectual activity was an elaboration of a common meal as a ritual in the attempt to overcome the gap or distance we have been noting between common everyday practice and its ritualization. The result was a ritual of thanksgiving (Eucharist) for the salvation revealed in the gospel in which the people could now participate. With the elements taking on such significance, one can understand that the "proper" way to celebrate the Eucharist became an issue for debate. An excellent example of a leading bishop trying to keep up with the top-level forum of myth interpretation, while being concerned most of all with the interpretation and practice of the meal ritual, can now be given.

The citation I have in mind is from Irenaeus, bishop of Lyons during the last two decades of the second century. There had been a furious conflict over ways in which the meal ritual was being interpreted in relation to the myths of Jesus' martyrdom. Bishops such as Irenaeus thought of themselves as guardians of the true tradition having to fight all of the "heresies" that had been springing up. The Docetists, a strong dissident movement in North Africa, would not agree to the idea that Jesus was a combination of divinity and human nature. They did not reject the idea of Jesus as the son of God; without that there could be no revelation of the transcendent realm and how to think of it as one's true home and destiny. But they found it impossible to think of the divine revealer becoming a man of flesh and blood. Instead, they worked out several ways to think of Jesus as a spiritual being who only "appeared" in human form. Thus they refused to give thanks at a memorial meal when told they were eating the body and drinking the blood of the Christ. This was serious business, and Irenaeus introduces the following definition of the Eucharist by rather lengthy tirades against both Docetists and Jews, who, since they deny the reality of Jesus as the Christ, have no right to give thanks to God for anything:

> Inasmuch therefore as the Church offers [the Eucharist] in simplicity of heart, her gift is rightly considered a pure sacrifice with God...For we are bound to make our oblation to God and in all things to be found grateful to God the creator, with a pure mind and faith without hypocrisy...And this oblation the Church alone offers pure to the creator, presenting to him with thanksgiving from his creation. The Jews offer it not for their hands are full of blood: for they did not receive the Word through which [thanksgiving] is offered to God. Nor do any of the synagogues [churches] of the heretics. For some of them say that there is another Father besides the creator, and so, in offering to him, they show him to be desirous and covetous of another's goods...How again do they say that the flesh which is nourished by the body and blood of the Lord passes into corruption and attains not unto life? Either, then, let them change their opinion or let them abstain from offering the aforesaid things [bread and wine]. But our belief is in accord with the Eucharist, while the Eucharist confirms our opinion. For we offer to him the things that are his, proclaiming harmoniously the unity of flesh and spirit. For as the bread of the earth, receiving the invocation of God, is no longer common bread but Eucharist, consisting of two things, an earthly and a heavenly; so also our bodies, partaking of the Eucharist, are no longer corruptible, having the hope of eternal resurrection. (*Adv. Haer.* IV, xviii, 4–6; in Bettensen, *Documents of the Christian Church*, 104–5)

One can see that the attempts to think critically about the Eucharist as the way to define Christianity were compromised irreparably by (1) taking the gospel literally as history, (2) wanting to be simple, practical, and definite as a shepherd of the flock, (3) engaging in haphazard theological debates about God and his son with school traditions marked by comprehensive systems, (4) trying one's hand at using Greek philosophical categories to explain mythic equations and conundrums, and (5) in general searching for ways to put individuals in contact with a meaningful world other than the one in which they were living. As one reads the treatises of the next one hundred years (third century), the embarrassment of this kind of fuzzy, polemical thinking does not recede. These theologians were thrashing about in vigorous position-taking with regard to systems of thought with cosmic scope, working with structures of social formation and interests not fully understood, and driven by the desire to transcend their social experimentation. It is difficult to imagine a religion supported by its own worldview, canopy, mythic grammar, culture, and mentality ever coming into existence. It may be that we shall have to think of the arrangements made between Constantine and Eusebius as the accidental origin of Christianity as a universal establishment. Is it possible that a Roman emperor was the one who created Christianity as a state religion?

Establishment

Constantine was born in Naussus (Nis in modern Serbia) to an aristocratic Roman family of the military governing class. Naussus was an important center of Roman provincial administration on the main road from the Roman province of Pannonia at the head of the Adriatic Sea, through Singidunum (modern Belgrade), to Byzantium, and during his youth Constantine was introduced to Roman military courts and their system of administration in an eastern province of Asia Minor. In the course of his career as a military leader, then general, and in battles fought against other Roman generals and contenders for the position of emperor, he apparently came to look upon Jesus Christ as his patron deity, just as others fought under the patronage of Apollo, Dionysos or some other god. At the decisive battle of the Milvian bridge (312 A.D.) he is said to have put the name or monogram of Christ on the shields of his troops. This raises the questions of whether or not, when and how, Constantine came to be a Christian, and what he thought about Christianity. There are no records of his "conversion," though there are two reports of the military victory at the Milvian bridge under the banner of Christ. The one just mentioned is from Lactantius, who wrote that Constantine was told in a dream to put the sign on his shields. The other is from Eusebius, his biographer, who relates that Constantine was given a "sign" of the Christ in the sky, saying, "In this sign, conquer." Both are answers to our question in the genres of omen and oracle. Constantine "saw," and made sure his opponents "saw," that Christianity and the Roman empire were good for each other. This does not satisfy the questions Christians have had about Constantine's conversion, thinking automatically of such in terms of a personal religious experience or philosophical change of mind, but it does show that the ancient genres of revelation and prophecy were all Christians had to account for the remarkable changes in religious and political structures introduced by Constantine. Both writers recognize that it was a military victory and power in the hands of a Christian emperor that made the changes possible.

One year later the famous Edict of Milan (313 A.D.) was released, granting Christians throughout the empire freedom from prosecution as well as personal and civic privileges. The Edict of Milan was Constantine's response to the recent persecutions of Christians under Diocletian (303–11 A.D.). The problem had been that the Roman Empire was experiencing decline from invasions and rebellions, and Rome had become the site of political, religious, and ideological confusion. With their roots in the older traditional Roman religion, tolerance for religions from the Eastern provinces had worn thin among the aristocratic Roman families and senators. Apparently the penetration of Christians into the higher echelons of civic service and the army had become enough of a threat for Diocletian to order sanctions against the religion. It was Diocletian who had reorganized and strengthened provincial control under military authority. Even though his edicts promised not to spill blood, confrontations of the military administrations with Christians throughout the provinces got out of hand, producing anger and martyrs. On becoming emperor, Constantine put a stop to the prosecutions and began to issue a series of edicts and laws that restored the property of Christians taken during the Diocletian persecution. He also granted special civic privileges and financial support to bishops and their urban programs. There are letters from Constantine to both bishops and provincial administrators to the effect that Christians should be supported because they were of benefit to the empire. Apparently Constantine had taken note of the networks of bishops and their flocks of Christian devotees who might provide some stability to the administration of the empire. But he did not leave the shaping of the new religion of state up to the bishops. How could he? They had not achieved agreements among themselves on any matter of myth, ritual, cosmology, history, or how to live with the Romans and other peoples in the empire. Constantine took charge in a series of moves. His first move was the construction of basilicas for the Christians that would eventually replace the temples of the older systems of religion. This was followed by such things as convening councils of bishops, demanding that they agree on a creed, instigating the formation of a canon of scriptures, deciding on a date for the annual festival of Easter and thus inaugurating the Christian calendar, creating civic posts for bishops, and supplying funds for dioceses and bishoprics on the model of state-supported religious institutions. In the course of two decades, Constantine succeeded in bringing centralization and structure to a new state religion. And even though the images of sovereignty, king, kingdom, obedience, governance, and judgment were not unfamiliar to Christians, nothing in the first three hundred years of fussing with these concepts could have prepared them for the changes introduced by Constantine. They were now to take their place as the religion of a kingdom in and of this world.

Building Christian basilicas was more than a sign that some great change was taking place. As Smith has shown (*To Take Place*, 74–95), it was the change itself that would restructure both the networks of Christian churches and the Roman Empire. In Rome, Constantine deeded imperial property to the bishop for the construction of the Basilica Constantiniana (now San

Giovanni of the Lateran); in Constantinople, newly named after him and called the "new Rome," he supervised the building of the Basilica of the Apostles; and in at least a dozen other urban centers throughout the provinces he encouraged and supported the construction of Christian basilicas, at Trier, Aquileia, Cirta in Numidia, Nicomedia, Antioch, Gaza, and Alexandria. The basilica was an imperial civic structure and could be monumental. Provided with a dome above the transept of a central aisle (nave), a Romano-Byzantine architectural style came into being for the new state religion. Plain on the outside, the Christian basilicas were soon ornate inside, with mosaics depicting biblical themes in the apse and in the dome showing the heavens where Jesus was enthroned. A chair for the bishop in the apse announced the new position of ecclesial power; Constantine now referred to the clergy as "priests"; and the meetings of Christians, until now in private houses unobserved by non-Christians, were suddenly a matter of public display.

It was in Jerusalem, however, that the construction of basilicas introduced a profound and lasting twist to the emerging practices and mentality of Christianity. There the rationale was not simply to provide a meeting place for public Christian ritual, add a Christian monument to the other "historic" temples and buildings as in Rome, or to mark the center of a newly planned city with a Christian basilica as in Constantinople, but to seek out the "proper" sites for the memorials and celebrations of the major events in the gospel story. It may have been Constantine's mother, Helena, who came up with this idea. In any case, basilicas were soon built at Bethlehem (the "Nativity"), the Mount of Olives, the "Holy Sepulchre" (*Anastasis*), and at Mamre, where according to Christian interpretation Jesus as the Son of God or *logos* appeared to Abraham. There is no indication that Christians had marked these places for special veneration. Constantine's request of Makarius, the bishop at Jerusalem, was to "seek out the sites" for the basilicas. Thus, it was clearly an imperial interest, with Constantine in the ancient role of the king with responsibility for the construction of temples, that claimed the land of the Bible and the gospel for Christian occupation.

One can only wonder how this was possible. Christians had been the illegitimate children of the Greco-Roman mix of cultures. They had been looked upon as anti-social for not participating in public festivals. Their claim to be a new religion of recent revelation was odd in the mix of Greco-Roman cultures, all of which harked back to antiquity for their wisdom and origin. Their account of the resurrection was incredible, their cosmologies weird, and their strident polemics in philosophical and theological battles with one another struck a much harsher tone than traditional school debates among Greek philosophers. As we have seen, Christians did not yet agree upon a coherent Christ myth, much less a common worldview, myth system, social structure, ritual practice, or mentality. At the time of Constantine, for instance, the Donatists in North Africa were refusing to accept the ordination of bishops accused of compromising with the Romans; and Arius in Alexandria had been excommunicated for his view that Jesus should be seen as subordinate to God the Father. There were by now Marcionites, Gnostics, Manichaeans, Jewish Christians, and the beginnings of monastic communities, as well as streams of persuasion named for a particular theological view. How was it possible that the "persecuted" peoples, cultural aliens in the *oikoumene*, and embroiled in debates about a spiritual kingdom revealed in Jesus, so quickly took their place as the favorites of the Roman emperor?

It will help to reconstruct the events surrounding the construction of the basilicas in Palestine which are available in the accounts of Eusebius. Eusebius was bishop at Caesarea, a center of learning and biblical manuscript research at least since the residence there of Origen (231–54 A.D.), and also the Roman provincial capital. It was what we might call a center of "liberal" Christian thought, disliked by other bishops, including the bishop of Alexandria and Makarius of Jerusalem, whose dioceses were larger and more powerful. Origen had been hounded for his views by Demetrius, bishop of Alexandria at the time, and imprisoned and tortured under the emperor Decius (250 A.D.). Eusebius had raised the hackles of Alexander, bishop of Alexandria, for defending Arius when he was excommunicated for his views on the "subordination" of Christ to the Father by virtue of becoming a man. Constantine, however, understood the value of Eusebius and the manuscript center at Caesarea for his program of establishment. He used Eusebius to prepare copies of "authoritative" scriptures for his basilica in Constantinople, and he convened the council of bishops at Nicaea (325 A.D.) to give Eusebius the opportunity to defend his views and, he thought, to resolve the Arian controversy by means of the formation of a creed to which all bishops would agree. Constantine's council did not resolve the Arian controversy, which continued to boil just as other theological controversies would continue unabated for the next several hundred years, and Eusebius was eventually condemned by the seventh ecumenical council (787 A.D.). Nevertheless, Constantine had his way. Makarius was all he needed to find the proper sites for the Jerusalem basilicas. And at the council of Nicaea, even though Eusebius lost the argument, he compromised on the "identical substance" language upon which Makarius insisted and agreed not to rock Constantine's boat.

So Eusebius, the first church historian, scholar of the Hebrew scriptures, and defender of the faith, whose many writings became primary documents of the Christian church, caved in on a point of theology he thought very important. One would never know it, however, when reading his glowing accounts of Constantine's construction of the basilicas and establishment of Christianity as an imperial religion. He and the other bishops had, after all, responded dutifully to Constantine's requests, and they had accepted willingly his upgrading of the bishops to civic prestige and his largesse with respect to the building and ornamentation of the basilicas. In his *Life of Constantine*, Eusebius credits Constantine with arranging for the discovery of the "holy places," especially the site of the "Holy Sepulchre," which had to be unearthed in order to shine forth into the light of day (Smith, *To Take Place*, 78–81). The transition was made possible by casting Constantine in the ancient role of kings who were both slayers of dragons (in this case the "pagans" and "demons" who had tried to hide the holy place) and also sacred rulers in charge of building and maintaining the temples of the gods. It was a matter of royal power, now to be celebrated for its recognition of Christianity as the official religion of the empire.

Neither Eusebius, nor the bishops, nor Constantine could have imagined the consequences of this historic transformation. In retrospect, and viewed from the perspective of the historian of religion, it was this transformation that created Christendom, the structure of a religion that was to last through many changes of empires until modern times. The claim to Palestine as the place in the real world where the gospel events could now be memorialized with basilicas, monuments, and shrines created a kind of "land" (even if not yet called the Holy Land) from which Christians could trace their beginnings and spread throughout the empire. The reader will recall our discussions of land as territory in Chapter 2, its importance as a mythic construction upon the natural environment, and the social interests related to it. I have emphasized the difference between early Christian associations and other Hellenistic formations in regard to not having a country and culture of origin. In some ways, this mythic claim upon the land of Palestine answered the question of cultural extraction. It also provided the opportunity to "go back" to their land of origin and visit it. Pilgrimage to the land and sites of the gospel events soon began, with priests at all the sites to guide the pilgrims, ready with a reading of the scriptural account and appropriate prayers. A kind of liturgical pattern developed in which an itinerary followed the sequence of the biblical and gospel stories, stopping at sites for a reading and a prayer. It was not long before a calendar added appropriate dates for the celebration of the divine events, starting with Constantine's request of Eusebius for a definite date for Easter and his rule that Sundays be given to Christian worship, presumably in all basilicas throughout the empire.

The pilgrimage liturgy was soon transferred to basilicas elsewhere as an easily transposed pattern of memorial. Basilicas became microcosms of the mythic world of the Bible and the gospel. Mosaics provided images of the apostles. The last supper could be reenacted by priests at the altar overseen by images and symbols of the divine figures inhabiting the heavens above. Christian ritual was decidedly a matter of memory and memorial in the presence of depictions of the scriptural accounts. Historians of religion have always argued about the relation between myth and ritual, especially after finding so many examples among other religions where each functioned independently. The reason for the debate is that the tight combination of myth and ritual in the Christian religion was assumed by scholars as definitive of the phenomena. Now we can see that the combination was created by the anchoring of the mythic events in a particular time and place. Christian ritual became a reenactment of the mythic events, whether at the appropriate location or in basilicas that replicated the world of the imagination giving significance to those events.

Constantine's address to the bishops at the council of Nicaea was intended to resolve theological conflicts that he regarded as foolish and insignificant. The bishops went along with his request that they spell out in brief and simple terms what Christians taught and believed. This did not keep the bishops from their serious preoccupation with "foolish and insignificant" debate, as Constantine saw it, but it did result in a brief statement upon which, at the moment, those bishops attending tried to agree. The result was what we now call the Nicene Creed. The reader will no doubt know, however, that councils and creeds of various configurations filled the subsequent histories of theologians at their work. This work might be compared to the preoccupation of intellectuals engrossed in a puzzle or game consisting of a system of abstract signs, such as mathematicians play while working with equations in quest of prime numbers. How could it be otherwise when the puzzle was the Christian gospel, unsolvable because mythically and logically untenable, yet held as definitive in creedal form? How could the Son of God be both human and divine? If both, was he of two natures or one? If divine, did he really die? And does the Holy Spirit come from God only, or from God and from the Son? So the questions occurred, and so the debates raged. Contested terminology such as *homoousios* ("of one substance") marks the junctures of temporary agreements reached by subsequent councils in this long history. And yet, despite the arcane language and the embarrassing attempts to translate the myth into abstract philosophical categories, something of a core recital of Christian propositions came into being as a creed, or propositions that defined Christian belief. Theologians sometimes call this the *credo*, referring to the liturgical practice of its recitation that begins with "I believe." Scholars know that Christians have to "believe" their creed because it refers to a myth taken as history, that is, as fact. No other people require creeds and belief in order to practice their religions.

In order to make a few observations about the Christian creed, I shall cite a version of the Nicene Creed from Epiphanius (c. 374 A.D.) because it omits the anathemas in the original formulation on those such as Arius and Eusebius who wanted to use the language of "subordination" for the Son instead of saying that he was "of one substance" with the Father.

> We believe in one God the Father All-sovereign, maker of heaven and earth, and of all things visible and invisible;
> And in one Lord Jesus Christ, the only-begotten Son of God, Begotten of the Father before all the ages, Light of Light, true God of true God, begotten not made, of one substance with the Father, through whom all things were made; who for us men and for our salvation came down from the heavens, and was made flesh of the Holy Spirit and the Virgin Mary, and became man, and was crucified for us under Pontius Pilate, and suffered and was buried, and rose again on the third day according to the Scriptures, and ascended into the heavens, and sitteth on the right hand of the Father, and cometh again with glory to judge living and dead, of whose kingdom there shall be no end;

> And in the Holy Spirit, the Lord and the Life-giver, that proceedeth from the Father, who with the Father and Son is worshiped together and glorified together, who spake through the prophets;
> In one Holy Catholic and Apostolic Church;
> We acknowledge one baptism unto remission of sins. We look for a resurrection of the dead, and the life of the age to come.
> (Ancoratus, 118; Bettenson, *Documents*, 37)

The creed encompasses both cosmos and history and reaches from creation to the Eschaton. The pivot of history is a focus on the gospel story that ends with Jesus' ascension into heaven and installation as the viceroy of the Father, eventually to come again for a judgment of the living and the dead when the glorious kingdom will appear. In the meantime there is the Holy Spirit, the Holy Catholic and Apostolic Church, and the remission of sins. This does serve as an answer to many of the conceptual attempts to rationalize the identity and place of Christian associations within the Roman world during the second and third centuries. The concepts of the sovereignty, rule, and kingdom of God have been parceled out and distributed to various locations of the comprehensive worldview: the sovereignty of God to the creation and heavens above, the rule and domain among humans to the Church on earth, and the glorious kingdom that will combine both to the age to come. The problem of conceptualizing the resurrection and destiny of Jesus has been answered by treating it as an ascension to heavenly status as a cosmic installation as king. No longer is Jesus the teacher of divine wisdom, the martyr for the kingdom idea, the "first fruits" of the resurrection from the dead, the good shepherd of the flock, the hero who vanquished the cosmic spheres and made it up and out to the realm of light, the Gnostic guide to enlightenment and eternal life. He is the Son and viceroy of the sovereign God installed in the heavens to oversee the church in the world. As for the Holy Spirit, its work has been contained within the gospel events on the one hand, and infused into the work of the Church on the other. The Spirit is the life-force of the Church's liturgy of memory and memorial. It can be "worshiped together" with the Father and the Son. No need for esoteric or Gnostic experiences as the way to belong to God's kingdom.

Furthermore, the Holy Catholic and Apostolic Church has now been added to the list of items to be believed. This is a strange and striking recognition of the radical changes introduced by the Constantinian revolution in the conception of the Church as a mythic, social, historical, and political institution. To "believe" in the Church on a par with "believing" in God and the Christ is truly extraordinary. It is, of course, possible to understand some of the thinking that must have led to such an addition. The bishops at Nicaea were working on definitions of the "right" way to understand the gospel in opposition to all of the "wrong" ways that many held. They were also interested in marking the "right" way to be known as a Christian, the "right" kind of congregation, the "right" kind of bishop with the "right" kind of ordination, in distinction from all of the other wrong ways of being Christian and/or pagan.

To link the right way to think of the gospel with the right group and its institution was exactly what the situation needed. But to do it by adding the Holy Catholic and Apostolic Church to the creed meant that a concept of the Church was in effect taken up into the newly formed and solidified mythic worldview. This was more than an acknowledgment that the concept of a single, universal institution was a new and important idea or ideal. It gave the Church a mythic status, easily ontologized as belonging to the realm of reality populated by the gods, a divine order of reality. And yet, the Church was also a very real social entity, with basilicas to mark its presence, and bishops and their roles to play as part of the Roman Empire. Christian gatherings were no longer associations with their own teachings, congregations with their own leaders, or single churches with their own bishops. They were now to be seen as part of a single, universal entity that belonged to the world of the gods still hovering around in peripheral vision, as well as a real institution of social significance in the Roman world.

The emphasis upon one God, Lord, and Church is also astounding. This can be understood as a reasonable summing up and paring down of the open-ended issues of mythic and social identity that were confusing the second- and third-century intellectuals and leaders, but the creedal form suggests more than a statement of the way a particular people happen to view themselves and their deities. It is not that "our one god is named such and such, and has certain attributes that distinguish him from others." It is that "There *is* only one God, the supreme sovereign and creator of all things." And more than that, "It is the God who fathered our Lord, the heavenly sovereign, who commissioned apostles to create the Church in which we believe." In the context of the Constantinian revolution, that is monotheism with a vengeance. The creed does not have to go on and say that there are no other gods. It does not any longer have to call all of the other gods of the Roman world demons, or their devotees pagans: that is taken for granted. So it is not surprising to learn that the other gods, temples, and peoples were in trouble. Imperial funds in support of them dried up; on occasion Christians became marauders of pagan shrines and temples; and later in the century Theodosius used the power of the emperor to prohibit the worship of pagan gods (edict of 392 A.D.). Only those who believed in the consubstantiality of God the Father, Son, and Holy Spirit were to be considered Catholic Christians (edict of 380 A.D.; Council of Constantinople, 381 A.D.). Strengthened by a military victory against "pagan usurpers" in 394 A.D., the Christian God won out over all other gods of the old empire even while the empire was in the process of being dismantled. From this time on, Zeus and his pantheon were no more, Mithras disappeared, and Isis faded away.

The establishment of Christianity as a social institution was a matter of royal power. The mythic imagination of Christianity centered on power, and the administration of the church was now invested with a peculiar kind of civic and religious power. It has sometimes been thought that the relation of the church to the empire replicated the ancient Near Eastern model of the temple-state with its king and priest presiding over two intertwined social structures, one of executive power (the king) and one of social status (the high priest). In some ways this is a very helpful analogy, if not homology. That is because the church and the empires that ensued did become integral components of a single domain that we have called Christendom. But the differences need to be kept in mind. The hierarchy of clergy in the Christian church was more elaborate than that of the hereditary priestly castes in the temple-state model, and it was organized more by power than status. There would be canon law and a chief bishop (pope) with a staff symbolizing ecclesial power in parallel to the scepter of the king. Thus the church was a kingdom within an empire more than a temple at the center of a kingdom. Instead of providing the rules for status and purity in the daily life of a Near Eastern kingdom, the church provided rules for grades of personal piety and devotion to the mythic realm of the church itself.

Thus the worldview canopy that was finally imagined was vast. Its horizons were in keeping with the scope of the cosmic and historic imaginations of the Greco-Roman age, but the picture painted on this canopy was extremely focused and narrow in its social interests. In other chapters I have mentioned the two environments that form the backdrop for the mythic imagination or worldview of other peoples. The one environment was that of the natural world; the other that of the social world. Where social interests found them intersecting in ways that impinged upon the well-being of a people and its productions, the personifications of the mythic imagination and the rituals of perfection provided ways to think about, rationalize, and engage situations. In the case of Christianity's worldview, the natural order is all but effaced. It is there, to be sure, under the rubric of "creation," but "creation" as a mythic image is more about God and his power than about the natural world. It will not be surprising, therefore, to find that those who later turned their attention to the natural world had trouble with the Christian mythic canopy and the authority of the church. So what kind of social interest was involved in the imagination of the Christian canopy, and what kind of society does it sustain? Those are the questions to which we must turn. To answer them will require a tracking of what I have called Christian mentality through sixteen hundred years of history. The major displays of Christian presence and the main events to be considered are well known, and the observations to be made are in keeping with our overall quest. A few words about martyrs, relics, monastic communities, cathedrals, the mass, Christian art, political arrangements, and missions can prepare us for observations about Christianity's reactions and responses to the Renaissance, Reformation, Industrial Revolution, the natural sciences, and the rise of the nation-states and democracies. We need to see how the mythic world of the Christian imagination has been transformed and yet survived the long duration, and how it can be that Christian mentality continues unexamined in our own time.

6 The Social Formation of Christendom

With Constantine the foundations of an edifice were laid that we call the Church. In this chapter those foundations will be noted, the subsequent construction of the edifice will be discussed, the imagined world created by its systems of myth and ritual will be described, some transformations and reproductions throughout its history will be analyzed, and the question of a Christian mentality will be raised. From Constantine to the present is a long stretch of Christian history, much too vast to be summarized in a chapter. Thus the focus will fall on just those topics and moments that allow us to apply the categories from our emerging social theory of religion. We want to analyze the social interests of the church and the myth and ritual systems of Christianity as structures of an imagined world in order to ask about the mythic grammar that underlies certain ways of thinking about the social worlds.

The Foundation Stones

At the end of the last chapter the establishment of Christianity as an institution of the Roman Empire was briefly described as a remarkable and innovative turn of events for the bishops of Christian congregations and for the relation of the Roman Empire to its erstwhile religions and cultures. We can now position the foundation stones laid during that brief period of change, and ask about the construction of the edifice built upon them during the next several hundred years.

I use the metaphor of edifice with a double reference, not only to the construction of the church as a social institution, but also to the building of basilicas for public Christian presence in the Roman world. Building basilicas for Christians was the first and major move made by Constantine in the transformations he planned for establishing Christianity as the religion of state. Basilica was the name of a civic building of Roman design, with two colonnades, set near the forum, and used as a courthouse, market, and place for public gatherings. It was apparently thought to be close enough in design to older Greco-Roman temples to suggest an appropriate building for the new religion, while it retained its primary association with the emperor, for *basilicus* meant "royal," and *basilica* "the emperor's building." In the writings of Constantine and Eusebius during the period of construction, the terms used for the basilicas dedicated for Christian use reveal the novelty of the new arrangement between the Christians and the state. At first, it seems, the

Christian basilicas were thought of as "temples" and their sites as "sacred precincts." These were new ideas for the Christians who did not have a name for their places of meeting, only for their gatherings, called "assemblies" (*ekklesiai*), a term taken from the Greek *polis* in reference to its council, a meeting together that did not need a temple. The notion of a "sacred site" was a brand-new idea, but one worth thinking about now that Constantine needed to know the proper locations for the Christian basilicas he wanted to build in Palestine. Come to think of it, Jerusalem and the Jerusalem temple were right there in the gospel story, weren't they? And was not the proper name for the Jerusalem temple "God's house"? What if the basilicas, buildings that belonged to the emperor, could be called "houses" for the Christian God? That would take care of several conceptional problems at once. It would distinguish Christian basilicas from pagan temples. It would announce the succession of Christianity to the Jerusalem temple and its religious heritage. It would sanction the building as an approved place for Christian congregations to assemble. It would honor the emperor for dedicating his house to the Christian God. And it would glorify the Christian God as the ruler of the universe who was now recognized by the ruler of the empire. Eusebius was apparently fascinated with those ideas. We cannot be sure he was the very first to translate *basilica* by the Greek *kyriakos*, meaning "a master's house," with the connotations of royalty and ownership. There is, however, a remarkable passage in Eusebius' oration "On the Sepulchre," noted by Jonathan Z. Smith in private correspondence. The passage runs as follows:

> [Constantine] dedicated temples and sacred precincts to the one God, the Ruler of All, surely the Master of the Universe. For which reasons the dedications are deemed worthy of the Master's title, since they come into their surname not from men but from the Lord of the universe, and so they are deemed worthy of the title *Kyriakôn*. (Oration 335, xvii, 4, in *In Praise of Constantine*, Drake, 124)

Thus the building of Christian basilicas was not taken for granted. It was the sign of a transformation of the religion. Christianity could now be understood as an imperial construction (*kyriakos*) as well as a social formation (*ekklesia*). It is the term *kyriakos*, forming words in the Slavic and Germanic languages, from which comes our term *church*.

The building of basilicas in Rome, Constantinople, and Palestine announced the new arrangements of royal power and ecclesiastical authority, and set the agenda for the work of turning networks of Christian congregations into an institution of empire. Roman largesse provided funds not only for the continuing construction of basilicas in cities throughout the empire, but also for the maintenance of bishops, clergy, and their local programs of social welfare. The social interests of Constantine and subsequent emperors are not difficult to discern. With Christians providing shepherds for the people in all urban centers who expressed their loyalty to the Roman authorities, with pulpits and attendant clergy offering instruction to the people in matters of belief and obedience, and congregations providing help in times of need, a layer of responsibility for civilized governance was achieved for the Romans in one stroke.

The ease with which this arrangement took place can be understood as a belated reproduction of the ancient Near Eastern traditions of the temple-states and the Greek tradition of city-states. Thus the basilicas represented not only a place for Christians to congregate, but also the civic functions of temples in the older models of empire. These functions included schools, supervision of economies, civic governance, the keeping of records and accounts, composing myths, edicts, and laws, as well as care for temple accoutrement and activity. Since the Romans already had a system of supervision for keeping order and procuring taxes, the bishops were not expected to fulfill those functions. But with the new arrangement, the reasons for being a bishop suddenly shifted from preoccupation with a mythic kingdom of God and toward responsibilities for the order and stability of the kingdoms of this world. It may actually have been that there was a subliminal lust for power in the earlier Christian experiments, a secret desire that could now surface and be fulfilled (Vaage, "Why Christianity Succeeded"). In any case, there does not seem to have been any hesitation on the part of the bishops about letting the emperors build basilicas for them, moving their flocks into these new houses for their Lord, taking their seats of authority in the apses of the new basilicas, and celebrating the Eucharist in their own *kyriakoi*. There was no conceptual problem about this social arrangement with its division of labor in the interest of the empire and all of its designs. The scepter/staff liaison was taken for granted, and the financial support from the emperor's treasuries must have been considered fully appropriate for the church's new role as a fundamental structural component of the empire.

The bishops did have to make a few changes in order to satisfy the emperor. It was, after all, his idea to establish the Christians as the religion of empire, and the bishops would have to learn what that might require of them. As Constantine investigated the organization of the new religion, he found that there were several structures not yet in place that he thought necessary in order for the state religion to take its place in the world with presence and authority. For one thing, the bishops were constantly carping at one another about theological minutiae of no consequence for a civic institution. It was also the case that the bishops ruled over their own cities and churches as independent dioceses and did not have a sense of fitting into a single, empire-wide administration. That wouldn't do. To make matters worse, they couldn't even agree on which books contained authoritative teachings, or on what all Christians were supposed to believe. Constantine said that the bishops would have to agree on the canons (norms, rules): the texts to be included in the Bible, the format for a regular Sunday liturgy, the date for Easter and other days in the Christian calendar, a clear and succinct statement of what Christians were to believe, and a start on what eventually would become canon law, namely, rules governing the organization and operation of the church as an empire-wide institution. Poor bishops. They accepted the emperor's "invitation" to meet together at Nicaea for council, and the records show that they tried to keep their theological consciences even while compromising with one another and with Constantine's demands for a common statement of faith. But, of course, the disputes over the creed continued for another four hundred years, for the councils and the creeds had become official forms of governance and authorization within the single institution of the one catholic church. A chuckle would not be inappropriate when thinking about the administrators of a civic institution working out their differences over the fine points of abstract creedal formulations, trying to solve conceptual problems related to the "two natures" of the Christ or the triune character of the one God. What did they think was the purpose of this church–empire arrangement?

At the level of a working institution, hierarchies of status and authority soon determined roles. Within the church the main distinction was between bishops who supervised many congregations from a central urban basilica, and the local resident clergy of those congregations. It was not long before the clergy itself was variously deployed according to special tasks, such as parish priests, guides for tourists at major shrines and sites in Palestine and elsewhere, and the governance of life in the monasteries that now burgeoned with monks. Among the bishops, ranking was contested and related more to the importance of their cities within the structures of the empire than to their authority over matters pertaining to the church. Ranking would change in keeping with the histories of Alexandria, Caesarea, Antioch, Byzantium, and Rome as centers of both Roman and ecclesiastical powers. The centralization of ecclesiastical authority in leading cities of the Roman Empire eventually produced bureaucracies strong enough to survive the demise of the empire, and in fact to continue the governance of the several Catholic churches still in existence today.

And so, what used to be a few loose networks of the congregations of the Christ were transformed by becoming the official religion of the Roman Empire. The status of the erstwhile Christians as antisocial atheists for refusing to participate in the traditional religions and their temple festivals was a thing of the past. Those who had been prosecuted on occasion by the Romans, who were suspicious of their *collegia* and political plans, were no longer threatened. No longer victims but victors, Christians were now recognized as a positive influence in the society and as worthy of imperial support. However, their organization was quite different from other cultural traditions of the time with their priests, temples, and festivals open to participation by the populace at large. The church was open to all, but it now had its canons such as baptism, a common creed, authoritative texts, common liturgy, and calendar that defined its myths and rituals, and one had to become a member to participate. It had its own basilicas, bishops, councils, and administrative structures. It could recruit clergy for secure and attractive positions of service within its many offices for the care and welfare of the people. And as for the administration of the empire under the control of the emperor and his armies, the church offered the rulers counsel, occasional reminders of a high moral standard when waging war or engaging opponents, and, most important, a guarantee of loyalty on the part of the populace.

The Christian Empire

Christians and their congregations had been living with non-Christians as a matter of course for more than two hundred years. Thus there was no great push to rise up against the non-Christian populace as pagans or to invite the populace at large to become Christians. Some Christian bishops, such as Tertullian, had been ranting and railing against the godless pagans and their orgies for over a hundred years, so Christians were fully aware of their differences from the world around them. Just because the Roman emperor had accepted Christianity, and the church was now the official religion of the Roman Empire, did not mean that everyone was expected to become a Christian, at least not at first. The Romans had received many non-Roman religions and allowed temples to be built for them in Rome for over five hundred years. Think of the devastating effect upon public life and festival were the traditional temples, shrines, and special days suddenly to cease. That would have been unthinkable. Indeed, what could the Christian church have to offer in the place of urban festivities, markets, processions, shrines, theaters, and centers of learning generated by traditional religions?

It was also the case that becoming a Christian was different from attending a pagan temple or festival, different even from being initiated into one of the mystery cults, cults that did not mind at all if you also found other gods or goddesses to be attractive. To become a Christian, one had to be baptized, instructed in the creed, agree to a code of ethics, and submit to the supervision of the clergy and bishop. Theoretically, at least in the preaching of the bishops and clergy, a Christian was not supposed to have any other gods but the Father of Jesus Christ. Despite these hurdles, however, the number of Christians did grow. Given the opportunities for access to Christian welfare and Roman governance, the attraction of the church should not be surprising. Some bishops were actually uneasy about the numbers wanting to become Christians. It was not always clear whether newly baptized Christians were truly convinced of the faith and its canons, or whether taking the vows seemed the thing to do under the changing social and political circumstances. What to do about insincere Christians or those who lapsed in their loyalty to the Christian God was an agonizing question for the bishops who spent much time on refining the canon laws with respect to such matters as readmissions or rebaptisms. You cannot play around with a rite of spiritual transformation, baptizing the same person twice. So of course the doors were open to all, but what if they remained unruly?

At the state level, the making of decisions with respect to multiple religions was one of political interest and clarity about the effective differences these religions made in a society. The first move was to realize that the traditional supports for the shrines, temples, and festivals did not have to be continued. These supports had been financial and political. The rounds of religious activities in cities throughout the empire had been supported and protected by the Romans in several ways. Only in the case of a festival getting out of hand, such as the Bacchanalias in Rome, did the Romans step in and close them down by outlawing them. But now that these supports were no longer a matter of course, some traditional practices began to wither. Some temples and shrines were left vacant to deteriorate. Some festivals were no longer held. And some Christians took advantage of these situations to desecrate shrines and maraud temples with impunity. Other unfortunate actions on the part of Christians against the religions and traditions of non-Christians are well known, such as the burning of the library at Alexandria in 391 A.D. The end of paganism was by no means certain or celebrated, however, least of all by those leading families with stakes in their cities and religions. In Italy, the Roman aristocracy and political leadership, including leading generals and circles of potential contenders for the office of emperor, had reason to be upset with Constantine's creation of the Christian church and his preference for Byzantium (Constantinople) as the major city of the empire and the central diocese of the church. It took most of the fourth century to work out these conflicts over Rome's attitude and legal policies with respect to religions. It was during this time, for instance, that the emperor Julian, "The Apostate," decided to rescind the privileges granted to Christianity and to restore the traditional Hellenic and Roman temples and rituals.

Toward the end of the fourth century, however, the Christian emperor Theodosius, residing in Constantinople, thought to settle the matter with edicts. The political situation had become exceedingly complex. The Visigoths were pressing hard at the borders of the empire from the north; the church was hopelessly divided in hard and hostile battle between Arians and Orthodox Christians; the Roman aristocracy in Italy was divided on the issues of Rome versus Constantinople as well as Christian versus traditional religions; and questions about the power and authority of the bishops and the emperors had come to a head in the excommunication of Theodosius by the bishop Ambrose because Theodosius had ordered a massacre at Thessalonica. That Theodosius did penance and was reinstated by Ambrose as a confessing Christian has often been viewed as evidence for the incursion of ecclesiastical authority and power into the "secular" authority and governance of the empire. In any case, the times were exceedingly troubled, and Theodosius, though moving energetically on all fronts, could not settle all the issues. He sought to solve the Arian/Orthodox conflict by imperial edict (380 A.D.), stating that only persons who subscribed to the Nicene creed, with its insistence upon Jesus being "of one substance" with the Father, were to be considered Catholic Christians. This hardly settled the matter, for the missionary to the Goths had been Ulfilas, an Arian, not an Orthodox Christian, and the Goths and other northern tribes would be heard from in the subsequent machinations of political and religious intrigue. It was the edict of 391 A.D. that scholars have considered a precedent for the unimaginable power and authority of the church throughout the kingdoms that emerged after the demise of the Roman Empire. This edict prohibited the worship of pagan deities, including the visiting of pagan temples, the performance of ritual offerings, and attendance at festivals. That subsequent kings from European tribes and would-be emperors of the Holy Roman Empire did accept the fact that they should be Christians, that their kingdoms should be Christian, and that their people should acknowledge Christianity as the only religion of the kingdom, is one of the most curious and startling facts of Western history. But it probably had nothing to do with Theodosius's edict. His edict was a proscription dealing with the Greco-Roman religions of the past and their relation to the Christian Empire, mainly because the pagan temples in Rome were still creating problems in Italy. The emergence of Christendom in Europe has therefore to be explained in some other way. Three or four observations concerning this history are now in order.

The first is that the Roman Empire, though no longer in the hands of the Roman aristocracy, was still present in memories, monuments, and patterns of district administration, from the Limes (western frontier) to the Euphrates. Its extent, military successes, administrative structures, legal traditions, and illustrious history of civilization defined a concept of empire that was still thought to be in place and active. Most of the subsequent warriors, kings, and emperors who vanquished and took charge of various parts of the empire had done battle precisely for this legacy. When the Visigoths sacked Rome in 410 A.D., the rationale was said to be punishment for the Romans relinquishing the old Roman traditions and losing control to the wrong Christians, namely, the Orthodox, who were thought of as centered in Constantinople. Since Alaric was Arian, it was assumed that the right Christians were now in charge. Thus, the concept of the Roman Empire was still in place.

The second observation is that the church was already deeply involved in the far-flung districts of the Roman Empire. Missionaries had ventured beyond the urban centers of the Mediterranean to convert the "rustics" (the original connotation of "pagans") to Christianity. There they built shrines on the model of small basilicas and other buildings to serve as schools and administrative centers for vast areas of countryside. They had followed the Roman armies and, for the most part, worked in league with the Romans in the interest of what they understood as "civilizing" the natives. The lands of the Roman Empire of the fourth century were vast, and Christian missions had spread throughout the entire expanse.

Lacking the Greco-Roman traditions of education, the rustics could not be expected to understand the Christian creed or its theological significance, but they could be shown depictions of the gospel story, the martyred saints, and the Christian emperors. They could be instructed in fundamental rules of civilized behavior. And they could be baptized and invited to church. Actually, being baptized was the only thing that really mattered in these lands far from Rome. It meant that you had said "Yes" to the missionaries and acquiesced to the institutions of religion, instruction, and governance that they represented. If, in the course of time, cities, trade routes, and kings came along, the foundations for kingdoms would already have been laid by the Christian missionaries.

Finally, when cities did rise in Europe as new centers of governance, the Christian basilica and its bishop were taken for granted as belonging to the model. They took their place at the center of the city as if the social domain of the district was theirs. Here the Christians did not have to compete with the vibrant public life of the Greco-Roman city and its many temples. Instead, they were able to elaborate the Eucharist into impressive performances on the models of pilgrimage and procession. These performances marked the difference between the newly urban culture of Christianity and the traditions of rural rituals among the country folk.

Pilgrimage and procession were the result of the Constantinian creation of Christendom. Both were related to the remarkable effect of Constantine's construction of Christian basilicas in Palestine. For the first time, Christians could claim a homeland, a real place in the world from which they had come. They could return, at least for the period 335–638 A.D., to visit the sites mentioned in the Bible and especially in the gospels where the events of significance in the life of Christ were said to have happened. Pilgrimage to these sites did start almost immediately, forging a link between text, site, and prayers that took place right there on the very spot. Thus was created a distinctively Christian combination of myth and ritual, the significance of which we will look at more closely in the next section of this chapter. Here we can point out that a proper sequence to the visitation of the sites was soon worked out, a narrative sequence that followed the biblical and gospel accounts, thus producing patterns of procession. Since these patterns of pilgrimage, procession, and rituals of memorial were easily copied, and since the sites in Palestine were now marked by basilicas, churches elsewhere soon became the sites for liturgies that replicated pilgrimage, memorial, and procession on the model of practices in Palestine. One can imagine the impression Christian ritual must have had upon the country folk throughout Europe.

This transposition of biblical–gospel sites to the basilicas in Europe was achieved by means of architectural arrangements and ornamentation. Mosaics on the inner walls and dome of the apse depicted biblical figures and scenes. This created an enclosed space within which the biblical stories could be told, the Eucharist could be celebrated, and the portraits of martyrs and Christian emperors of the subsequent histories could be included. The early replication of Christian myth and ritual on the model of pilgrimage to

Palestine, the land of the gospel story, can still be seen in the fifth- and sixth-century churches of Ravenna. As Christendom unfolded throughout Europe, the basilica at the center of the city soon became the Romanesque church, then the Gothic cathedral, each more elaborate and expressive in depicting the gospel story and providing the space and place for processional pageantry. Even at Ravenna, at the beginning of the Christian use of the Roman basilica for its gospel liturgies far from Palestine, the impression one has is that of entering a microcosm of the world of the Bible and subsequent Christian history. One can therefore imagine monks, clergy, and bishops presiding over liturgical reenactments of the gospel story in such an atmosphere throughout Europe, perhaps with local kings and generals in attendance and attire. Such liturgies marked the present performance as a reenactment and memorial of a history stretching from the present moment back to the gospel events and before. It was a history of the church into which kings might be integrated who ruled on the model of Constantine and the Christian Roman Empire. By themselves, the post-Constantine kings of Europe could not claim that kind of history for their kingdoms. Only by ruling in league with the bishops could a king have a kingdom on the model of the Roman Empire.

Thus the history of Christianity and of the many kings, kingdoms, and emperors that fought each other over lands and peoples during the next several centuries did not raise questions about, much less weaken, the place and authority of the Christian church in the social structures of governance. The balance of powers between the bishops and the kings was more or less divided between civic and spiritual administrations. But given the fact that the church had acquired lands, supported monasteries and their production of goods, employed clergy, received offerings, and maintained buildings, there was always some confusion about the lines separating the administrations of the two social institutions—kingdom and church. Each contested the other over lands, finances, and the control of the people. Kings frequently wanted to appoint their own bishops. Bishops wanted to tell their kings how to rule. The amazing thing about this history, however, is that neither questioned the other's authority over his respective domain.

The histories of the medieval period are less clear and detailed about the effects of Christendom upon the populace, especially in the country villages and farming communities. These people would have accepted the various changes of sovereignty as long as their way of life was not disrupted. One imagines that the rise of cities, their commerce, and the pageantries of the Christian liturgies may well have drawn the people from the European countryside to the cities, on occasion, in order to taste the flavors of Christendom. As noted already, however, the interest of the earlier Christian missionaries was focused on the civilization of rustics, guaranteed by the agreement to being baptized. Since the church took its place mainly as an urban institution with an interest in the culture of kingdoms and empires, the question has been raised about the ways in which the populace of the countryside may have changed its practices and thinking in respect to rituals and belief. What seems to be clear is that the old agrarian festivals and seasonal celebrations of village life continued, as well as the rites of passage on traditional folk models, throughout the entire time. Frazer's collection of folk rituals still practiced in nineteenth-century Europe is telling evidence for the coexistence of folk rituals and Christianity among many of these people.

There was, however, one other development of some importance for the practice of piety among the populace, and that resulted from an obsession with the relics of martyrs that occurred soon after the Constantinian establishment. The fact that Christians had been prosecuted and killed by the Romans during certain periods of the pre-Constantine period is not particularly noteworthy. That is because Roman concern with what they saw as Christian intransigence regarding the making of sacrifices for the emperors, the customary sign of loyalty to the empire, is understandable. The sword had always been used that way in times of desperation on the part of those in power. What turned that history into memorable event and then into a cult is that, even before Constantine, Christian authors had begun writing biographies of some of those killed by the Romans. They called them *martyrs*, a Greek legal term meaning "witness," and understood their "confessions" of faith at the time of martyrdom to be "witnesses" for the truth of the Christian faith. After Constantine there were to be no more martyrs. Among the many edicts and canons issued during the period 313–20 A.D., from which we also have Constantine's letters to Eusebius corroborating his views, it was stated clearly that there were to be no more crucifixions or bindings of criminals of any kind, and that from now on the "long-suffering" of Christian piety would be rewarded by God in lieu of martyrdom. But what, then, were Christians to think about the martyrs of the pre-Constantine period? They became heroes of the faith from the earlier times, and the sites of their martyrdoms and burials became destinations for pilgrimage. While it is far from clear that the deaths of the martyrs were always viewed on analogy to the crucifixion of Jesus, lore accrued about their souls being rewarded with eternal life as a result of their faithfulness. Thus they became "saints" and their bodies and burials became places where contact might be made with their spiritual powers.

One of the curious results of building basilicas on the sites of Jesus' martyrdom and resurrection, basilicas called "At the Cross," "On Golgotha," and "Anastasis," was the thought that it would be appropriate for Christian sovereigns to be buried within the basilicas of their capital cities. Thus Constantine was buried in the church "Of the Apostles" in Constantinople as the "thirteenth apostle," as he said, and the Empress Galla Placidia had her mausoleum attached to the narthex of the basilican palace church of Santa Croce, slightly later restored as San Vitale, in Ravenna. It was not long before relics from the burial sites of the martyrs were also being taken to basilicas throughout Christendom for a kind of reburial in shrines that gave the churches upgrades in status. These shrines became destinations for pilgrimage, and the prayers and meditations at these sites were often requests for healing. Thus the long-standing tradition of shrines throughout the pre-Constantine Greco-Roman world, a tradition that Walter Burkert has called "votive religion" (*Ancient Mystery Cults*, 12–17), was again available to the people by means of a reproduction of folk piety, a transformation of Christian mythology, and a transposition of Christian ritual. Christian saints now marked the shrines instead of Greco-Roman deities.

Our description of the structures of Christendom as a social institution can now be used to ask some questions about the imagined world so created and the way that the imagined world supported a mentality assumed by church and state alike for several centuries. Reading the histories of Christian thought and practice from the perspective of the present time, one cannot help but notice the degree to which the imagined world was taken for granted as self-evident at all levels of thought, action, negotiation, and planning. This is true of what we read about bishops and their sense of mission, clergy and their sense of duty, generals and their sense of purpose, and sovereigns and their sense of authority to rule. They never asked about their imagined world as imagined, although they were prepared to quickly label other worlds of non-Christians and heretics as delusions or fantasies. Their own imagined world was simply taken for granted as the way things were. We need a better understanding of that imagined world.

The Imagined World

The imagined world of the late medieval Christian is there to be studied, graphically displayed in the entrance archways, painted domes, mosaic-covered apses, carved altars and pulpits, and shrines of Europe's cathedrals. All who have had the opportunity to visit a European cathedral will know what the cosmos looked like, how the Christ ruled in heaven above, what the gospel story was about, who Jesus's disciples were, and who were the saints of history, both from the Old Testament accounts and from Christian history since gospel times. This picture need not be repainted here. But there are some observations to be made and some questions to be asked.

Is this picture all there is to the medieval imagination of the world? If so, what about the natural orders, what about the social orders? How do these important features of the world fit into the picture, or what are we to make of them in light of this picture? What about the Bible? Does this picture stem from the Bible, agree with the Bible, depend upon the Bible, or bring many other interests to its own interpretation of the Bible? And how does this picture help as the setting for prayers, for the Mass, for the recitation of the creed, or for baptisms? And what about the place and space within which these depictions are displayed, this cathedral? Does it represent the world? The everyday world? If so, what is one to think about it? These questions rise from our quest to develop a social theory of religion and to analyze Christianity according to the categories we have been using to understand its system of myth and ritual.

In Chapter 4 we began with the concept of two environments, the natural and social worlds, and their intersections where social interests and activities encountered impingements from beyond the empirical and manageable everyday worlds. We found that both the natural and social worlds were much too large to grasp and manage by humans in the everyday world, and that myths and rituals could be devised in order to craft scenes, agents, and activities with the purpose of attending to these interests when set in their imaginary worlds in order to gain some distance from them and ponder their significance as human activities. We need now to ask about the social interests focused upon by the Christian myths and rituals, their environments, and the reasons Christians structured their imagined world the way they did. In order to do so we will have to recall some of the history we have already considered, following the development of some features of its myths and rituals that still need to be mentioned. These include the Bible, the creed, and the rituals of the established church.

The Bible

Various collections of early Christian and Hebrew writings were made during the course of the second and third centuries, but the Bible as a special collection, closed and considered authoritative for use throughout the Church, was not an urgent matter for common agreement until the fourth century. However, the social logic at work in the discussions that produced the Bible was already there in the mythologies of Paul and Mark, in Justin Martyr's research of the Hebrew scriptures, and in the myriad sermons and essays of the bishops during the third and fourth centuries. It took some time to agree on the selection of texts from Hebrew, Hellenistic-Jewish, and early Christian authors, and to arrange them in such a way as to suggest a continuous history from creation to the Eschaton. But once they were selected and arranged, the logic was quite simple, namely, that the God of Israel had had Christians in mind from the beginning of Israel's history, that the Hebrew scriptures prophesied the advent of Jesus just before the end of that history with the destruction of Jerusalem, and that Christians were now God's people with a mission to convert the nations by telling them the gospel story and warning them of the final judgment. What this added to the origin myths of Paul and Mark, and to the imagined world of the creed, was the sense of a universal history, the center point of which was the advent of Jesus and the origin of the Church. It also added a sense of verification in that the Bible was a written record to be taken literally as documentation of that history. Combined with the cosmic world of the creed and cathedrals, the imagined world could now be seen to encompass all time and all space. It had room for both the heavenly kingdom of the realms above the earth and the appearance of the kingdom at the end of time. It also positioned the Church squarely between the gospel events in the past and the Eschaton in the future, thus producing a sense of orientation that was dynamic. To the axis up and down of the heavenly/earthly worlds, there was now a horizontal pull from creation to the Eschaton.

The Creed

As for the creed, we have already noted the strange addition of the church to the list of items to be believed. Now that we have considered the social interests of the origin myths of Paul and Mark coming to focus on the social formations of the Jesus associations, this addition no longer seems so strange. The church turns out to be a mythic entity, linked as it is to the history and destiny of the kingdom of God. The church may well be thought of as some kind of agent active in the drama of salvation, as the creed has it, on a par with the other divine agents of the story. This remarkable inclusion of the church in the list of essential beliefs was no doubt intended by the council that created the creed as a political move in the interest of bringing together disparate and competing bishoprics. It reveals, nevertheless, the absolute seriousness with which the bishops were taking themselves, as well as their naiveté about matters philosophical and theological. Despite the overlay of philosophically loaded terminology, the creed is not a philosophical composition. It is a reduction of the myths created by Paul and Mark to a short list of the divine agents in their narratives. There was, however, a bit of elaboration of these myths in keeping with their cultivation during the second and third centuries. The inclusion of the Church was one of these elaborations, this one based on the realization that the concept of the church was integral to the kingdom theme of the origin myths.

Other elaborations included the sovereignty of the one God and his making of the heaven and the earth, the emphasis on Jesus being "begotten" by God the Father, and the awkward statements about the Holy Spirit, the "Lord and Life-giver," "proceeding" from the Father, speaking through the prophets, and being "worshiped and glorified together with the Father and Son." It is obvious that the Holy Spirit had taken a place in the creed in order to imagine ways in which the heavenly and earthly worlds could be linked. Once the atmospheric deities of the Greco-Roman cosmologies had been dispensed with because of the one God emphasis, something had to take their place in order for contacts to occur. The ubiquitous concept of spirit and spirits would work well as long as it could be limited to just those functions required by the church. The embarrassment for subsequent generations of theologians is that a trinity of deities resulted, a notion difficult to fuse with the concept of the one God. At the level of concepts, separately defined and in need of logical relations and arrangements on the game board of philosophers and theologians where abstractions are the playing pieces, the creed has always been an intriguing logical puzzle incapable of resolution. However, its incredibility has never resulted in discounting its authority for Christians. That is because its authority is not related to philosophical persuasions. Its authority stems from the imagined world of the kingdom of God, the mythology required to account for the Christian church and its claims to represent the kingdom in this world.

The emphasis upon the figure of Jesus and his many names and designations indicates that the early theologians had some trouble making the links between Jesus and the Father God. This is not surprising, given the absolutely impossible conceptual solutions to such a link. As in the case of the Holy Spirit, however, the link had to be made for reasons other than those of satisfying conceptual logics. The strategy of the creed seems to have been a stacking up of the many formulations suggested by the several creedal traditions represented at the council. That in itself was bound to be overwhelming and so would have made the relationship unavailable for further logical questioning. But that would not have mattered, given the mythic importance of Jesus at that juncture of history where the heavenly kingdom world, the Jesus associations, and the social orders of the real world converged. Thus the section of the creed devoted to Jesus is actually a summary of the gospel story won by a collation of all four canonical gospels. Even though the Father–Son link received the most embellishment, it is the conclusion of Jesus' mythic biography that is more telling. It is imagined that he "ascended into the heavens, sat on the right hand of the Father, and will come again with glory to judge the living and dead, of whose kingdom there shall be no end." As one can see, the kingdom myth was the frame that gave the Jesus myth its significance and rationale.

The Rituals

The rituals of the medieval church were the way in which the mythic structure of the imagined world was available for contact and contemplation by the individual. The intellectuals and priests of the church honed both the myth and the ritual to perfection over the twelve hundred years of Catholic Christendom (the fourth to sixteenth centuries), and the focus on the individual was by design. We can make a few observations about baptism, confession, devotions, the Mass, and last rites in order to analyze the way in which ritual practice and experience enhanced the imagined world.

Although baptism was originally a rite of initiation for adults during the early periods of history when the church was not the major religion in the Greco-Roman world, in the later Catholic Church it became a rite of reception for infants and children. It took place at a font in the back of the nave just inside the entrance portals, and so symbolized the entrance of an infant into both the social world and the church's domain. This marked the child as a Christian and announced the fact to the world. Being a Christian was taken for granted by most adults, since there were no alternative religions or identities available from which to choose. However, an individual could be reminded of the fact that he had been baptized, and therefore was expected to act as a Christian.

From the fifth century the hearing of a person's confession of sins by a priest was a ritual practiced in preparation for the Mass, at first limited to the

Mass on Holy Thursday before Easter. Soon, however, confession, with its priestly response of forgiveness or absolution of sins, came to be practiced as the appropriate, if not required, preparation for participation in any Mass. The gesture of kneeling before a seated priest and the submission of one's self-analysis to the judgments of the church were understood as signs of obeisance and loyalty to the church and to God, as well as a request for forgiveness, blessing, and recognition as a committed Christian. The focus on the adult individual is obvious in this ritual, and the function of the confession in relation to participation in the liturgy of the Mass indicates just how significant the ritual was considered to be for the individual's sense of incorporation into and orientation within the imagined world of Christianity.

Since the medieval cathedral has provided us with the large-scale picture of the imagined world of Christendom, and since the cathedral was clearly arranged in order to perform the Mass, it might be that the performance of these rituals would tell us something more about the imagined world than we have been able to sketch by means of the mythologies and iconographies. The early myths of meals with Jesus as memorials of his death were not written as scripts for rituals of reenactment. They were at most suggestions for using the normal practices of association meals as occasions for the announcement and recognition of the group's rationale as a Jesus association, just as in other associations it was customary at the beginning of the meal to pour out some wine for their patron deity to acknowledge who they were. And, as discussed in Chapter 5, not all early Jesus schools and associations remembered Jesus' death in such a way. It seems that the myths of Jesus' death as a martyrdom did not produce rituals of memorial or reenactment until some time in the third to fourth centuries, about the time when the Constantinian revolution provided basilicas for the public performance of a Christian ritual. It is at least the case that the development of the Mass is related to the history of the arrangements within the church for the performance of rituals. It was then that the ritual reenactment of the Last Supper in the gospel story was celebrated separately from the eating of common meals together. A priest now took Jesus' place at the "table" and offered the bread and wine as symbols of eternal life.

The Mass became the single most important ritual of Christendom. It was the occasion for the individual to participate in the imagined world of Christianity. If we recall the setting for the Mass, surrounded by images from the gospel and the cosmic canopy where the ruler of the world reigned in sovereignty, the ritual can be understood as a reenactment of the events portrayed in the church's myth of origin. In the history of iconography, the central figure was not always the crucifix with which we are now familiar. Jesus was at first depicted as teacher and then as the good shepherd who ascended into heaven and could therefore guide the way. Shortly after the establishment of the church under Constantine, Jesus could be depicted in the mosaics of the apse as a royal figure enthroned in heaven. As the religion of empire, it was now possible for Christianity to acknowledge publicly its long-standing interest in the kingdom of God and its representation of that kingdom in the world. The focus fell upon the ascension of Jesus to kingship in the heavens. But, in time, a remarkable reversal took place in the portrayal of Jesus and in the ritual of reenactment. Instead of a meditation on the ascension to sovereignty, the crucifixion of Jesus as a martyr and sacrifice for sins became central. This has been understood as a kind of compensation for the real power that the church actually had in the world, a reversal similar to that attending the pre-Constantine martyrs who came to be venerated as victors and saints, and whose burial sites became shrines where divine powers were understood to lodge. As the Eucharist turned into the Mass, however, a mode of meditation developed which had to do with the vicarious suffering and sacrifice of the divine Son of God for the sins of the world. It was in this posture of meditation beneath the crucifix in the apse that the individual Christian was invited to partake of the eternal life offered by the Church.

We have already considered the effect of the Constantinian revolution at the point of creating the early Christian liturgies in basilicas throughout the empire on the model of pilgrimage to the memorial sites of the gospels in Palestine. We have also mentioned the work of Jonathan Z. Smith on ritual theory, and on the unusual character of Christian ritual as a reenactment of myth. We can now see the consequences of this curious combination of myth and ritual. By performing the Mass in the context of the church as a replication of the imagined world of the divine kingdom, the "pilgrim's" approach to the altar to be present at the reenactment of the sacrifice of Christ according to the gospel story placed the pilgrim within the ambience of the gospel story and at the intersection of its historical and cosmic axes at the same time. A sense of presence was created, and as a matter of fact, the notion of presence was consciously cultivated and applied not only to the importance of a person's "attendance" at the ritual, but also to the "reality" of the transubstantiation of the bread and wine into the body and blood of Christ. In the later Protestant Reformation the doctrine of transubstantiation came to be viewed as superstition, but the debate about the "real presence" of Christ at the ritual continued at the level of theological abstraction.

We should linger here a moment, for it is just this moment of "participation" in the mythic event of Christ's death and resurrection by means of ritual reenactment that has defined "religious experience" for Christians and determined the definitions of religion, myth, ritual, spirit, and personal experience with which most scholars have been working. We can now see why scholars have had such difficulty in understanding the religions, myths, and rituals of other peoples, for the tight combination of Christian myth and ritual and the notion of transformation as the sign of divine agency and presence are peculiarly Christian. This tight combination of myth and ritual does not tap into ordinary social interests, sensibilities, and intellectual labors that accompany other myths and rituals. It collapses the spaces between the "then" and the "now" of myth and the "here" and "there" of ritual. It also erases the differences between the spiritual and empirical worlds and results in the notion of "identification" between mythic agents and human beings. The reader may have noticed that there was little difference between the notions of "authentic experience" indicative of Modernism discussed briefly in Chapter 1 and the popular definition of religion as "personal religious experience." Both are engrossments difficult to understand without knowing about the powerful concentration of myth and ritual in medieval Christendom and its application to the individual in attendance. We need to see that the Christian myth–ritual combination shifts attention away from the everyday and onto the interior world of the individual as if in confrontation with a divine agency of transformation. The theory of ritual with which we have been working says that ritual creates an occasion for paying close attention to the action performed in the interest of reflection upon the same action commonly performed in the course of everyday life. In the case of the Mass, the ritual is no longer reflective of common meals, and its express reference is to a mythic event, not to a common human practice, the mythic event of the death and resurrection of Christ that is imagined to reoccur in its present reenactment. The myth contains the script for the ritual. The environments of the social and natural orders have been elided and reduced to the personal experience of an individual encompassed by the ambience of the Church's world.

As for the last rites, we can now see just how important they were as a confirmation that the individual will continue to be a citizen of the imagined kingdom.

The Mentality

I want now to describe the mythic structure of the imagined world of Christendom as a grammar for thinking about the real world and making judgments about circumstances and situations that arise. The mythic structure is, of course, a result of intellectual activity within the church for the sake of the church. One could argue that it reflects the thinking only of the theological elite, or perhaps the elite per se, inside or outside the church, during the medieval period. And yet, the Christian myths, rituals, and patterns of governance provided a framework for negotiating the world that everyone had to understand in some degree or way. It is that framework, largely taken for granted by most, the result of natural enculturation, and, like the grammar of a language, hardly ever raised to the surface of consciousness for analysis, that provided a common structure for social discourse. Like the grammar of a language, the mythic structure both made possible and constrained the conceptual arrangements and sensibilities that were used to understand a situation, and that allowed for communication. The mythic structure of the medieval imagination was a grammatical schema used to interpret the world.

The Structure

The structure of the imagined world is given with the myth–ritual system. The imagined world itself is a large-scale expanse of cosmos and history within which the myth–ritual system provides the framing as well as the schema for its application to the real world. The cosmos is a totalizing environment despite the fact that it is devoid of the customary astronomical and geophysical entities and has no markers for meditation on real-world activities or environments. The cosmic setting has to be there in order to imagine the transcendent realm for the sovereign God and his domain as a perfect and eternal part of the created order. This God is the only one there is, creating the world and human beings at the beginning and presiding over the history of humankind until its perfection. When that happens, the earthly orders will no longer exist, for the heavenly kingdom will have received the perfected human beings into its eternal glory. Thus there is a history running through the imagined world, from beginning to end, a history of the human race and God's designs to make it perfect. This history is essentially mythic. It structures the imagined world of God's purposes and thus takes the history of the human race up into the light of the spiritual or cosmic order where God reigns. However, built into the mythic structure is the acknowledgment of the repeated failures of humans to recognize this God, obey his commands, and follow his guidance. This history of failures to render obedience and achieve perfection introduces a very serious element of ignorance, intransigence, and sin into the picture at the level of human history.

This problematic history results in a set of dualisms that complicate the otherwise monodimensional world. The first duality is that between the heavenly realm where God is located and the earthly where humans find themselves. This has often been regarded as a cosmic dualism distinguished as spiritual and material realms. However, the mythic dualism is not a simple ontological distinction, because the transcendent realm is the location of sovereign power that impinges upon the earthly order in "breakthrough" events (such as "miracles," dramatic reversals of circumstances, personal "transformations," natural disasters interpreted as "divine judgments," etc.). A second dualism is more complicated still, for it has to do with the problem of human history and its distinction between those who recognize and obey the divine plan and those who do not. This distinction is absolute theoretically, for there is no middle ground between obedience and disobedience (godly and ungodly, good and evil), and there is no mechanism by which to overcome the oppositions except a breakthrough event. Nevertheless, since breakthrough events are built into the schema, the dualism at the level of human history is not static. The obedient can falter, the disobedient can come to their senses, and so forth. A third dualism is the curious division of the history between the time of Israel according to the Old Testament accounts and the

The Christian Myth and Imagined World

	GOD	
	Sovereignty	
	Father; Christ–King	
Creation	**Christ Event**	**Eschaton**
Commandments	Mission	Judgment
History of **Israel**	History of the **Church**	
Prophets and Kings	Bishops and Kings	
Obedience	The righteous	Redemption
Disobedience	Sinners	Destruction

time of the Church since the Christ event storied in the New Testament. This dualism creates a schema, for the "time of Israel" is, like human history in general, a time of testing under the criteria of knowledge/ignorance and obedience/disobedience. But it is also the time before the Christ event, a period of time "on the way to" the Christ event, and so it is charged with temporal signals such as promise, prophecy, plan, and approach. This doubly charged period of human experience in relation to the divine plan can easily become that part of the schema capable of reapplication to all other humans who are not Christians but who can be considered candidates for conversion as "pre-Christians." The period between the Christ event and the end of history is also charged with a double dualism. The first is between Christians and pagans, a theoretical opposition between the godly and the ungodly. The second is between the "righteous" and "sinners," a distinction that describes the tension underlying the Christian's sense of imperfection. This distinction is absolute in light of the final judgment, but unresolved in the meantime. Thus the structure of the mythic world of the imagination is dynamic. It outlines in large scale the designs of a sovereign God for the human race, but also acknowledges the problematic dualisms of human history. In the diagram above the structure of the imagined world combines the mythic structure of the world from both the divine and the human points of view. The primary characteristics of the divine are sovereignty, agency, and commandment; those of the human are knowledge, obedience, and/or sinfulness. The biblical history is evident and the cosmic axis of the medieval portrayals can be imagined. The primary intersections of the divine with the human take place on both the horizontal and the vertical planes, and they are events of transformation: Creation; Christ event; Eschaton. These events of transformation have primary significance, but there are many other significant events that follow from them. These are found in the biblical narratives of each, which produce a myriad of additional nuanced connotations that do not appear on the diagram but are familiar from the histories of iconography and theology. The primary events of transformation and their narrative embellishments are mythic images that serve as mythic markers.

Mythic images are narrative in form and signal features of the imagined world that can be taken as indicators of divine purpose, power, or plan. In the Genesis account of creation, for instance, the mythic images on the intersection of the vertical and horizontal axes at the point of creation are signs of sovereignty and power in the creation of the natural world; creation of the human and a divine commandment; human disobedience and banishment from "paradise," an odd mythic image combining features of both the natural and the divine worlds. It is also possible to notice such features as the male–female sequence and relationship; the phrase "in the image of God"; the commandment to "have dominion"; the commandment to "be fruitful and multiply"; and so forth. Each of these narrative images has been fastened upon by Christians as a sign of consequence affecting the entire mythic system, interpreted as having structural significance for the imagined world and its application to the real world. In contemporary evangelical Christianity, some conservative Christians have associated God's curse on the earth and humans shortly after the creation with their eventual destruction imagined to take place at the end of time, from which they conclude that current environmental concerns for the earth are of no importance or consequence. The association reveals the totalizing and systemic aspects of the Christian's imagined world. A subsequent set of stories tells of God's change of mind about the banishment and destruction of the human race; his selection of Abraham and his posterity as a people of promise; the revelation of the divine laws to Moses; his leading the people to the promised land; and the history of kings and prophets in the land of Israel. Unfortunately, from the Christian point of view, the story of Israel is mainly one of disobedience.

The mythic images at the intersection of the divine and human realms at the point of the Christ event are even more dense and complicated. The Christ event is pictured at the middle point of history, designed to take care of the problem of disobedience. The primary features are sovereign power, human martyrdom, divine sacrifice, and transformation under the signs of resurrection and ascension. Sequel events and interpretations suggest that the divine sacrifice answered the problem of human sinfulness, thus retrojecting the Christian conception of sin back onto the "disobedience" problem of the history of Israel as that which had to be remedied. Other later interpretations understood the appearances of the resurrected Jesus to the apostles to inaugurate the time of the church and its mission to convert the world to Christianity. The way in which the gospel account of the Christ event supports these interpretations has never been clarified, despite the agonizing attempts of theologians for seventeen hundred years to explain its logic. It is enough for us to say that these interpretations are standard as theological constructions upon the mythic images in the imagined world as a system.

We may now add the Christian ritual of the Mass to this staged history and its status diagram. We said that the ritual reenacts the mythic event of the Christ and thus produces a sense of presence at the intersection of the vertical cosmic axis and the horizontal history where the priest and the communicant happen to be. This curious sense of participating in the cosmic, historic, and personal effects of the gospel story is clearly an elaboration of the earlier replications of the Palestinian pattern of pilgrimage and meditation transposed to the basilicas throughout the Roman Empire. We see here that the function of place, fundamental for our theory of ritual's distinction between a "here" and a "there," was transformed in the notion of the "proper site" for memorial basilicas inaugurated by Constantine. The result was the concept of the ritual replication of divine events, located not only in Palestine and other Christian basilicas wherever they might be built, but also in the experience of individuals. I can now suggest that this pattern of ritual replication was not limited to the death and resurrection of the Christ. The entire biblical and subsequent Christian history of important events and heroes of the faith, anchored as it was in the imagined world, was present in the parallel series of Israelite and Christian figures in the graphics and iconography of the medieval church. Thus, the structure of the Christian myth and history turns out to be a complex schema, capable of superimposition upon different time–place locations and dramatic events. It is a structure with whorls enough to cover both the territory of the imagined world and the escapades of the human world as long as these escapades fall within the interests of God's plan for his kingdom.

The Church is another mythic image of significance, located between the Christ event and the Eschaton. It is the only image on the level of human history that enjoys the guarantee of salvation by virtue of its knowledge of the divine plan, its representation of the kingdom of God in the world before the grand finale, and its tight control of Christians and their piety. It is this privileged location in the imagined world that gives the Church its authority to speak for God.

The mythic images at the Eschaton are events of divine sovereignty, power, and judgment in the division of the human race between the righteous and the sinners. It also includes the salvation of the righteous, variously imagined, the damnation of the sinners, also variously imagined, and the destruction of the old world order. The Eschaton is the event when the kingdom of God will be fully revealed to receive Christians, exclude sinners, and thus overcome all the preceding dualisms of the mythic schema.

The Grammar

The diagram of the imagined world on page 201 can now be seen as a grammar. It functions similarly to the grammar of a language except for two differences. One is that it governs mythic thinking, not speech. The other is that its logics are narrative sequences and consequences, not syntactical rules. I have called the major events listed therein, as well as their many narrative embellishments, *mythic images*. Within the structure of the diagram the images are integrally related. Each is significant only in relation to the others. However, the relations are not static, as if the grid pictures the state of the world once and for all. As in any novel or schema, the diagram is dynamic, understood to make room for movement and event, and sequence is important for significance. The relations among terms do not consist of equations, as in mathematical calculations. They are governed by a narrative logic and thus are to be seen as a set of factors of consequence.

It is therefore necessary to imagine the diagram as a description of consequences at two different levels, the divine and the human. On the human level, moreover, there is a second bifurcation of levels, depending upon the human response to the divine plan. On the one human level, where obedience is the factor of consequence, a constructive sense of the events of transformation and final judgment is imaginable. A sense of forward movement is given, typical of pilgrimage and the proper way of approaching events of divine breakthrough and transformation. On the other human level, where sin and disobedience are the factors of consequence, forward movement is fraught with danger, and conversions are needed. The imagination of movement forward is derived from the biblical history and gospel narratives. In the case of the Old Testament history on its way to the Christ event, the factors of consequence are obvious in traditional Christian interpretation. They are the usual contrasts between obedience and sin and their consequences. The sense of movement is given with prophecies and promises. In the case of the gospel, the story is designed in such a way as to take the reader back before the event of transformation in order to "follow" Jesus on his way to Jerusalem. Thus the narrative notion is given of approaching or coming to the pivotal event as an event of consequence about which one must make a decision. Finally, in the time between the Christ event and the Eschaton, the church governs the sense of movement. Pagans are asked to convert or be threatened with divine judgment; Christians are expected to stay faithful and pure in order to pass the test of the final judgment. The sense of movement now shifts toward the Eschaton. If Catholic, the confessor hears the words, "Go and sin no more." If Protestant, one can flaunt one's status as a "bornagain" Christian, but then, because one cannot be positively certain about the final judgment, live in "fear and trembling," as Kierkegaard put it, or work hard and succeed in business in order to prove one's election, as Max Weber's study, *The Protestant Ethic and the Spirit of Capitalism*, concluded.

I am now ready to suggest that this mythic grammar has determined a Christian mentality. The mentality governed by this mythic schema is much more difficult to document than the schema itself. The mythic system is objective in the sense that its manifestations in texts, iconography, and ritual practices are available for review. The grammar of the system is a bit less obvious, but still available for review in the sermons, theologies, and applications of the system throughout Christian history. The resulting mentality is a feature of enculturation, thus a matter of the ways in which the grammar has been used to apply the logic of the mythic worldview to the real world. As such, it is a largely unconscious factor in determining common discourse. And yet it is just at the level of common discourse that the influence or use of the mythic grammar can be spotted and analyzed. I have used the terms *mythic images* and *factors of consequence* to name features of the mythic system that function as a grammar for thinking and discourse within the social world. It is the automatic application of this grammar to situations in the social world of the everyday that alerts us to the presence of a mentality. In the next chapter I will provide several illustrations of contemporary Christian thinking and discourse that can be understood as expressions of a mentality based on the logic and grammar of the mythic system. Here it will be sufficient to note a number of mythic images and the grammatical rules they govern in order to help conceptualize the function of this myth–ritual system as a grammar.

Monistic thinking The overriding mythic image pervading all of Christian mentality is that of the one God. Since this God is imagined both as a divine being (Greek conceptuality) and as a personal agent (Jewish derivation), monistic thinking encapsulates sovereignty and agency in relation both to the natural world as the creation, and to human history as plan and demand. Thus there can be no other agencies of significance either in the natural orders, such as evolution or astrophysical explanations, or in the human realm, such as human ingenuity or social formation as a human achievement. For Christian mentality there is only one sovereign, one ultimate agency, one revelation, one divine plan, one divine standard for humans, one right way of thinking, and one right way of living. Monistic thinking is not only pervasive, it is taken for granted, and thus is seldom noticed as the problem that keeps Christians from considering and appreciating differences within a pluralistic world.

The singularity of monotheism, monarchy, the concept of universe, and confidence in universal principles is so self-evident to Christians that it provides the basis for entire systems of logic and explanation without being questioned. One result of this monistic thinking is the notion of the unique. This takes the concept of the single to the level of singularity where it can be applied to the Christ event or any other aspect of Christianity and its canons in order to claim incomparability in relation to other events, religions, and myths. Although this might be seen as an implicit recognition of plurality in the world without having to abandon the monotheistic claims of Christianity, the notion of the unique puts Christianity into a separate category, all by itself, and thus protects monistic thinking. In New Testament scholarship the use of the term *unique* has meant two things. One is that the claim to divine origins is somehow credible. The other is that the scholar need not try to explain this origin by comparison with other religions or by means of human logics and explanations.

The problem with the concept of the singular is the acknowledgment of other humans and their failures to recognize the one God that also have to be in the picture. This acknowledgment is in fact built into the schema. It sets up a very interesting logical mechanism for dealing with all others who are not Christian: the logic of opposites and opposition. Opposition presents a problem for Christianity in the real world, but it does not threaten the mythic system, because the schema includes the mechanisms of breakthrough events, conversion, and final judgment to resolve all oppositions. And yet, the dualisms implicit within the mythic system do register a problem, not only for God and his plan, but also for human thought. Neither a dualistic cosmology of the Christian kind nor the separation of humankind into two separate categories has been fruitful of further intellectual elaboration. Nevertheless, these dualisms persist in Christian thinking as oppositions that can be resolved eventually only by means of divine agency.

The dualisms During the second and third centuries, when the Christian myth was in the making but not yet given creedal form, the "logic of the singular" was obvious in the literature and arguments of the theologians. We noted this in the previous chapter and discussed its difference from other logics in which the dual and the plural determined constructive ways of thinking. Now we see that a principle of dualism is integral to the grammar of the Christian myth and ritual system. This dualism refers to social distinctions as opposites and can be expressed in a series of paired contrasts, such as enlightened/ignorant, obedient/disobedient, righteous/sinful, Christians/all others, good/evil, saved/damned, etc. These contrasts are thought of as two kinds of status in relation to the sovereign God, thus integrated into the grammar determined by the logic of the singular. We might ask how that can be, how the logic of the dual works in a system determined by the logic of the singular.

Normally the logic of the double, the paired contrast, or the plural works to mark differences and distinctions that give rise to thought. In tribal societies, as indicated in a previous chapter, the division into two or more clans or moieties, each consisting of two or more clans, marks differences of importance for thinking about the working relations of the tribe as a whole. In the case of paired contrasts common to human observation, such as up/down, right/left, male/female, light/dark, and so forth, the contrasts mark differences that function as a basic system of classification. They can be used to mark distinctions between and among many objects under observation, sharpen description, and enable description and thinking. They serve as second-level categories in which each term is relative to the other. Thus the earth can be "female" in relation to the sky ("male"), but "male" in relation to the sea ("female"). In Western thinking we tend to interpret contrastive pairs as if they are definitional and ranked, marking an opposition instead of a relative difference. This may be an indication of the influence of the Christian grammar with its preference for absolute dualisms of opposition. If we add the observation that the contrastive oppositions of the Christian grammar mark moral differences that are absolute determinants of ultimate destinies, we come close to an explanation for the way in which the explicit use of dual language tends to be limited to moral distinctions. We need only remind ourselves of the many ranked pairs in current public discourse, such as right/wrong, white/colored, nativist/anti-immigrationist, us/them, right/left, etc. This works as long as the Christian period of time between the Christ and the Eschaton is in mind, the inferior term is not considered permanent, and the inferior group is not considered an enemy. Then inferior status can be understood to mark candidates for instruction, missionizing, and/or conversion. This, however, does not result in a "symmetrical relation between two hierarchical evaluations [that] combines the claim of encompassment of the Other with the reversibility of that claim, made possible by the dualistic structure of the system," as in Valeri's study of the Siwa-Lima system of inverse and reciprocal moieties among the Central Moluccas ("Reciprocal Centers," 137). Should the rejection of Christianity and its right way be seen as definite and final, the contrast easily turns into an opposition with potential for conflict. Then an assessment of the contrast takes the form of a final judgment on the absolute determinant of ultimate destiny (as in "Go to hell," or "axis of evil"). When this happens, the distinction between the two terms of contrast becomes sharp and hard. This logic of opposition is not a matter of "on the one hand" and "on the other." It is a logic of the "either/or" variety in which certain absolute values are not subject to deliberation or compromise.

Dramatic events The mythic grammar attributes significance to events. The paradigmatic events are those of divine creation, transformation, and judgment. All are double-edged in that oppositions are inverted in a two-staged sequence. The first event, Creation, has usually been seen solely as the unimaginable inversion of nothingness into the creation of the world. Left at the divine level of the diagram, that works as a demonstration of God's creative power and claim to sovereignty. However, the Genesis story comes to focus on the creation of humankind. At this level there is the first interchange of divine command and human disobedience. The result is expulsion from paradise, consignment to labor, family conflict, violence, and the time of testing. The Eschaton also contains two movements. One is the end of human history and the judgment of the righteous and ungodly; the other is the destruction of the ungodly and the redemption of the righteous. The most graphic image of an event that matters is, of course, the Christ event, the crucifixion and resurrection of Jesus. It is this image that controls all of the nuances of divine event for Christian mentality and reveals the radical inversion required to overcome oppositional contrasts. The inversion is a transformation from death to life, from victim to victor—an event of transformation possible only by the intervention of God.

Christian mentality is sensitized to events and thinks of an event as the location of significance and meaning. As a matter of fact, the preferred designation for a human situation is an event. We know, however, that human situations can combine many interests, issues, and relationships that are significant and meaningful other than in terms of eventfulness. Christian mentality eschews the banal but pays special attention to events in which transformations occur. One would think that processes of analysis, factoring, ranking, comparing, deliberating, and suggesting theories and policies for understanding and/or solving questions or problems related to a situation would be the reasonable approach. However, Christian thinking has demonstrated an amazing impatience with the analysis of multiple factors in a human situation. This is especially true of social situations where deliberation, negotiation, and compromise are necessary. Instead, the focus is always on those features of a situation where the decisive event takes place, or on the actions of those in control, constructed if possible in the direction of the dramatic and sensational, if not as a crisis. That is because significance for Christian mentality is a function of dramatic change and/or transformation, usually with a moral coefficient.

Sovereignty The Christian myth–ritual system assumes sovereignty as the only imaginable power to create social worlds and keep order. For worlds to come into being in any other way, whether the world of the universe or that of human society, is largely unimaginable, because the concept of sovereignty allows for the notions of creation, of ownership, and of ruling one's domain, in such a way as to make the demands of a sovereign legitimate, and the control of a sovereign to be expected and desired. If no order, no sovereign; if no sovereign, no order, so the thinking has been. This logic was first transferred from the sovereignty of God to the emperors and kings of the Roman Empire and its successors. Kings were the legitimate heirs of divine privilege and had a mandate to govern their peoples and lands and keep order. Now that there are no longer kings on the old monarchical model, the question of sovereignty has been passed to the secular nation-states, and the use of divine power to control a people has become problematic. The Protestant Conservative Right in the United States has not been willing to give up on the notions of divine sovereignty and control at the level of political governance, but most Christian churches have shifted the arena of divine control from the political to the personal, where God can still be in control of morals. Of course, this is an arena over which the church has always had control, but to limit divine control to the arena of morals is a reduction of erstwhile kingdom and social fantasies. The desire for law and order is not thereby met. Thus one detects a sense of disenfranchisement on the part of the mainline churches in America. It therefore remains to be seen whether the old triad of Christian controls over kingdom, power, and piety can last. At the present time, at the level of mentality and sensibility, the triad is still in place.

Problem solving The Christian imagination is at work between the Christ event in the past and the Eschaton in the future. These two events are understood to be God's solutions to human problems. They do not reflect well on the character of God and his capacity for solving human problems, for in both cases the logic is that of redemptive violence. Violence is not redemptive, and even if one wanted to justify the two events of the Christ event and the Eschaton on the basis of some special consideration for divine power and purpose as imagined in other periods of history, as paradigms for the present time they are hardly a good model for solving human problems. They are, however, the only model Christians have, which is to project guilt and call for confession, conversion, and obedience. The Catholic church can mediate forgiveness to individual persons, but it gets confused about solving the social problems of context, while the Protestant church has mainly the pulpit to charge the troublemakers with immorality and call for a return to the traditional fold. In neither case is there a mechanism for solving social problems that calls for deliberation, negotiation, and compromise. These are all taken to be signs of weakness on the part of those from whom the defense of righteousness is expected.

The Christian grammar makes it difficult to handle human conflict. The Christian categories of classification are not adequate, since they are all beholden to the imagined world of human history in relation to divine sovereignty, not the human worlds in relation to one another. The best that can be managed when human conflict becomes critical is the contrast between superior and inferior, then good and evil. This is obviously not helpful, and especially not in times of war.

Encounters with Others

Thus far in our essay we have focused upon the church as an institution and its imagined world as clergy, kings, and Christians have seen it from within. It was possible to do this because the formation of medieval Christendom produced such an encompassing culture, and its myth–ritual system has continued to be cultivated even in the twenty-first century. From the medieval period to the present, however, the church has had encounters with many other cultures, peoples, histories, logics, human interests, enterprises, and political formations whose social interests did not need the church, and in fact could not be made to fit into the church's world. This history is exceedingly complex, and its massive documentation is such that it can be mastered only in small segments by specialists and historians. Nevertheless, the general outlines of the history are, if not well known, readily available for perusal in any number of studies and encyclopedia entries. These will be sufficient in order to make some observations about a number of these encounters and the ways in which they challenged the church's authority. We will not be able to keep track of or account fully for the church's response as an institution. It will only be possible to take note of the remarkable resilience of this institution throughout a history when other social formations were dislodged and/or radically restructured. Of more importance for our study will be to question the resilience of the church's imagined world. It is the fate of the myth–ritual system that we want to discover, whether it was found capable of answering the challenges of social and worldview changes or not, and what contemporary Christians might be doing with its logic in a world that is radically different from the Roman and medieval worlds in which it was first imagined. Why, in fact, do Christians continue to cultivate and invest in an imagined world that has no grammar for thinking constructively about the present configuration of the human world?

Peoples and Cultures

There were always other peoples and their gods around the edges of the Roman and medieval church, but none were regarded as threats to the imagined world. At most they were considered either an inconvenience or a fertile field for missionary expansion. Only on occasion has conflict with another religion become an occasion for war, and those were matters of political conflict more than religious ideological differences. Nevertheless, the imagined world of Christians has no place for other peoples, gods, and religions, and that has brought about a variety of responses depending upon circumstances, near–far relations, possible accommodations, and whether in some cases the other peoples were willing to convert.

The gods and religions of the Greeks and Romans were banned and died. The gods of the Scandinavians were reduced to folklore figures when their tribal chiefs "converted" to Christianity under the sword. The Jews were allowed their ghettos because they had no tribal chiefs with warriors, and could in any case be related to biblical history as "Old Testament" people in whom God might still be interested. They were certainly not a threat to any sovereign, and their "No, thank you" approach to Christianity was hardly offensive. It was mainly in times of social crisis such as the Plague and the Nazi insanities that the gospel account took over to target the Jews as scapegoats. These were not insignificant moments of Christian far-reaching, to be sure. The gospel at the center of the imagined world had to be there for the rationalizations to work.

With Islam the story has been a bit different. As with Judaism, Islam was difficult to classify because it laid claim to the biblical heritage, descent from Abraham, a monotheistic sovereign, and a universal mission. All of these marked similarities to Christianity that were too close for comfort and were recognized as competing claims. In distinction from Judaism (until the twentieth century), it also produced chieftains with armies, missionary conquests, and political confrontations just like the Christian rulers. It was at this level of challenge to royal power that the crusades were undertaken. However, the customary Western construction of this threat has been exaggerated. There was no single threatening event that triggered the crusades. Rather, the fragmentation of the Roman Empire had resulted in wars among the European kingdoms, social and economic decline, and a sense of lost energy and glory. A resurgence of political and ecclesiastical control of lands and peoples had been building for some time by redirecting the wars against one another within Europe to target the "infidels" on the borders. The crusades marked a surge in this marshaling of energies under the aegis of the Church that organized armies and rabble from the several European kingdoms in a concerted effort to regain lands lost to the Muslims. Recent studies have documented the period of the crusades as "products of an increasingly aggressive and energetic society bent on strengthening politico-religious authority at home and extending its reach abroad" (Lazare, "God's Willing Executioners"). Reading the histories of this period is a very painful experience (Tyerman, *God's War*). It is painful because of the religious zeal and exuberance of the Christian armies in their many massacres all the way to Jerusalem, where in 1099 the Muslim and Jewish defenders were indiscriminately slaughtered and the victory of the Christians' triumphant God was celebrated in a religious gathering at the Church of the Holy Sepulchre.

It is painful for another reason as well. That is the way in which Christians have justified the crusades by laying the blame on Muslims who practiced "conversion by the sword." The implied contrast, of course, is that Christians do not, as Pope Benedict XVI stated at Regensburg in September 2006, but the truth is that no other religion in combination with political powers has unleashed such a history of violence and war as Christianity. The justification of this history in the name of a righteous sovereign who wants to govern a universal peaceable kingdom is nothing less than an offense to human reason and dignity. We need not deny that there are reasons for taking offense at Islamic law and similar atrocities in its own histories in order to acknowledge the elegance of the Byzantine court at the time of the crusades, the remarkable Islamic civilization at the time, with its sciences and learning, or the contributions of its intellectuals and social philosophers such as Ibn Khaldun to the Renaissance (Stone, "Ibn Khaldun"). Thus Muslims were less quickly consigned to pagan fates by Christian scholars in Europe at the time, who often received them into their centers of learning. However, this recognition of Muslim achievement in science, historiography, and philosophy did not result in a realignment of the Christian grammar, much less the logic of its myth–ritual system.

We have already had occasion to mention the church's interest in other peoples and their religions during the Age of Discovery and colonization. We have already noted that tribal cultures have consistently been regarded as inferior, much in need of civilization and conversion to Christianity. We have also mentioned that a curiosity about tribal culture and religion never led to a questioning of the definition of religion that stemmed from familiarity with Christianity on the part of historians of religion. We can now observe that Christian missions worked in tandem with other Western interests abroad, such as trading, colonization, and the exploitation of natural resources. This means that the church has continued to think of itself on the old staff/scepter model of civilization right up and into the nineteenth and twentieth centuries. Eventually, when the real scepters of the nation-states looked less and less like sovereign emblems of righteousness, the church apparently found ways to accommodate other forms of political power as its partners. Its mission was then reduced to building churches, converting the natives however that could be managed (by force if necessary), and supporting the increasingly secular powers in the interest of social control and stability. This liaison with "secular" governments, their powers, and their missions abroad has never been radically challenged. Only much later, in the late twentieth century, did Christian missionaries begin to wonder about the political and corporate interests they had customarily supported and defended.

The Natural World

At some point, usually dated somewhere around the thirteenth century, the imagined world of Christendom was found inadequate to contain, much less explain, the learning that increased during the Renaissance. The Renaissance has customarily been associated with the rediscovery of Greek and Latin texts, and renewed interest in the arts and cultures of late antiquity. However, it was also a time when the empirical world caught the attention of intellectuals and scientists. Its hallmark has frequently been called an exploration of humanism, an interest in seeing a recognizably human figure in the setting of the natural world without halos or flying angels. In every case there was an awareness of violating the church's taboos against stepping outside the atmosphere and vision of the imagined world. The confessions of Petrarch, a fourteenth-century humanist, are a clear example of this awareness right at the point of different views of the natural world, that of "creation" vs. "nature." But Galileo's caution, Copernicus's daily devotions, and Newton's obsession with the Bible are all examples of the continuing effect of the church's imagined world even for those intellectual giants whose sciences were breaking it apart. One might think that the new sciences should have altered the church's cosmology. But no. The sciences were simply rejected by the church, and the scientists threatened with excommunication. Only later and by degrees would theologians make the attempt to incorporate the new learning into the Christian view of the world. Aquinas kept the heavenly world in place by separating it from the natural world, letting "reason" have the natural world for its arena, thus leaving the heavenly world to "faith," a form of persuasion not amenable to rational criticism. Teilhard de Chardin took the natural world and its cosmology up into the abstract world of divine mystique and mystification in order to satisfy Christian sensibility. And Protestants have devised a menagerie of "spiritualities" in order to let the heavenly world trickle through the natural and social environments.

We know, of course, that the conflict between the natural sciences and religion has never been resolved. It is the Christian's imagined world that is at stake. Even after generations of scientific research into some physical matter, the results can just be dismissed by Christians if it appears that the imagined world is under attack. A current example is the debate between evolution and creationism in the United States. One hundred fifty years of research in physical anthropology, cultural anthropology, geology, the evolution of marine life, animal species, and botanical species does not count. It is the biblical story of creation by the one sovereign God of Christianity that is preferred.

Other Creeds

The Protestant Reformation can serve as another example of the continued cultivation of the Christian myth and ritual system despite serious differences of opinion about the patina of the imagined world. These differences occurred in the wake of the Renaissance. The literatures of late antiquity included the biblical texts. Learning Greek suggested new ways to read those texts. The growing awareness of historical roots in Greco-Roman culture suggested ways to imagine Christian origins other than through the lens of the imaginary world overlaid with Catholic embellishments, which were now regarded as superstitions. A new orientation to reason, appreciation for the arts and Greek culture, and the importance of the social dimensions of "community" accompanied the reformers' disgust at the extravagant mystifications of Roman Catholicism, especially the selling of indulgences (discounts on time required in Purgatory), and the Mass as a miracle of transubstantiation. The reformers directed their criticisms at the Catholic Church, but their efforts at reformation were directed to the construction of new congregations that were independent of Catholic governance. Their reconstructions of the Christian church were radical if compared with Catholicism and judged in light of their subsequent social effects. And yet, as the reformers said, the church is present wherever (1) the word is proclaimed and (2) the sacraments are performed.

This combination of congregation, Bible, and sacraments (referring especially to the "Lord's Supper" in distinction from the Mass) was the way in which Protestants wriggled free from the dense and singular environment of Catholic Christianity. It can be seen as a remarkable intellectual effort in rearranging and resignifying the objective signs and symbols of the mythic markers of the Christian's imagined world. The emphasis on congregation was intended as a corrective to the Catholic concept of the Church as a spiritual and universal ethos encompassing the worlds of nature and society. The Protestant conception of the congregation introduced a social and historical, real-world dimension to Christians gathered for worship. The local congregation became the place in the world where Christian experience and life were located. The Bible transferred attention to text and history, away from the Catholic orientation to the cosmic world with its ontologies of heaven and hell. The celebration of the Lord's Supper was now framed by the preaching of the Word with its emphasis upon doctrinal propositions basic to the

Christian faith. The individual Christian was now addressed as a believer, one who was required to assent to the truth of the Bible and the Christian faith, and who would need to struggle with the truth claims of the gospel in order to be a true Christian. Hence the shifts in the objective symbols of the Christian religion: from Mass to Lord's Supper; from altar to pulpit; from iconography to credo; from visual and aesthetic ambience to preaching; from priest to preacher. All were moves that pared down the mystique of the medieval imagined world. Nevertheless, these moves did not dismantle the myth–ritual system itself. Its logic of replication shifted from Mass to memorial, from ritual to myth, but it was not set aside.

As may be well known to the reader, the Catholic Church reacted to the Protestant Reformation with a Counter-Reformation, using the weapons of authority, power, and intellectual intimidation to bring Protestant Christians to their senses. It did not work. The main reason was that the times were ready for a more rational and sociological interpretation of Christianity. It was, however, also the case that the old pattern of staff and scepter could be transferred to the kings and rulers of northern Europe, who saw the advantage of supporting and protecting the Protestant leaders and their churches. As a matter of fact, it was the rulers of the various lands and peoples of northern Europe who decided between Protestant and Roman loyalties for their countries. The rule was "As the ruler, so the church," meaning that the people were expected to conform to their ruler's choice of church, be it Protestant or Catholic. Thus the notion of Christendom was still in place.

The Reformation produced a variety of Protestant movements and churches, some conforming to the circumstances prevailing in various countries at the time. Thus the Lutherans became the dominant church in Germany and other northern European countries. The Reformed tradition of Calvin and Zwingli started in Switzerland, where the city-state of Geneva turned against its Catholic rulers and asked Calvin to lead its experiment in forming a Protestant city. Then the Reformed tradition jumped to Scotland, where John Knox and the Presbyterians became dominant. In England the Reformation produced a shift in the thinking and leadership of the Catholic Church without dismantling the institution. The king was recognized as the head of the Anglican Church as well as sovereign of the state, and the prelate Thomas Cranmer became the first Anglican archbishop of Canterbury. He introduced the English Bible into all of the churches, composed the new Book of Common Prayer, and devised litanies for Anglican worship. Thus there were many ecclesiastical formations to counter the overreaching authority of the medieval church. And there were soon many attempts by non-clerical intellectuals to explore Renaissance thinking in relation to the Protestant conception of the Christian faith. John Locke's treatise *The Reasonableness of Christianity* can serve as an example of attempts to come to terms with the new anthropologies, while Deism was one of the ways in which philosophers held on to the idea of a supreme being while acknowledging the new scientific cosmologies. Protestants have frequently thought that the acceptance of

The Social Formation of Christendom

reason and science purified Christian faith of its need for mythic thinking. Unfortunately for this view, both Locke's arguments for the miracles of Jesus because they were so unique as to be inexplicable and the notion of creation by the supreme deity that was not relinquished by the Deists reveal the persistence of mythic thinking that continued through the Enlightenment.

Other Kings

The last three centuries have witnessed the Enlightenment; the American and French revolutions; the Industrial Revolution; the rise of the nation-state; the separation of church and state in the United States; the influence of political philosophies and ideologies, such as democracy, communism, capitalism, and fascism; wars in the interest of political domination of other lands and peoples; and the emergence of global corporations and polycultural societies. One might think that the imagined world of Christianity and its several denominational churches as institutions would have been found wanting, if not counterproductive, for the intellectual labors called for by rapidly changing social circumstances. In a sense, that is exactly what has happened. The churches have not been able to address a long list of social, political, environmental, and cultural issues that are obviously in need of some discussion, if not deliberation and solution. One would think that would be of concern and interest to Christianity as the dominant religion of the Western nations. In Europe, however, the Christian state churches have found it possible to retire from the political arena and be satisfied with presiding over important state occasions and religious holidays, as well as serving the needs of individuals for ceremonies of baptism, marriage, and funerals. This contrasts with the situation in the United States, where Christian coalitions are engaged in political action committees, and conservative Christians, concerned about the moral state of the nation, seem to be in fear and trembling about the future, and are not embarrassed to say in public that they believe in the imminent end of the world, or that believing in "Jesus Christ and him crucified," as one scientist put it on Bill Moyers's talk show, will decide the fate of all peoples for eternity. How can that be? Do the imagined world and its myth–ritual structure still provide the grammar for Christian mentality and thinking currently in the United States? The thesis in this study is that the grammar is still very much in place, both in the postures of the institutional churches, and especially in the thinking and behavior of individual Christians.

We are therefore ready to argue for this thesis in the next chapter, which is an analysis of the current notion of the United States as a Christian nation. The break-up of the church–kingdom arrangement in Europe was followed by the secularization of the nation-states, and that has been followed by multiethnic and polycultural states. Thus the imagination of a cosmic kingdom of God, represented in the real world by the church–kingdom arrangement, is no longer available as a civic projection of the churches for scholarly analysis. This means that the search for the myth–ritual system of American Christianity and a documentation of its mentality will present us with a different kind of challenge. The transformation of European models when applied to the United States will have to be worked out in terms of the history of Christianity in the United States, and against the background of a general lack of interest in social theory among Americans. In the United States, a very definite turn to individualism needs to be recognized. What that means for social concepts such as freedom, equality, fraternity, and democracy, as well as for what Christianity has come to mean for individuals, will have to be explored. Nevertheless, a close look at the rhetoric and conceptuality of the Christian nation as expressed in public practices and discourse will allow us to assess the degree to which a Christian mentality still exists on the model of the traditional imagined world. It will be important to describe this mentality as it now works in America, in order to assess the chances for Christianity in a social and cultural world that it is no longer capable of addressing.

7 The State of the Christian Nation

We have traced the imagined world of Christianity from its beginnings into the modern period and analyzed its myth and ritual structure at the point of medieval Christendom. It was relatively easy to do that, for the documentation was evident, public, and still available to us in texts, architecture, art, and the myth–ritual practices of the Christian churches that continued after the medieval period. On the basis of this analysis we theorized a mentality based upon the myth–ritual system as a kind of conceptual grammar. This was possible because of the way the church and its imagined world were taken for granted. We also noted the remarkable fact that, as the Roman Empire came to its end, and subsequent would-be emperors carved up the empire into separate and competing kingdoms, the church continued to function as a single, imperial institution of fundamental conceptual and structural importance. No monarch thought to rule any European kingdom that was not Christian.

From the period of the Reformation to the present, however, marked by the Enlightenment, the Industrial Revolution, and the rise of the nation-state, keeping track of the imagined world became more difficult. There were now many different Christian denominations relating variously to several new configurations of political domain and social structure. We noted that the church was still taken for granted in all European nations of the modern period, and that the myth–ritual pattern was still extant whether Protestant or Catholic. One might have thought that the Western history of intellectual enlightenments, social revolutions, scientific discoveries, and industrialized technologies would have set aside the Christian myth–ritual system as archaic, for according to our theory the social interests of the nation-states no longer required such a mythology, and the social interests of the church were largely reduced to assuring its own survival as an institution of private religion. Yet it seems that Christian mentality continued to influence thinking, both in Europe and in America, as our spot check of mythic markers has indicated. This raises the question of the ways in which Christian mentality and the Christian churches have worked out their accommodations to their new social situations.

In the case of the European nations one might begin to answer this question with the observation that the state churches are taking advantage of a cultural lag. Just as with the retention of the monarchy and the name United Kingdom in England, for instance, so the Anglican Church continues to be appreciated as a reminder of continuity with an illustrious history. As with the monarchy, the church is more a cultural emblem than an active participant in the political aspects of the society. Without it, certain historic moments of significance and glory would not have their monuments and celebrations, nor would the traditional rites of passage have their priests. As Raymond Williams found in his study of the intellectual tradition in England during this period, the issues under discussion revolved around the ugliness of urbanization caused by the Industrial Revolution, whether democracy had any chance of working as an answer to monarchy and the social issues of the industrial age, and the threat to the cultural values held dear by the intellectuals who continued to think of the pre-industrial time as civil, their own time as tarnished. The Christian church was not up for criticism or discussion. On those few occasions when the Christian tradition was mentioned in these learned essays, always in the context of other discussions, the church was appreciated solely as the vehicle for nurturing civility, where civility meant traditional English culture. It appears that the Christian grammar we have been theorizing may have seeped into a cultural mentality that substituted a colonial governance for the older Holy Empire.

In this chapter, however, I want to move across the Atlantic and explore the question of the resilience of Christian mentality in the United States. The question has become important because of the Christian influence in politics and public discourse in recent years, leading to debates about the United States as a "Christian nation." In order to explore this concept and the questions it has raised about religion and society in America, we need to keep four different concepts of society in mind. There is (1) the popular notion of America as a Christian nation, (2) the understanding that America is a nation-state, sometimes called a republic or a federal union, functioning as a democracy, (3) the concept of the Christian kingdom embedded in the traditional mythic grammar of Christianity, and (4) the concept of society as described in our study, namely, as a social construction in which religions (myths and rituals) rationalize collective social interests of importance to the working of the society as a whole. This chapter will analyze each of these concepts in relation to the others in order to explore the ways in which Christian mentality has influenced thinking about religion in America.

First, it will be important to acknowledge that the popular notion of religion as personal experience has seldom found it necessary to think about these social conceptions. One reason for this circumstance was discussed at the end of Chapter 1, namely, that a focus upon the individual has been a mark of Western cultures since the Enlightenment, and that this focus has resulted in a wide range of psychologies and philosophies of what has been called "authentic experience." The point was that religion was not the only cultural tradition affected by this interest in exploring personal subjectivity. A second reason can now be given. It is that Christianity has expressly addressed the individual from the very beginning of its history. This fact, together with the modern, cultural focus upon the individual in general, can help us understand the difficulty many Christians may have in thinking critically about the social logic of the Christian mythic grammar. A brief review of this history of Christianity's interest in the individual may serve as a counterpoint to our analysis of the interest Christians have recently taken in our society.

The early associations of the Jesus schools were "voluntary" organizations, independent from Roman control. Associations served the social interests of particular people, of course, but "membership" was in some sense a matter of "choice," at least in the sense of taking a particular place or position within the larger social order. In the transition to a religion of empire, the association language of personal choice was not discontinued even when there were no longer alternative religions from which to "choose," and the medieval system of Christian ritual was expressly focused on the individual. It was in fact polished as a performance that climaxed at the point of an individual's "participation" in the reenactment of the divine event of transformation. The Protestant reformations introduced a complication into the public/private equation, but they did not relieve the address to the individual. The complication was that, instead of the Catholic Church providing continuity from one kingdom to another, as had been the case throughout medieval history, people found themselves having to change religions as determined by the king. The Augsburg formula to end the wars unleashed by the Protestant reformations was "as with the king, so the religion" (*cuius regio, eius religio*), meaning in effect that the king will decide whether to be Protestant or Catholic, and as he decides so will all his people decide. That left little room for "choice" on the part of the individual, but the new arrangement did not exempt the individual from responsibility for his or her personal salvation. The shift from ritual experience to being addressed by preaching and the demand for believing meant that Christians were now responsible for understanding as well as "accepting" (or experiencing) the Christian message solely as individuals. A remarkable combination of intellectual agony and psychological interiorization resulted in some circles as the definition of "religious experience." This was especially true in Calvinistic traditions. It is this mode of "experiencing" the Christian religion that is now being taken for granted in conservative Christian churches in the United States.

In Germany there was some relief from such an address to the individual by means of the "two-kingdom" concept, which left matters of "faith" and "piety" to the church and let the kings control society. This arrangement provided a space between the two worlds within which the individual Christian need not worry too much about personal beliefs or religious experiences. As Luther said, "Soak up those suds and preach the gospel." In England the two-kingdom concept was not enough, mainly because the Anglican solution to the Reformation could not quiet voices of dissent. The political decision of importance was the Toleration Act of 1689, in which the distinction was made between "public" and "private" religion. Dissent in matters of personal religious belief was allowed in private (or limited to assemblies of dissenters), but forbidden in the form of public and political activities.

As the Industrial Revolution quickened, yet another social structure came into being that widened the gap between personal piety and participation in social and political activities: that was the nation-state. A *de facto* separation of state from church occurred, as we have seen, allowing new modes of production, finance, and political control of social infrastructures to organize apart from Christian institutions. The result, even for Enlightenment intellectuals such as Hobbes and Rousseau, was a retention of the Christian belief in a transcendent God, the guarantor of morality, together with the cultivation of personal religious sentiment with respect to one's spiritual well-being. Russell McCutcheon has called this the "interiorization" of religious belief, sentiment, and self-identity. He has helped us see how complicit this development was in the support of what can now be called the "secular" state. His point is that the "agreement" to limit religious experience to the "zone" of the personal, while it may have been the only way to continue thinking of oneself as a Christian, in effect supplied the secular interests of the nation-state with a religious justification in the name of tolerance (*The Discipline of Religion*, 252–90).

In the United States it was this tradition of tolerance and the definition of religion as a matter of personal and private experience and opinion that found its way into the Constitution. The arrangement worked quite well as long as both the governments and the churches thought of each other as complementary domains and the individual Christian could be governed in matters of morals and values. It allowed the formation of sects (separatist denominations), as well as letting individual Christians experiment with various ways of thinking about private experience and religiosity. These experiments were not solely aimed at personal religious experiences, for they also focused on individual moralities and ethics as the "outward" signs of Christian belief and character. It was when Christians no longer saw their personal values reflected in the practices of individuals, society, and government that "dissent" was organized by conservative leaders for political action. The cultivation of Christian beliefs and practices by individuals provided a huge reservoir of motivation, now aimed at cleaning up the iniquities in the world that had accumulated by letting non-Christians have their way. Unfortunately, the only vision of a cleaned-up world available to these Christians was that of a righteous kingdom on the model of the imagined world of medieval Christendom. It is this combination of personal piety and social concern that we need to analyze.

The Christian Nation

The misleading but standard popular account of its history has assumed that the United States was from the beginning and continues to be a Christian nation. It is possible to follow some of the expressions of that assumption in a reconstruction of the nation's history. There is the account of the pilgrims who fled religious persecution in Europe and colonized New England as puritans. That was clearly before the Revolutionary War, and is much more to our credit as a nation with religious purpose, it seems, than accounts of Jamestown, the Virginia Company, the land grants in Virginia and the Carolinas, where plantations were developed for profit, or the founding of New York as a commercial enterprise. As for the founding fathers, it has been taken for granted that they read and studied the Bible, as indeed some of them did, even though it has been convenient, if not necessary, to overlook its reduction to the "pure Deism" that Jefferson wanted to find in the teachings of Jesus. The Great Awakenings of the eighteenth century, the first in New England, the second in the Virginias, both spreading out to the west and south, have also often been rehearsed as signs of a basic Christian religiosity and piety. Francis Scott Key could praise "the Pow'r that hath made and preserved us as a nation" for the victory of the States in the War of 1812 as well as the image of the "Star-Spangled Banner," waving "O'er the land of the free and the home of the brave." Samuel Smith, a Boston minister, had no trouble when composing "My Country 'Tis of Thee" in 1831 in thinking of "Our fathers' God" as the "Author of liberty" and "Great God, our King." By the time of the Civil War, the author of the "Battle Hymn of the Republic" could discern the "truth" of the Christian's God and Christ in the victories of the Union army as its soldiers "marched on," ready to "die to make men free." The popular account also includes the circuit riders and other evangelists of American Protestant church history, as well as the flourishing of denominational churches and media evangelists throughout the twentieth century. In our recent history, the polls that suggest that more than 80 per cent of Americans believe in God and 60 per cent go to church have been cited as evidence for the nation being Christian.

Christian denominations have written their own versions of this history of Christianity in America in order to emphasize their own presence and influence in American society. Knowing that they are one of many other Christian denominations enhances the sense that Christianity is pervasive throughout America. The individual Christian thinks of religion in terms of this picture. One's own denomination is understood as a national institution with networks of local churches, governing bodies, and other organizations in contact with one another. Transferring membership from one denomination to another has not required major shifts in systems of belief or commitment. The many "community churches" are taken for granted as a sign that different denominations are variants of the same Christian religion. Do not all of them regard the Bible as the gospel, believe in Jesus as the Christ, and worship the Christian God? The result has been the perception that all or most Americans are Christians and that America is therefore a Christian nation.

It is not that Christians are unaware of the social world as a challenge. That the social world may not always look like a Christian community or Christian nation is the reason for the missions of the church. The church is charged with responsibility for the inculcation of religion among the people, oversight of social morals in society at large, care for the needy, and ethical counsel related to national policies. The energies required by these missions are taken for granted, just as the needs for them are somehow accepted as the way the world works. Thus the difference between the ideal of a Christian nation and the reality of the social world is acknowledged without calling the concept of a Christian nation into question. An excellent example of this perception can be found in the life and lecturing of William Jennings Bryan (1860–1925). He has been remembered mostly for his progressive social programs, political career as a Democratic Senator and three-time candidate for the presidency, and for his passionate oratory calling for social change in the interest of the rural Midwestern populace. His arguments against "Darwinism" in the Scopes trial have frequently been thought curiously out of character for a person with such a career. But a recent study by Michael Kazin, *A Godly Hero*, lets us see Bryan's life-long self-understanding as a Christian and his view of the Bible as literally true. This helps to explain his position at the Scopes trial as that of a biblical Christian's fear of evolution. It also presents us with an example of the way in which Christians at that time had no trouble thinking of the United States as a Christian nation and Christianity as the moral fabric of the United States, even though the struggle to make sure it conformed required constant attention.

This standard story is woefully inadequate as a comprehensive history of the social and political interests and practices of America. Most of the versions are oriented to Protestant thinking and interests. Left out of account are large portions of American history filled with vigorous debates and projects hardly touched by Christianity at all, as well as the French and Spanish Catholic influence in New Orleans and the early South, the Catholic missions in the Southwest, native American religions, Black slave religions, and the many immigrant waves of different peoples and religions throughout the nineteenth and twentieth centuries. We need therefore to retell the history with a different concept of America in mind.

The Birth of the Nation

In distinction from the emergence of the nation-states in Europe, the United States did not have an illustrious history of being a Christian kingdom with a state church as its only religious institution. It became a nation after a number of discrete English colonies had developed their own means of production and councils of administration in the New World. Most of these colonies were experiments driven by economic interests, not quests for religious freedom as the myth asserts. All had some remnant of Christianity from their European extractions, to be sure, and the particular denomination of that remnant was sometimes important as one of the markers for membership, privilege, or proprietorship in a colony: Protestant dissenters were okay; Catholics not welcome; and so forth. And it is true that some of the colonists in Massachusetts, now referred to as pilgrims, had been dissenters in England before coming to America (Worrall, "Pilgrims' Progress"). But that way of telling the story is fatally flawed. It has been replaced by more detailed historical reconstructions such as that of the Wampanoag civilization in Massachusetts that was decimated by European incursions in the early seventeenth century (Mann, *1491*, 33–67). Reading Mann one learns that the colonists were neither pilgrims nor puritans, as those terms are commonly understood, but European adventurers and settlers intruding upon and colonizing lands already occupied by native Americans. During the next one hundred fifty years the story of the colonies is one of conflicting and competing positions on matters of finance and the administration of lands, production, and the marketing of goods. As for the causes of the eventual break from English rule, the story is one of strong position-taking, opposing views on matters of loyalty to kings, contrasting ideologies of governance, and the rise of dominant leaders and parties unwilling to compromise on questions of independence and control. Thus, the process of formation of the United States was very different from that of the nation-states in Europe, which emerged from kingdoms by means of internal structural changes.

The difference this made for religious bodies and their relations to the state was significant. Social construction at the level of government was being negotiated as a union of erstwhile independent colonies (now states) with separate legislatures. No kings, whether deposed or in waiting. No state church taken for granted and automatically supported by the Federal government. The Christian churches of European extraction would now have to find ways to support themselves as independent and voluntary organizations. Most of them found ways to do this by authorizing "tithes" and "offerings" as religious obligations and by raising funds for building schools and churches as philanthropic endeavors. Thus there were now two distinctly different foundational documents for Christians in the United States: the Bible and the Constitution. Neither of these contained a clear charter for the construction of a Christian church in America as a Christian nation.

The social formation of the new nation in America as a federal republic was founded on practical considerations of independence and political thought engendered by the Enlightenment, not by direct appeal to the Christian gospel or biblical epic as charter. In the minds of the founding fathers, the principles of both the American and French revolutions were "freedom" from monarchial and autocratic rule, "equality" of all citizens under the law, or equal access to justice, and "fraternity," or the recognition of a common stake in the well-being of the people or of a class of people as a whole, based on the "laws of Nature and Nature's God," as Thomas Jefferson phrased it in the Declaration of Independence (1776). James Madison's Preamble to the Constitution of the United States put the formation of "a more perfect union" (fraternity), the establishment of "justice" (equality*)*, and the securing of the "blessings of liberty" (freedom) in the hands of those identified as "we the people of the United States" (1787). Both Jefferson and Madison included religious liberty among the freedoms intended, but the primary focus was on freedom from British monarchial rule. Religion was mentioned because intolerance was a problem already manifest among the several colonies, not because the colonies were joining together to guarantee the freedom of religion for all. Becoming a federal republic was a matter of hard political bargaining, as the Federalist Papers of Alexander Hamilton reveal, not an attempt to create a Christian nation. The notion of the separation of church and state, a cliché in modern parlance thought to be a constitutional guarantee of religious freedom from the state, was originally a policy formulated in the interest not of religious freedom from state control, but of freedom of the state from control by religion. Since these are the documents that attended and rationalized the events of the birth of the nation, and since they appealed to collective human capacities for social formation on the basis of natural law, there was very little need or chance in immediate retrospect to credit the Christian myth with the founding of a Christian nation. As a matter of fact, the earliest official statement on the United States as a Christian nation actually denied it. In the Treaty with the Barbary Pirates of 1797, Article XI states that "the government of the United States is not in any sense founded on the Christian religion" (Meacham, *American Gospel*, 19).

How, then, did the notion of a Christian nation come about? The answer is by means of many rationalizations over a long period of time. The story of America as a Christian nation is one of mythmaking by degrees, as is the story of the various interpretations of the Constitution in American history. The Christian myth was already in place in the minds of some colonialists, who brought it with them from Europe. It did not have to be invented but its application to the very different social situation in America as a nation was not immediately possible. What happened was a process of reinterpretations both of the Constitution and of the Christian myth in the course of many moments of social change, political crisis, and the rationalizations called for by the social histories of the nation. Thus the reconstruction of the mythmaking that eventually produced the concept of a Christian nation has to follow the history of two themes or threads, parallel for the most part, but brought together on occasion in attempts to combine them. In due course the two myths of origin converged in the minds of some Americans, but the two strands have never actually meshed. In order to illustrate this thesis we can follow portions of the history of the nation and note places where attempts have been made to join the Christian myth to the concept of equality, one of the philosophic principles of the Constitution. This can only be an illustration of a much more complex history in which other constitutional and humanistic concepts, such as freedom, fraternity, democracy, and social justice would also need to be tracked in parallel with Christian thinking about them. However, this illustration should be sufficient for our purpose. It will lead us to some honest observations about the way in which Christian mentality has worked in the American experiment of constructing a social democracy.

The History of the Nation

As the Civil War progressed, Abraham Lincoln found it necessary to think through the consequences of a war for the sake of the Union (fraternity) in relation to the issue of slavery that had sparked the secessions. The result was the Emancipation Proclamation of January 1, 1863, in which the slaves then held by citizens of southern Confederate states "in rebellion" against the United States were declared free by the United States. This joined the principles of union (fraternity) with freedom (liberty) in a new way, for the freedom envisaged was clearly that to be accorded to African-Americans who had been slaves. This "act of justice," Lincoln wrote, was "warranted by the Constitution upon military necessity." This is hardly a strong indication that considerations of the right to equality (justice) had played a significant role in his deliberations. At Gettysburg, however, ten months later, when Lincoln thought to honor the Union soldiers who "gave their lives that the nation might live," the "new nation" was said to be "conceived in Liberty, and dedicated to the proposition that all men are created equal." That was mythmaking in action. Jefferson's reference to equality, which had to do with bourgeois legal and economic freedoms, was now redirected to encompass the social anthropology of a nation divided over principles of democracy, states' rights, and federal jurisdictions. Garry Wills (*Inventing America*) has given us a remarkable meditation on this historic moment as a shift in Lincoln's language from that of the Constitution to that of the Declaration of Independence. If we put that together with Julia Howe's "Battle Hymn of the Republic" (1861), which says, "As He [Christ] died to make men holy, let us die to make men free," the convoluted mergers of Christian myth and the founding documents of the United States are obvious. What about Christian thinking in the South? What about the equality of African-Americans as free citizens of a Christian nation?

Slavery

The story of the nation that included Africans among its many peoples can begin with the observation that they were imported as slaves to work the plantations of the South. The first boatload of African slaves landed in Virginia in 1619, one year before the *Mayflower* arrived in Cape Cod, and one hundred years after the start of the African slave trade in the middle Americas and the Caribbean. The Spanish colonialists had already depleted the native Indian work-force early in the sixteenth century and the Catholic bishop in Chiapas prevailed upon the Spanish crown in 1516 to allow the importation of Africans as slaves for the missions and plantations in the New World. The request was granted and the trade began, eventually to expand into the North American colonies. By 1750 there were approximately 250,000 African slaves in the colonies, and by 1860 a census counted 4,441,830 in the United States. When Thomas Jefferson wrote the Declaration of Independence in 1776, combining contemporary French thought with what he understood to be a biblical basis for a free and enlightened society, the fundamental truth held to be self-evident was that "all men are created equal." It was a grand concept and a serious statement of tremendous consequence for the history of the United States. But it was not taken from the Bible, and it did not apply to African-American slaves. Jefferson himself was a slave-owner, as was James Madison, and though Madison let it be known that he was troubled about the institution of slavery, neither he nor Jefferson nor the Congress of the United States expressed conceptual problems over the conflict between the practice of slavery and the principle of equality. Part of the reason for this was that the principle of equality in its French derivation was never intended to apply to humanistic anthropology in general. It was actually a political slogan in reference to a social class. "Equality" pertained only to the bourgeoisie, not to the peasants. In the Declaration of Independence, equality was a high-sounding argument based on "the Laws of Nature and Nature's God," but in support of a revolution at the level of governance and law in the interest of economic and political freedom from England. Slavery was the institution that made possible the Southern plantation, and it provided the economic foundation for the wealth of the new nation. Thus it apparently never occurred to the fathers of the country that slavery was wrong because it violated the principle of equality. But by stating that equality was grounded in "creation," and counted as a "law of Nature's God," Jefferson unwittingly invited subsequent interpretations that were quite different.

As questions were raised about slavery by French humanists and English pietists, abolitionist movements increased during the eighteenth century. In America, however, this merely resulted in pitiful attempts by the Congress of the United States to prohibit trading in slaves on the high seas. Several acts of legislation were enacted between 1794 and 1820 with little effect on the slave-trading in American ports and none on the institution of slavery in the states, including those of New England. The story has been told by Don Fehrenbacher in *The Slaveholding Republic*. Each act of the Congress focused on some feature of the practice of the slave trade, such as carrying slaves from one country to another (1790, 1800), slave-trading between Africa and America (1807), and outfitting ships for slave-trading in foreign ports (1818). Finally, in 1820, slave-trading became a capital offense. Yet, from the beginning of the Republic to the end of the Civil War (1865), the slave trade continued and flourished, although the sea captains and American ports had to learn deceptive ways to smuggle slaves into the country. Even so, many captains were apprehended during this period, but few were fined, and only one eventually was executed in the shadow of the Civil War (1862) as an "example" of the seriousness with which the Federal laws should be taken. As Ron Soodalter explains in his book, *Hanging Captain Gordon*, the laws were against slave-trading, not against slavery, and the reasons were more economic than humanitarian.

As the debates about slavery came to focus on the Federal Union of the states, a discussion was forced about the legality of slavery and how the new federation could govern a union of states both "slave" and "free." As tensions over this issue increased, and the institution of slavery had to be defended in the South, history shows that the Bible became an important argument and source of ideology. All through the South, the rhetoric found in sermons, newspapers, essays, and interviews was the same. "The Bible said" that slavery was ordained by God. One might wonder where in the Bible it said that. From the Old Testament the proof text was Genesis 9:20–27, God's curse on Ham, one of the three sons of Noah, interpreted to say that Africans would be slaves of the other peoples of the earth. From the New Testament the proof text was from "Paul's" letter to the Colossians in which he enjoined wives to be subject to their husbands and slaves to obey their masters (Colossians 3:18–22). The standard homiletic interpreted this to say, "If a wife is to be subject to her husband, *how much more* a slave." What could the Christian abolitionists say? All they had in their quiver were abstract principles about the fatherhood of God and the brotherhood of man to argue for the morality of the constitutional statement about equality in the Declaration of Independence. And so the debate about slavery took place in the United States Congress over policies concerning the admission of newly formed states from the territories of the Louisiana Purchase (1805) and whether slave-owners would be allowed to settle there. The Missouri Compromise (1820), the doctrine of popular sovereignty embedded in the Kansas–Nebraska Act (1854), and South Carolina's Act of Secession (1860) that occasioned the Civil War (1861–65) were all driven by desires for political and economic privilege and power, not issues of Christian morality grounded in the Christian myth as charter or in the statement about equality in the constitutional papers. So it was that the Gettysburg Address launched a startling idea to accompany the revolutionary results of the Civil War.

One year after the war, in 1866, the Protestant white supremacist Ku Klux Klan emerged as an underground resistance movement to the Reconstruction of the South, and the era of intimidation, lynching, and burnings began. Apparently the Christian myth and Bible would continue to be read and applied to the social situation in a way quite different from that of the "Battle Hymn of the Republic." The social situation was different, devastatingly so. The foundations and structures of an entire way of life cultivated to perfection during the preceding two hundred years of social and cultural formation had been destroyed. When the Reconstruction period ended ten years later in 1877, Jim Crow laws were enacted throughout the South. The rule was "separate but equal," or "equal, but separate." Thus the legal principle of equality was given token acceptance even though the social principle was not. The fiction of supporting the *principle* of equality actually resulted in the construction of a social system that refused to allow freed blacks full participation in the civil rights of white society for the next seventy years. Lynchings continued as ritualized exorcisms of the danger freed blacks represented to the Christian purity of whites. Plantation owners were no longer in control of their slaves and thus were awash in a social chaos that frightened the white woman and threatened the manhood of the white male (Harris, *Exorcising Blackness*; Singleton, "Christian Rationalization for Lynching"). As Rebecca Felton, a southern white woman from Atlanta, wrote in her letter to the *Boston Transcript* in 1897:

> When there is not enough religion in the pulpit to organize a crusade against sin, nor justice in the court house to promptly punish crime, nor manhood enough in the nation to put a sheltering arm about innocence and virtue—if it takes lynching to protect women's dearest possession from the ravening human beast—then I say lynch, a thousand times a week if necessary. (cited in Singleton, 7)

Civil Rights

In the meantime blacks found ways to keep their dignity despite the humiliations of this demeaning social system. They did this by turning the Bible into a charter for liberation, by creating music that sang in the face of oppression, and by going to war for America as Americans. Yet another reading of the Bible emerged, this one reaching back into the Old Testament to pit the God who ordained freedom against the God who ordained slavery. When the black troops returned to America after World War II, many having earned high praise and medals of honor, Jim Crow finally became unbearable and ridiculous in the eyes of enlightened whites. Rosa Parks refused to sit in the back of the bus and the demonstrations against segregation and for civil rights began. The 1950s mark a major turning-point in the social history of the United States. The concept of equality had been enriched by adding human respect and civic value to the notions of equality under the law. The administration of justice in the South was now a matter of concern and scrutiny throughout the rest of the United States. African-Americans had found a way to let the rest of America know that something was wrong with the system. Martin Luther King, Jr., had a dream, and the liberation movements of the 1960s carried the wave of reform from liberation for blacks to women, gays, native Americans, impoverished Latin Americans, and the poor in the United States and beyond.

After the civil rights movement of the 1950s, and especially after the Supreme Court decision in 1954 to desegregate the public schools in America, the goal was integration. Some progress was made in the restructuring of social and legal systems called for by the principle of equality rooted in enlightenment anthropology. Voting rights, jury rights, welfare rights, affirmative actions based on equal opportunity rights, workplace rights, open housing, educational programs, and more were instituted. Christians responded in different ways, some wanting to be involved and to give Christianity the credit for humanizing advances, others, however, by digging in their heels to stop the slide of a Christian nation into social decadence and immorality. This resistance to the liberation movements of the 1960s was sometimes talked about as a "Third Great Awakening" of evangelical Christian religiosity.

What, then, about integration? What about equality? Well, the track record is not good. Despite some obvious and helpful changes in the domain of politically correct attitudes and behavior on the part of persons in public, legislation intended to guarantee integration, such as open housing or school busing, did not work. Gated communities, private schools, and white flight to the suburbs left inner-city schools crowded with African-Americans and poorly supported. As for the welfare system, it came under attack because, as they said, "The black woman [who for two hundred fifty years, we should remember, exemplified a work ethic that kept both black and white families together and provided for their sustenance] is lazy, content to produce children just in order to receive more welfare." The workplace left the inner city, and for African-Americans the highly touted American dream turned into a nightmare.

The suspicion must be that this resistance to the Civil Rights movement and civil liberties legislation is the result of a deeply ingrained mentality in the American people. Christianity has regularly accommodated the social interests of the dominant classes in Western cultural history, of course, and given its blessing to such enterprises as colonialism (as "mission"), capitalism (as "Protestant ethic"), and the taking of the West in America (as "manifest destiny"). But this observation about privilege granted to the elite interests of a society is not enough to unravel the convoluted sets of interests swirling around the issue of African-American equality. Issues of race, culture, and moral values are involved that threaten the Christian concept of a Christian society. Notice that we have come to this impasse after sketching the history of the concept of equality only in relation to the question of our acceptance of Africans as Americans. It would be possible to do similar sketches of other concepts important for our self-understanding as a nation, such as freedom, justice, or fraternity (as in "we the people" of the Constitution), but the result would be to land at the same impasse. Christian engagement would again include both accommodation and resistance, depending upon circumstances and personal interests. We could also trace the histories of our treatment of peoples other than African-Americans, such as Amerindians, Asians, and Mexicans, without gaining more clarity about Christian mentality and the effective difference it is making in the current social projects and policies of the United States.

We need to stop here for a moment and notice the difference between the two concepts of the United States as a society—a Federal Republic and a Christian nation. The difference has been illustrated in the histories we have sketched. We have emphasized points where attempts to apply one feature of the Constitution (equality) has run into Christian resistance, sometimes on the basis of appeal to the Bible. We have imagined this history as an acceptance of the two founding documents whose concepts of society do not easily mesh. The Constitution is the more official and legal document, but its concept of society is that of a state rather than of a culture concerned with the quality of life. In the case of the Christian myth, a concept of society is integral to its medieval grammar, but buried in the modern Christian's mentality. That is why the reasons for the Christian resistance we have followed have been unspoken, more a matter of attitude than articulation. And that is why the Bible has served as the "founding document" for the Christian's sense of the social. It has not always been noticed that the Bible functions in the minds of Christians as a charter for the state as well as the church, or that the concept of the Christian nation, drawing upon the medieval model of Christendom, dare not be spelled out because it cannot be made to fit a nation-state as a federal union. So, even though the history of the nation has not readily conformed to the Christian ideal, the thought of America as a Christian nation has not been set aside. It is attractive to Christians because it belongs to their imagined world and the sense of the social implicit to it, even though its concept of the social no longer makes sense for a modern nation-state.

The Righteous Nation

During the last half of the twentieth century and the first decade of the twenty-first the popular and unexamined notion of the Christian nation took the form of a political concept. America was or should be a "righteous nation," not only at the level of personal religion and its churches, but also at every level of society including our governments. This was not a matter of conscious intellectual and ideological attention. It happened slowly in the course of a new awareness of America as a nation and the role it had come to play in the world after World War II. Under President Dwight Eisenhower, the Congress of the United States acknowledged our newly confirmed sense of rightness, power, and divine approval by adding the phrase "under God" to the pledge of allegiance (1954), and the sentence "In God we trust" to our dollar bills (1956). This left the question open as to whose God we were under, but it did reveal a move in the direction of making "official" the definition of America as a religious nation. As Eisenhower said, "Our form of government has no sense unless it is founded in a deeply felt religious faith, and I don't care what it is" (Gibbs, "The Religion Test," 41). That Eisenhower did not care "what it is" was apparently his way of acknowledging the variety of religious faiths among us, but it did not mean that he himself was confused about which God we were under. It was Eisenhower who presided over the first National Prayer Breakfast and started a tradition of prayer breakfasts which Protestant preachers such as Billy Graham were regularly invited to lead. John F. Kennedy was more cautious about the relationship of church and state, as cited in our Introduction, but he also took it for granted that Americans were a religious people. Both Eisenhower and Kennedy understood personal religious faith to be an important fact in the way Americans constituted a nation.

Then there were the "culture wars" of the 1960s and 1970s, unleashed by concerns about the Vietnam War, the treatment of minorities at all levels of our society, and the life-style experiments of a younger generation that was unimpressed with traditional social mores and distressed by the attitudes of superiority and sovereignty projected by our governments. Dissidents demonstrated and the forces of law and order came to the support of traditional "values." Christian sensibility was offended by these signs of social conflict, and during the 1980s Jerry Falwell, a conservative Protestant preacher, coined the term "Moral Majority" in order to put the immoral minority in their place. Christians were the moral majority in his view, and they needed to make sure that the "sinners" and "liberals" of the dissident generation did not dismantle the moral fabric of the nation. His vigorous support for Ronald Reagan has been acknowledged as a major factor in Reagan's election to the presidency, as well as the shift in the political orientation of Southern voters from Democrat to Republican. Reagan was attractive because he was a Christian, understood atheistic Communism as a danger, was "tough on crime," and thought creationism should be taught in the public schools. As the 1990s loomed, other Christian leaders added their flocks to the Moral Majority and televangelist Pat Robertson founded the "Christian Coalition." Networks of Christian churches and organizations were soon forming Political Action Committees interested in Christian representation on school boards, city councils, and in county, state, and federal government. They sought to stop what they understood as the slide of America into "liberalism" and immorality by making sure that Christian values were recognized as the norm for social ethics. They were particularly interested in finding ways to control social practices and behavior thought to violate biblical laws and injunctions.

In retrospect, this was an extremely troubling chapter of our history from the 1960s through the 1990s. It was also historic and significant as a violation of the traditional principle of the separation of church and state. Recalling the words of Kennedy, cited in the Introduction, America was a land where "no religious body seeks to impose its will directly or indirectly upon the general populace or the public acts of its officials." In the history of the nation traced above, the notion that America was a "Christian nation" was more an assumption taken for granted than a clearly defined social concept. Christian sensibility sometimes bumped into the social issues that emerged as our democracy shaped its infrastructures based on the Constitution, but the churches seldom thought to influence political policies and structures in order to define the federal union as a Christian nation with legal and ideological standards and controls. Instead, the notion of the "Christian nation" and the "Constitutional democracy" traveled along together on somewhat parallel but separate tracks, crossing over each other a few times and finding such occasions somewhat tense, but assuming that the separate tracks would continue in parallel and mostly in the same direction. To erode this distinction as many Christians intended during the late twentieth century meant in effect to collapse the two ways of thinking about American society into one definitive concept: the righteous nation. Its proponents thought the "Christian nation" had been ravaged by "liberals" because America as a democratic nation-state had not been able to control our morals. The way America was functioning as a democracy gave the liberals the freedom to get out of hand, and the way to reconstitute the country as a civil and moral society was to establish Christian values as the essential ingredient at all levels of our society, from the composition of its governments to their influence in social structures, practices, and personal pieties.

We need not rehearse in detail the many Christian statements, behaviors, and programs that took our attention during the latter part of the last century and into the first decade of the twenty-first. However, it is just these statements and programs that present us with a remarkable opportunity to document the resilience of the Christian mythic grammar in American mentality. They have exposed the mythic mentality of Christians in America by bringing its grammar and social logic to the surface of public expression and debate. Since mythic grammar resides at an unconscious level, and since in the case of religions in America expressions of religious persuasion have always been taken as a matter of personal and private conviction, it has not been easy to document or describe American Christian mentality. Because the public discourse about religion and society available to us from this chapter of our history is largely from the conservative or evangelical wing of Christianity, we will need to notice at every turn that the mythic markers in question apply to the thinking of Christians in general. This is not unreasonable, given the fact that the older popular notion of the Christian nation was inclusive of all denominations, and that these all share common beliefs about Jesus Christ and the worship of the Christian God. It is also the case that the Bible, a mythic marker of fundamental significance for the imagined world and its grammar, is an authority common to all Christian churches and in continuity with the markers of the European Christianities that produced the imagined world. That the Bible is prominent in all forms of Christianity far beyond the so-called Bible Belt will make it possible to use the Bible as a template for the imagined world described in the diagram. This will enable a description of Christian mentality in America in general even though the evidence for its public expressions is found mainly in the conservatives' discourse about the "righteous nation." The positions taken by conservatives can be understood as extreme and exaggerated forms of mythic thinking made possible by the Christian myth.

The Christian Grammar

Recalling the diagram of the Christian's imagined world (on page 201), we can use its mythic markers as an outline for a discussion of the statements expressed and positions taken by Christians in this latest chapter of our history. Examples of the logic of the grammar of this diagram can be pointed to in applications of Christian thinking that the reader will have no trouble recognizing.

Creation

Among the many myths of world-making in the Hebrew Bible, the Genesis story tells of a god like one of the gods of the pantheons of the ancient Near East *separating* the heavens from the earth by cutting them apart (*bara'*) and *fashioning* the earth as if from the mud of the watery chaos below, just as he *fashioned* Adam (humankind) from the "dust of the earth" (Genesis 2:7). Similarly, the Greek and Latin translations use terms that refer to making the world by fashioning it (*poiein; facere*), as well as allowing the connotation of *causing* it to be. In the account in 2 Maccabees, from the second century B.C., however, the notion of God making the world out of material that already existed is rejected (7:28). In later Christian thinking it is this image of "creation out of nothing" that demonstrates the incredible power of the sovereign God. He creates the entire world simply by saying, "Let there be..."

The combination of absolute power, the sovereignty of God, and the creation of the world out of nothing mark the event as unimaginable and unthinkable. Nevertheless, it is precisely this image that Christians have in mind when thinking about God, and this image of creation has affected Christian mentality in two important ways. One is that meaning tends to be found in dramatic events rather than in relationships, thinking, intellectual labor, manual labor, and construction. The other is that human creativity is thought of on the model of the creation story as an inexplicable matter of genius not amenable to analysis. The image of the creation of the world by God results in notions of awe in the presence of power and the mystique of events unexplained.

In recent Christian interpretation it is this story that challenges scientific theories of evolution. The issues have to do with the concept of God, the truth of the Bible, and the origins of humankind. Evolutionary theories do not need a divine creator to account for the physical and natural worlds, or a miraculous event to distinguish humankind from other primates. Therefore, Christians have argued against evolution and demanded that "creationism" be taught in the public schools. What they are protecting is the imagined world of Christianity, one that requires a divine sovereign, creator of the world and lord of history. They have proposed the teaching of creationism as a scientific theory in the public schools, but they have no real interest in the scientific logic of creationism. Arthur McCalla has analyzed this issue in *The Creationist Debate: The Encounter Between the Bible and the Historical Mind*. We can see that the drive to include creationism in the curricula of our public schools is rooted in a concern that our children continue to think of the world in terms of the Christian myth.

That is about as far as Christian interest in the natural world goes. We are now producing huge amounts of scientific knowledge about the natural orders of our world. We are focusing on the uses that can be made of these natural orders for a variety of human and social interests. Ranging from investigations of galaxy formations, sub-atomic particles, nuclear energies, and molecular biologies, to electronic communication and genetic engineering, our scientists are producing a bewildering array of information and technology for understanding and manipulating natural processes. We are discovering that some of the intersections of human interests and natural systems have become problematic. Technologies used for the exploitation of natural resources are creating pollution and natural-order changes of unimaginable dimensions and consequences, while we have not found a way to control the steady increase in exploitation driven by interests in company profits and wealth accumulation. The churches seem to be confused on these issues because the Christian grammar does not provide categories for thinking critically about this kind of human activity. Insofar as the Christian interests in the creation are limited to (1) proofs for a transcendent God, or (2) justifications for humans having "dominion over every living thing that moves upon the earth" (Genesis 1:26, 28), the silence is understandable. There is little in the Bible or in the myth–ritual system of the Christian's imagined world to provide a framework for taking a Christian position on our techno-economic interchanges with the natural environment. That is because, for Christians, creation is a theological category. The silence of many of the churches on eco-issues is a kind of negative proof that the medieval grammar is still in place.

One might be sympathetic, for the Christian myth has sustained exceedingly rich cultures of social construction, ethical norms, and profound explorations of human being and personal experience. The world in which we find ourselves is indeed vast and mysterious. It is the concept of creation that has located an ultimate agent to make the world seem a livable place for humans. This means that the issue of creationism and science should not be seen as a simple matter of debate about the "truth." The issue strikes to the core of human self-understanding and can only be addressed by a fundamental shift in our anthropology.

Moral Classifications

The diagram of the imagined world contains a period of human history stretching from the creation of the world to the Christ event. As Hebrew epic this history is a complex, remarkable, and intriguing story of social and intellectual labor in the interest of constructing a theocracy in the midst of other kingdoms. In Christian interpretation, however, it is the story of disobedience to God's plan for his kingdom and of the divine judgments that follow. The Christian sequel to this history, from the Christ event to the Eschaton, results in a division of humankind between Christians and all other peoples, who are ranked in relation to their knowledge of and response to the divine plan. Some are ignorant pagans, some are disobedient sinners, and some are evil enemies. The Christian code words for this major division of the human race are "sin" and "righteousness." Current public discourse on "morals," "sin," and "evil" alerts us to this orientation. Just as the story of Adam and Eve has served to characterize the entire history of the human race as one of disobedience, so the particular act of disobedience imagined there has given the notion of sin its peculiarly Christian sexual connotations. Thus it is that the earmarks of our immorality are thought to be sexual promiscuity, pornography, homosexuality, abortion license, the use of condoms, and so forth. One does wonder at the energies expended in the attempts to legislate, control, and punish offenders in matters such as these. It seems as if this is all that is required in order to shape up as a Christian nation. It is at least such an obvious and recurrent theme in public discourse that we can safely take it as an indication that this Christian mythic marker is still in place.

Another obvious indication that the grammar is still at work is the pervasive use of the diagram's system of classification into those who are okay (righteous, obedient, Christian) and those who are not. This division into opposites was noted in the previous chapter as a mark of the logic embedded in the Christian grammar. In current applications this comes to expression in many ways: Christians/pagans; good/evil; righteous/immoral; conservative/liberal; believers/unbelievers; natives/immigrants; ethical/licentious; civilian/terrorist; us/them; and so forth. The oppositions are clearly understood to be definitive categories, mutually exclusive terms, and descriptions of a state of affairs requiring a radical corrective. The thinking is that oppositions occurring within the nation need to be addressed by legislation although, as we know, many Christians have not waited for legislation. Thus there have been incidents involving guns, bombs, and fires that have had a moral rationale in mind. Killing abortion doctors in order to save babies comes to mind, and, if the immoral are crashing the gates, a strange spate of nativism and anti-immigration arguments and strategies can surface. In the case of "third-world" peoples who stay in the third world and who are not Christians, the strategy of mission to the unenlightened can still slip into place, and all appears to be well as long as the natives are content to be subservient to the Christian missionaries and the other interests of the empire that accompany them. Should the natives become restless, intransigent, or worse, the efforts at instruction and enlightenment come to an end. Non-Christians can easily turn out to be enemies. Then we have to destroy them in order to save them, as the saying from Vietnam went, or destroy their regime in order to "free" the people for "democracy," as the righteous rationale has sounded in support for our wars in the Near East.

It is a bit more difficult to be sympathetic about this penchant for moral classifications than with the issue of creationism. We know, of course, that many peoples have thought of themselves as the standard for the right way to live in distinction from others who live differently, but the Christian distinction between the good and the bad is based on a moral rubric that consigns the other to a position in need of rectification. Sympathy in this case is limited to what moderate Christians say about "concern" for the other. This concern has produced a large number of Christian missions in which non-Christian peoples have been treated kindly without immediate castigation as immoral. A good example of this is the history of Christian medical missions, and yet, even in these cases, a "civilizing" and Christianizing purpose has usually accompanied the missions. The recent rhetoric about Christian values in the United States has therefore to be seen as an unfortunate regression to the moral dualisms integral to the Christian's mythic grammar, and the recent use of Christian categories to justify our wars in the Near East and elsewhere is an obvious case of constructing a moral distinction between Americans as good vs. the "enemy" and "evil."

Christ Event

The Christ event marks the center of the imagined world and its myth–ritual structure. It is a very complex and compact cluster of mythic notions because so much hinges upon it for Christians. It marks the place where a second major manifestation of divine power and purpose "entered" human history. It is that entrance, and the changes imagined to have occurred because of it, that turned the gospel story into a complex mythic marker. Scholars and theologians have reduced the many significant features of the gospel story to the concept of the Christ event. For Christians the Christ event is the "hinge of history," the event that brought the Old Testament history of disobedience to an end and inaugurated the Christian time. How the crucifixion of Jesus as the Christ did that has never been explained, but all of the designations and descriptions are ways of saying that it did. References to the significance of the Christ event include Jesus as the Christ or son of God, his crucifixion as a martyrdom or sacrifice, his resurrection from the dead as a demonstration of God's power and vindication, and the Pauline references to "Christ crucified" as the core of the Christian message (*kerygma*). In each case the designation indicates some feature of the event that emphasizes the importance of Jesus' "appearance" in the world and translation to rule in heaven, together with God's powerful intervention in raising Jesus from the dead. That such an event could also change the course of history by changing the character of Christians through conversion and transformation is the mystery encapsulated in the medieval ritual. Protestants also regard an individual's encounter with the sacrifice of Christ as the point at which conversion, faith, and new birth take place, but the means is understood to be the preaching of the gospel rather than ritual reenactment. Protestants are understandably wary about trying to explain this in public. As a matter of fact, the term *sacrifice* as a description of the crucifixion of Jesus creates more conceptual problems than it solves, as shown by the long history of failed attempts by Christian theologians to explain it. Thus we have only the cliché about being born again, and other informal references to conversion, becoming a Christian, or believing in Jesus as one's savior, to register acknowledgment of this mythic marker. This is somewhat different from the ways in which the other markers are referred to without embarrassment in public. In evangelical circles the "testimony" of a person who has been born again is, of course, a public genre that has been found to follow a conventional form. But this focuses upon the changes that have taken place in a person's life rather than an explication of the logic of the Christ event. I have therefore used the term *Christ event* to refer to the many functions of this mythic marker in the context of the diagram and its logic. This is the point at which Christians think of the gospel as an event to be reenacted in personal religious experience, but also as an event of cosmic and historical significance that anchors the reality of the salvation history patterned in the Bible.

We can therefore be quite certain that the Christ event is still in place in the Christian's imagined world. Without it there would be no answer to the punishment of Adam and Eve, being exiled from Paradise, and the history of disobedience that followed. There would be no way to be prepared for the final judgment. Both the Creation marker and the Eschaton marker (the final "judgment" of the world) are obviously being taken very seriously by American Christians, which means that the gospel story is the mythic marker for Christians in demonstration of God's intervention in human affairs. Without it, both the imagined world and the everyday world would turn very ugly, not an arena within which God's purposes for humankind could be imagined as constructive.

There are, of course, occasions, namely, Passion week and Easter, when a crucifixion/resurrection pageantry or scenario may be made public. There is always a strange naiveté on the part of the performers or producers about these productions. There is an expectation that everyone watching will understand and applaud the performance as a solemn and significant ritual occasion. One cannot detect any sense of the ugliness and offensiveness of such a performance for those who are not Christians.

Eschaton

If the Christian myth–ritual system is structured as God's plan for a salvation history, the Eschaton is the goal toward which God's plan is directed. It is the third and final breakthrough event, the set of which is designed to inaugurate the divine plan (Creation), rectify human failures (Christ event), and finally guarantee the establishment of the righteous kingdom (Eschaton). It may not work well as a teleological theory for tracking human history as a developmental narrative, but it is certainly there in the Christian's imagined world. Which scenarios belong to the end of time varies with interpretations of the encoded biblical ciphers, but two or three features are more or less constant throughout all interpretations. One is that there will be a final war between the forces of good and the forces of evil, often called Armageddon. A second is that there will be a final judgment presided over by Christ or by God, a judgment that will separate the righteous from the ungodly. The righteous will be "saved"; the ungodly "damned." A third is that the world as humans have known it will be destroyed and a "new heaven and new earth" will appear to receive the righteous for eternity. As preposterous as these scenarios are, there can be no question about an apocalypse being a mythic marker in the Christian's imagined world. Its logic is a kind of futuristic theodicy on the one hand (a justification of God's power and righteousness), and a mythic warrant for the eventual justification of Christians on the other. We know that this mythic marker is still firmly in place for individual Christians because of the current hysteria created by radio preachers, television evangelists, and the publication of books about the "rapture" and the end of the world. The notion of Armageddon has surfaced in discussions of conflicts in the Near East at high levels in our current administration. The historian may be appalled, but she or he cannot say that the apocalyptic myth does not belong to the Christian's imagined world. From James Watt's famous retort that the exploitation of the natural world did not matter because Jesus was coming soon to destroy it anyway, through the many thousand copies of the *Left Behind* series read avidly by Christians (Frykholm, *Rapture Culture*), to the influence of John Hagee at the White House (Posner, "Pastor Strangelove"), an imminent apocalypse is as far into the future as many Christians can see. Hagee's book, *Jerusalem Countdown*, and his preachments on his program called *Praise the Lord* on Trinity Broadcasting Network, agitate for war with Iran on the basis of biblical prophecy about the final war between the righteous and the ungodly, called Armageddon.

Even though periods of apocalyptic fear and hysteria have dotted the history of Christianity, we need not think that this exaggerated form of perturbation is characteristic of all Christians. Protestant preachers with radio and television programs can be divided into two classes: those that point consistently to the books of Daniel and Revelation in the Bible, and the many others who seldom do. It is also the case that many "mainline" Christians are embarrassed by apocalyptic preachments. However, the mythic grammar does not provide any alternative scenario for the ending of the Christian epic. The incidence of apocalyptic hysteria among us reveals the consternation caused by confronting a social world and history that contradict the Christian vision. For those who resist thinking of the end of the world apocalyptically, we may nevertheless assume that the thought of a "final judgment" of some sort can be a constant reminder of the way one's life will be remembered, if not judged.

The Kingdom of God

The period between the Christ event and the Eschaton is the time of the Church. Christians are to fill the horizon with enlightenment and righteousness. That some concept of the church belongs to the Christian's imagined world, and is still in mind, probably needs no demonstration. After all, there are churches galore across the nation and the mythic system of the imagined world positions the church in relation to the reign and kingdom of God. Thus the church is a very important social institution in the minds of Christians. The church is in charge of making sure that the spiritual kingdom of God is represented in the social world. But because the state is now separated from the churches, and because there are now many different denominations of churches in America, and because the concept of one church has become problematic, this is exactly the place at which the myth–ritual system of the imagined world has run into trouble. Without a state church to represent Christianity in the structure of the nation, who is in charge of providing enlightenment and supervising righteousness? This was not a problem as long as the Christian churches in America could think of the nation as Christian, as long as they saw the ethos as civil and in keeping with Christian morals. It was not a problem as long as the mainline churches could think of themselves together as having effective authority to influence moral standards and ethical decisions in the lives of the people. But when circumstances changed in the last half of the twentieth century, the assumed moral link between the church and the nation snapped, and Christians found themselves living in a nation threatened with immorality. There were now many non-Christian people with different religions crossing the borders, and there were "liberals" within, promulgating practices and even legislation that Christians found offensive, if not immoral. Thus there was confusion between personal and social ethics, church and state responsibilities for making sure the nation was moral. Some Christian leaders encouraged the members of their churches to take some steps into the political arena in order to address the ethical state of the nation. One result of this was the emergence of the Moral Majority and the Christian Coalition. The code word was righteousness. Righteousness was what God wants. Righteousness was possible because of the Christ event. Righteousness was the solution to sin and immorality. And righteousness was the standard for the final judgment.

Attempts to introduce God's law from the Bible into state and federal legislation are examples of the church's interest in shaping the moral fabric of the nation. Most of the "family values" thought to be in need of legislation are, of course, not values that were part of all the ways in which families have valued living together in the past, but strictly issues of sexual mores found threatening to Christian sensibilities regarding sexuality. Attitudes toward gender, the body, sexual behavior, and racial purity sparked the issues of the so-called culture wars. It is, however, not clear that these issues about family values struck to the core of the Christian's dis-ease. Something about the Christian's unexamined notion of the kingdom of God, a haunting ideal for the collective, was threatened by the "secular" society we had become. We followed some of the history of the Christian's struggle with the notion of equality in relation to the issue of slavery. Now we can mention the ironies that finally surfaced at the end of the twentieth century. White politicians were preaching family values to African-Americans whose families once were split up and sold separately by white slave-owners. Affirmative action initiatives, set in place to rectify the consequences of the long history of racial injustices, began being used by whites to claim discrimination. Racial profiling was finally seen as wrong, but not before our prisons were overcrowded with black males and became a financial burden. And then we started profiling Arabs and Mexicans. Even in the case of federal legislation purporting to be a constructive response to the problem of inequality at the level of public education, the No Child Left Behind program, the Christian twist found a way to come out on top. When the Secretary of Education, Margaret Spellings, was asked about drying up federal funds for public schools that did not make enough progress in improving the grades of minority students, she said, "I think that's the righteous thing to do" (*The News Hour with Jim Lehrer*, April 7, 2005).

These confusions about moral standards, divine law, the Bible, and the kind of legislation appropriate for a polycultural nation-state are a direct result of attempts to apply the archaic grammar implicit in the Christian's myth–ritual system to a world that is no longer medieval. It is clear that the presence of Christian thinking at the highest levels of the administration of the United States cannot be credited or blamed as if it were the sole factor in practices and policies that have gone wrong for the world, but the overlay of Christian thinking as rationale for other interests is not to be discounted. Other interests, all overlaid with Christian-sounding rhetoric, include being the world's superpower (think divine sovereignty), creating a global military empire (think one world "under God"), ridding third world nations of their tyrants (think evil rulers), spreading democracy by force of arms (think "converting the godless"), preaching to the world about human rights (think missions), treating the nations of the United Nations as subordinates (think city on a hill), demanding that others lay down their arms so that only we and our friends will have them (think righteous kingdom), and justifying preemptive conquests because our enemies belong to an axis of evil (think holy war). It has not been difficult for critics to see the conceits and deceits in all of these policies that cover for another set of interests having to do with the exploitation of natural resources abroad, the accumulation of wealth at home, and the expansion of the global market in ways that support our capitalistic economy. What critics have not been able to do is sort out the rationalizations for critique that appeal to Christian mentality. That is because the imagined world of the Christian myth–ritual system has not been available for description and discussion.

The Christian mythic grammar imagines the social world on the model of medieval Christendom. This conception of the social world is even less clearly or consciously in mind than that of the Christian nation. It is, however, intrinsic to the imagined world of the Christian myth. The concept is that of a kingdom ruled by sovereign powers within which everyone is supposed to be a Christian. The cosmic dimension of the kingdom is ruled by Christ the king; the earthly kingdom is ruled by a Christian king; the spiritual kingdom on earth is ruled by the Church; and the ultimate establishment of righteous rule will be the kingdom of God at the end of history. In some ways American Christians know that this concept of the kingdom of God is no longer thinkable, and there are ways for Christians to imagine the influence of the Christian's God in the world other than with the kingdom of God model. The Christian churches have often thought of themselves as the sufficient representation of the kingdom of God in the world. Pentecostals have cultivated the notion of God's spirit as a more diffuse form of divine presence in the world than that of a church or a kingdom. But in other ways the concept of the kingdom of God continues to be haunting. It is there in the underlying reasons for the Christian missions. It is there in the vision of a universal Christianity. It is there in the concept of God as creator of the universe and Lord of all human history. And it is there in the concept of the righteous nation.

A particularly trenchant example of such thinking in application to our federal government can be found in the speech George W. Bush addressed to the nation from Ellis Island on the first anniversary of the September 11 terrorist attacks. Elizabeth Castelli has analyzed this speech in her article "Globalization, Transnational Feminism, and the Future of Biblical Critique." She noticed that Bush "repeatedly invoked a range of Christian theological categories, the American myth of a nation chosen by God, and images of biblical temporality and utopian eschatology." In the Bush Administration the use of Christian language had been so obvious that its apparent acceptance on the part of the media and the American people tells us that it did count for something. It is at least the case that Christianity was the main source for the rationalizations put forth by the Bush Administration for its policies and master plan. Castelli cited the closing paragraph of the speech as follows:

> Tomorrow is September the 12th. A milestone is passed, and a mission goes on. Be confident. Our country is strong. And our cause is even larger than our country. Ours is the cause of human dignity: freedom guided by conscience, and guarded by peace. This ideal of America is the hope of all mankind. That hope drew millions to this harbor. That hope still lights our way. And the light shines in the darkness. And the darkness will not overcome it. May God bless America.

Noting that his speech creates a series of equations between "the ideal of America," "the hope of all mankind," and "the light [that] shines in the darkness," Castelli draws the conclusion that, in Bush's mind, the "ideal of America" *is* "the light [that] shines in darkness." She then reminds us that the statements about "the light [that] shines in the darkness" and that "the darkness will not overcome it" are taken from the Prologue to the Gospel of John. The Prologue is about the *logos* that was with God at the creation, a god itself, the light and life of humanity. Mapping the two sets of claims, Castelli sees "a rather astonishing intertextual assertion that 'the ideal of America' is the same as the light/life that is present within the *logos* (the organizing principle of all creation)" (73). It is not necessary to think that Bush realized what he was doing with this biblical text in order to be astonished. The text is well known among Christians, and it goes on to describe the alienation of the light from the world. Castelli is able to illustrate our astonishment by substituting "the ideal of America" for the *logos* in the biblical text:

> The true ideal of America that enlightens every person was coming onto the world. The ideal of America was in the world, and the world was made through the ideal of America, but the world knew the ideal of America not. The ideal of America came to its own home, and its own people did not receive it. But to all who received the ideal of America, who believed in its name, it gave power to become children of God. (73–4)

Castelli sees this naïve merger of biblical language and the ideal of America as "a dizzying and unsettling juxtaposition of nationalism and theological determinism." She can do that because, in the speech, Bush said, "I believe there is a reason that history has matched this nation with this time," and soon afterward asserted, "We do know that God has placed us together in this moment, to grieve together, to stand together, to serve each other and our country." It is this convergence of history, God, Bush, and the "ideal of America" as the "light [that] shines in darkness" that astonishes. And yet, knowing that the language of the "ideal of America" is a cover for a set of "national interests" that are self-serving, we can see that the special claim to be the light of the world is an embarrassing and disgusting disclosure of a political deception. It can be taken, however, as a demonstration of the Christian mentality used to justify the self-righteousness driving the leaders of the Christian nation. As David Rieff put it, cited in the Introduction: "For the Bush Administration, American leadership is a self-evident moral right [with] the conviction that America has a special mission based on the universality of its values" (Rieff, "We Are the World," 34).

We need to pause here, for this speech is an illustration of the Christian mentality in America allowed to work its way up to the top of our administration. The influence of the mythic markers of the Christian grammar is obvious. There is the Bible, taken for granted innocently and as self-evident truth. There is the concept of the one God, Lord of creation and history. There is the double revelation of this God's entrance into human history, referred to without question. One revelation is that of the light (of the *logos* that came into the world in Jesus). The other is that Bush "knows" that "God has placed us together in this moment." There is the dualism of the light and the darkness, clearly referring to a division of humankind into two opposite classes of people. There is the claim that the "ideal of America" is that "light" and the "hope of all mankind." There is the Christian language of "mission" to spread "freedom guided by conscience." And the concepts of sovereignty and kingdom are evoked in the languages of "strength," "confidence," and the assertion that the darkness "will not overcome" the light. From other speeches we know that Bush believed God told him to be president, a not-so-subtle claim to messianic election. And in this speech he said that he believes "there is a reason that history has matched this nation with this time."

The Christian Empire

This manifestation of Christian mentality in the thinking of the president of the United States is not the whole story. Instead of turning its attention to our exceptional social experiment in creating a social democracy, the federal government at the beginning of the twenty-first century has been obsessed with the notion of an American empire. We heard rumors of the plan developing in secret enclaves of the federal government, especially in the Department of Defense, since the end of the so-called Cold War with communist Russia. The accidental emergence of America as the only superpower to survive the twentieth century of wars and terror was apparently taken as a sign that the time had come to spread "democracy" around the world. Our status as a superpower was thought to give us the right to impose our will on other nations, and our executive and military officers assumed the posture of the sovereign when addressing and dealing with the other nations of the world. We simply told them what to do, or else. And our armies started to roll. We now have military bases in strategic positions around the entire globe to guarantee our control of the entire world, and we have pinpointed enemies for liquidation—those resisting our interests in controlling their economies, resources, and governments. We now have a book about that plan called *The Architect: Karl Rove and the Master Plan for Absolute Power* (Moore and Slater, 2006). As we know from such studies there is absolutely no awareness of or interest in the social-structural consequences of the plan's execution abroad or at home. Our leaders have been interested only in the procedures necessary to assure that our powers take control of other countries to advance our "national interests." We have already seen enough to know that these national interests do not include interests in the future of planet Earth as an ecosystem, an environment for living things, a place for rewarding human habitat, experiments in renewable energy, sustainable social systems, and control of exploitation. Obsessed with the notion of absolute power, the Bush Administration has been incapable of attention to such things as human well-being, quality of life, the appreciation of cultural differences, sustainable global economies, and a sense of the longer run. And there is no ultimate concern for what happens to the enemies, opponents, and peoples who get in the way of our national interests. These national interests are no secret, even though those in power never admit to them. They are the interests of those who benefit most from the control of government, corporations, industry, and financial institutions. What they want is free rein to expand their control throughout the world, using both carrots and threats of military incursion in order to have their way. The accumulation of wealth at the top is the real interest, and we now know how the system works. At home the well-being of the poor and the working class is simply dispensable. Around the world, when the people of a foreign nation whose natural resources we have exploited, and whose territory we have invaded, find their traditional social structures coming apart, a kind of awakening can occur. When leaders who have benefited from cooperation with us at the expense of their own people are exposed, rebellions can take place. It is then that we use our power to launch a military response to crush the insurgents and keep those in power who cooperate with us. So it is that the use of power to protect corporate exploitation has become a major issue in our time. The history of this kind of incursion into other countries around the world is now available in Stephen Kinzer's book *Overthrow: America's Century of Regime Change from Hawaii to Iraq*. We have apparently not found a way to criticize the assumptions of sovereignty, power, and the moral right of America to spread "democracy" around the world. That is because the rhetoric is rooted in a Christian mythic grammar that is not recognized as anachronistic.

The Consequences

The Christian's imagined world and its grammar have been the frame of reference for addressing human social problems that come along with the construction of nation-states and the conflicts between societies that require compromise and negotiation. It does not contain any mechanism or grammar for solving such problems. With the Christ event behind and the Eschaton before, the only model Christians have for solving problems of social conflict is violence. It makes little difference who ends up victim or victor, the enemy or the righteous, because violence is redemptive and God's final show of destructive-redemptive power will solve all ambiguities. In the meantime there is victorious conquest or martyrdom, each capable of justifying the myth of mission and righteousness. Even soldiers who sacrifice their lives in a wrong and disgraceful war can be considered martyrs as long as the enemy is thought of as evil.

The Christ event is a crucifixion; the Eschaton is a war. Both result in the "redemption" of the righteous and the destruction of the wicked. The model is "salvation" from "damnation," and both "solutions" to the problem of human sinfulness are costly. "Redemption" connotes the payment of a ransom (to whom?), and crucifixion is understood to be a vicarious "sacrifice" for sins, as Paul's formulation reads:

> Since all have sinned and fall short of the glory of God, they are now justified by his grace as a gift, through the redemption that is in Christ Jesus, whom God put forward as a sacrifice of atonement by his blood, effective through faith. He did this to show his righteousness, because in his divine forbearance he had passed over the sins previously committed; it was to prove at the present time that he himself is righteous and that he justifies the one who has faith in Jesus. (Romans 3:23–26)

Christians accept their redemption at the cost of vicarious violence because it is God's solution to the problem of sin, and the gospel story of Jesus' sacrifice/martyrdom does not help to suggest any alternatives. To be a "follower" of Jesus is to "take up one's cross." The history of Christian experience on the model of the *imitatio Christi* is a profound but troubling internalization of the sacrificed one as a victim. But Mark's gospel has two parts: part one is the appearance of the man of power; part two is the story of obedience unto death. The sequence of the two parts can be turned around. If you start with the sacrificed one, he then becomes the man of power, this time glorified and with a mandate to return to destroy the ungodly. The only logic of this paradigm of sacrifice, as if "for others," is that of mythic reversal. And the only agency capable of reversing such completely oppositional destinies as life vs. death is the power of the sovereign God. This is not helpful as a model for solving social conflicts. Violence is not redemptive. Violence does not solve problems. And yet, this logic embedded in the Christian grammar is the only model Christians have for dealing with "sinners," social issues, and international conflict. Thus we have prisons, punishments, executions, assassinations, wars, and ethnic cleansings, all as attempts to cleanse society from those who do not conform to some standard of rightness. In the last chapter the logic of sacrifice embedded in the Christian's mythic grammar was applied to the Christian on the side of the victim as a martyr. The convoluted logic of martyrdom and sacrifice was not able to say how it could be that a vicarious violence could change the character of another person or the course of history. Now we have to look at the Christ event and Eschaton from the side of the agent of violence. And we have to say, especially in the light of the century of wars, ethnic cleansings, incarcerations, tortures, and destructions of enemies, that neither God nor his representatives on earth can be justified. Violence is not redemptive. This model for solving human social problems can only spell disaster, not redemption.

We have already made the point in the course of our study that the imagined world of the Christian myth is not adequate to address the social issues of modern working societies. Left out of the picture and its applications is the entire range of human interests in the natural and social worlds.

The medieval myth–ritual system focused on the church and the individual, expecting the church to treat the kings and their peoples as Christians under the church's moral control. Thus there was no need to worry about what we have been calling the social interests that occur at the intersections of the natural and social environments of pre-Christian and working societies. The myth–ritual system of medieval Christianity was not created to rationalize the social interests of such intersections. It was interested only in the church taking its place as the dominant religion in Christian empires and kingdoms. And so, left out of the picture and its applications is the entire range of current human interests in the natural world, the natural sciences, the human sciences, the social sciences, and the issues of social well-being taken up by social philosophers, cultural historians, economists, politicians, and other intellectuals.

Because there is no room in the Christian's kingdom picture for noticing the importance of these new social configurations and interests, much less evaluating them in relation to some vision addressed to issues of natural, social, and global governance, the superimposition of the Christian grammar of sovereignty, power, and domination merely exacerbates problems related to these real-life areas of interest. It does not address them in a constructive way. It does not have the categories for thinking critically about the social enterprise. That, of course, is the fundamental problem with the notion of the righteous nation. We have had a Christian administration that did not believe in global warming, refused to hold industry accountable for pollution, was speechless in the face of catastrophes affecting the poor, turned its back on the problem of poverty, gave privilege to the wealthy, allowed the exploitation of natural resources without controls, put down those who called for environmental controls, cut provisions for social welfare, ignored the outpouring of rage from Muslims under our occupation and guns, and could not imagine that wars were not working, all the while preaching to the other nations of the world about doing things our way and calling for a celebration of the American dream based on a boot-strap approach to personal achievement. The rhetoric of concern for justice, freedom, democracy, and America as a light to the nations leaves no room for criticism of such an administration, debate about political systems, or deliberation about policies. A "war on terrorism" only exacerbates the reasons for it among those whose territories we have occupied abroad and creates a reign of fear among those at home who are supposedly being protected.

Thus the notion of one God in charge of creation and history, and Christians in charge of his dominion on earth, has produced a mentality that is incapable of dealing with complex social issues, multiple cultures, a global world, and differences among various ways of living in and accounting for the world. People whose cultures, ways, and ethnic extractions differ from the European Christian profile, imagined as the righteous leaven in a troubled and angry world, are seen either as candidates for conversion to American ways or as threats to our dominion. There is little interest in or appreciation of other social formations or cultural systems as exemplary products of the human enterprise in the construction of societies. Christians simply have a difficult time embracing the world in its display of many colors, performances, productions, constructions, skills, logics, and profundities.

This inability to deal with difference and complex issues cannot be brushed aside as a common characteristic of all human societies, which automatically think of themselves as doing things the right way. No. The inability is rooted deeply in the logic of the Christian grammar. We have mentioned the particular formulations of the logics of the "singular" and the "dual" in the Christian grammar. We now need to emphasize that neither is capable of dealing with complexity. This is the reason why compromise, negotiation, and deliberation are eschewed as the means for solving differences of opinion and interest in the construction of social policies.

We should now be able to see more clearly why the maneuvers in the interest of a Christian nation unleashed such a troubled recent history. The application of the Christian's imagined world to a nation-state was anachronistic. The identification of democracy with the notion of a righteous nation was unthinking. The attempt to add righteousness to power in the governance of a constitutional democracy was inappropriate. And the uncritical support of the financial interests and practices hiding behind the rhetoric of "national interests" has been cynical and egregious. Nevertheless, a kind of mythmaking took place that was able to draw upon the hopes and fears of Christians, and that supported the plans for an American empire. The myth was called the "American Way," and the Christian notion of a mission to the world allowed our incursions into other nations a kind of divine legitimacy. We thought of ourselves as a light to the nations and "democracy" became the code word for justifying regime change. But other peoples and nations are now in the process of resisting our incursions. Some are countering our military forces, others our economic exploitations, and still others our cultural values and implicit attitudes of superiority and dominance. Not many have censured Christian mentality as the cause.

The combination of uncontrollable executive power, self-righteousness, and the accumulation of wealth at the top levels of our society has succeeded in damaging congressional deliberation, the judicial system, the military, the economy, state governance, and the infrastructures concerned with welfare, health care, education, jobs, small businesses, pensions, pollution control, environmental protection, and quality of life. This means that the social world has become difficult to manage in terms of the imagined world of the Christian's myth–ritual system and its global scope and mission. It is no longer possible to think of the whole world converting to Christianity. And it has become most problematic to think of the United States shaping up as a Christian nation. The political antics of the conservative Christian Right and the policies of the recent administrations they have put in power have to be seen as desperate attempts to combine Christian thinking with social control. The consequences have been disastrous. Not only has the infrastructure of the democratic experiment in the United States been ravaged, an infrastructure in the process of construction and refinement for more than a century, but the deceit involved in the exportation of democracy, as if that were the real social interest involved in our foreign conquests, has only succeeded in the destruction of nations, peoples, and goodwill abroad. This is a serious situation for America and for American Christian mentality, a mentality accustomed to thinking that liaisons between religious authority and political power should produce and control moral order and well-being in the world. So, it is no wonder that, from the perspective of Christians who do find themselves thinking about the state of the world, it is an ugly scene. Whether or not these Christians notice that the ugliness is the very result of the American attempt to rationalize political power and economic interests with the Christian rhetoric of sovereignty, superiority, and righteousness, the ugliness has meant that the failure of the imagined world of the church to succeed in transforming the real world of the state has to be taken as a critical challenge. Christians who think of the United States as a Christian nation are not capable of managing our nation-state and should not be in charge.

It thus appears that the concept of the Christian nation can no longer be sustained. We have followed the history of the attempts to imagine the United States as a Christian nation. The road has been bumpy, the criteria for thinking that we are a Christian nation have been mythic and vague, and the emergence of the Christian Right at the level of political action has been alarming. One of the problems has been that the structures, social interests, and agenda of a nation-state require modes of thinking, deliberation, and governance that are very different from those assumed by a Christian mentality and grammar. Another is that the social interests generated within a nation-state create issues at junctures of social and natural world transactions, requiring an altogether different worldview from that of the Christian's imagined world. And a third problem is that, especially in the United States, the people have come from many lands, ethnicities, and cultures. Living within a polycultural nation-state requires concepts of the state, the common good, social belonging, and social identities that challenge Christian mentality and the notion of a Christian nation. These concepts are exactly those that define the social interests appropriate for the construction of social democracies in our time. And so, since we cannot be a Christian nation, the question is, what then? It will take another chapter to explore this question.

8 Religions in a Polycultural World

The concept of a "Christian nation" registers a problem for thinking about the social situation in which we find ourselves in the United States in the first decades of the twenty-first century. The designation is a misnomer, and the concept does not provide a program for a constructive engagement with the social issues facing us. The mythic world of Christianity imagines society on the model of a kingdom in which the Christian church is the only religion. Conservative Christians may have coined the term "Christian nation" with this model in mind. The history of the nation reveals the extent to which Christians and others have assumed the dominant influence of Christianity to indicate that the United States was a Christian nation. However, the history has shown the degree to which other concepts and social interests reveal structures and practices that are not rooted in the Christian's imagined world. During the last half of the twentieth century the disparity between the assumption of a Christian nation and the reality of our situation as a nation-state rooted in other interests and views became obvious. It was then that conservative Christians sought to shore up the moral values they imagined definitive for Christianity and for a Christian nation. The result was a remarkable violation of the principle of the separation of church and state. The Christian Right succeeded in putting many Christians into positions of leadership from local school boards to state systems of governance, and in convincing the Republican Party to formulate an agenda of moral issues that eventually put a born-again Christian in the White House and a Republican Congress in charge of the federal government. We have now seen what the combination of righteousness and power can produce if given free rein. The combination is not only inappropriate, given the actual state of the nation and its peoples, but also dangerous as a prescription for dismantling infrastructures at home and eroding influence and programs abroad in the interest of the powerful and privileged.

Given our study of Christianity and its mythic mentality, it should be clear that Christian-nation discourse and the entrance of conservative Christians into politics have written an exceptionally anachronistic chapter of our history. This discourse brought to the surface the erstwhile unacknowledged Christian mentality that otherwise resided below the surface unexamined, anchored in the mythic grammar of Christian uniqueness, superiority, monotheism, sovereignty, and global mission. The notion of a Christian nation was and is a terribly unfortunate and unthinking attempt to apply this grammar to the modern world without any appreciation or understanding of the social circumstances, practices, and interests that created the nation-state and the multicultural world we inhabit. That social circumstance is a challenge for

Christian mentality. Conservative Christian political activity is only an exaggerated example of the incommensurability of this mentality and the modern world, but it is a very important example for our study. As a public discourse that many now see as problematic, it lets us document the grammar at work in public thinking and policy-making that otherwise would be very difficult to delineate. My study is not aimed at conservative Christianity *per se*; it is aimed at an analysis of the underlying Christian mentality in keeping with my social theory of religion (revealed in myths, rituals, social interests, and social formations). There are many Christians who think that this conservative brand of their religion is a travesty that real, authentic Christianity cannot condone. However, most of such critiques, though well meant and hopeful as a sign that rethinking is under way, seldom strike to the core of the issue I want to highlight in respect to the mythic grammar and social interest of the Christian mentality at work in the United States at the present time. For a recent documentation of this thinking at the highest levels of our corporations and government, see Jeff Sharlet's study *The Family: The Secret Fundamentalism at the Heart of American Power*.

This chapter presents an alternative proposal for seeing the United States as an experiment in democracy that need not be a Christian nation. The reader will immediately notice the irony of a book about religion ending with a chapter on democracy, but this is necessary, given the study we have pursued. As we have seen, it was Christianity that defined the concept of religion in the first place, a definition that was not capable of explaining the myths, rituals, and social interests of other peoples. In order to explain them we had to develop a new set of categories related to a social theory of religion, and limit the discussion of religion to the function of myths and rituals. It was when we finally took up the task of analyzing the social logic of Christianity's myth–ritual system that the familiar features of the popular concept of religion reappeared. Now that we have explored those features and discovered why Christian mentality has become inappropriate for addressing such a social situation as that which exists in the United States, it is the social situation itself that requires some redescription. Please recall that our study of the logics of the myths and rituals of other peoples focused on the social interests that pertained to the social structures of peoples living in their social worlds. The social logics of Christian myth and ritual can no longer do that. We will therefore have to spend some time analyzing the social interests, issues, and composition of the people of the United States against the background of the concept of the Christian nation. Only later, in the course of this chapter, can the question be raised of how the various religions among us, including Christianity, can be imagined to function constructively in a nation-state that does not privilege a particular religion. This will bring us back to our social theory of religion, so as to conclude the study with a reimagination of myths and rituals appropriate for the social interests of a democratic society.

The Social Situation

Five features of the social situation can be identified. The United States is (1) a *nation-state*, (2) experimenting with a *social democracy*, (3) troubled by the balance between "national interests" and *social interests*, (4) awakening to its *polycultural* constituency, and (5) exploring its *religions* in light of its multicultural constituency and hopes for the future. These features are integral to the social formation of the society. All are social facts of importance to the society as a whole. Each is intertwined with the others in ways that make the social formation dynamic. None is sufficient as a definition of the society. The interaction among the systems is liable to cause tension and is governed by what can be called the self-interests of each. However, in public discourse and practice, policy-making in regard to these special interests is not evenly represented. That is because the people and institutions aware of and pursuing these interests are distributed in different ways to various levels and classes throughout the society. It is also because each of these systems has its own set of concepts, rules, and practices that defines its self-interests and operations. Many of these self-definitions have their own rationalizations as self-evident ideologies or mythologies.

When thought of as independent systems, each of these social factors can interact with the others in contention for recognition, authorization, and influence. And yet, none is easily accommodated by the others. That is because their social interests and logics often collide. American society as a whole has not yet found it possible to restructure its working relations among all of these interests as a projection of a common vision for the common good. It is this fact that has made it so difficult to think clearly and critically about religion and society and why our social theory of religion has resulted in a cultural critique of Christian mentality and the notion of a Christian nation. The five features of the social situation do not readily mix and match and are not complementary to one another. This describes a society and a social situation that is greatly different from the societies we have reviewed in our history of religions.

The reader will have noticed that the societies we reviewed were largely unified systems in which religious functions (myths, rituals, and their performances) were integral to the patterns of life of a single social world or a political system thought of as a single organizing mechanism. The one exception was the fragmentation and mix of cultures during the Greco-Roman period, when the social and political histories dismantled traditional arrangements of social structures and cultures. This created a new situation within which the cultivation and transformation of traditional myths, rituals, and cultural emblems characterized the responses. Our theory could explain the responses of peoples wanting to retain contact with traditional cultures, the desire of the early Christians to imagine themselves belonging to a universal kingdom of God, and the eventual liaison between Christians and the

Roman imperium that formed Christendom. The Christian missions subsumed many of the erstwhile cultures of the ancient Near East just as the Alexandrian and Roman expansions had subsumed their kingdoms and countries, but the single kingdom/single empire concept remained. It was the creation of Christendom and its claim to be the only religion permitted for the empires and kingdoms of the Western civilizations that surprised us. We were not surprised at the underlying conception of society as a kingdom and its religion as integral to its governance, life, and practice. That was understandable both in terms of the past history of the kingdoms of the ancient Near East and in terms of our findings about religions and societies in general. What surprised us was the emergence of a mono-mentality and system on the archaic model as the response to the vibrant multicultural mix of the Hellenistic world. It was this superimposition that curtailed the opportunities for experimenting with new, non-royal social formations during the Hellenistic period and restricted the otherwise normal human capacity for creative thinking generated by dealing with difference. And, as we have seen, that Christian mentality has survived the modern emergence of the nation-state and influenced the way in which we Americans have conceptualized our culture as Christian.

Thus it is that the separation of church (religion) and state in the United States and the emergence of many interests not directly addressed by the government of the nation-state, a single religion, or a common culture have created an exceedingly vigorous and open arena for social and religious experimentation. The question is whether the many streams and institutions of social interests can find ways for their logics to complement one another in the quest for social structures productive for a common good. With this in mind, it will be helpful to describe briefly each of the five features of our social situation and outline the reasons for their mutual incompatibilities. This can prepare us for a discussion of religions in a polycultural democracy.

The Nation-state

Anthony Giddens has helped us see that the structure of a nation-state is very different from the shape and organization of previous societies. Kingdoms and empires were centralized but their borders were more like frontiers, their systems of authority were concentrated in courts and bureaucracies at the top, and their control of their peoples was partial and intermittent, especially throughout rural areas and villages far from the capital city. Nation-states mark and police their borders, exercise control over all people within their borders, control the accumulation of information, preside over the information made available to the public, claim sovereignty, and have armies prepared for war in the national interest (Giddens, *Nation-State*).

It was during the period of modernity that nation-states emerged. Nation-states developed their own mechanisms for pursuing a set of interests made possible by the new technologies, industries, patterns of trade, and modes of marketing. These interests came to focus on economic factors that the governments of the nation-states soon realized were basic for the new patterns of production and social arrangements. Modes of production and marketing were used to compare the strength and competitive advantage of one nation-state with others. Profit was used to measure the success of industries and trade, and the location of wealth shifted from the properties of the landed aristocracies to the accumulation of capital by industrial and business entrepreneurs. The rather drastic changes that industrialization and urbanization created for all classes of people involved many social problems and inequities. But neither the churches nor the governments were quite prepared or able to control the pursuit of independent enterprise and the emergence of capitalism rationalized as the way to produce the wealth of nations. To take but one example, trading in rum, slaves, and cotton was an independent enterprise that provided England with capital and the Americas with wealth for about two hundred years without much government control except for various attempts at taxation. During the eighteenth and nineteenth centuries the value placed on trade and profit simply trumped critical deliberation about slavery, colonization, the "taking" of the lands in the Americas for private development, and the treatment of Amerindians. The importance of the slave trade for trading was the only category that mattered.

So it was that the interests driving the social changes that occurred in the wake of the Industrial Revolution were mainly economic. A new class of industrial and business entrepreneurs was created which eventually achieved political influence and power at the highest levels of government. The social location and effect of this class of persons bore little relation to the functions of former kings, clerics, and professionals. As a class they have found it difficult to think in terms of the well-being of a society on any other model than its financial system and strength. Success is measured in terms of the economic strengths of nation-states, businesses, and more recently global corporations. In the United States persons of this sort have been honored by the society as a kind of hero or celebrity, revered for entrepreneurial success and, if not persons to be envied, at least as models for the aspirations of all Americans. Some have suggested that the political philosophies, economic theories, and popular ideologies that support these interests can be thought of as our modern mythologies.

The United States was crafted in the period of the Industrial Revolution, French Revolution, and the Enlightenment, but without the history and experiences that forged the European nation-states. A national identity was not in place. The monarchy was far away, ill-informed about life in the colonies of America, and hardly the matrix society within which the colonies worked out their differences and formed a union. The emergence of industries in America was yet to come, a feature of the modern state that played an important role in the European experiments. The urban–rural division of interests was not yet as critical here as it was in Europe. Enlightenment discourse at the level of political philosophy was not a match for the debates pertaining to colony rights and representation, slavery, land ownership, financial matters, and taxation. The structures of a federal constitution and the governance of the colonies as a federal union were mainly matters of practical considerations, experimentation, and compromise, to say nothing of the various ways in which conflicts were actually resolved. The United States became a nation-state, taking its place among the nation-states that emerged during the eighteenth and nineteenth centuries, but the history of its beginnings marks it as distinctive. It did not emerge from a monarchy as others did and it did not have a state religion to give it continuity with a particular cultural tradition belonging to a specific people. It is this formation of the United States as a nation-state that presents a challenge for Christianity, the notion of a Christian nation, our polycultural constituency, and the need for a vision of the common good as the purpose for government and statecraft.

Social Democracy

The idea of democracy came along with the French and American revolutions, and it was the idea of democracy that made possible the creation of the United States as a federal union with a constitution and a representative form of government. As we have seen in the last chapter, the framers of our Constitution drew upon the concepts of democracy forged in the French Revolution. We should note, however, that the elite of industry or wealthy family estates and those of high-culture sensibilities in Europe were never completely comfortable with the idea, as Raymond Williams has shown for England (*Culture and Society*) and William L. Shirer has documented for the troubled histories of Germany and France up until the Second World War (*The Collapse of the Third Republic*). Those in control of governments and financial institutions have always been afraid of democracy. Democracy means the "power of the people," and those invested in other kinds of power have imagined people power to be rowdy, chaotic, destructive of culture, and unworkable. We like to think that the idea of representative democracy in the United States has included the balancing of powers, resources, and human energies in the interest of social constructions that enhance well-being and environmental policies that keep the natural world a living, healthy, and lovely place for humans to live. As John McGowan says in his book *Postmodernism and Its Critics*, social democracy is our best bet for constructing a working society, given the place to which our several histories have brought us. However, the democratic ideal is not a guarantee that a nation-state will function as a social democracy controlled by a vision of the common good. It all depends on the definition of citizenship, the ways in which deliberation and legislation take place, and the means by which the state controls the loyalty of its people.

The term *social democracy* can certainly be used to describe our experiment with social construction in the United States. I know that the term is not commonly used, and in fact is highly suspect on the part of many as an ideology in opposition to the more comfortable thought of being a republic in the form of a Christian nation. The term *democracy* is not the main problem. Though it can be misused by an administration in its designs upon other nations, and abused by those who want to justify practices that otherwise are merely self-serving, it is still the acceptable term for our form of government. So it is the *social* notion that has often been resisted. It has been used as a designation of the social democracies of Europe that are considered "Old World" and "secular," and therefore ranked as second-class, and it has been resisted in its use as a self-designation of our own democracy. Several reasons are frequently given for this resistance. One stems from the term's association with communism and the experience of the cold war years. Another starts with the statement that we are a nation of free individuals, not a social entity. But the basic reason has to do with fears that social interests threaten the interests of the nation-state and the freedom of individuals to pursue their own goals without having to worry about what happens to others. It is this interpretation of democracy and freedom that corporations and administrations have used to justify their exploits. There is, however, no reason not to use the term social democracy for our longstanding social experiment. We might take a moment to let the image congeal, for there is no other that describes our democracy as well, or lets us join the human race as easily. While our study of other peoples has encountered many with structures that cannot be called democratic, we did not find any without *social* interests. Even in the case of aristocratic empires where the view was from the top and the interests of empire outran the interests of smaller social units subsumed under their aegis, the social interests basic for their myth and ritual systems had the people and society as a whole in view, and ways were found to accommodate diverse cultural traditions. Our challenge will be to translate what we have learned about religions and societies in ways appropriate for a nation-state experimenting with a polycultural social democracy.

Social Interests

Our theory of myths and rituals (religions) started with observations about the two environments (natural and social) that coalesce in an imagined world. Myths and rituals mark those intersections of the two environments that a people has selected as important for the social formation of its society. They represent the interest people take in their social and natural worlds and mark features of their practices held to be significant for the structure of their society. We have used the term *social interests* to describe this collective investment in a people's social world and its practices. We have also emphasized the ways in which myths and rituals enable critical thinking about a people's practices and situation, and that changes in practices and situations result not only in new mythmaking and ritual performance, but also in new selections of interests of importance for new social formations.

We can use this term to analyze a set of problems critical for our social situation in the United States. A nation-state operates with its own set of interests, as we have seen. These interests are primarily driven by the desire for power, control, financial strength, and defense. The structure of a nation-state does not automatically make room for the interests of religions, democratic practices, ecological concerns, or the enhancement of the quality of life of all its citizens. All of these interests are alive and vibrant, however, and together they define the dynamic process of our social situation. To call all of them social interests lets us see them as important ingredients in the experiment under way, an experiment in the construction of a social democracy.

Think of the many experiments in process aimed at solving social and environmental problems in which the federal government of the United States has not taken leadership or even interest. Cities are learning to control development, create local stay-at-home businesses, make sure the working population has a livable wage and health care, and that the city is a wholesome and happy place for all to live. These interests and many others are documented and discussed in an issue of The Nation called "Urban Archipelago" (June 20, 2005): from Los Angeles to Palo Alto, Boulder, Ann Arbor, New York, and many other American cities, there are urbanist mayors and others working on solving social and quality-of-life issues at the local level. All of our energies have not been drained away by fixations on morals, weapons, fear, and superpower dominance. The issues are very clear. At the people level there is nothing at all wrong with the ideas that the administrations of our nation-state have found troublesome: "liberal," "union," "social," "social democracy," "living wage," "single-payer health care," "financial market controls," "social security," "transparency," and "justice." At the level of foreign policy and international relations, the United States has trouble with "United Nations," "international law," "world courts," "Geneva Convention," "Kyoto Accord," "nuclear disarmament," "bilateral negations," and so on. All of these belong to the social interests of a social democracy with a vision for the common good. There is nothing wrong with wanting the world to be a good place to live for everyone. Nothing. Other countries with nation-state structures are in the process of creating social democracies, as the examples from Europe and elsewhere prove, and there are now several Central and South American countries trying to wrest free from domination by the so-called national interests of the United States in the interest of creating their own social democracies.

It is true that we have not yet rationalized a comprehensive vision for the social interests of importance for our social democracy. It is perfectly possible, however, that we might find the challenge of identifying and ranking our social interests to be a rewarding intellectual labor. These interests would surface at the critical pinch points in what we have been calling the intersections or overlaps in our several environments, now having added the polycultural configuration to the social environments we have discussed. What about a listing of social interests of structural significance for a polycultural democracy? Several lists of social issues now under discussion among us have already been given in both this chapter and Chapter 7. These issues might be analyzed in terms of our category of social interests to determine ranking and relevance for the society as a whole. What about a thorough discussion of the intersections between human society and the environment, the rich and the poor, the several interests in economic systems that now clash, states' rights and the national interests, developers' interests and communities' interests, the people's interests and the administration's interests, the media and the people's interests? These social interests would look somewhat different from those traditional in single-culture societies. But they would name issues not being addressed as of structural importance for our society, and they could lead to very constructive exploration and discussion. They could be focused on the common good and well-being for all in the real world. The challenge for our society as a whole will be the development of a public forum and discourse aimed at the honest description and penetrating analysis of our social systems in relation to the concept of the common good. The challenge for Christianity and the other religions among us will be not only to help construct a vision of the common good, but also to explore their traditional notions of social interests to address the full range of social issues confronting our social democracy.

A Polycultural Society

The United States has been a polycultural society from its beginnings in Jamestown and throughout the seventeenth and eighteenth centuries. It was not long before the waves of immigration began to create noticeable communities of peoples with different religions, languages, and cultural traditions. As long as most of the early immigrants were from European countries, and thus familiar with some form of Christianity, the "melting pot" approach obscured the fact that distinctly different "ethnic" and cultural communities were shaping the fabric of the American people. But then there were the native Americans and the African-Americans to deal with as segments of the population, and in time they were joined by Asians, mid-Eastern Indians, Jews, Arab-Muslims, Mexicans, and peoples from Polynesia, all of whom migrated to America and became Americans. Thus our nation-state is polycultural. It is not a Christian nation, as if Christianity can or should provide the religion that determines citizenship or defines our culture. Those of European extraction who have thought of themselves as the main ingredient in the society will soon be in the minority. In any case, all of us, with the possible exception of the American Indians, are here as immigrants. Thus the double identities: Asian-American, African-American, American-Muslim, American-Indian, and so forth. As for the earlier ridiculing of "Pollacks," "Dagos," "Norskes," "Jews," "Irish," and others, it was always a matter of poking fun at their double identities. Those who have railed against the hyphenated nomenclature, impatient with immigrants who, it was thought, should assimilate to a monolithic American culture, simply betray their lack of appreciation for the ways in which cultural identities are formed, sustained, and cultivated, including their own. Double cultural identities are exactly what all Americans live with and cultivate.

If America is not a people of common ethnicity rooted in a land of origin and cultural memorials, is not a Christian nation, and is not a mere happenstance collection of adventurers, entrepreneurs, and do-gooders, what kind of a nation-state is it? The answer I have suggested is that we are an experiment in constructing a polycultural social democracy. The fact that we are a modern nation-state without a state religion might actually be considered one of the factors that has made the United States attractive for immigrants from other countries and cultures. It is, in any case, a fact that the composition of the people of the United States is polycultural. Most of us have found this experiment in creating a world worth living in to be a precious and important, if fragile and frustrating, investment. That it is supposed to work for the benefit of both individual and collective interests as well as contribute to social structuration is taken for granted. The unstated goal has always been to find practical solutions to social or physical problems in the interest of making life together worthwhile. It is true that our polycultural composition has not been thought of as a resource for social construction, and that our exceptional experiment in constructing a social democracy has not been consciously and vigorously pursued as a social vision of singular consequence and merit. However, if in the United States we could create a *polycultural* democracy, it would be the most rewarding and spectacular accomplishment of the era. It is almost as if, despite the accidental character of our social formation as a nation-state, and despite our failures to recognize and value our social experiment, the United States occupies a distinct position among the nations and countries of the world. We are not special because of our rise to being a military and economic superpower, as Gabler thinks (discussed briefly in the Introduction). No. But we may be special as the very place where an experiment in social democracy can encompass a polycultural people.

We already know that religions of all kinds have had little trouble taking up residence in the United States. We need only think of the synagogues, mosques, temples, shrines, monasteries, and retreat centers from all the major world religions that are in evidence among us. It seems that all of them have taken their place as a matter of course, without apology or embarrassment, content to serve as cultural markers and reminders for peoples cultivating a particular identity in the midst of a pluralistic society. Most of these markers are proudly displayed for the public to see. They are displayed as a way to cultivate their traditional cultures in a new social situation with a new mix of peoples. The ability to cultivate a cultural tradition in the context of a multicultural society exhibits a marvelous human capacity. What this achieves is a sense of particular identity, a knowledge of who one's people have been and are, where one finds oneself on the map of a mixed society, and a position from which a special perspective upon and response to the social situation are possible. This sense of personal identity as one who belongs to a particular social and cultural tradition makes it possible to analyze and negotiate social situations with insight, clarity, and decision. The difference between the two identities, cultural tradition and American, is apparently not an obstacle for negotiating the larger world. The gap between the two social arenas sharpens insight, invites critical thinking, and makes exchanges interesting. As for the skills required to negotiate such a gap, especially when experienced as the control of a dominant culture or system by those of subordinate status, Michel de Certeau, in *The Practice of Everyday Life*, studied them from just such a perspective. He found that practices he called "tactics" were automatic maneuvers in situations where different views and agenda required negotiation. A kind of awareness about one's projects could be detected that marked the human spirit as extremely capable of responding to difference. So a polycultural composition of our society is not a problem for our social democracy as long as the social democracy is structured and governed in ways that make living together possible and rewarding, and as long as a given cultural tradition can modify its imagined world to entertain and appreciate the many other religions and cultural traditions among us. This does not yet fully answer the question of the contribution a given culture might make to a polycultural experiment in which the quest for a common good and ethos requires a comprehensive social vision, but it does describe a situation in which such questions can be explored.

Religions in a Polycultural Democracy

Our study of religions has worked with a number of concepts that are important to keep in mind. The concept of social interests took us to myths and rituals where arrangements had been worked out with the two environments, the natural and social worlds. These arrangements were partly celebrative because the society had found ways to live constructively by selecting certain practices where its natural and social environments overlapped, and by creating myths and rituals to acknowledge their importance for the society as a whole. In the societies we have reviewed, the myths and rituals that focused upon these arrangements were also acknowledgments and celebrations of the structures of the societies that had been developed. Thus the social practices of hunting, farming, herding, building, crafting, questing, commanding, defending the territory, creating kingdoms, working together, and remembering the ancestors all became objects for recognition, reflection, and celebration by means of myth and ritual occasions. Thus the social interests and practices featured in a round of myth and ritual occasions could be taken up into a system of symbols that marked the social structuration of a people. We have called that its culture. We also discovered that myths and rituals were not only the creations of intellectual labor in the interest of recognizing social interests. They also served as rationalizations for features of a social formation impinged upon by influences and forces located in the environments that were beyond the reach of control by means of present energies and initiatives. These rationalizations, kept collectively in mind by means of mythic markers and symbols, were found to support mentalities grounded in what we have called their mythic grammars.

The place and function of religious myths and rituals in the United States are quite different from this description of traditional religions, societies, and cultures. The combination of a single society with its single religion is no longer applicable. Instead, there are many religions that cultivate their myths and rituals in separation from the state. This bifurcation of religion from the state has been accepted as a fundamental principle of our society. It has not been recognized as a problem for the practices of a religion or the significance of a religious system's beliefs, myths, and rituals. Local congregations and communities form highly valued and active social units that support a wide range of family and personal interests. Networks emerge that encourage mutual support in matters relating to employment, business, and social services available in the society at large. Rites of passage, rituals of celebration, cultural traditions, emblems, and markers of particular cultural identities can all be cultivated. It is therefore not surprising that individuals understand religion as a private and personal matter, a way of experiencing a particular identity by means of internalizing and cultivating a cultural tradition. And yet, given the social interests and social ideals rationalized in the imagined world of traditional religions and cultures, living in a society that is structured quite differently is bound to present a challenge.

The Challenge

The challenge is to live in a dynamic social situation that does not correspond to the mythic mentality and grammar of the imagined world of a given religion. The social situation must be engaged even though its social interests may differ from those rationalized and valued in a particular religion and traditional culture. The human capacity for negotiating social and cultural differences is a remarkable resource that can be called upon in such a situation. Many examples of this have been noted in the course of our historical review. And yet the challenge is real. The mythic grammars of a particular cultural tradition provide logics and ways of thinking about the world that may find it difficult to appreciate and comprehend other cultures and the social interests of a larger superordinate society. We have focused on Christian mentality as the prime example of this problem in relation to the social situation in the United States. But the imagined worlds of other religions will also have their mythic grammars underlying the mentalities of their cultures. As we have seen, these mythic grammars function largely at an unconscious level and, as with any grammar, would need to be explored, studied, and analyzed in order to work out their logics. The challenge, then, of living in a polycultural social democracy requires the recognition of other ways of thinking about the world as well as skills in negotiating social relations where differences in the practices and interests of others have to be engaged. There are signs that such accommodations are in fact under way.

An example of pursuing a particular cultural tradition in the context of our multicultural society can be seen in the way American-Muslims have responded to conflicts in the Near East, to the Bush Administration's stereotyping of Muslims there as enemies, and its treatment of Muslims among us as potential subversives. One can hardly imagine a worse situation for straining loyalties to the breaking point. And yet, American Muslims have made it clear that they are Americans as well as Muslims, that they have found ways of interpreting Islam in the interest of their double identity as Americans, and that we have nothing to fear from them just because they are Muslims. As a matter of fact, they have gone out of their way to explain to us how they understand several red-flag concepts found in the Quran. In every case, the translations may or may not be technically correct, historically proven, or transparent. But that cannot be the issue or point. The point is that what we have called a transformation and reproduction of a cultural tradition in conversation with a cross-cultural situation is obviously under way. American-Muslims may turn out to be 110 per cent Americans in the process, without having to discontinue being Muslims, because they will have had to analyze both their traditions and our polycultural situation in depth in order to make their responses to it.

Other examples of the transformation and reproduction of cultural traditions quickly come to mind. Jews, Amerindians, Asians from many countries, African-Americans, Mexican-Americans, Indians, and others have made their arrangements with life in the United States while keeping their distinctive identities. It might be helpful to notice that all these cultural traditions have negotiated our polycultural society using different strategies, which are the result of the various social circumstances in which the representatives of a cultural tradition have found themselves in America. Different strategies are also the result of the various cultural grammars that determine different ways of thinking about social life and values.

In the case of Judaism, for instance, there is a long history of cultivating identity by means of family rituals and community centers (synagogues) where teachers (rabbis) provide instruction in their traditions of religious and philosophical thinking, and preside over the adjudication of ethical and community issues. Rabbinic Judaism has found it possible to embrace the United States as a society in which the full range of civic activities and personal interests can be pursued without compromising its traditions. Only since the dreadful events of World War II, the rise of Zionism, and the establishment of the state of Israel has American Jewry become divided over questions of religion and society. These questions are now being addressed at the level of social theory and historical analyses (Brian Klug, "The State of Zionism").

Amerindians are finding other ways of keeping native traditions alive while coming to terms with the devastating histories of mistreatment by American governments, and Mexican-Americans are now in the process of negotiating the two cultural traditions at the level of civil rights and political power.

Since we have focused primarily on the challenges facing Christians as the result of social issues that have finally surfaced for attention, we should notice that many Christians have been working at the task of rethinking their myths and rituals with our polycultural society in view. Given our emphasis upon conservative forms of Christianity, one might suspect that Christians would have more trouble thinking of themselves as a subculture, mainly because a kind of nativism supports their self-understanding, but thinking about the hundred and fifty years of small-town Midwestern American history reveals another story. In any town there would be five to ten churches of different denominations plus a synagogue here and there for the people to attend once a week, a weekly mechanism of social segregation. After that, it would be life as usual, with tolerance for differences and maybe some humor on occasion, for example, because old farmer Jones played the banjo at the barn dances but couldn't play music at his church because they didn't believe in it. And so, it may be only when the shift to an urban and polycultural democracy puts pressure on Christian mentality that the task of critical analysis and a search for ways to reinterpret the myth system without losing the tradition can get serious. Nevertheless, there are "mainline" churches that have become uncomfortable with traditional and conservative Christian theologies. An example would be the way in which Methodists have toned down the logic of sacrifice built into the Christian Eucharist, and have therefore recast the ritual in the direction of a family meal. Church membership is no longer necessary to come to the table in these churches, and the confession of being unworthy, as in the old Anglican liturgy, is no longer necessary in order to hear the words of welcome to the family of God. Others have learned to prefer folk guitar to cathedral anthem and to gather in the round instead of sitting in pews. Some see this as an attempt, not merely to translate traditional Christian practices into a more modern idiom, but to turn away from traditional forms of ritual, with their symbols of obeisance before divine sovereignty, and substitute instead the ambience of "community" grounded in human freedom and integrity.

We might pause here to notice that changes such as these are taking place as transformations of ritual. This is significant. Ritual is the place where practice determines attention to social formation and mythic symbols. Changes in ritual practice can be made that challenge traditional mythic grammars. The transformation of mythic grammars requires changes in the narrative accounts, and most changes of this sort require time to be recast and let the erstwhile plots fade away. Rituals are more available for manipulation, and ritual changes, even if subtle, immediately evoke critical thinking in response to their significance for social formation.

Another example of ritual transformation is taking place among progressive Christians, who are definitely worried about the effective difference Christianity is making in the social and political arenas. They find evangelicals talking about saving souls an embarrassment; and the conservative Christian Right is seen as even more of a problem because of its intolerance for liberal

Christian views. Many of these progressives have formed networks for promoting their eight-point program, in which a social vision of inclusiveness counters traditional Christian prejudices against ethnic, gender, and moral differences. The Center for Progressive Christianity includes in its program such statements as "[We] invite all people to participate in our community and worship life without insisting that they become like us in order to be acceptable." A recent brochure says, "We are developing strategies for evangelism that do not assume the absolute superiority of Christianity so that we do not contribute to the world's tragic divisions" (www.tcpc.org).

There are also many organizations on the fringes of Christian churches engaged in liberation programs and social services called for by interpretations of the kingdom of God as a caring community or a social ethic understood to be rooted in Christianity. An example would be the Heifer Project, a program started by a Christian farmer that provides farm animals and plants to impoverished peoples, together with instructions on their care, reproduction, and use. Recipients are required to expand their domestic production and give "starts" to a neighbor. Other examples would be Habitat for Humanity, Physicians without Borders (Médecins sans Frontières), and many other humanitarian organizations.

Not all of these arrangements have been matters of reciprocal interests and concern on the part of Americans in general, as we know. That means that many Americans have not yet learned to appreciate our society as polycultural. Our many religions and their mentalities, or ways of thinking about the world, have seldom been seen as a precious resource for thinking creatively about the construction of a multicultural society.

Rethinking Religions and Society

Everyone is involved in the dynamic process we have described as the social situation in the United States. We have emphasized the challenge of living in the social world with a distinctive cultural grammar given with a particular religious tradition. We have described this challenge as the limitations of a given cultural grammar to comprehend and negotiate the larger social world with its diverse patterns of peoples and interests. We now need to recognize that the challenge is not merely one of living with a double identity and mentality, as suggested, of finding one's particular place in the larger society. The challenge of thinking about one's place in the larger social world is compounded by the fact that there are many other religions, cultural traditions, and mentalities at work in our society, all of which require particular skills in negotiation in order to be adequately understood and addressed. If we turn the perspective around in order to ask about the challenge that faces the society as a dynamic configuration of the many interests outlined above, including those of the many religions and cultural traditions at work, the consequences of our being polycultural can more easily be seen. A polycultural social democracy requires some vision of society as a whole based upon the concept of the common good, conscious of the need to rank and control all of the interests energizing its several practices with the common good in mind, and working out processes of deliberation and legislation that can draw upon the interests and intellectual resources of its many constituencies. The question is whether traditional religions can not only manage such a society but make constructive contributions to such a social program.

Recalling what we have learned about religions and their societies, we see that there are a number of observations relevant to this question. Myths and rituals are ways in which peoples have selected practices and interests of importance for social constructions. We have noted that these selections are the result of both practical and intellectual investments. The practices of myths and rituals were also found to be occasions for critical thinking. This thinking was no different from the intellectual activities of humans in general except in terms of its focus upon practices and images of particular significance for the conception of their societies. The basic grammar of human intellectual activity works with an interest in classifications, noticing differences, the making of comparisons, marking relationships by means of two systems of differences, using analogy to derive meaning, ranking roles in terms of social place and function, and forming images, emblems, and symbols to guarantee tuition and the collective celebration of a common way of life. Myths and rituals have been formed and practiced by means of these intellectual activities. They did not prohibit the exercise of these capacities in application to the many other interests pursued by a people, but they did mark particular and distinctive practices and concepts characteristic for their societies, which defined them. We have called the cultivation of such practices and concepts, manifest especially in myths and rituals, a culture, and we have seen that a culture produces a mentality the grammar of which can be analyzed by asking about the social logics of its myths and rituals.

We can use this intellectual anthropology of religion to analyze the social situation of our polycultural democracy and note that the many religions among us are actually resources for thinking critically and constructively about the social project under way. The challenge would be to tap the thinking already invested in a mythic grammar, compare it with the new social situation, analyze both sets of interests, and reveal their social logics for discussion. We have already noted the rethinking of many religions and cultures that have learned to accommodate the social situation in the United States. It is, however, not clear that critical analysis has been given to their mythic grammars in comparison with the social reasons required to imagine a social democracy. The move from accommodation to constructive participation in the formation of a social democracy would be enhanced by such critical thinking. What we have called the transformation and reproduction of a culture often takes place automatically in the course of making compromises related to the practical interests and requirements of a new situation. However, such transformations could also lead to critical analyses of a culture's myth system and grammar. Through the surfacing of such analyses, critical thought could be focused on both the grammar and logic of a given culture as traditional, as well as on the new social situation and its own sets of interests, rationales, and ideologies. Supposing a people found it constructive to engage in such analyses and made them available for public discussion, an exceptionally rich resource for thinking about our experimental project could be imagined.

Recognizing the fact of our polycultural society; listing its social interests; rendering a critique of sovereignty, capitalism, and war; assessing our human resources; and projecting a vision of the world as a good place to be, are ways in which we can finally suggest an answer to the question about what our traditional religions might contribute to the making of a polycultural world. Recall that our theory of myths and rituals emphasized the gaps they created between the imaginary world and the situations they addressed in the everyday world. Recall also the mode of thinking evoked by these gaps. It was the difference between the two worlds so experienced and imagined that called for comparison, using the differences to note features of the social world that might otherwise be overlooked or taken for granted. This invited critical thinking about the social situation. All of our religions have worked that way in their traditional societies and cultures. The new situation in our polycultural society demands more, but the demands are actually constructive. They are a challenge for critical thinking at a new level, where our religions could become a major resource for our experiment, yet the gaps we have to work with multiply. Not only are there differences among the several religions that can be compared in terms of their mythic grammars and mentalities, the gaps between each religion's imagined world and the social situation in which we find ourselves are different from those in the other religions. These gaps are exactly what we can use to advantage for thinking critically about our situation and for proposing solutions for our experiment. All of our religions can be recognized as the result of a people's interest in social well-being. We can ask each one to describe the features of its concept of social well-being. The wisdoms of their cultural histories are encapsulated in their myths and rituals. Each could work at the task of translating its myth–ritual system in application to our new social situation. Such a translation is called for in any case by the need to adapt, but thought of as a contribution to the public discussions we need to have about our experiment, these translations could easily become proposals from which we might take topics for consideration in the quest for a general vision.

Were several religions analyzed in this way, the differences among them with respect to social interests would be an invitation not only to critical thinking but also to public forum and debate. Seeing the differences in terms of what might be called proposals for conceptualizing the common good could take advantage of the differences for deliberation and discussion. Such a discussion could take place at the social level of common interest in the workings of the society. Revealing a given culture's thinking about what made a traditional society work in ways that reward human interests need not be a matter of sacrificing its distinctive values to the social vision of a polycultural democracy. It would actually enhance a people's sense of dignity and partnership in the experimental project. It would, however, require the giving of reasons for such values, and that would open the discussion to debate and create a social arena in which each religion and culture could begin to see what it looked like to the others. That could be an invitation to reproduce traditional identities appropriate for the new polycultural situation.

Visions of the Common Good

The reader alert to public and political discourse in the United States will know that a vision of the common good seldom surfaces as a consideration or argument for policy formation. As a matter of fact, there may not be a common vision of the common good in the United States to which reference can be made. We lack a concept of our society as a culture and a collective of the kind typical for traditional single-culture societies. Our thinking has been determined largely by the "Rights" to "Life, Liberty, and the pursuit of Happiness," as the Preamble to the Declaration of Independence has it. Freedom has been the emblem and motto for a society encouraging individual pursuits. We therefore find ourselves locked into a thoroughly individualistic anthropology or way of thinking about what it means to be a human being.

Our social situation now requires a concept of the common good able to entertain another anthropology. Freedom has been abused as a political slogan at home and abroad, and as an argument for allowing financial institutions and multinational corporations free rein without social accountability. As individuals we have thought of ourselves largely as being personally responsible for successful accomplishments in our own interests in a competitive world. It is not that we do not know about all of the many other ways in which individuals take interest in the world and construct their lives as human accomplishments. The problem is that the social world is pictured as a collection of individuals intent on their own pursuits. Left out of the picture is the entire range of interests in the world of which humans are capable, a configuration of the social that projects and calls for the celebration of being human, and a focus on the intersection of the social world with the natural environment that can rekindle a sense of wonder and respect.

What if we were to imagine a world that did not reward the strong man, the autocrat, predation, the acquisition of wealth as a great human achievement, the exploitation of natural resources as justifiable in the interest of corporation profits, or the display of luxury in order to think of oneself as successful and important? The motivations driving such projects are not necessary for meaningful and rewarding human existence. They are the values of a worn-out anthropology and the result of our own mesmerizement with the mono-mythologies of power and accumulation. There are other motivations, reasons, and rewards for engaging in human projects that are possible, interests that can rise to the top of a social system and its consciousness and make living worthwhile. And there is a ground swell of energies at the people level now being driven by just such interests. The reader will know of the many movements, leaders, thinkers, and agencies among us that are working to restructure our social systems in the interest of the common good. The social issues focused upon by these movements are frequently quite specific, but the larger picture is always in view, and the reasons for the movements clearly have the larger picture in mind. These movements are called for because the way our society is presently structured and functioning and the way our federal administrations have promoted their policies are not conducive to the common good. This means that there is a huge gap between the picture projected from the top and the social realities experienced at the people level, a gap into which more and more thinking is being poured. I will take but two examples of such thinking, both coming from the highest levels of thoughtful social analysis.

The first is a book published by Ralph Gomory, President of the Alfred P. Sloan Foundation and for many years a senior vice president at IBM, on *Global Trade and Conflicting National Interests*. Gomory's point was that two distinctly different "national interests" needed to be distinguished. One was the federal government's interpretation, which imagined the government's purpose was to make possible our capitalistic economy and support corporations as exemplars of our society of freedom (National Interests A). The second concept of "national interests" was the more popular and standard notion that the purpose of the federal government was to look after the well-being of our society (National Interests B). William Greider recently interviewed Gomory and asked him to comment on our free trade policy from the perspective of his earlier study, a study that has been "overlooked" by our representatives and government. Gomory's response was that the policy was not working to the benefit of the national interests at home (B), but only for the benefit of our multinational corporations (A). Even though these corporations are American, they are not held accountable by our government and are not concerned with the national interests here at home (B). The problems were systemic, he said, and resulted from a "divergence of interests." According to Greider, "If nothing changes in how globalization currently works, Americans will be increasingly exposed to downward pressure on incomes and living standards" ("The Establishment Rethinks Globalization," 13). Gomory's thinking has not gotten to the level of social theory and the analysis of the logics involved in each of the two "national interests" he has identified, but he has seen the different effects of the two, and he has started to worry about the system not working right. That is something, coming from a scientist, mathematician, and executive of a major successful American corporation.

The second example of critical thinking is a rather large number of studies in criticism of the ideologies of war. They suggest that we might be able to imagine a world without war and violence. As already indicated, Anthony Giddens says that war as it is now being pursued is directly related to the structure and interests of the nation-state (*Nation-State*). Others have suggested that the nation-state as it is now configured may not be right for the future of the world as a global congeries of peoples (Kumar, "A Civilizing Mission"). It means that there is an inherent tension between the structure of a nation-state and the practice of a democracy in a global age. In the case of our experiment with a polycultural social democracy the problems we are having with an administration that justifies war in the "national interest" might also be problems with the rationale and structure of our nation-state. In any case, Jonathan Schell thinks it possible to imagine a world without war and violence, because the "war system," as he calls it, has finally been damaged beyond repair (*The Unconquerable World*). Reviewing Schell's book in the *Los Angeles Times*, Jaroslaw Anders said, "The war system has been a set of actions and counter actions throughout the ages that made practically every developed state prepare for war, expect war and accept war as the final arbiter of international conflicts of interest." However, the mind-boggling investments in destruction without anything of value to show for them throughout the twentieth "century of terror" and the fact that the war system no longer solves problems of conflict, but makes them worse, are now obvious to anyone willing to analyze the strategy. The system is finally bankrupt in its attempt to use military power and violence to solve international conflicts. The war system has not solved the problem of terrorism, but actually unleashed it. "The unprecedented brutality and scale of the war system, its proliferation of weapons of mass destruction, the trillions of dollars poured into high-tech armaments, the festering of old conflicts newly provoked by wars and new ones springing up in the most unusual places, warlords with weapons of mass destruction, and crumbling international institutions" have become the marks of our insanities, not our wisdom. And so it may be time to call a halt. Anders put it this way: "If we play our cards well, we may retire war for good and enter an era of lasting peace and cooperation." Playing these cards may not be easy without a radical rethinking of the interests and logics driving our traditional assumptions about the purpose of government, but the criticisms of war as a means of solving conflict are coming close to an analysis of the social structures that take war for granted.

What if we shifted our attention from our problems with the authorities and interests at the highest levels of power and privilege and turned instead to the ground swell of constructive energies at the people level? That is where the ingredients for a concept of the common good are being generated. That is where thousands of community leaders, thinkers, and activists are at work with the conviction that a society structured to enhance the common good would be a most rewarding world in which to live. The trick will be to imagine a world worthy of its celebrations. We might think of this imagined world of the common good on the model of our traditional myths and rituals. Myths and rituals have been the ways in which a people acknowledge, celebrate, and rationalize their societies as being for the common good. We might even want to think of the concept of the common good gathering up the many myths and rituals of the many religions among us to acknowledge the multicultural fabric of our society. We have already considered the contributions that our many religions might make to the construction of a new vision of the common good if only they were to let their traditional mythic grammars surface for social analysis in public forum.

If we did this with a sense of humor to accompany the seriousness of the social situation we need to address, we might actually entertain the thought of the traditional gods in their traditional worlds unable to handle our multicultural world and our experiment in constructing a social democracy. If we had a Jewish sense of humor we might have some fun putting all of the gods and all of the prophets of all the gods into the same imaginary world to see what might happen. Just think of Yahweh, Allah, the Christian God, Marduk, the Buddha, Moses, Mohammed, Jesus, Confucius, some Zen Master, maybe a *kami* if we could catch one, and of course the Native American's trickster coyote, all in the same imaginary world together, just as all of their followers are together in the real world here on earth. What would they say to one another? Could we get them to talk? Would they recognize one another? And would they know what has happened in the human world since their followers first imagined them alone in their own imaginary worlds? If we could get them to talk to one another with all of us poised to listen in on the conversations, maybe we could have them explain themselves and their histories to one another. Maybe we could ask them to discuss social interests, intellectual anthropology, and the transformation of religious grammars. It would be very good to listen in on such a discussion. Yahweh might want to explain his many changes of mind in the course of his history, especially about temples, priests, and kings. Jesus might have to revise his notion of the kingdom of God. The Christian God might have to wince about the "sacrifice" of his son and say that he really didn't mean it when he inspired John to write the Revelation of the end of the world. The Buddha might be silent for most of that, but would probably not have too much trouble understanding the coyote, of course. And Moses could chuckle about it all for a change, explaining that, as a fictional character, his intention in writing the five books was really that of an epic poet. Mohammed might sniff, sneeze, and cough a bit when asked about jihad. Whether the *kami* could find his garments in the mix-up might be a problem. Of course, the very concepts of social formation and intellectual anthropology might seem so old hat to these denizens of human history that we would not learn anything new from them at all except for their wondering why it took us so long to figure it out. But at least we could imagine them all talking together instead of wanting to break up the conference and rush out to preside over their separate peoples and domains. That would be something.

A better approach, however, would be to focus on our experiment in the construction of a social democracy and notice that it depends upon human agents rather than the gods. The gods involved in our traditional myths and rituals are already symbols of importance only for particular cultural traditions. These myths and rituals are incapable of celebrating the social democracy of a collective, multicultural society. What then? Might it not be possible to entertain a social anthropology in which the human agents at work in the interests of the collective, which in some ways would include all of us, could be honored as the agents that matter most, as heroes of the human spirit? Although we have not thought about remarkable examples of being human as our heroes of the human spirit, nor of our heroes making a contribution to thinking and theory about the common good, they are there all around us, all the time, presenting us with opportunities to reimagine ourselves as capable of making the world a good place to live. Supposing our polycultural democracy, working with the structures of a non-religious nation-state, actually achieved a social structure that made the world a good place for everyone to live, the stories about our heroes in the construction of the common good could well become our myths. If so, their celebrations could well become our rituals.

And so we come to the end of our study. Do religions matter? Yes. In the histories we have reviewed religions have mattered very much, serving social formations by providing myths and rituals to rationalize and celebrate life together. Do religions still matter in our modern world of nation-states and global economies? Yes, but no longer in the same ways. Some matter as subcultural formations in the service of personal pieties and family rituals. It remains to be seen whether they will want to make a difference as well for rationalizing and celebrating our secular and multicultural democracy. Some still continue to think of themselves as the only religion right for our society. These have been making a difference for the society at large, but a difference that is destructive. The tragedy is that one of these monotheistic religions, Christianity, has become the rationalization for sovereignty, defense, war, and violence in the service of interests that do not contribute to the common good. Can religions still matter constructively in our polycultural situation in the United States? Well, as we have seen, the possibility does exist that religions willing to take their places alongside the many other religions among us might actually make a significant difference in our quest for a vision of the common good. Were they to tackle the task of transforming their myths and rituals in order to contribute to the social formation of a polycultural social democracy, the difference they could make for our society and its culture would be very significant indeed.

Conclusion

We have traced the history of thinking about religion from the Age of Discovery to the present, during which time the concept of religion has changed several times. Its first definition was provided by familiarity with medieval Christianity, conceptualized consciously when the New World was discovered and Columbus found that "the natives had no religion." A kind of bewilderment settled in, for medieval Christian mentality had no way to classify humans without religion. During the next two centuries, missionaries, explorers, and scholars struggled with this conundrum, finding traces of what they thought were religious sensibilities, but without being able to identify or conceptualize anything similar to what they understood religion to be. When scholars and ethnographers finally focused on tribal myths and rituals, they triggered a shift in the concept of religion that broke away from its Christian connotations. Religion was understood no longer as a matter of belief and piety interested only in contacting a realm of the gods, but as one of symbolic representations of social interests and structures.

In Part I of the book I was able to develop a social theory of myths and rituals and explain the ways in which their imagined worlds created a common mentality for a people and a grammar for thinking together about themselves and their world. Then, taking some time to document and describe the Christian system of myth and ritual, we found that its imagined world and resulting grammar were created during the ages of empire and that its transformation into the institution of the Church enabled it to survive the social changes of the modern world. Nevertheless, the resulting mentality was found to be inadequate to comprehend the polycultural society we have become in the United States. It was then possible to see why it was wrong to think of the United States as a Christian nation, and why the rhetoric, plans, and practices of a Christian administration had created such danger and devastation at home and around the world. The imagined world of Christians did not have room for the kind of world we had become. The myth and ritual system had a social logic that did not fit, and the Christian grammar determined ways of thinking that were arrogant and destructive.

This critique was based on scholarly considerations, documentation, and argument. It was not a matter of ideological debate. Because that left us with another conundrum, namely, what then to think and do about Christianity and the other religions in our polycultural democracy, I wrote a final chapter on the intersections where our several environments create social issues that impinge upon social interests of importance for our experimentation with a social democracy. Using what we have learned about myths, rituals, and social formation, about the transformation and reproduction of traditional cultural systems, and about the anomaly of traditional religious systems in a secular and polycultural nation-state, I dared a further meditation on the chances for a shift in our ways of looking at our world, away from our traditional mythic grammars anchored in the imagined worlds of the gods, and toward a re-imaging of our polycultural social worlds by taking delight in human agency and values. I even wondered about a new social formation experimenting with new genres of myth and ritual in the quest for a social vision of the common good. If our social democracy took our attention, and the social interests and issues that had to do with its construction focused our thinking about it, why not consider turning some of our stories about human agents into stories of the human spirit and their achievements into celebrations of our lives together? We would then have "myths" and "rituals" that focused upon heroes of the human spirit rather than upon the traditional gods.

The reader will know that the focus upon religions in our polycultural society has not adequately addressed a large number of social issues that were briefly mentioned in the description of our social situation. Many of these are matters that impinge upon the structures and practices of our governments. Entertaining the notion of the common good results in concerns about the control of financial interests, guaranteeing democratic procedures in the formation of laws and policies, rethinking the function of our police and military, criticizing foreign policy driven by "national interests" and the new colonialism, rendering a critical assessment of war and violence as ways to solve problems, and so forth. And yet, all of these issues stem from different ways of thinking about the world, different interests involved in the human enterprise of social construction, and various ways for individuals and institutions to find their investments rewarding. That means that addressing these issues requires new myths (worldview grammars) and rituals (attention to practices recognized as having human and social value), as well as action on the political and practical fronts where strategies and tactics aim at changing social structures. So I dared the hopeful outlook, not only in recognition of all the activities that mark the American experiences aimed at making the world a good place to live, but also in the knowledge of the human capacity for mythmaking and the transformation of mythic grammars in situations of social and cultural change.

The first response to this uncommon scenario by people invested in their religious and cultural traditions might be to think this preposterous and decide to make do with the old grammars. I therefore suggested that transformations and reproductions of a traditional religion might make it possible to continue its cultivation in some way, and that having double identities was a human capacity common to many peoples. I did wonder whether the Christian myth–ritual system, focused upon monolatry and sacrifice, was pliable enough to manage the new world, and whether some double identities based on traditional religions could survive. In the meantime the public presence of many cultural traditions could become an interesting, colorful, and constructive enhancement of our common life if only their peoples found it rewarding to live in a social democracy and could manage the skills of double identity without rancor.

The second response, this one not from the religious right but from the realist right, is that the picture is dreamy, fantastic, and completely irresponsible. That is because all peoples have always gone to war, disparate interests in a society automatically create conflict, the need for leaders and the drive for power are necessary, and the acquisitive, competitive instinct is natural. So the argument hangs on "natural," "necessary," "automatic," and "always." What kind of an argument is that? It is an argument from the top, a voice that tells us to get over it, a statement of satisfaction with the status quo on the part of those who are reaping its benefits. It is a mind-set comfortable with the status quo of war, conflict, power, and acquisitive overreach. But these are the very problems we are having with our world, problems that have gotten out of hand. They are exactly the issues confronting us, issues we are having a difficult time comprehending, much less addressing. As for the status quo being natural, that is exactly what the studies in this book have argued against. Mind-sets are not natural. Social configurations are not manifestations of divine plans for humankind, cosmic powers of determination, or natural laws that prescribe how a society has to be structured. Societies are human constructions. Myths and rituals are human constructions. Mentalities are the result of living with a set of myths and rituals as a grammar for the activities and maintenance of a society that humans have constructed. All that can change. All the several layers of societies, their structurations, and their mythic rationalizations have changed many times in the history of the human race. There is no divine or natural law that says the only way to construct a society is with an autocrat, domination, and violence. Violence is thought to be necessary in our society because it has been justified by our traditional mythologies and mind-sets. Change the myths and mind-set, and violence need not be thought necessary.

So now the third critical response can be heard. It is that, while the picture I have painted might be granted as an interesting consideration of some relevance to our situation in the United States, it is foolish and silly to think that creating a polycultural social democracy here could solve the problems of our relations with the whole world of nations. If it cannot, we would be making ourselves vulnerable to the predatory interests of other nations that might want to take advantage of our weakness. This criticism is actually helpful as a way to bring our studies to a conclusion. It raises intellectual and logistical questions that we have not touched upon, that are still outstanding, and that are serious considerations for those who may be wanting to rethink our cultural resources. At the level of political and industrial exchange and negotiation it is not clear what would have to happen for a shifting in human values to make a difference in practices. That is why this study is an attempt to suggest a rethinking of our own culture, not a program for execution. It does not pretend to offer a practical plan for a social democracy or the steps that may be required to work toward one. It does not pose as having answers to the myriad issues of social construction and the balancing of the many interests that are constantly being encountered both at home and abroad. It is an analysis of our cultural Christian mentality in the interest of understanding why we think the way we do, why we think of ourselves the way we do, and why we look different in the eyes of other peoples from the way we look to ourselves.

And yet, suppose we took both the study of our mentality and the proposal for a social democracy seriously and then got worried about what might happen to us in the larger world of nations. Reasons for the cautionary advice about staying strong lest our enemies take advantage of our "weakness" might well bring to mind problems that appear intractable. However, the problems that come to mind are the very same problems that we now have because of our "strength." Since our posture of self-righteousness and military might in support of our national interests has contributed to, if not caused, much of the current conflictual and violent state of the world, staying strong and providing the rest of the world with weapons so our economy can stay strong cannot be the answer. Were we, as a social democracy, to shift from unilateral to bilateral thinking in keeping with what would be our own internal practices in deliberation and governance, it is conceivable that our very change of posture would result in finding ways to solve the many international problems now before us. Learning to appreciate cultural differences, analyze social problems, and compromise in matters of exchange is not the mark of weakness. It is the greatest achievement of the human spirit of which we are capable as social beings. It is worthy of the highest honor, reverence, and reward. Myths and rituals of the human spirit would be wondrous mechanisms for creating a rich and beautiful social democracy, and for realizing that the world is a good place to be.

Thus we come to the end of a study about religions and social interests. Our social theory has focused on myths and rituals, and the essential ingredient throughout has been critical thinking. Critical thinking is what myths and rituals make possible, and myths and rituals are themselves the products of critical thinking. Most have been generated slowly over long periods of time. Thinking collectively about social interests has always been involved as well, but thoughts generated collectively about social interests work themselves out in myths, rituals, and practices that lose their conscious voices. Social issues that arise also call for critical thinking. Myths and rituals may be called upon to rationalize this or that approach to a new social circumstance or social issue. In the hands of those in charge, myths and rituals may well be abused or transformed by self-serving manipulations, and, as we have seen, mythic systems can become archaic and dangerous grammars for thinking about the real world. But as the gaps between a myth–ritual system and the social world it addresses widen, the arena for critical thinking can entertain a critique of the system itself. Especially critical are times when traditional myths and rituals no longer help because they continue to cultivate thinking that stems from social interests and their rationales that have become obsolete. It is then that they themselves may suffer critique. Hence, this book is not only a study about religions and social interests as they have been seen and created throughout human history. It is also my attempt to render a cultural critique of the Christian mentality at work in the United States at the beginning of the twenty-first century. I would like to leave the reader with an invitation to join me in this venture of critical thinking about religion, society, and our social situation.

Bibliography

Althusser, Louis, *For Marx*. London: New Left Books, 1969.
Althusser, Louis, *Lenin and Philosophy*. New York: Monthly Review, 1971.
Althusser, Louis, *Philosophy and the Spontaneous Philosophy of the Scientists*. London: Verso, 1990.
Althusser, Louis, *Politics and History*. London: New Left Books, 1976.
Althusser, Louis, and Etienne Balibar, *Reading Capital*. London: New Left, 1970.
Anders, Jaroslaw, Review of *The Unconquerable World* by Jonathan Schell. *Los Angeles Times*, Book Review, June 1, 2003.
Apuleius, Lucius, *The Golden Ass*, trans. P. G. Walsh. The World's Classics. Oxford and New York: Oxford University Press, 1995.
Armstrong, Karen, *The Battle for God*. New York: Knopf, 2000.
Beck, Roger, *The Religion of the Mithras Cult in the Roman Empire: Mysteries of the Unconquered Sun*. Oxford and New York: Oxford University Press, 2006.
Benedict, Ruth, *Patterns of Culture*. Boston: Houghton Mifflin, 1961 (first published 1934).
Bettelheim, Bruno, *The Uses of Enchantment: The Meaning and Importance of Fairy Tales*. New York: Random House, 1977.
Bettenson, Henry, *Documents of the Christian Church*. London and New York: Oxford University Press, 1947.
Bettenson, Henry, *The Early Christian Fathers*. London and New York: Oxford University Press, 1969.
Boas, Franz, *The Mind of Primitive Man*. New York: Macmillan, 1938 (first published 1911).
Boas, Franz, *Race, Language, and Culture*. New York: Macmillan, 1940; Free Press, 1966.
Bonnet, Hans, *Reallexicon der Aegyptischen Religionsgeschichte*. Berlin: De Gruyter, 1952.
Bourdieu, Pierre, *Esquisse d'une théorie de la pratique*. Geneva: Droz, 1972 [*Outline of a Theory of Practice*, trans. Richard Nice. Cambridge Studies in Social Anthropology 16. Cambridge: Cambridge University Press, 1977].
Braun, Willi, and Russell T. McCutcheon, *Guide to the Study of Religion*. London and New York: Cassell, 2000.
Bruner, Jerome, *Actual Minds, Possible Worlds*. Cambridge, MA: Harvard University Press, 1986.
Burkert, Walter, *Ancient Mystery Cults*. Cambridge, MA: Harvard University Press, 1987.
Burkert, Walter, *Homo Necans: Interpretationen altgriechische Opferriten und Mythen*. Religionsgeschichtliche Versuche und Vorarbeiten 32. Berlin and New York: Walter de Gruyter, 1972 [*Homo Necans: The Anthropology of Ancient Greek Sacrificial Ritual and Myth*, trans. Peter Bing. Berkeley: University of California Press, 1983].
Cameron, Ron, and Merrill Miller (co-editors and commentators), *Redescribing Christian Origins*. Symposium Series 28. Atlanta: Society of Biblical Literature, 2004.
Cameron, Ron, and Merrill Miller (co-editors and commentators), *Redescribing Paul and the Corinthians*. Symposium Series. Atlanta: Society of Biblical Literature (forthcoming).
Carr, Pat, *Mimbres Mythology*. Southwestern Studies Monograph 56. El Paso: University of Texas Press, 1987.
Castelli, Elizabeth, "Globalization, Transnational Feminisms, and the Future of Biblical Critique," in Kathleen O'Brian Wicker, Althea Spencer Miller, and Musa W. Dube (eds), *Feminist New Testament Studies*, pp. 63–76. New York: Palgrave Macmillan, 2005.

Certeau, Michel de, *The Practice of Everyday Life*, trans. Stevan Rendall. Berkeley: University of California Press, 1984.

Columbus, Christopher, *The Diario of Christopher Columbus's First Voyage to America, 1492–1493*. Abstracted by Bartolome de las Casas; transcribed and translated into English, with notes and a concordance of the Spanish, by Oliver Dunn and James E. Kelley, Jr. The American Exploration and Travel Series. Norman: University of Oklahoma Press, 1989.

Comte, Auguste, *Discours sur l'ensemble du positivism*. Paris, 1848 [*A General View of Positivism*, trans. J. H. Bridges. Stanford, CA: Academic Reprints, 1953].

Darwin, Charles, *On the Origin of Species*. London: John Murray, 1891; New York: Modern Library, 1936 (first published, 1859).

Diamond, Jared, *Collapse: How Societies Choose to Fail or Succeed*. New York: Viking Penguin, 2005.

Diamond, Jared, *Guns, Germs, and Steel: The Fates of Human Societies*. New York: Norton, 1999.

Drake, Harold A., *In Praise of Constantine: A Historical Study and New Translation of Eusebius' Tricennial Orations*. Berkeley: University of California Press, 1976.

Dubuisson, Daniel, *The Western Construction of Religion: Myths, Knowledge, and Ideology*, trans. William Sayers. Baltimore and London: Johns Hopkins Press, 2003.

Dumézil, Georges, *L'Idéologie tripartite des Indo-Européens*. Brussels: Latomas, 1958.

Durkheim, Émile, *Les Formes élémentaires de la vie religieuse*. Paris, 1912 [*The Elementary Forms of the Religious Life*, trans. Joseph Ward Swain. New York: Free Press, 1915].

Eliade, Mircea, *Encyclopedia of Religion*. New York: Macmillan, 1993.

Eliade, Mircea, *From Primitives to Zen: A Thematic Sourcebook on the History of Religions*. New York: Harper and Row, 1967.

Eliade, Mircea, *A History of Religious Ideas*, trans. Willard R. Trask. Chicago: University of Chicago Press, 1978–1985.

Eliade, Mircea, *The Myth of the Eternal Return: Cosmos and History*, trans. Willard R. Trask. With a new introduction by Jonathan Z. Smith. Bollingen Series 46. Princeton and Oxford: Princeton University Press, 2005.

Encyclopedia Britannica, 15th edition. Chicago and London: Encyclopedia Britannica, Inc., 1977.

Enuma Elish, see Pritchard, *Ancient Near Eastern Texts*, pp. 60–72; 501–3.

Epiphanius, in Wilson, *Sacred Books of the East*. London and New York: The Colonial Press, 1902.

Erman, Adolf, *The Ancient Egyptians: A Sourcebook of Their Writings*, trans. Aylward M. Blackman. New York: Harper and Row, 1966.

Evans, Sara M., and Harry C. Boyte, *Free Spaces: The Sources of Democratic Change in America*. New York: Harper and Row, 1992.

Fehrenbacher, Don E., *The Slaveholding Republic: An Account of the United States Government's Relation to Slavery*. Oxford and New York: Oxford University Press, 2001.

Felton, Rebecca Latimer, *Country Life in Georgia in the Days of My Youth*. New York: Arno Press, 1980.

Fisher, Loren, *Genesis, A Royal Epic: Introduction, Translation and Notes*. Xlibris, 2000.

Fontenelle, Bernard Le Bovier de, *De l'origine des fables*. Edition critique avec une introduction, des notes, et un commentaire par J. R. Carr. Paris: Alcan, 1932 (first published 1724).

Frankfort, Henri, H. A. Frankfort, John A. Wilson, Thorkild Jacobson, and William A. Irwin, *The Intellectual Adventure of Ancient Man: An Essay on Speculative Thought in the Ancient

Near East. Chicago: University of Chicago Press, 1977 (first published 1946). Baltimore: Penguin, 1949.

Frazer, Sir James George, *The Golden Bough: A Study in Magic and Religion*, abridged edition. London: Macmillan, 1963 (various editions from 1890 to 1922).

Frye, Northrop, *Anatomy of Criticism: Four Essays*. New York: Athenaeum, 1957.

Frykholm, Amy Johnson, *Rapture Culture: Left Behind in Evangelical America*. Oxford and New York: Oxford University Press, 2004.

Gabler, Neal, "An Eternal War of Mind-Sets," *Los Angeles Times*, October 7, 2001.

Geertz, Clifford, *The Interpretation of Cultures*. New York: HarperCollins, 1973.

Geertz, Clifford, *Local Knowledge: Further Essays in Interpretive Anthropology*. New York: HarperCollins, 1983.

Geertz, Clifford, *Negara: The Theatre State in Nineteenth-Century Bali*. Princeton, NJ: Princeton University Press, 1980.

Gibbs, Nancy, "The Religion Test," *Time Magazine*, May 21, 2007, pp. 40–2.

Giddens, Anthony, *The Nation-State and Violence*. Volume 2 of *A Contemporary Critique of Historical Materialism*. Berkeley: University of California Press, 1987.

Gomory, Ralph, *Global Trade and Conflicting National Interests*. Cambridge, MA: MIT Press, 2000.

Gould, Stephen Jay, *Wonderful World: Burgess Shale and the Nature of History*. New York: Norton, 1989.

Grant, Frederick C., *Hellenistic Religions: The Age of Syncretism*. New York: Bobbs-Merrill, 1953.

Greider, William, "The Establishment Rethinks Globalization," *The Nation*, April 30, 2007.

Grimm, Jacob Ludwig Carl, and Wilhelm Carl Grimm, *The Complete Fairy Tales of the Brothers Grimm*, trans. Jack Zipes. New York: Bantam, 1987 (first published in German, 1812–22).

Hagee, John, *Jerusalem Countdown*. Dallas: Strong Communications Co., 2006.

Harland, Philip, *Associations, Synagogues and Congregations: Claiming a Place in Ancient Mediterranean Society*. Minneapolis: Fortress Press, 2003.

The HarperCollins Dictionary of Religion, ed. Jonathan Z. Smith. San Francisco: HarperSanFrancisco, 1995.

Harris, Trudier, *Exorcising Blackness: Historical and Literary Lynching and Burning Rituals*. Bloomington: Indiana University Press, 1984.

Hultkranz, Åke, *The Religions of the American Indians*, trans. Monica Setterwall. Berkeley: University of California Press, 1979.

Hume, David, *An Inquiry Concerning Human Understanding*. New York: Liberal Arts Press, 1955 (first published 1748).

Hume, David, *A Treatise of Human Nature: being an attempt to introduce the experimental method of reasoning into moral subjects, and dialogues concerning natural religions*, edited by T. H. Green and T. H. Grese. London and New York: Longmans, Green, 1898 (this edition first published 1874). Oxford and New York: Oxford University Press, 2000.

James, William, *Varieties of Religious Experience: A Study in Human Nature*. London: Longmans, Green, & Co., 1902.

Jay, Martin, *Songs of Experience: Modern American and European Variations on a Universal Theme*. Berkeley: University of California Press, 2005.

Jensen, Adolf E., *Hainuwele*. New York: Arno, 1978.

Jensen, Adolf E., *Mythos und Kult bei Naturvölkern*. Wiesbaden: Franz Steiner Verlag, 1951 [*Myth and Cult among Primitive Peoples*, trans. Marianna Tax Choldin and Wolfgang Weissleder. Chicago: University of Chicago Press, 1973].

Jensen, Tim, and Mikael Rothstein, *Secular Theories on Religion: Current Perspectives*. Copenhagen: Museum Tusculanum Press, 2000.

Kazin, Michael, *A Godly Hero*. New York: Knopf, 2006.

Kennedy, John F., "Address of Senator John F. Kennedy to the Greater Houston Ministerial Association," Rice Hotel, Houston, Texas, September 12, 1960. John F. Kennedy Library and Museum. (jfklibrary.org)

Kinzer, Stephen, *Overthrow: America's Century of Regime Change from Hawaii to Iraq*. New York: Henry Holt, 2006.

Kirk, G. S., *Myth: Its Meaning and Function in Ancient and Other Cultures*. London: Cambridge University Press; Berkeley: University of California Press, 1973.

Kloppenborg, John S., "Collegia and Thiasoi: Issues in Function, Taxonomy and Membership," in John S. Kloppenborg and Stephen G. Wilson (eds), *Voluntary Associations in the Graeco-Roman World*, pp. 16–30. London and New York: Routledge, 1996.

Klug, Brian, "The State of Zionism," *The Nation*, June 18, 2007, pp. 23–30.

Kosmin, Barry A., "Who Is Secular in the World Today?" *Religion in the News*, Fall, 2006.

Kumar, Amitava, "A Civilizing Mission," *The Nation*, November 27, 2006, pp. 32–6.

Lang, Andrew, *The Making of Religion*. London and New York: Longmans, Green, & Co., 1898.

Lawson, E. Thomas, and Robert N. McCauley, *Rethinking Religion: Connecting Cognition and Culture*. Cambridge: Cambridge University Press, 1990.

Layton, Bentley, *The Gnostic Scriptures*. Garden City: Doubleday, 1987.

Lazare, Daniel, "God's Willing Executioners" (review of Tyerman, *God's War: A New History of the Crusades*), *The Nation*, December 11, 2006, pp. 44–9.

Lears, Jackson, "Keeping It Real" (review of Martin Jay, *Songs of Experience: Modern American and European Variations on a Universal Theme*), *The Nation*, June 12, 2006, pp. 23–30. Berkeley: University of California Press, 2005.

Lévi-Strauss, Claude, *Introduction to a Science of Mythology*, 4 vols, trans. John and Doreen Weightman. New York: Harper and Row, 1973–1978.

Lévi-Strauss, Claude, *The Savage Mind*, trans. George Weidensfeld. Chicago: University of Chicago Press, 1966.

Lévi-Strauss, Claude, "The Story of Asdiwal," in *Structural Anthropology*, Vol. II, trans. Monique Layton, pp. 146–97. New York: Basic Books, 1980.

Lévi-Strauss, Claude, *Structural Anthropology*, Vol. I, trans. Claire Jacobson and Brooke Schoepf. New York: Basic Books, 1963.

Lévi-Strauss, Claude, *Structural Anthropology*, Vol. II, trans. Monique Layton. New York: Basic Books, 1980 (first published 1976).

Lévi-Strauss, Claude, *Les Structures élémentaires de la parenté*. Paris: 1948 [*The Elementary Structures of Kinship*, trans. J. H. Belle and J. R. von Sturmer and ed. R. Needham. Boston: Beacon, 1949.

Lévy-Bruhl, Lucien, *La Mentalité primitive*. Paris: Alcan, 1922 [*How Natives Think*. London: Allen & Unwin, 1926].

Lincoln, Bruce, *Authority: Construction and Corrosion*. Chicago: Chicago University Press, 1994.

Lincoln, Bruce, *Discourse and the Construction of Society: Comparative Studies of Myth, Ritual, and Classification*. New York and Oxford: Oxford University Press, 1989.

Locke, John, *An Essay Concerning Human Understanding*. Oxford: Clarendon, 1975 (first published 1700).

Locke, John, *The Reasonableness of Christianity*. Dulles, VA: Thoemmes Press, 1997 (first published 1695).

Mack, Burton L., *The Christian Myth: Origins, Logic, and Legacy*. New York: Continuum, 2003.
Mack, Burton L., *Logos und Sophia: Untersuchungen zur Weisheitstheologie im hellenistischen Judentum*. Studien zur Umwelt des Neuen Testaments 10. Göttingen: Vandenhoeck und Ruprecht, 1973.
Mack, Burton L., *The Lost Gospel: The Book of Q and Christian Origins*. San Francisco: HarperSanFrancisco, 1993.
Mack, Burton L., *A Myth of Innocence: Mark and Christian Origins*. Philadelphia: Fortress Press, 1988.
Mack, Burton L., "Rereading the Christ Myth," in Ron Cameron and Merrill Miller (eds), *Redescribing Paul and the Corinthians*. Atlanta: Society of Biblical Literature (forthcoming).
Mack, Burton L., *Who Wrote the New Testament? The Making of the Christian Myth*. San Francisco: HarperSanFrancisco, 1995.
Malinowski, Bronislaw, *Magic, Science and Religion, and Other Essays*. Boston: Beacon, 1948; Garden City: Doubleday, 1955.
Mann, Charles C., *1491: New Revelations of the Americas before Columbus*. New York: Vintage Books, 2006.
Mannhardt, Wilhelm, *Wald- und Feldkulte* [Forest and Field Cults]. Strasburg: Tübner, 1875–77; Darmstadt: Wissenschaftliche Buchgesellschaft, 1963.
Marett, R. R., *The Threshold of Religion*. London: Methuen, 1909.
Martin, Luther H., "Cognition and Religion," in J. Hinnells (ed.), *The Routledge Companion to the Study of Religion*, pp. 473–88. London: Routledge, 2005.
Martin, Luther H., *Hellenistic Religions: An Introduction*. New York and Oxford: Oxford University Press, 1987.
Marx, Karl, *Contributions to the Critique of Political Economy*, trans. from 2nd German edn by N. I. Stone, with appendix containing Marx's Introduction recently published among his posthumous papers. Chicago: Kerr, 1911.
Marx, Karl, *Das Kapital: Kritik der politischen Oekonomie*. Hamburg: Meissner; New York: Schmidt, 1867 [*Capital: A Critique of Political Economy*, trans. Samuel Moore and Edward Aveling and ed. Frederick Engels. New York: Modern Library, 1906.
Mauss, Marcel, *Essai sur le don, forme archaïque de l'échange*. Paris, 1925 [*The Gift: Forms and Functions of Exchange in Archaic Societies*, trans. Ian Cunnison. New York: Norton, 1967.
Maybury-Lewis, D., and V. Almagor (eds), *The Attraction of Opposites: Thought and Society in the Dualistic Mode*. Ann Arbor: University of Michigan, 1989.
McCalla, Arthur, *The Creationist Debate: The Encounter Between the Bible and the Historical Mind*. New York: Continuum, 2006.
McCutcheon, Russell T., *The Discipline of Religion: Structure, Meaning, and Rhetoric*. London and New York: Routledge, 2003.
McCutcheon, Russell T., *Manufacturing Religion: The Discourse on Sui Generis Religion and the Politics of Nostalgia*. New York and Oxford: Oxford University Press, 1997.
McCutcheon, Russell T., "Myth," in Willi Braun and Russell T. McCutcheon (eds), *Guide to the Study of Religion*, pp. 190–208. London and New York: Cassell, 2000.
McGowan, John, *Postmodernism and Its Critics*. Ithaca: Cornell University Press, 1991.
Meacham, J., *American Gospel: God, the Founding Fathers, and the Making of a Nation*. New York: Random House, 2006.
Miller, Merrill, "The Anointed Jesus," in Ron Cameron and Merrill Miller (eds), *Redescribing Christian Origins*, pp. 375–415. Symposium Series 28. Atlanta: Society of Biblical Literature, 2004.

Miller, Patrick, "The MRZH Text," in Loren R. Fisher (ed.), *The Claremont Ras Shamra Texts*, pp. 37–49. Analecta Orientalia 48. Rome: Pontificium Institutum Biblicum, 1971.
Montaigne, Michel, "Of Experience," in *The Complete Works*, trans. Donald M. Frame, pp. 815–57. Stanford: Stanford University Press, 1958.
Moore, James, and Wayne Slater, *The Architect: Karl Rove and the Master Plan for Absolute Power*. New York: Crown, 2006.
Mueller, Max, *Sacred Books of the East*. See Epiphanius.
Murphy, Joanne M., "Ideologies, Rites and Rituals: A View of Prepalatial Minoan Tholoi," in Keith Branigan (ed.), *Cemetery and Society in the Aegean Bronze Age*, pp. 27–40. Sheffield Studies in Aegean Archaeology 1. Sheffield: Sheffield Academic Press, 1998.
Otto, Rudolf, *Das Heilige* [*The Idea of the Holy*], trans. John W. Harvey. New York and Oxford: Oxford University Press, 1961 (first published in German in 1917, in English in 1923).
Pettazoni, Raffaele, *The All-Knowing God: Researches into Early Religion and Culture*, trans. H. J. Rose. London: Methuen, 1956.
Pettazoni, Raffaele, *Essays on the History of Religions*. Leiden: Brill, 1954.
Plutarch, *De Fortuna Romanorum* [The Fortune of the Romans], Moralia IV. Loeb Classical Library. London: William Heinemann; Cambridge, MA: Harvard University Press, 1962.
Posner, Sarah, "Pastor Strangelove," *The American Prospect*, June 2006, pp. 39–43.
Pritchard, James B. (ed.), *Ancient Near Eastern Texts Relating to the Old Testament*, 3rd edn. Princeton, NJ: Princeton University Press, 1969 (first published 1955).
Radcliffe-Brown, A. R., *The Andamen Islanders*. New York: Cohen and West, 1954 (first published 1922).
Radin, Paul, *Primitive Religion: Its Nature and Origin*. New York: Dover, 1957 (first published 1937).
Radin, Paul, *The Winnebago Tribe*. Lincoln: University of Nebraska Press, 1970.
Raffaele, Paul, "In John They Trust," *Smithsonian*, February 2006, pp. 70–7.
Rappaport, Roy A., *Pigs for the Ancestors: Ritual in the Ecology of a New Guinea People*. New Haven: Yale University Press, 1984 (first published 1967).
Resch, Robert Paul, *Althusser and the Renewal of Marxist Social Theory*. Oxford and Berkeley: University of California Press, 1992.
Rieff, David, "We Are the World," *The Nation*, July 3, 2006, pp. 31–6.
Rousseau, Jean-Jacques, *Discours sur l'origine et les fondemens de l'inégalité parmi des hommes*. Paris, 1754 [*Discourse on the Origin and Foundation of Inequality among Mankind*. London: Dodsley, 1761].
Sahlins, Marshall, *Culture and Practical Reason*. Chicago: University of Chicago Press, 1976.
Sahlins, Marshall, *Historical Metaphors and Mythical Realities: Structure in the Early History of the Sandwich Islands Kingdom*. Association for Social Anthropology in Oceania, Special Publications No. 1. Ann Arbor: University of Michigan Press, 1987.
Saussure, Ferdinand de, *Cours de linguistique générale*. Paris, 1906; 1915 [*Course in General Linguistics*, ed. Charles Bally and Albert Sechehaye and trans. Wade Baskin. New York: Philosophical Library, 1959].
Schatzki, Theodore R., *The Site of the Social: A Philosophical Account of the Constitution of Social Life and Change*. University Park, PA: Pennsylvania State University Press, 2002.
Schell, Jonathan, "Too Late for Empire," *The Nation*, August 14/21, 2006, pp. 13–24.
Schell, Jonathan, *The Unconquerable World: Power, Nonviolence, and the Will of the People*. New York: Metropolitan Books, 2003.
Schleiermacher, Friedrich, *Der Christliche Glaube*. Berlin and New York: Walter de Gruyter, 1960, 2003 [critical editions of 1830 publication] [*The Christian Faith*, edited by H. R. Mackintosh and J. S. Stewart. Edinburgh: T & T Clark, 1960, 1999].

Schmidt, Wilhelm, *The Origin and Growth of Religion*. London: Methuen, 1931.
Sharf, Robert H., "Experience," in Mark C. Taylor (ed.), *Critical Terms for Religious Studies*, pp. 94–116. Chicago: University of Chicago Press, 1998.
Sharlet, Jeff, *The Family: The Secret Fundamentalism at the Heart of American Power*. New York: HarperCollins, 2008.
Shirer, William L., *The Collapse of the Third Republic: An Inquiry into the Fall of France in 1940*. New York: Simon and Schuster, 1969 (Pocket Books, 1971).
Singleton, Carrie Jane, "Christian Rationalization for Lynching: A Correct Interpretation of the Gospel of Mark." Masters thesis, Claremont School of Theology, 1987.
Smith, Jonathan Z., "The Bare Facts of Ritual," in *Imagining Religion: From Babylon to Jonestown*, pp. 53–65. Chicago: University of Chicago Press, 1982.
Smith, Jonathan Z., "The Domestication of Sacrifice," in Robert G. Hamerton-Kelly (ed.), *Violent Origins: Walter Burkert, Rene Girard, and Jonathan Z. Smith on Ritual Killing and Cultural Formation*, with an Introduction by Burton Mack and a Commentary by Renato Rosaldo, pp. 191–205. Stanford: Stanford University Press, 1987. (Reprinted in Jonathan Z. Smith, *Relating Religion: Essays in the Study of Religion*, pp. 145–59. Chicago: University of Chicago Press, 2004.)
Smith, Jonathan Z., *Drudgery Divine: On the Comparison of Early Christianities and the Religions of Late Antiquity*. London: School of Oriental and African Studies, University of London; Chicago: University of Chicago Press, 1990.
Smith, Jonathan Z., *Imagining Religion: From Babylon to Jonestown*. Chicago: University of Chicago Press, 1988.
Smith, Jonathan Z., "Manna, Mana, Everywhere and ///," in *Relating Religion: Essays in the Study of Religion*, pp. 117–44. Chicago: University of Chicago Press, 2004.
Smith, Jonathan Z., *Map Is Not Territory: Studies in the History of Religions*. Leiden: E. J. Brill, 1978; Chicago: University of Chicago Press, 1993.
Smith, Jonathan, Z., "A Pearl of Great Price and a Cargo of Yams," in *Imagining Religion: From Babylon to Jonestown*, pp. 90–101. Chicago: University of Chicago Press, 1988.
Smith, Jonathan Z., *Relating Religion: Essays in the Study of Religion*. Chicago: University of Chicago Press, 2004.
Smith, Jonathan Z., "Religion, Religions, Religious," in Mark C. Taylor (ed.), *Critical Terms for Religious Studies*, pp. 269–84. Chicago: University of Chicago Press, 1998. (Reprinted in Jonathan Z. Smith, *Relating Religion: Essays in the Study of Religion*, pp. 179–96. Chicago: University of Chicago Press, 2004.)
Smith, Jonathan Z., "Sacred Persistence," in *Imagining Religion: From Babylon to Jonestown*, pp. 36–52. Chicago: University of Chicago Press, 1982.
Smith, Jonathan Z., *To Take Place: Toward Theory in Ritual*. Chicago: University of Chicago Press, 1992.
Smith, Jonathan Z., "What a Difference a Difference Makes," in *Relating Religion: Essays in the Study of Religion*, pp. 251–302. Chicago: University of Chicago Press, 2004.
Smith, Jonathan Z., "When the Bough Breaks," in *Map Is Not Territory: Studies in the History of Religions*, pp. 208–39. Leiden: E. J. Brill, 1978; Chicago: University of Chicago Press, 1993.
Smith, Mark S., *The Origins of Biblical Monotheism*. New York: Oxford University Press, 2001.
Soodalter, Ron, *Hanging Captain Gordon: The Life and Trial of an American Slave Trader*. New York: Simon and Schuster, 2006.
Stark, Rodney, *The Rise of Christianity: A Sociologist Reconsiders History*. Princeton, NJ: Princeton University Press, 1996.

Stark, Rodney, and William Sims Bainbridge, *A Theory of Religion*. Toronto Studies in Religion 2. New York: Lang, 1987.
Stone, Caroline, "Ibn Khaldun and the Rise and Fall of Empires," *Aramco*, September–October 2006, pp. 28–39.
Stowers, Stanley K., "Greeks Who Sacrifice and Those Who Do Not," in L. M. White and O. L. Yarbrough (eds), *The First Christians and Their Social World: Studies in Honor of Wayne A. Meeks*, pp. 295–335. Minneapolis: Fortress, 1995.
Suggs, Robert C., *The Island Civilizations of Polynesia*. New York: Mentor Books, n.d.
Taylor, Mark C. (ed.), *Critical Terms for Religious Studies*. Chicago: Chicago University Press, 1998.
Teresi, Dick, *Lost Discoveries: The Ancient Roots of Modern Science, from Babylonia to the Maya*. New York: Simon and Schuster, 2002.
Toorn, Karel van der, *Family Religion in Babylonia, Syria, and Israel: Continuity and Change in the Forms of Religious Life*. Leiden and New York: Brill, 1996.
Turner, Victor, *The Forest of Symbols: Aspects of Ndembu Ritual*. Ithaca, NY: Cornell University Press, 1967.
Turner, Victor, "Mukanda: Rite of Circumcision," in *The Forest of Symbols: Aspects of Ndembu Ritual*, pp. 157–279. Ithaca, NY: Cornell University Press, 1967.
Tyerman, Christopher, *God's War: A New History of the Crusades*. Boston: Harvard University Press, 2006.
Tylor, Edward Burnett, *Primitive Culture*, 2 vols. London: Murray, 1877.
"Urban Archipelago," *The Nation*, June 20, 2005.
Vaage, Leif, "Why Christianity Succeeded (in) the Roman Empire," in Leif E. Vaage (ed.), *Religious Rivalries in the Early Roman Empire and the Rise of Christianity*, pp. 253–78. Studies in Christianity and Judaism 18. Canadian Corporation for Studies in Religion: Wilfrid Laurier University Press, 2006.
Valeri, Valerio, "Reciprocal Centers: The Siwa-Lima System in the Central Moluccas," in D. Maybury-Lewis and V. Almagor (eds), *The Attraction of Opposites: Thought and Society in the Dualistic Mode*, pp. 117–41. Ann Arbor: University of Michigan Press, 1989.
Van der Leeuw, G., *Religion in Essence and Manifestation*, 2 vols, trans. J. E. Turner. New York: Harper and Row, 1963 (first published 1938).
Van Gennep, Arnold, *The Rites of Passage*, trans. Monika B. Vizedom and Gabrielle L. Caffee. Chicago: University of Chicago Press, 1969 (first published as *Les Rites de passage*, 1909).
Vernant, Jean-Pierre, *The Origins of Greek Thought*. Ithaca, NY: Cornell University Press, 1982.
Weber, Max, *The Protestant Ethic and the Spirit of Capitalism*. London: Unwin, 1971 (first published in German 1905).
Wheatley, Paul, *The Pivot of the Four Quarters: A Preliminary Enquiry into the Origins and Character of the Ancient Chinese City*. Chicago: University of Chicago Press, 1971.
Williams, Raymond, *Culture and Society: 1780–1950*. New York: Columbia University Press, 1983 (first published 1958).
Wills, Garry, *Inventing America: Jefferson's Declaration of Independence*. Garden City: Doubleday, 1978.
Wittfogel, Karl August, *Oriental Despotism: A Comparative Study of Total Power*. New Haven: Yale University Press, 1959.
Worrall, Simon, "Pilgrims' Progress," *Smithsonian*, November, 2006, pp. 88–97.
Younge, Gary, "The Illogic of Empire," *The Nation*, February 5, 2007, p. 10.

Index

Adonis 110
agency 79, 85–7, 90, 205
Alexander the Great 104, 114, 118
Althusser, Louis 49, 50
Ambrose (bishop) 188
American Revolution 19, 215, 223, 254
Amerindians 16, 17–18, 20, 21–2, 27, 28–9, 37, 88, 261
    social interests 54–5, 60, 63–4, 68, 69–70
ancestors 9, 53–4, 68–2, 85, 138–9
Anders, Jaroslaw 268
Anglican Church 217–18, 219
animism 22–3, 24
anthropology 25, 28–31, 34–41, 51, 270
Apollonius 104
apostles, **see disciples**
Apuleius, Lucius 115–16
Aquinas, Thomas 212
Aranda myths 53–4, 60, 62–3, 68, 90
Arianism 176–7, 179, 188–9
Armstrong, Karen 5
asceticism 26
Asdiwal stories 37, 69–70, 88
Ashcroft, John 3
associations
    early Christianity, see Jesus schools and associations
    Hellenistic world 105, 108–9
Athenagoras of Athens 168
Australia 27, 53–4, 60, 62–3, 68, 90
authority, see power
Aztecs 18, 64

baptism 190, 196
base/superstructure model 49–51
basilicas 175–6, 177–8, 183–4, 185, 190–1, 192, 197, 198, 203
Beck, Roger 115
belief 8, 27
Bettelheim, Bruno 88
Bettenson, Henry 180
Bible 21, 100, 194–5

Christian nation 223, 227, 228, 229, 230, 232, 242, 245
    Hebrew scriptures, see Judaism
    New Testament accounts 12, 20, 148, 151–2, 154–5, 161, 162–5, 170–1, 194
Boas, Franz 28–9, 42
Bonnet, Hans 56
Bourdieu, Pierre 42, 77, 141
Bruner, Jerome 89, 123
Bryan, William Jennings 222
Burkert, Walter 65, 66, 193
Bush, George W. 3, 241–3, 261

Calvin, John 214
Calvinism 26, 219
Cameron, Ron 155
cargo, myth and social change 132–5
cargo cults, myth and social change 135–9
Carr, Pat 54
Castelli, Elizabeth 241–2
Center for Progressive Christianity 263
Ceram 63, 132–5, 136–7
Certeau, Michel de 259
Chicago school 34
China 16, 17, 27, 69
Christ event 21, 24, 201, 202–3, 204, 207, 209, 236–7, 239, 244, 245
Christian Church 12–13, 42, 147–8, 182, 183–216, 271
    Christian nation 221–2, 239–43
    and empire 13, 187–93
    foundation of 181–2, 183–7
    imagined world 182, 183, 193–216, 217
    medieval 191–9, 209, 246
    relations with others 206, 209–16, 235
Christian Coalition 2, 231, 239
Christian grammar 12, 146, 203–9, 211, 215, 230, 232, 233–48, 249, 271
Christian mentality 12, 147–8, 182, 193, 199–209, 216

Index

Christian nation 2, 6–7, 13, 41, 217, 218, 225, 230, 232–48, 249–50, 251, 252
   inadequate for social situation in USA 260, 262, 271, 274, 275
Christian missionaries 18, 136, 189–90, 211–12, 235–6, 241, 243, 247
Christian myth–ritual system 12–13, 24, 44, 66, 130, 143, 146, 148–74, 178, 179, 181, 183, 190–1, 193–209, 250, 271
   and Christian nation 13, 217, 224–30
   rethinking in polycultural society 262–3, 272–3
Christian nation 1, 2–5, 7, 13, 46, 91, 147, 215–16, 217–48, 249, 271
   Christian grammar 232–44
   consequences of Christian mentality 244–8
   and empire 243–4, 247
   mythmaking in history of 224–30
   political concept 230–2
Christian Right 2–4, 5, 41, 202, 208, 215, 219, 232, 247, 248, 249, 250, 262
Christianity 7
   model for definition of religion 11, 17, 20–1, 24–5, 27, 31, 32, 33, 42, 66, 110, 133, 136, 146, 211, 250, 271
   types 146
   see also Christian Church; early Christianity
church fathers 100, 160–70, 172
church/state separation 2, 44–5, 46, 219–20, 224, 231, 249, 252
city-states 97–104, 185
civil rights 228–30
Clement of Alexandria 164, 168
Code of Hammurabi 94–6
Codrington, Robert Henry 23
colonization 24, 211, 212, 222–3
   myths and social change 125–39
Columbus, Christopher 16–18, 271
common good 248, 251, 254, 256, 257, 263–270, 272
community 262
Comte, Auguste 21
confession 196–7
Constantine, emperor 12, 174–82, 183–7, 190, 192

Cook, James 126–31
Copernicus, Nicolaus 18, 212
Corn Mother and Corn Maidens 20, 54–5, 64, 88
Cortez, Hernando 18
cosmogonies 53–8, 92–7, 102
cosmologies 33–4, 35, 90, 102–4, 107, 111–12, 117, 233
   Christian 157, 160–4, 165–6, 172, 180, 200–2
Council of Nicaea (325 A.D.) 177, 179, 180, 186
Counter-Reformation 214
Cranmer, Thomas 214
creation
   Christian nation and 233–4, 237, 238, 246
   Christianity and 182, 212–13
creation myths 53–8, 92–7
   Christianity 201–2, 205, 207, 233
creationism 202, 213, 231, 233–4
creeds 177, 179–81, 188, 195–6
critical thinking 6, 8, 50–1, 250, 251, 264–6, 271–5
   common good 267–70
   possible responses to 272–4
cultural anthropology, *see* anthropology
cultural differences 140, 274
cultural identity 108, 140–1
cultural traditions 83–5, 118–19, 137–9
   modification in polycultural democracy 259–63
cultural values 25, 217–18
   see also moral classifications and values
culture 259
   mythic mentality 139–43, 218
   religion as 1, 26, 35
   transforming myths 125–39
culture wars 5, 46, 91, 231, 239
Cybele 109, 113
Cyprian, bishop of Carthage 171

Darwin, Charles 20, 23
Deism 214–15, 221
deities 9, 27, 42, 146
   and common good 269–70
   mythmaking 12, 82, 84, 85–7, 90, 93–103, 105, 106, 108–10, 111, 113–19

and social change 120–1, 122, 124
  see also God
Demeter myth 64–5, 80, 84, 109, 113–14
democracy 101, 218, 250, 268
  identified with Christian nation 243, 244, 247, 248
  see also polycultural social democracy; social democracy
Diamond, Jared 43, 63, 135–6
differences 38–40, 59, 124, 130, 140, 170, 206
  Christian nation 246–7
  dealing with 260, 274
Diocletian, emperor 175
Dionysius of Corinth 168
Dionysos 86, 109, 110, 113, 124
disciples, early Christian 100, 161, 162, 164–5, 181
Docetism 173
Donatism 176
dualisms, Christian 200–1, 206–7, 235–6, 242–3, 247
Dumézil, Georges 42
Durkheim, Émile 26–8, 42, 49, 51, 59

early Christianity 12, 20, 66, 90, 100, 146–82, 219, 251–2
  establishment as state religion 174–87
  philosophy and theology 100, 160–70, 172
  social interests 66
Edict of Milan (313 A.D.) 174–5
Egyptian myths 55–56, 57, 100, 115–17
Eisenhower, Dwight 230, 231
Eliade, Mircea 31, 32–4, 35, 54, 56, 65, 132, 133, 134
empire
  Christian 13, 187–93
  Christian nation 243–4, 247
  Roman, see Roman empire
England 25, 64, 88, 214, 217–18
Enlightenment 6, 19, 21, 24, 99–100, 215, 217, 220, 223, 253
Enuma Elish 93–7
environments, natural and social
  Christianity 182, 194
  imagined world 84–5, 120–2, 141, 142, 255, 259–60
  mythmaking 83–5, 86, 89–90, 97, 119

epiphanies 33
Epiphanius 179
equality 223–30, 240
Erman, Adolf 56
Eschaton 180, 201, 203, 204, 207, 209, 237–8, 244, 245
ethnography of religion 18–41, 51, 82, 88
ethnology, see anthropology
Eucharist 170–4, 190, 262; see also Mass
Euripides 57
Eusebius 174, 177–8, 179, 183–4
evolution 20, 21, 29, 33, 213, 222, 233–4
exchange 22, 74, 126, 128, 130–1, 136–7

fairy tales 88
Falwell, Jerry 231
family religion 91, 99
family values 239–40
Fehrenbacher, Don 226
Felton, Rebecca 228
Fisher, Loren 71
folk tales and rituals 19, 20, 64, 134, 192–3
Fontenelle, Bernard Le Bovier de 19
food production
  mythmaking 83, 84, 92, 98–9
  social interests 54–5, 63–8, 72, 78, 80
France, sociology 26–8
Frankfort, Henri 97
Frazer, Sir James George 20, 23, 24, 64, 110, 192
French Revolution 19, 25, 223, 253, 254
Freud, Sigmund 49
Frye, Northrop 88
Frykholm, Amy Johnson 3, 238
functionalism 34–6
funerary rites 23, 61, 71–2, 80

Gabler, Neal 5–7, 258
Galileo 18, 19, 212
Galla Placidia, empress 192
Geertz, Clifford 35, 42, 81, 141
Germany
  early sociology 25–6
  mythmaking 88
  two-kingdom concept 219
Gibbs, Nancy 230
Giddens, Anthony 141, 252, 268
Gilgamesh Epic 96

Gnosticism 165–6, 177, 180
God 71–2, 86
  Christian 90–1, 153, 157, 161–2, 166, 167, 180, 181, 195, 200, 205–6, 208–9
  Christian nation 233, 242, 245, 246
gods, *see* deities
Gomory, Ralph 267
Gospel of Thomas 149, 151
Grant, Frederick C. 116
Greece and Greco-Roman world
  mythmaking 84, 88, 97–104, 109–10, 118, 150, 165, 185, 251–2
  myths in social structure 124
  social interests in myths and rituals 64–8, 70–1, 80
  see also Hellenistic world; Roman empire
Greek philosophy 6, 100–4, 107–8, 151, 153, 162, 164, 165, 167, 168, 169
Greider, William 267

habitus 77, 81, 141
Hagee, John 238
Haida people 30, 37, 55, 69–70
Hainuwele myth 88, 132–5, 136–7
Hamilton, Alexander 224
Harris, Trudier 228
Hawaii, myth and social change 126–31, 136, 138
Heifer Project 263
Hellenistic world
  early Christianity and 150, 151, 153, 158, 167, 251–2
  mythic imagery and social structure 124
  mythmaking 82, 88, 90, 97, 103, 104–9, 118, 119
heresies 169, 173
Hipparchus 104, 165
Hippolytus of Rome 168
history 33, 68
  Christianity and 179, 180, 194, 200, 202, 203, 205, 236, 246
Hobbes, Thomas 220
holy, the, *see* sacred, the
Hopi people 54–5, 64
Howe, Julia Ward 221, 225
Hultkranz, Åke 43
Hume, David 19

identity
  early Christian 154–5, 157, 158, 159, 163, 171, 180, 181
  imagined world 108, 121, 140–1
  polycultural world 248, 257, 258–9, 260, 261, 263, 272–3
  religion and 10
imagined world 8–9, 68–9, 76–9, 82–7, 120–2, 140–2, 255, 271
  Christian nation 232–48, 249
  Christianity 182, 183, 193–216, 217
  of common good 268–70
Incas 18
India 17, 27
individualism 45, 46, 73, 122, 216, 218–20, 246, 266
Indonesia, myth and social change 132–5, 136–7
Industrial Revolution 6, 19, 24, 25, 217, 218, 220, 253
initiation rites 60–2, 110, 114, 117
intellectual anthropology of religion 37–41, 264, 269
intellectual interests 75–6
Irenaeus, bishop of Lyons 164, 168, 172–3
Isis 86, 109, 110, 115–17, 162, 181
Islam 17, 86
  Christianity and 100, 210–11
  extremism 3, 4–5
  in polycultural democracy 261

James, William 46
Japan, social interests 55, 56, 57
Jay, Martin 45
Jefferson, Thomas 221, 223, 224, 225, 226
Jensen, Adolf E. 31, 132–5
Jesuits 18
Jesus
  Christian nation 232, 236–7, 244, 245
  in early Christianity 12, 148–58, 161, 162, 165–6, 167, 169, 170–3, 180
  later Christian Church 195, 196, 197–8, 202–3, 207
  see also Christ event
Jesus schools and associations 12, 148–64, 171, 178, 180, 197, 219
Judaism 17, 21, 70, 86

early Christianity and 100, 153, 154, 155, 156, 158, 159–60, 162–3, 166, 167
Hebrew scriptures 57, 58, 61, 64, 71, 100, 166, 167, 194, 233
later Christian Church and 210
in polycultural democracy 261
Jung, Carl Gustav 49
Justin Martyr (Justin of Samaria) 164, 166–8, 194

Kazin, Michael 222
Kennedy, John F. 2, 230–1
Key, Francis Scott 221
Kierkegaard, Søren 204
King, Martin Luther, Jr 228
kingdom of God
Christian nation 239–43
in early Christianity 12, 152–8, 163, 251
later Christian Church 195, 196, 198
in polycultural democracy 263
kingdom schools, see Jesus schools and associations
kingship
Christianity and 208
mythmaking 82, 91–7
social interests 55, 65–6, 70
kinship systems 22, 27, 29, 37, 44, 58, 78
Kinzer, Stephen 244
Kirk, G. S. 49
Klug, Brian 261
Knox, John 214
Kumar, Amitava 268

Lactantius 174
Lang, Andrew 23, 24, 31
language 20, 36, 44, 73–4
Las Casas, Bartolomé 18
Lawson, E. Thomas 85
Layton, Bentley 166
Lazare, Daniel 211
Lears, Jackson 45
Leeuw, G. van der, see Van der Leeuw
Lévi-Strauss, Claude 30, 31, 37–8, 42, 49, 55, 58, 59
Lévy-Bruhl, Lucien 31
liberalism
early Christian 177

US Christianity 4, 5, 231, 232, 239, 262–3
Lincoln, Abraham 225
Lincoln, Bruce 51
Locke, John 19, 214–15
logos 5–6, 167, 168, 242
Lono myth 128–31, 138
Los Angeles Times 5
Luke, apostle 148, 151–2, 161, 164–5
Luther, Martin 18, 219

Madison, James 223–4, 226
magic 23, 24, 26
Makarius, bishop of Jerusalem 176, 177
Malinowski, Bronislaw 29–30, 84
mana 23–4
Mann, Charles C. 63, 223
Mannhardt, Wilhelm 20
Marcion of Sinope 164–5, 166, 167, 177
Marco Polo 16
Marduk 93, 94
Marett, R. R. 23, 26
Mark's gospel 148, 151–2, 154–5, 162–3, 170–1, 194
Martin, Luther H. 58, 65, 86, 115
martyrdom 155–6, 160, 170, 171, 173, 192–3, 197, 198
Christian nation and 244, 245
Marx, Karl 25, 49
Marxism 49–51
marzeah 71–2, 80
Mass 196–8, 199, 203; see also Eucharist
Mauss, Marcel 26–7, 42
Maya 64
McCalla, Arthur 234
McCauley, Robert N. 85
McCutcheon, Russell 49, 220
McGowan, John 51, 254
Meacham J. 224
Melanesia 23–4, 29–30
Melito of Sardis 168
Mexico 18, 64, 138
Miller, Merrill 155
Miller, Patrick 71
Mithras 109, 110, 114–15, 181
Modernism 46, 199
monism and monotheism 23, 24, 31, 181, 205–6
Montaigne, Michel 45

Moore, James 243
moral classifications and values 2–3, 4, 231–2, 234–6, 239–40, 249
Moral Majority 2, 231, 239
Mueller, Max 19
Muhammadanism, see Islam
multicultural society 45, 104–9, 118, 119, 215, 246, 269
    early Christianity 149, 169, 170, 176
    see also polycultural world
mystery cults 65, 109–17
mysticism 26
mythic grammar 146, 260, 262, 273, 274
    and common good 269
    see also Christian grammar
mythic imagination 12, 82–119, 249
    Christian 200–9; see also Christian myth–ritual system
    rethinking in periods of social change 12, 119, 120–43
mythic mentality 9, 139–43, 260, 271
    see also Christian mentality
mythmaking 11–12, 49, 82–119
    Christian nation 224–30, 232
    in early Christianity 12, 148, 152–8, 160–70
mythos/logos distinction 5–6
myths 44, 48
    and common good 268–70, 272
    early studies of religion 19–44
    meaning and function 8–9, 48–9
    as narratives 87–91, 123
    new role in polycultural democracy 13, 260, 264, 265, 271–4
    and social change 10, 12, 49, 122–43
    social interests 11, 52–81, 121–2, 255, 259
    see also Christian myth–ritual system

Nation, The 256
nation-state 10–11, 19, 220, 248, 268
    Christian Church 208, 212, 215–16, 217–18
    Christian nation 222–5
    polycultural world 251, 252–4, 256
national interests 5, 12, 242, 243–4, 247, 251, 255–7, 267, 268, 274
native Americans, see Amerindians
natural world
    Christianity and 182, 212–13, 238
    primitive religion and 21–2
    see also creation; environments
Ndembu 61–2
Near East, ancient 252
    mythmaking 88, 90–7, 98–9, 101, 109, 111, 117, 118, 165, 181–2, 185
    and social interests 55, 56–7, 58, 64, 65, 66, 70, 71–2
Near East, modern 5, 238
new age spirituality 46
New Testament accounts, see Bible
New World, religion and discovery 16–19, 20, 21–2, 41, 271
Newton, Sir Isaac 19, 212
Nicene Creed 179–81, 188

offerings 63, 64, 92, 99, 100
Origen 168, 177
origins 20–1, 29, 33
    myths of 53–4, 57–8, 59–60, 68, 78, 127, 133, 195
Osiris 110
Otto, Rudolf 31

Pacific Islands 23–4, 29–30, 63, 125–39
Parks, Rosa 228
Paul (apostle) 20, 151, 152, 154, 155, 165, 194, 195, 245
Paul III (pope) 18
Pentecostals 241
Persephone myth 64–5, 80, 84, 109, 110, 113
personal religion 1, 2, 42, 44–7, 51, 199, 208, 260
    Christian nation 218–20, 231, 237
Petrarch 21, 212
Pettazoni, Raffaele 31
piety 42
    Christian 159, 192–3
    Greek and Hellenistic 99, 100, 101, 103, 105, 107, 109
pilgrimage 190–1, 192, 198, 203
Pindar 70
Pizarro, Francisco 18
Plato 165
Plutarch 106, 112, 116
polis, mythmaking 97–104

political power, *see* power
polycultural social democracy 13, 41, 258, 269–70, 271–4
　challenge of social situation 251, 260–3
　place of religion 251, 259–66
　rethinking religions and society 263–6, 272
polycultural world 215, 248–70, 271; *see also* multicultural society
Polynesia, *see* Pacific Islands
polytheism 23
Posner, Sarah 238
postmodernism 50–1
power
　Christian Church 181–2, 183–87, 188, 208, 210–12, 215
　Christian nation 243–4, 246, 247, 249
　social order and mythmaking 91–109
primitive religion, study of 19–34, 37–8
Pritchard, James B. 56, 93, 95, 96
Protestant Reformation 18, 24, 45, 100, 198, 213–14, 219
Protestantism 20, 21, 26, 212, 219
Ptolemy (Ptolemaeus, Claudius) 104, 165

Radcliffe-Brown, A. R. 42
Radin, Paul 60
Raffaele, Paul 137, 139
Rappaport, Roy A. 30, 81
Reagan, Ronald 231
redemption 244–5
relics 192
religion
　characteristic features 7–10
　and common good 268–70, 272
　comparative study 26, 28
　definitions 1–7, 20, 24–5, 44, 51, 82, 271; *see also* Christianity, model for definition of religion
　function, *see* functionalism
　importance 270
　intellectual anthropology of 37–41, 264, 269
　　past explanations 11, 16–47
　　peoples without 16, 17–19, 20, 41
　　possible transformation of 272–4
　　role 10–11
　　as social construction 44, 46–7, 48

　social theory of 7, 11, 40–4, 47, 51, 250, 251, 271
religious studies 7, 51
Renaissance 18–19, 21, 100, 212, 213
Resch, Robert Paul 50
Rieff, David 5, 242
rites of passage 59, 60–3, 192
rituals 44, 48
　Christian, *see* Christian myth–ritual system
　and common good 268–70, 272
　early studies of religion 19–44
　function 8–9
　and mythmaking 89, 92, 96, 97, 98, 99, 110, 113, 118
　myths and social change 122–5, 126, 128, 132–9, 141
　new role in polycultural democracy 260, 264–5, 271–4
　social interests 11, 52–72, 76–81, 255, 259
Robertson, Pat 231
Roman empire
　Christianity in 159, 161, 167–8, 169, 183, 187–91, 192, 208
　establishment of Christianity as state religion 174–82, 183–7, 252
　myth, ritual and social interests 65
　mythmaking 90, 106, 111–17, 118
Romanticism 19, 45
Rousseau, Jean-Jacques 19, 220

sacred, the 28, 31–34, 35, 59
sacrifice 23, 24, 39, 40, 63, 66–8, 92, 99
　Christian 171, 172, 262
　Christian nation 237, 245
　social structure and social change 124–5, 132–5, 136
Sahlins, Marshall 126, 129–31, 136
saints 192–3
salvation 26, 110, 169
Saussure, Ferdinand de 36
Sayings Gospel Q 149, 151
Schatzki, Theodore R. 74, 141
Schell, Jonathan 268
Schleiermacher, Friedrich 46
Schmidt, Wilhelm 31
science 6, 18–19, 212–13, 233–4
September 11, 2001 attacks 3, 6, 241

shamanism 30
Sharf, Robert H. 46
Sharlet, Jeff 250
Shirer, William L. 254
shrines 192–3
signs, systems of 36, 37–8, 43, 48, 49, 73, 76, 79, 81
Singleton, Carrie Jane 228
singularity, Christianity's logic of 169–70, 205–6, 247
situation 12, 39, 123, 141
Slater, Wayne 243
slavery, Christian nation and 225–8, 240
Smith, Jonathan Z. 17, 24, 30, 38–41, 43, 48, 49, 53, 59, 60, 63, 66, 77, 80, 89, 100, 111, 122–3, 124, 125, 132–3, 136–7, 141, 157, 170, 175, 177, 184, 198
Smith, Mark 70
Smith, Samuel 221
social anthropology, see anthropology
social change 9–10, 25, 253
 Christian Church 187, 210, 215, 217
 Christian nation 2–3, 224, 239
 mythmaking and 82, 104, 111–12
 rethinking mythic imagery 12, 119, 120–43
 social interests and 72–3, 79
social conflict 209, 244–5
social construction 12, 43–4, 46–7, 48, 51, 73–6, 80, 97, 223, 273
social control 247
social democracy 11, 13, 225, 243, 251, 254–5, 256; see also polycultural social democracy
social ethics, see moral classifications and values
social formation 48
 concept 11, 49–52, 269
 early Christianity 154, 158–60, 174
 later Christian Church as 146, 183–216
 mythmaking 49, 86, 90, 95, 96, 101, 102, 104
 social interests 72–6, 77–8
 social situation in USA 251–9
 social structure 12, 120–43
social interests 11, 49–72, 146, 217, 259, 271, 274

Christian nation 245–6, 248, 250
Christianity 153, 174, 178, 182, 183, 194
 concept 72–6
 mythmaking 84, 87, 89, 90, 91, 97, 99–100, 101, 108, 109, 111, 112, 117–18, 120, 121
 relation to myth and ritual 52–72, 76–81, 82
 social situation in USA 251, 253, 255–7
 social structure 49–52, 54, 58–60, 73–6, 77, 79, 80–1, 140, 141, 250
social practices 3, 8, 39–40, 122–3, 141, 259
 social formation and social interests 49–72, 76, 79, 81, 274
 and social structure 43, 48
social problems, Christian Church and 209, 244–5
social roles, social interests and 60–3
social structure 26, 28, 30, 40, 42–3, 48, 259, 271
 Christian nation 243–4
 mythmaking and 83, 89, 117, 120–43
 and social interests 49–52, 54, 58–60, 73–6, 77, 79, 80–1, 140, 141, 250
 see also social change; structuralism
society
 Christian nation 230
 as dynamic concept, see social formation
 and religion 4, 34–6, 42–3, 273
Society for the Propagation of the Gospel in Foreign Parts 18
sociology 25–8, 51
Soodalter, Ron 227
soul 22–3
Spellings, Margaret 240
State, see nation-state; temple-state
Stoicism 103, 107–8, 167
Stowers, Stanley 67–8
structuralism 36–8
Suggs, Robert C. 126
syncretism 118

taboos 23, 128, 130
Tanna, John Frum cult in 137–9

Tatian 157, 168
Teilhard de Chardin, Pierre 212
temple-state
  mythmaking 91–7, 98–9
  relation to establishment of
    Christianity 100, 154, 181–2, 185
  territory, and social interests 52–7, 78,
    178
terrorism 3, 6, 246, 268
Tertullian of Carthage 164, 168, 187
Theodosius, emperor 115, 188–9
Theophilus of Antioch 168
thusia 67–8, 80, 99
tjuringas 27, 62–3
Tlingit people 30, 37, 55, 69–70
Toltecs 64
Toorn, Karel van der 70, 91
totemism 27, 28, 30, 37, 58–9
tribal societies 22, 27–8, 29, 30, 37–8,
  53–5, 58–60, 118, 211
Trobriand Islands 29–30, 84
Tsimshian people 37, 55, 69–70
Turner, Victor 30, 42, 61
Tyche (chance, fate) 106, 107, 108, 112,
  117
Tyerman, Christopher 211
Tylor, Sir Edward Burnett 22–3, 24

Ulfilas 189
United States
  alternative to Christian nation 250,
    259–70
  Christian Church and nature 213,
    238; *see also* creation, Christian
    nation and
  Christian Church and political power
    208, 215, 243–4, 246, 247, 249
  as Christian nation, *see* Christian nation
  cultural critique of Christian mentality
    271–5
  cultural identity 140
  features of social situation 13, 251–9
  neglect of common good 266
  personal religion 44–7
  as polycultural social democracy, *see*
    polycultural social democracy
  study of primitive religion 28–9
  urban ritual 80–1

Vaage, Leif 185
Valentinus of Alexandria 164, 165–6,
  167
Valeri, Valerio 207
Van der Leeuw, G. 31–2, 35
Van Gennep, Arnold 42
Vanuatu, myth and social change 137–9
Vernant, Jean-Pierre 101–2
violence 209, 211, 244–5, 267–8, 270,
  273, 274
Vitoria, Francisco de 18

war 3–4, 246, 267–8
Watt, James 238
Weber, Max 25–6, 51, 204
Wheatley, Paul 42, 80–1
Williams, Raymond 25, 218, 254
Wills, Garry 225
Winnebago people 30, 60
worldview, *see* imagined world
Worrall, Simon 223

Zeno of Citium 107
Zumárraga, Juan de, archbishop of
  Mexico 18
Zuni people 54, 64
Zwingli, Ulrich 214

Series Editor: Russell T. McCutcheon, University of Alabama

Myth and the Christian Nation
A Social Theory of Religion

Burton L. Mack

'This book is vintage Mack. It is Mack at the height of his powers—of analysis, argumentation, communication. I find especially poignant his argument that a critical accounting of "religion"—especially including the modern historical "christian" instantiation of it—must come to painful honest terms with what pertains to the "discovery" not of the ancient text but the "other." We have hardly begun critical work on such basis. All serious explorers should reference this book as they chart their courses.'
Vincent L. Wimbush, Professor of Religion, Director, Institute for Signifying Scriptures, Claremont Graduate University, and editor of *Theorizing Scriptures*

'Burton Mack is the most interesting and the most important scholar of ancient Christianity working today. His work has redefined and continues to redefine what it is we do when we study ancient Christian writings. Yet he continues to expand his—and our—horizons. This work expands his insights on Christian origins to the arena of religious studies in general, and, most remarkably, shows what the study of the religions of "others" can do for our understanding of Christianity, both ancient and contemporary.'
William Arnal, Associate Professor of Religious Studies, University of Regina

This is a book on a social theory of religion and culture. A survey of the meanings of the term religion from Columbus to Jonathan Z. Smith sets the pace. Examples are taken from ethnography, the ancient Near East, the Greco-Roman age, and Christendom to develop the concepts of "imagined world," "social formation," "mythic grammar," and "cultural mentality." What has been learned from the study of other peoples and their religions about the function of myths and rituals is then applied to an analysis of the Christian myth-ritual system and its social logic. The odd combinations of mythic world and ritual presence, monotheism and sovereignty, righteousness and power, all peculiar to Christianity, are analyzed historically and followed into the twenty-first century. This study offers a meditation on the recent public discourse about the "Christian nation" in light of the current social situation in the United States and ends with an invitation to rethink the role of religions in constructing a polycultural social democracy.

Burton L. Mack, now retired, was formerly John Wesley Professor in Early Christianity at the Claremont School of Theology and Graduate University in California. He is the author of numerous publications on Hellenistic Judaism, ritual theory, classical rhetoric and Christian origins from the viewpoint of cultural anthropology and the history of religions.

Front cover image: Albert H. Stegall, BurntHand Metal Art (sculpture)
Cover design: hisandhersdesign.co.uk

Printed in the USA

ISBN 978-1-84553-373-1

www.equinoxpub.com